ANIMATING CENTRAL PARK

Weyerhaeuser Environmental Books

PAUL S. SUTTER, EDITOR

Weyerhaeuser Environmental Books explore human
relationships with natural environments in all their variety
and complexity. They seek to cast new light on the ways that
natural systems affect human communities, the ways that
people affect the environments of which they are a part,
and the ways that different cultural conceptions of nature
profoundly shape our sense of the world around us.
A complete list of the books in the series appears
at the end of this book.

ANIMATING

CENTRAL

PARK

A MULTISPECIES HISTORY

DAWN DAY BIEHLER

University of Washington Press

SEATTLE

Animating Central Park is published with the assistance of a grant
from the Weyerhaeuser Environmental Books Endowment, established
by the Weyerhaeuser Company Foundation, members of the
Weyerhaeuser family, and Janet and Jack Creighton.

Copyright © 2024 by the University of Washington Press

Design by Erin Kirk

Composed in Adobe Caslon Pro, typeface designed by
Carol Twombly, based on original by William Caslon

28 27 26 25 24   5 4 3 2 1

All rights reserved. No part of this publication may be reproduced or
transmitted in any form or by any means, electronic or mechanical, including
photocopy, recording, or any information storage or retrieval system,
without permission in writing from the publisher.

UNIVERSITY OF WASHINGTON PRESS   *uwapress.uw.edu*

LIBRARY OF CONGRESS CATALOGING-IN-PUBLICATION DATA
Names: Biehler, Dawn, author.
Title: Animating Central Park : a multispecies
history / Dawn Day Biehler.
Description: Seattle : University of Washington Press, [2024] |
Series: Weyerhaeuser environmental books | Includes
bibliographical references and index.
Identifiers: LCCN 2024014100 | ISBN 9780295753195
(hardcover) | ISBN 9780295753201 (ebook)
Subjects: LCSH: Animals—New York (State) —New York. |
Human-animal relationships—New York (State) —New York. |
Central Park (New York, N.Y.)
Classification: LCC F128.65.C3 B54 2024 | DDC 974.7/1—dc23/eng/20241009
LC record available at https://lccn.loc.gov/2024014100

♾ This paper meets the requirements of ansi/niso z39.48-1992
(Permanence of Paper).

TO MY FAMILY:
Brigid, Alice, and Nathan

Contents

Foreword: Central Park's More-than-Human History
by Paul S. Sutter   ix

Acknowledgments   xv

Introduction   1

PART 1: Creating and Contesting the
Animated Landscape

1. Reassembling a Rural City   29

2. Free Animals in a Changing Landscape   70

3. Captive in the City   111

PART 2: Human and Animal Claims on a Plural Park

4. Freedom, Joy, and Privilege in Multispecies Spaces   159

5. Modern Childhood and Modern Captivity   199

6. Animals Out and In   234

Conclusion   269

Notes   281

Selected Bibliography   327

Index   347

Foreword

Central Park's More-than-Human History

PAUL S. SUTTER

On February 2, 2023, an intruder snuck into the Central Park Zoo and cut a hole in the steel mesh enclosure that held a male Eurasian eagle owl named Flaco, allowing him to escape. Flaco had come to the zoo thirteen years earlier, after being hatched at a North Carolina bird park, and he had endured a lonely existence in his cramped cage. But once liberated, this massive owl became larger than life. Zoo officials, concerned about how strong a flier Flaco would be after years of confinement and skeptical about his ability to feed himself, initially tried to recapture him. But when they saw that Flaco was fending for himself, they suspended their efforts. Over the following months, Flaco made the city his home, splitting time between the northern part of Central Park and the Upper West Side of Manhattan, where he often perched atop water towers, slept on fire escapes in sheltered courtyards, and stared into apartment windows from AC units and windowsills. Flaco became an avian celebrity, attracting huge crowds and a fierce social media following. More than that, he became a symbol of freedom and wildness in an intensely built environment where many human residents feel cramped and contained. While zoo officials and other bird conservationists worried about Flaco's well-being in an urban environment filled with hazards, many New Yorkers forged strong emotional ties to this unusual owl, rooting for him to make it in the big city.

Flaco's freedom lasted only a year. On February 23, 2024, he was found lying on a sidewalk on West Eighty-Ninth Street, mortally injured from colliding with a building. A necropsy revealed that Flaco had died from blunt trauma injuries, but he was also a victim of preying on rats and pigeons. He had contracted pigeon herpesvirus and had harmful levels of four kinds of anticoagulant rat poison, both of which affected his ability to navigate the city safely and likely would have killed him eventually. New Yorkers mourned Flaco's demise, constructing a makeshift memorial under one of his favorite oak trees in Central Park and starting a petition to create a monument in his honor. For a brief period, Flaco had animated Central Park and its surrounding neighborhoods, and his death reminded New Yorkers that their lives were necessarily entangled with those of other animals.

As Dawn Biehler shows us in her timely new book, *Animating Central Park: A Multispecies History*, Flaco's saga is only the latest in a long line of such animal stories. Biehler insists that multispecies relationships have been a consistent and ever-shifting component of Central Park's history and that New Yorkers have often claimed space in the park, or denied belonging to others, through their relationships with nonhuman animals. While Flaco seems to have brought New York City residents together, the history of animals in the park has not always inculcated such a sense of common belonging.

The famous Greensward plan created by Frederick Law Olmsted and Calvert Vaux—the plan that gave form to Central Park—had little room for animals. As such, it was in keeping with a larger set of processes designed to make New York City sanitary and modern. Indeed, the nineteenth-century "taming of Manhattan," as the historian Catherine McNeur has shown, had the removal of economically useful animals as one of its core components. Yet the city never became been quite as modern, or human, as many came to assume. In her wonderful first book, *Pests in the City* (which also appeared in the Weyerhaeuser Environmental Books series), Biehler chronicled the lives of several pest species—flies, bedbugs, cockroaches, and rats—that have long foiled our sense that urban environments have mastered nature. In *Animating Central Park,*

Biehler has turned her geographer's eye to one of New York's great outdoor landscapes and the surprising persistence of human-animal interactions within it, showing again that our relationships with other species are almost always about our relationships with each other as well.

Animals and their labor were essential to the construction of Central Park, but from its inception, the park was off-limits to the kinds of private animals that antebellum New Yorkers had long let run rampant. Pigs, goats, and cows were kept out of the park to protect fragile landscaping, even as they continued to populate surrounding neighborhoods. But surprisingly, livestock soon reappeared in the park, albeit under different auspices. Southdown sheep grazed under highly regulated conditions and served as objects of quiet contemplation, symbols of improved livestock breeding, and sources of revenue for the fledgling park. Meanwhile, goats pulled carts with joyful young passengers in the park's Children's District, while wealthy New Yorkers promenaded though the park on horseback or in horse-drawn carriages. There was even a vision for a working dairy in the park, to provide wholesome milk to visitors at a time when swill milk scandalized the city. As Central Park's custodians replaced one version of the more-than-human city with another, the park became an arena for the revaluation of animals. No longer the economically useful creatures that augmented the subsistence of many poor New Yorkers, pastoral creatures became prized for their encounter value.

Meanwhile, New Yorkers animated Central Park in other ways as well. They stocked park ponds and reservoirs with fish; they let loose exotic birds such as swans, house sparrows, and starlings; they intentionally released chipmunks and squirrels, while escaped woodchucks and hares also thrived; and they sought to control feral dogs and cats to protect these other species. And as park vegetation matured, wild species came of their own volition. To these pastoral and wild species park officials soon added captive species as well. Central Park had its own menagerie, with park supporters donating animals, including bison and other species provided by Lt. Colonel George Armstrong Custer and his Seventh Cavalry. Its collections were haphazard, and there were ongoing controversies about whether the menagerie, which was popular with working-class and immigrant visitors, even belonged in Central Park. But these caged animals connected New Yorkers to numerous other parts of the world in both compelling and troubling ways. By the end of the nineteenth century, as Biehler brilliantly shows, Central Park was replete with animals—pastoral, wild, and caged—and the new multispecies relationships that came with their presence. More than that, the park's elite custodians had made animals essential partners in the symbolic work of sculpting the park's refining influences.

During the twentieth century, as the population in the neighborhoods around the park grew and diversified, Central Park saw new struggles over its animated green space. African American women from Harlem's growing middle and upper classes met white resistance when they began to ride horses on the park's bridle paths. Avian enthusiasts took to the Ramble, an area of dense vegetation and serpentine paths that attracted diverse populations of birds. So did members of the city's gay community, some of whom used it as a cruising destination—with birding as their cover. As a result, the Ramble's growing renown as a birding hot spot grew entangled with queer ecologies in ways that often troubled elite New Yorkers. "At a moment of increasingly visible human difference in the park," as Biehler incisively observes, "animal spaces became battlegrounds where white supremacist and heteronormative users attempted to maintain hegemony over the landscape."

The fates of pastoral and caged animals also shifted. By the early twentieth century, the park's menagerie had deteriorated as attention shifted to the New York Zoological Park in the Bronx, which opened in 1899. But an infusion of New Deal funding during the early 1930s underwrote a redesigned Central Park Zoo, one that catered to children and a belief that relationships with animals were critical to child development in the perilous city. Over the next few decades, as zoos evolved, more visitors felt a sense of sadness as they gazed at the zoo's animals, whose cages and enclosures seemed increasingly inadequate and cruel. These poor conditions led to further efforts at renewal, though, as the recent case of Flaco suggests, the fate of Central Park's caged animals remains a source of reformist concern. Central Park's sheep also faded from the landscape as visions of the modern city and the need for more recreational space drove them away. Today the sheepless Sheep Meadow and the famous Tavern on the Green restaurant, which occupies the former sheepfold, are the main vestiges of the park's pastoral past. In the northern part of the park, too often neglected by park officials, Black anglers increasingly made claims on the park's waters, releasing catfish as a new source of recreational fishing. In these and other ways, the park's evolution as a contested public space almost always involved animals, and the volition of the park's animals shaped human perceptions of the park and each other in turn.

Animating Central Park is a masterful multispecies history, a model not only for finding animals everywhere in our past but also for showing us how those animals have mattered to the stories we have too often told without them. To see Central Park animated is to see it anew. It is to recognize that humans have constantly remade this highly designed space in partnership with animals and that animals have sometimes escaped our designs in ways that challenge, inspire, and change us. "What the history of Central Park as an animated landscape shows us most clearly," Biehler concludes, "is that elites and privileged city dwellers have asserted great power to shape green spaces and animal life but that other communities, human and more-than-human, have also made places that are socially and ecologically consequential."

Acknowledgments

It has been a humbling journey to trace the far-flung paths of more-than-human life that join in the 843 acres of Central Park. I am humbled anew to think of the people—human and otherwise—without whom I could not have begun or completed this years-long project. The journey began many years ago under the mentorship of Bill Cronon, with a major assist from Lisa Naughton. Lisa began challenging me with her deep insights about animals, parks, and ecological politics back in the year 2000. Bill always asked just the right questions, saw the potential in a small idea, and inspired me with his love of place and the world. Matthew Turner, Gregg Mitman, Kris Olds, Jamie Peck, Leila Harris, and Bob Ostergren also shaped me as a geographer and historian and thereby shaped this book.

I am grateful to editors and staff with University of Washington Press and the Weyerhaeuser series: Mike Baccam, Andrew Berzanskis, Justine Sargent, Joeth Zucco, Regan Huff, and everyone who helped me craft my ideas and research into this book. Thanks to our series editor Paul Sutter for sticking with me as I muddled through the project's messy middle stages. This book would not be what it is without kind yet incisive comments from Paul and two anonymous reviewers. I can never thank you enough.

Many librarians and archivists have helped me access the historical materials that made this project possible. Most of these documents were housed at the New York City Municipal Archives, where Kenneth Cobb, Rossy Mendez, and other staff supported me with their extensive knowledge and many hours of their time. Major thanks also go to Cara Dellatte and staff at the New York Public Library; Madeleine Thompson and Sana Masood at the Wildlife Conservation Society Library and Archives; Erica Libhart at the National Sporting Library & Museum; A. J. Muhammad and other staff at the Schomburg Center for Research in Black Culture; Jill Reichenbach and staff at the New-York Historical Society. I have also benefited from the work of folks at the Museum of the City of New York, the Library of Congress (thanks Joshua Levy and many, many others), and the Museum of Chinese in America (thanks to Nancy Ng Tam and Yue Ma). Thanks to Logan Esdale at the Carl Van Vechten Trust. Thanks to Ken Lustbader and Amanda Davis at New York's LGBT Historic Sites, who helped me understand the landscape of queerness in the city. And of course I am grateful to the librarians at my home institution's Albin O. Kuhn Library, especially Semhar Yohannes and Drew Alfgren.

I am grateful to the Dresher Center for the Humanities at UMBC for granting me a residential fellowship that allowed me to focus on writing. Thanks to Jessica Berman, Courtney Hobson, and Rachel Brubaker for their support and to my co-fellows Theresa Runstedtler, Michelle Scott, and Katherine Bankole-Medina for helping make a vibrant intellectual community.

Many "writing buddies" worked on their own projects alongside me over the past several years, helping sustain me in virtual space and in person. Amy Smith Muise has been a steady and supportive friend, cheering me on when progress was slow and teaching me much about horses, sheep, goats, and cows. Yolanda Valencia, Chris Hawn, and Dena Aufseeser all shared my concern for life and justice in urban environments and greatly improved the book with their comments and insights on work in progress. I am also grateful to Hanieh Molana for organizing the Feminist Geography Writing Group, in which we all cheer each other on.

Other colleagues at my home institution (longtime or passing through) supplied encouragement, support, and ideas about more-than-human cities, culture, justice, and economies. Many thanks to Jaime Barrett, Chris Blume, Adriana DiSilvestro, Kate Drabinski, Amy Froide, Maggie Holland, Molly Jones-Lewis, David Lansing, Dillon Mahmoudi, Jared Margulies, Carole McCann, Andy Miller, Val Pasión, Liz Patton, JH Pitas, Ashanté Reese, Craig Saper, Mariya Shcheglovitova, Tissa Thomas, Fan Yang, and Alan Yeakley. A special thanks to Ohad Paris for taking time with me to discuss urban birds. Thanks to administrative staff members Robin Heckathorn Schmidbauer and Donna Dwayer, who helped arrange travel to archives and conferences.

The project benefited from support from several diligent research assistants: Bee Brown, Ari Cacic, Grace Krach, Em Schumacher, and Simon Winter. Thanks also to members of my Environment & Power seminar and my Animals & Society class in 2022 who formed wonderful communities for thinking about nature, justice, and place.

I am grateful to other scholars in many disciplines who have helped shape my thinking at key moments: Peter Alagona, Rafi Arefin, Mark Barrow, Steven Corey, Fritz Davis, Matthew Gandy, Shannon LaDeau, Nancy Langston, Catherine McNeur, Mars Plater, Mike Rawson, Tom Robertson, Kara Schlichting, Sherri Sheu, Kendra Smith-Howard, Lisa Uddin, Robert Wilson, Sacoby Wilson, and Carl Zimring.

Thanks to Sara Cedar Miller, who shared about her wonderful book when our paths crossed at the archives. Thanks to Suzanne Zywicki, Kristen Ellington, Alice Deutsch, and Robert DiCandido for welcoming me into the world of birding.

This project about the more-than-human world has constantly reminded me of my indebtedness to the web of life and the deep history to which we all belong. I honor the Lenape people who long stewarded Mannahatta (and who still endeavor to make place there) and the ecosystem on this island that connects to so many other places. I cannot name all the members of this web here, but a few notables whose paths I crossed in the park include hummingbirds, orioles, warblers, titmice, woodcocks, egrets, herons, ducks, crows, robins, cardinals, sparrows, dogs, turtles, squirrels, chipmunks, horses, fish, bees, dragonflies, and of course my fellow humans—riding horses, walking dogs, fishing, rescuing a turtle from the Drive, watching birds in the Ramble and the North Woods.

I am grateful to Brendan O'Brien, Amanda Segilia, and their lovely children for generously hosting me during one of my trips to New York City. Thanks to the staff at The Jane Hotel, where I usually stayed, and to the staff at the Old Rose who kept me fed during my stays.

Cherished friends provided respite throughout this journey: Stephanie and Brian Slattery; Tara Duffy and Chuck Wall; Giselle Hicks and Bill Ross. Joanne Savage and Mikey Weidman helped my family weather the pandemic; Emily Eldredge helped me see the park with fresh eyes.

My extended family provided love and comfort, shelter, food, fun, and free childcare. Thank you to Cristine and T. J. Kirsch, Eric and Karen Biehler, Stephen and Jayne Biehler, Sharon and John Day, Caitlin Day and Tess Abellera, Laura and Andrew Giarolo, and my nieces and nephews.

Alice, Brigid, Nathan, Cullen, and Jonesy have been living with this project for a long time (Brigid's whole life and the cats' too). Words can't thank you enough for bearing with me all these years, for your help with research and editing tasks, for your inspiring hope for multispecies and environmental justice, and for your constant love and support.

ANIMATING CENTRAL PARK

Introduction

As New York City suffered through the first wave of COVID-19 in spring of 2020, human New Yorkers—and often their dogs—sought relief from the pandemic lockdown on Central Park's winding paths, vast lawns, and other open spaces. While the park allows dogs to run unleashed within certain hours and spaces, some areas always require leashing, including the sensitive bird habitat of the Ramble.[1] As many New Yorkers took up birding for the first time, some veteran birders attempted to enforce the leash rules, often turning their cell phone cameras on those who released their dogs there. Some, including Christian Cooper, also sometimes goaded recalcitrant dog people to snap on a leash by offering treats to their canine companions. A naturalist, writer, and activist, Cooper had served on NYC Audubon's board, created Marvel Comics' first queer superhero storylines, ran an organization that supported pro-LGBTQ+ candidates, and appeared in the 2012 documentary *Birders: The Central Park Effect*.[2]

Illicit dog running seemed to peak during the lockdown. "In some thirty-five years birding in the park," Cooper wrote in his memoir, "I had never seen it like this." He attributed this "epidemic" of leashing violations to the closure of many official dog parks.[3] On the morning of May 25, 2020, late in the spring migration season, Cooper saw few birds (or other birders—many elders stayed home to avoid contagion) but did spot a cocker spaniel bounding off leash. He asked the white woman accompanying the dog to put it back on its leash, urged her to visit a nearby

OLD

RESERVOIR

Capacity 150,000,000

35 Acrs

THE RAMBLE
36 Acrs

THE LAKE
20 Acres

THE GREEN
15 Acrs

CENTRAL

PARK

THE PLAY GROUND

DRIVE

CENTRAL PARK
FORMERLY
MANHATTAN SQUARE

Wm. R Woolsey

Wm A Davis

Isaac Carrow

Isaac Jones

Wells

John Mullamphy

Kimberly

Cor. of N.Y.

F. Wood

John Bogert

F. Wood

J. Tallman

9TH AV

8TH AV

5TH AV

BROADWAY

ORNAMENTAL WATER

PLAN OF CENTRAL PARK

off-leash area, and then offered the dog treats when she refused. What happened next is well known because Christian Cooper recorded it all, and his sister shared the video via social media: the woman, Amy Cooper (no relation), called 9-1-1 to report that "an African American man" was threatening her life.[4] Ms. Cooper's attempt to weaponize racism and assert her presumed victimhood backfired on her, and Mr. Cooper has since achieved ever-greater platforms for promoting equity in the conservation field while sharing his joy in birds.[5]

Christian Cooper calls "dustup[s] between a birder and a dog-walker . . . the second-oldest story in the Ramble."[6] Indeed, Central Park's more-than-human archive is replete with stories of multispecies relationships in which beings assert power through space. In the park's early decades, dogs and cats mostly roamed outdoors, and many preyed upon small wildlife in the Ramble and even caged creatures at the menagerie. At the turn of the twentieth century, bird and squirrel lovers in the Ramble urged children and adults to cultivate gentle relationships with wildlife. Later, during the Great Depression, affluent Manhattan dog owners, many stuck in the city after relinquishing second homes in the country, pressured park authorities to open up space for their pampered pooches to roam. And around the same time, the singer Ethel Waters stood up to a gang of white equestrians who reported her to park police for nothing more than riding a horse while Black and queer. In spite of their attacks, Waters still reveled in exploring the park atop beloved horses, alongside other human and equine companions.

For as long as humans have inhabited Manhattan, their lives have been intertwined and interdependent with other-than-human beings, making

OPPOSITE: This plan map of New York City shows the southern half of Central Park as of 1867, including the Lake, Sheep Meadow, the Ramble, and the Arsenal, where the menagerie was located. As of the creation of this map, Manhattan Square to the west of the park was still planned for a formal zoological garden. Courtesy of the New York Public Library Digital Collections.

place together. Humans of many social identities have delighted in more-than-human encounters in the park, whether listening for birdsong in the park's forests, walking canine companions, trotting along the bridle paths, admiring sheep in the fold, or laughing at monkeys in the menagerie. For much of the park's history, affluent white men powerfully shaped its human-animal landscapes, although other New Yorkers—human and otherwise—asserted their attachment to places and to other species. This book argues that many New York communities have claimed urban public space through their relationships with animals, often in conflict with city authorities or other park users, and with varying effects on the animals themselves. Although authorities constructed the park as an enclosed patch of nature in the growing city, urbanizing spaces outside and beyond bore important consequences for human-animal relationships there. Furthermore, these other-than-human animals have helped remake the park, and often spaces beyond, with their bodies, behaviors, and relationships with human New Yorkers.

Humans, Animals, and the Park's Origins

Struggles over human-animal relationships in the place that is now Central Park date back long before the park itself. Communities of Lenape people had stewarded the land and waters of Mannahatta for over a millennium, managing vegetation to encourage deer populations and harvesting deer, beaver, turkey, fish, and oysters all around the island. Lenape hunters also created roads passing through what is now Central Park that connected living sites with hunting and fishing areas. The interdependence of Lenape and their other-than-human kin reminds us that animals are inextricably tied with human placemaking and mobility.[7] Beginning in the 1600s, Dutch and English invaders dismantled the more-than-human world of Lenapehoking, which stretched from Mannahatta to what we today call Philadelphia and Delaware. The Dutch West India Company enrolled Lenape people in the fur trade, buying beavers until they devastated the rodents' population. The Dutch, falsely claiming to have purchased the land, built Fort Amsterdam at the island's southern tip; some settled at the northern end, encroaching upon Lenape villages and naming one area "Otterspoor" for the tracks of another species living among them. Meanwhile, Lenape reeled from a smallpox epidemic and growing conflicts among these invaders and other Indigenous tribes. In 1640, the colonial director general blamed Indigenous people for theft of a settler's hog—a crime actually perpetrated by another settler—creating the pretext for massacres that killed hundreds of Lenape. Many survivors and their descendants made new homes as far away as Oklahoma, Wisconsin, and Ontario. Not only did settlers kill and displace Lenape people, but over the next two centuries, they depleted wildlife through hunting, fishing, and converting the land to industry, farms, and homes. The very existence of New York City and Central Park is predicated on this cultural, ecological, and territorial dispossession. By the mid-nineteenth century, the island's landscape was already a palimpsest in which Europeans had all but erased the Lenape people and their relationships with terrestrial, marine, and estuarine life.[8]

The Dutch—and then, after the 1680s, the English—built over Lenapehoking starting from the southern end of Manhattan, laying out numbered streets as far north as the lower Forties by the early 1800s. All manner of domesticated animals filled those streets, including horses and dogs who supplied muscle power for urban commerce and transport. Hogs, goats, and cows also moved to and fro, with or without human supervision.[9] In the nearly four miles between there and the Dutch village of Harlem, a few affluent members of New York society built estates on more upland areas, and others—African Americans, Irish Americans, and German Americans—established small communities too. Many kept domesticated animals for their livelihoods.

Health and planning authorities in New York, as in other US cities, increasingly restricted urban livestock agriculture, beginning with the hogs who roamed downtown and industrial dairy farms blamed for killing hundreds of infants with diluted and tainted milk.[10] The middle of the island remained a haven for animal husbandry and small-scale industry based on animal products until 1858. Then the dominant settlers emptied the center of the island of human residences and livestock, renegotiating human-animal relationships yet again after state and city authorities selected this site for a grand new park. They promised healthy green space to New Yorkers of all classes, unlike existing parks that were promenades for the privileged.[11] City authorities dispossessed Black residents of their formal land ownership in a community called Seneca Village and also evicted the German and Irish families that had rented or informally claimed land north of the built-up city with their domestic creatures.[12] Central Park enclosed more space as off-limits to these livestock. Real estate speculators and other New York elites bought up adjacent parcels, their value sent skyrocketing by their proximity to the new park.[13] Landowners and infrastructure development gradually squeezed farmers and their animals into Manhattan's ever-narrower undeveloped edges.

Calvert Vaux and Frederick Law Olmsted's Greensward plan for Central Park, adopted in 1858, completely reshaped these 843 acres that had for millennia teemed with wild animals and more briefly with creatures whom we might call "free-range" today. Olmsted wrote of the plan, "Every foot of the park's surface, every tree and bush, as well as every arch, roadway and walk has been fixed where it is with a purpose."[14] Olmsted omitted animals from this statement, and this omission is both representative of the Greensward plan and revealing about early park planning. Apart from the working horses implied by the bridle and carriage paths and crosstown roads required by the park design competition, Vaux and Olmsted's plan said little about nonhuman animals in Central Park. Other entrants in the design competition, however, greatly desired an "animated" park. They envisioned livestock exhibits, ponds full of waterfowl, landscaped zoos.[15] The elite Central Park Commission's majority chose the mostly unanimated Greensward not because of its lack of animals but for its strong design principles. Animals soon claimed space there, however, with their bodies and behaviors, from goats and cats to moths and warblers. Meanwhile, humans manipulated other animals' lives—from bison and swans to sheep and goldfish—by placing them in the park, some with official approval, others illicitly.

Thus, despite general inattention to animals in the Greensward plan, Olmsted and Vaux, park administrators, and New Yorkers in general grappled with new demands for animal spaces. How would humans and nonhuman animals fit together in this precious patch of green and blue gradually enclosed by buildings, roads, and other infrastructure? How and for whom should the city support urban livestock agriculture and potential fisheries in the park as urban growth edged out other opportunities to raise animals in the city? Who should decide what wildlife would get to inhabit this special green space? What resources should the city invest in an equestrian path that might be accessible only to a narrow segment of New Yorkers? How would pet dogs use the park as residential and business development filled up other spaces for play and exercise around Manhattan? Who should have access to what caged animals, under what conditions? (Few asked whether animals should be caged at all.) Olmsted and Vaux aimed to create a purposeful new landscape within central Manhattan that would mold New Yorkers' relationships with nature according to aesthetic ideals. However, they did not anticipate the ways that humans of many social positions and identities would remake space with other-than-humans there, seeking control or domination or struggling to belong and thrive together.

Humans, Animals, and Urban Green Space

Animating Central Park examines a specific urban public space over one hundred years of its creation and evolution. Four themes connect the stories of more-than-human communities across the history and geography of Central Park. First, as the brief prehistory presented here suggests, powerful humans have repeatedly *displaced* other beings by claiming territory within Manhattan. In more-than-human cities—which is to say, all cities—animals are essential to these dynamics of dispossession, erasure, exclosure, and gentrification. For example, after the city seized the land to make Central Park, the park commissioners allowed "gentlemen" farmers and butchers to select new livestock to graze on pastures once used by Seneca Villagers and immigrant pastoralists and their animals. In such moments, contestations over territory were shaped by animals' behaviors, perceived threats by or to them, and animals' cultural and material meanings for specific communities. This theme of displacement, however, is not meant to imply that urban space is a scarce resource that naturally elicits competition. Rather, urban societies create scarcity by failing to plan for the needs of all communities, human and other-than-human, and allowing systems of privilege to allocate resources.[16]

A second theme relates to *claims to space*. Scholars who examine human struggles over public parks argue that they are more than locations for recreation and contact with nature. For some humans and nonhumans who lack other places to carry out life functions, public spaces like parks are vital for their very existence. Practices such as fencing and policing limit certain activities and communities. In addition, public spaces become stages for mutual visibility where members of a pluralistic society may recognize one another's belonging. Those who gain access to public space may use it as a source of power. As geographers Lynn Staeheli and Don Mitchell write, public space can be "foundational in establishing who 'the people' are" through its rules accommodating or excluding various beings and behaviors.[17] How might a public space like Central Park expand "the people" to include nonhuman animals—for example, songbirds who rely on its sheltering spaces as migratory stopovers—and how might humans use their relationships with animals in public space to exert power? From the bridle path to the Ramble, from dog runs to the zoo, Central Park authorities and visitors have attempted to define which humans and other-than-humans belong in the polity of the city. Meanwhile, human groups from birders to equestrians to dog people have often cited the needs and vulnerability of favored animals in order to exert control over spaces and people within the park. Thus, here I explore how human groups' uses of power and affiliation with animals can help or hinder the creation of genuinely pluralistic more-than-human spaces.[18]

Third, this book examines how policies and practices *value* diverse humans, animals, and spaces, and how systems of value have changed over time. Indigenous cultures such as the Lenape's have long respected non-human animals as interdependent kin. Capitalist systems have carved up and commodified animals, calculating the worth of their material components—meat, milk, pelts, fiber, labor power, and their behavior and companionship as pets or entertainers. Other New Yorkers, including many immigrants and working-class residents, used animals to re-create rural traditions of fishing, farming, hunting, and vernacular bird-watching in the city. With the creation of Central Park, authorities and other city dwellers ascribed value to animals by making space and allocating resources for them there and simply by visiting them. Prominent New Yorkers in government, business, and reform movements believed that certain animals inspired city dwellers to learn about urban nature or that animals would provoke desired emotions such as kindness, contemplativeness, or excitement. In the nineteenth century, advocates for the park used the term *animated* to describe how nonhumans enlivened landscapes (hence this book's title). These advocates strived to populate the park with animals whom they believed would educate and enlighten the masses about nature and landscapes, from bison to Southdown sheep to English sparrows. At the same time, generations of New Yorkers of all backgrounds visited the menagerie for the thrill of seeing pachyderms and exotic cats up close. Today scholars call all such uses of animals "encounter value." It took decades for authorities and visitors to ascribe what we might call "intrinsic" value to some animals in the park.[19]

Finally, a fourth theme concerns the *mobility* of living beings, including both their power to move within the park and the way their movements (self-driven or forced by certain humans) connect the park space with other spaces, both near and distant. Once within the park, some animals, whether natives or newcomers, exerted their own life force by altering ecologies and landscapes or transporting humans or materials, sometimes in alignment and sometimes in conflict with park managers' aims. Powerful humans entangled this space with the global trade in animals designated as companions, educators, or entertainers, transporting creatures like bison, sheep, and chimpanzees from across the continent and around the world into New York's port. When menagerie captives reproduced there, the zoological department sometimes sold or traded their progeny around the region and country as part of economic and political relationships with farmers, networks of zoos, and others interested in animals. At a smaller scale, New Yorkers brought domesticated and wild animals into the park, both in cooperation with the park's zoological department and illicitly to fulfill their own needs and desires.[20]

Across all of these themes, humans of varied identities—by race, nationality, and class, gender, sexuality, and age—and nonhumans exerted power over space in important ways. The health and well-being of individual animals and animal populations were at stake as park authorities reshaped the city's land and water, as privileged New Yorkers dominated park attractions, and as immigrant, Black, poor, and queer New Yorkers made places for themselves there among the animals. These struggles over human-animal relationships and urban green space are not isolated from society beyond the park. Rather, struggles over animals in the park have often reinscribed histories and systems of domination—white supremacy, land appropriation, heteropatriarchy, colonialism, and exploitation of nature—upon this space.

Why Central Park?

Such more-than-human power dynamics play out in all urban public spaces, but this book looks to Central Park in part because of its iconic role in the history of landscaped urban parks, originating at a moment of rapid growth when city leaders anticipated conversion of land to industry, business, and residences. This process of urbanization obliterated wildlife habitat, constrained animal agriculture, and transformed other multispecies relationships.[21] Central Park also sits amid what became, in the twentieth century, a sprawling chain of cities and suburbs stretching along the East Coast. All around Central Park, urbanization converted wildlife habitats and farms, and rounds of disinvestment and redevelopment further displaced marginalized communities. In spite of initial inattention to nonhuman animals, the park became a haven for many wildlife species amid this sprawl; park patrons and authorities eventually claimed that this space was essential for promoting certain kinds of human-animal relationships.[22]

Central Park also became a crucible for ideas about urban landscapes that architects Frederick Law Olmsted and Calvert Vaux, their own sons as leaders in the subsequent generation of architects, and other followers spread across North American places. From Manhattan and Brooklyn to Washington, DC, Chicago, and California, Olmsted and Vaux's example reshaped multispecies cities.[23] Central Park thus plays a unique role in the history of animals in urban parks both materially and in terms of ideas and aesthetics.

Like so many green spaces, Central Park is at once beloved, vital, and marked by troubled histories. This book foregrounds struggles over more-than-human spaces while highlighting joy, survival, and hope for humans and nonhumans. It builds on critiques by scholars such as Roy Rosenzweig and Elizabeth Blackmar, Matthew Gandy, Stephen Germic, and Dorceta Taylor, emphasizing contradiction and complexity.[24] Central Park is a brilliant work of art *and* a space fraught with the baggage of western European empire, erasure of Indigenous history, gentrification, and cultural and spatial hegemony. Urban domesticated animals have been vital for immigrant communities' cultural survival and livelihoods, *and* they challenged worthy public health and environmental goals. Early park authorities and patrons mostly appreciated wild animals on instrumental terms rather than for their intrinsic value, *and* these authorities helped create critical wildlife habitat that persists today. Elites (who did not always agree with one another) powerfully attempted to shape the spaces and experiences of other groups while extracting value from urban space, people, and nature. Meanwhile, immigrants, people of color, working and poor folks, and queer folks exerted their own power in return. Amid these contradictions, animals have not been simply passive pawns. Central Park's more-than-human story reveals the long struggle among human communities and animals to shape urban space.

An Ethos and Vocabulary for Multispecies Historical Geography

Central Park—and indeed, all urban spaces—need more-than-human histories, but this kind of storytelling comes with challenges. Some studies of animals and environment lump all humans together as exploiters of animals. Instead, I have set out to emphasize the ways animals are enmeshed in struggles for survival and in evolving power dynamics among human communities and institutions. Birdsong from the trees, pounding hooves on the trail, bleating from the sheepfold, the caged cacophony of roars and chitters—these were all hard to hear in the historical evidence. It was often even harder to hear the voices of minoritized humans, whether they were displaced by the park or sought joy there. I have tried to center relationships—humans of all identities and communities have connections with animals, whether characterized by mutuality or violence, isolation or interdependence. Such relationships are never symmetrical, and each is unique. We cannot even assume that all members of a social group, such as white gentlemen farmers or Black equestrians, shared the same relationships with animals.

Human-animal relationships are plural, marked by varied interdependencies and assertions of power—ranging from subsistence hunting and fishing, to small-scale animal husbandry, to industrial dairy and meat production, to pet keeping, bird-watching, and zoo going, and even practices of avoidance. Political scientist Claire Jean Kim approaches such differences across race and culture by assuming shifting viewpoints in struggles over animals, and I try to follow her example. Furthermore, literary scholar Bénédicte Boisseron warns against equating the oppression of animals with that of minoritized human groups. Structures of oppression—for example, animal exploitation and the enslavement of racialized humans—are linked through global, hierarchical social systems, but oppressions are not strictly analogous. In New York City and Central Park, cultural hegemony, control and commodification of land, and policing of spaces have affected Black, immigrant, working-class, and queer communities along with certain animals, but each experienced and resisted these systems in distinct ways.[25]

Stories about historical animal "agency" also become complicated because we cannot assume that, say, a goat of today is the same as a goat in 1858 or even that all goats in 1858 performed their goat-ness in the same way. Furthermore, there is some peril in assuming what any nonhuman animal, historical or contemporary, experiences in terms of cognition, sensation, or the drives that propel their behavior. Historical records and observations can tell us what animals did and how they responded to their environments and fellow beings—where they moved or didn't move, what they ate, whether they bred and bore young, vocalizations and displays, defensive behaviors, or changes in their health.[26]

Finally, our language for referring to animals and human groups is ever imperfect, but I attempt to use terminology thoughtfully while acknowledging problematic categories. When possible, I refer to specific humans by their names and animals by their type; sometimes we know the name that humans gave to individual animals. When discussing animals generally, I often use the term *other-than-human* or *nonhuman* while recognizing that these label creatures by what they are not. These also risk lumping animals with beings from other kingdoms of life, such as plants or bacteria, and even nonliving entities such as rocks, water, buildings, and machines. The term *nonhuman* also inserts too sharp a break between humans and other species, denying what we all have in common. Even *animal* lumps together beings as varied as beetles, goldfish, and lions, and it often implies that humans do not belong to this category too. I often refer to groups of many kinds of beings as "multispecies" communities, but I prefer *more-than-human* to emphasize the expansiveness of life and relationships when more than one species is present. In using this term, I owe much to decolonial scholars who show that Indigenous societies have long conceived of other species as kin and refuse sharp categories separating humans and other beings.[27]

Animating Central Park: An Outline

Part 1 of this book traces the development of human-animal spaces in the park from its origins in the 1850s until about 1900. Over the park's first fifty years, powerful New Yorkers including the Central Park commissioners (especially Andrew Haswell Green), architects Olmsted and Vaux, zoological department director William Conklin, and many other park supporters exerted their power to reshape animal life and urban space. Meanwhile, humans from many communities marked by race, nationality, gender, and class, many of them unnamed in the historical record, along with numerous nonhuman individuals and populations renegotiated their place in remade fields, forests, and waters. They found themselves on either side of boundaries that now divided these pastoral and picturesque landscapes from private property and sprouting mansions, and eventually bustling streets and the churn of commerce and industry.

Rather than dividing this half-century chronologically, chapters 1 through 3 each examine a type of human-animal relationship that developed in the park. Chapter 1 tells the story of how elites displaced pastoralists and then used domesticated animals, particularly sheep, to re-create an idealized semblance of rural lifeways in the middle of Manhattan. Chapter 2 traces changing values related to wild animals, especially birds, squirrels, and fish that park patrons, authorities, and visitors released there, and other birds who through their own movements and perceptions found the new park's growing forests, fields, and waters to be suitable habitats. Chapter 3 examines controversies over the design and character of, and access to, Central Park's captive animal exhibits and how animals donated to the menagerie reflected the city's expanding urban footprint and economic connections. While these chapters classify animals as domestic, wild, and caged, they also show that creatures frequently crossed not only physical boundaries but also categorical ones.

Part 2 of the book picks up at the turn of the twentieth century and follows animal-human relationships through the 1970s, when the Central Park Conservancy began to assume several management functions for the park. Beginning around 1900, some policies toward animals in Central Park began to reflect greater concern for animals' existence and well-being and greater general attention to the park's role in supporting animals who lived and worked in New York. Yet the park also faced budgetary and logistical constraints that limited its ability to serve New York's expanding human populace *and* the many urban animals who needed the park too. Under these conditions, animal advocacy became a strategy for human groups—often white and affluent New Yorkers—to claim space and demand priority for the activities for which they used the park. Long-serving parks commissioner Robert Moses was not always a frontline decision-maker about animals in Central Park during this period, but his administration's policies, emphases, and exclusions nonetheless shaped human-animal relationships for nearly three decades.

As in part 1, part 2 of the book divides chapters based on spaces and relationships rather than chronology. Chapter 4 traces privileged park users' efforts to secure landscape rehabilitation on the bridle paths for the sake of horses' health and in the important bird habitat of the Ramble amid discrimination and even violence against Black and queer human users of these spaces. Chapter 5 follows the reconstruction of the Central Park Zoo and the way it centered an idealized vision of American childhood but concealed the suffering of animals living there. Chapter 6 examines three kinds of animals—sheep, fish, and dogs—whose belonging in the park was reshaped through urban development and varied human claims to space.

The main narrative of the book ends around 1980, in large part because of the changing governance of the park after that decade. Strapped to manage the park for much of the twentieth century, the City of New York arranged new relationships with private-sector organizations. The Central Park Conservancy formed to oversee preservation of the park's unique landscape. In the case of the Central Park Zoo, the 1970s and 1980s also saw the handover of the facility to the Wildlife Conservation Society. These new institutional relationships brought with them new human-animal relationships that will be stories for others to tell. In the conclusion of the book, I use a few more recent human-animal stories in Central Park to reflect on current efforts in cities to make more sustainable and just places for creatures.

While focused on Central Park, this history also tells us much about how plural humans and animals make, and could make, space in cities around the world. The nineteenth century's era of grand park building coincided with rapid urbanization and changing public health regulations in the United States in the mid- to late nineteenth century, altering human-animal relationships in cities. Many other large urban parks followed a similar trajectory, contemporary to or shortly after Central Park's origins, some of them designed by the same team of Olmsted and Vaux that had initially left animals out of the picture.[28]

Today we also see momentous urban changes, though of different sorts: human beings are flocking into some cities, leaving others, and everywhere reordering themselves within. Nonhumans still seek places in these remade urban worlds, often in relationship with humans. Older industrial cities of the early twenty-first century continue to see land use and social changes wrought by long-standing processes of racist segregation and deindustrialization. New efforts at urban greening may be just and community driven, or they may contribute to rising property values and displacement (often called eco-gentrification). Nonhuman animal lives are often at stake too. Some advocates hope that emerging green spaces, though often configured as more of a patchwork than New York's vast Central Park, will become migratory corridors for wildlife displaced by exurban development and climate change. Others have begun to raise livestock, whether as a hobby or to support community food security and environmental education. Similar processes of green space change, human power struggles, and animal occupancy mark cities from Manhattan to Mumbai, from Detroit to Dakar.[29] As a participant in efforts to make green spaces for everyone (I work with communities in Baltimore too), I see the present as another moment like the 1850s, when city dwellers attempted to preserve land for human recreation and health. Could the stories of multispecies struggles in Central Park help inform a more just and intentional politics for more-than-human twenty-first-century cities?

PART 1

Creating and Contesting the Animated Landscape

This view of Central Park from its southwestern corner shows urban development around the park as of 1895, along with horse-drawn carriage and train traffic on Central Park West (Eighth Avenue) and Central Park South (Fifty-Ninth Street). Courtesy of the Museum of the City of New York.

IN 1869, the Board of Commissioners of the Central Park touted the appeal of animal encounters to a wide spectrum of New Yorkers, stating that "the interest in animated nature is inexhaustible. There is something always fascinating to young and old in the endlessly varied aspects, the wonderfully diversified movements, and the almost infinite differences of instinct and intelligence displayed by the multitudinous inhabitants of earth, air and water."[1] The city had seized the land for the park just twelve years earlier, so many New Yorkers surely remembered the animal life that had recently teemed there.[2] According to park advocates, those goats, hogs, cows, and geese of middle Manhattan's informal commons roused none of the endless fascination now inspired by the park's beasts, birds, and fish. Colonization and settlement since the 1600s had already erased long-established human-animal relationships in Lenapehoking. Now the park displaced multispecies pastoralist communities in favor of new animal spaces designed for a growing metropolis.

Part 1 of *Animating Central Park* traces how park authorities, supporters, and visitors, along with a variety of animals remade a more-than-human public space, often in tension with one another, between the 1850s and 1900. Park boosters, administrators like Andrew Haswell Green and zoological director William Conklin, and (after initially neglecting animals in the Greensward plan) the architects Vaux and Olmsted all endeavored to create spaces in the park where New Yorkers could encounter nonhuman creatures. Over the course of the park's first fifty years, they along with hundreds of donors from New York, across the United States, and around the world filled those spaces with domesticated, free, and captive animals expected to gratify visitors' inexhaustible fascinations.

There is little evidence, however, that park authorities and patrons valued animated nature for animals' own sakes.[3] Even for earnest reformers, animals were educational tools; emblems of nature, nation, and empire; and models of healthful and peaceful contemplation of nature. Whether selecting a celebrated English sheep breed, importing swans and sparrows from Europe, or receiving a bison reserved from slaughter on the plains, park supporters valued animals for the emotional and intellectual capacities they were supposed to foster in other city dwellers. Furthermore, these "animating" ambitions extended Euro-Americans' ecological control over landscapes local and global.

In this context, other humans as well as animals used their own kinds of power to remake park spaces. In violation of park rules, young goatherds allowed their charges to wander in and dine on the bushes. Anonymous visitors released goldfish into the park's water features. Wildlife—from migratory birds and herbivorous insects to rabbits and raccoons—found their way in, to human visitors' delight and dismay. Some early environmentalists claimed space to protect wildlife and teach humans kindness and quiet. Throngs of visitors queued up to ogle monkeys and bears and protested when authorities threatened to move the menagerie farther away. The power of elites was not absolute, and many New Yorkers, human and otherwise, resisted displacement and hardened borders to make their own kinds of animated landscapes.

Human New Yorkers, and Their Animals, at the Park's Origin

As we embark upon this story, it will be helpful to understand the contours of New York society circa 1850, as discussions about a grand park for the city began. Elite and middle-class New Yorkers led the movement to establish a grand new park. The "Upper-Ten-dom," as the *Times* called them, included established white Americans, many of whom had made their fortunes in trade and finance. From stately homes along Fifth Avenue and from smaller parks already in use for fashionable promenades, elites eyed real estate north of downtown, believing that wherever a larger park was placed, its borders would see escalating property values.[4] A gridded street plan had existed on paper since the 1810s, promising avenues and cross streets spanning the island, but many parcels remained undeveloped in 1850. Furthermore, while many elites could afford to feed and outfit horses not just for business transport but also for leisure equestrianism, the island offered few scenic bridle paths for exercise, fashionable display, and socializing. A landscaped park would enable Manhattan's wealthiest to extract more financial value from the land, to see and be seen (perhaps on horseback or walking a dog), and to elevate New York's cultural status alongside European cities with grand parks. While this class often imposed rules and aesthetics that limited human-animal relationships in the city, they did not always act in agreement among themselves.[5]

Meanwhile, a growing middle class of clerks, educators, managers, artisans, and merchants also agitated for a park befitting their values and tastes. Andrew Jackson Downing, the country's foremost landscape designer, promoted the idea of a grand park for New York in his journal *The Horticulturalist* and in correspondence with city leaders from his offices north of the city. Downing attempted to translate the design and culture of European parks for what he saw as a more democratic society in the United States, promoting "popular refinement." His aesthetics appealed to elite as well as middle-class Americans.[6] These New Yorkers sought leisure recreation, healthy spaces for exercise, and refuge from the downtown's crowding and noise. Many, like their wealthier counterparts, sought green spaces far uptown.[7] These sites were miles away, though—a long ride on new horse-drawn trains stretching northward toward Harlem.

Affluent New Yorkers, including many philanthropists and reformers, extolled the benefits of a park for working-class folks—cartmen, manual laborers, domestic servants, factory workers, boardinghouse matrons—and the poor, many of them immigrants. Elites declared that a public park would provide the masses with fresh air, wholesome recreation on their Sunday holiday, and enlightening contact with nature—something better, to their minds, than the rowdy animal displays offered by showmen downtown. Such arguments were self-serving, justifying an enormous public expense whose benefits were defined by elites. Still, many fervently believed that the park would help Americanize immigrants, condition moral and orderly behavior, and perhaps mollify unrest over inequality. In 1864, the park commissioners also articulated their expectation that the park would unify a diverse immigrant populace: "The amusements and routine of the daily life of the Sicilian and Scotchman are dissimilar," but "there is ... a universality in nature, that affords a field of enjoyment to all observers of her works."[8] The working class swelled with immigrants fleeing oppression and deprivation in Europe; in 1850, nearly half of Manhattan's human residents were foreign-born. Many new Americans hailed from rural places—especially Ireland and southern German states such as Bavaria.[9] Most moved into the airless tenements of lower Manhattan and labored in commerce and industry. Some of the earlier arrivals released hogs to run in the streets and later butchered them.

Just under fifteen thousand Black people made their homes in Manhattan in 1850; many lived in "Little Africa" downtown and later moved to the area on the West Side known as San Juan Hill or to the east in Yorkville. Like the new immigrants, many were exploited by the financial and industrial juggernaut of New York City. Political parties favored European immigrants, however. Irish immigrants, although also targets of prejudice, eked out political and economic advantages, including some laws that excluded Black New Yorkers from competition for working-class jobs. In the 1820s, lawmakers courted Irish constituents by banning Black New Yorkers from obtaining licenses to operate horse-and-cart businesses, although many resisted the law.[10] New York also restricted the voting rights of Black men to those possessing a certain amount of property. Some two hundred Black Manhattanites, many of them property owners, lived in a community on the middle-west of the island that some called Seneca Village, established by Andrew Williams, Epiphany Davis, and Charles Treadwell in 1825. Williams identified himself as a cartman in the 1855 census.[11] Working-class and elite residents in Seneca Village built churches, schools, and businesses in a community dedicated to Black freedom and flourishing.[12]

While many Irish Americans saw themselves as competing with Black Americans, some lived in Seneca Village. All around Seneca Village,

German and Irish immigrants transplanted pastoral livelihoods from the old country, releasing hundreds of goats, pigs, cows, horses, and fowl to range across this unofficial commons.[13] These animals converted vegetation and humans' discards into flesh, milk, eggs, and labor power. For children who helped with animal-related chores, these creatures provided companionship too.

Through the 1880s and 1890s, Italians and Russians, including Jewish people from across eastern Europe, formed a growing share of immigrants to New York. Some Chinese immigrants also came east from California in efforts to escape racist attacks in mining and railroad towns; exclusionary legislation limited this community's growth after 1882.[14] In New York, these immigrants and native-born working-class and poor folks found new sources of illness and exploitation but also community in the tenements of the Lower East Side. Many later immigrants also came from rural areas and hoped to keep some animals to supplement their livelihoods, but city policies, access to land, and the judgment of their neighbors limited these practices.

Divisions of social class, race, and nationality shaped more-than-human New York in important ways, and differences of gender, age, and generation also intersected with these aspects of identity. In some working-class and poor families, women and children's work included caring for small animals like goats and geese. The Victorian era is often stereotyped as a time of gendered public and private spheres and the idealization of innocent childhood, but such ideals did not carry across classes, if they ever applied fully to anyone. Working-class girls and young women strained against family strictures, seeking fun in spaces like the menagerie. Middle-class reformers fretted about the moral standing of women, immigrants, and urban children, pointing out animal models for American motherhood and accusing rowdy boys of cruelty toward animals. Yet immigrants also made space for wild birds and other animals within their communities. And even among elite and middle-class naturalists, a

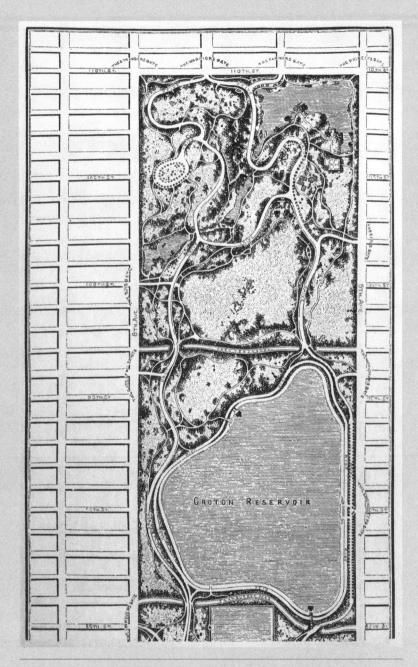

Map of the north end of the park from Clarence Cook's 1869 guide shows the Croton Reservoir, the North Woods, the Harlem Meer and other water bodies, along with bridle paths and transverse roads. As of the creation of this map, much of the street grid around the park remained undeveloped. From Cook, *Description of the New York Central Park.*

generational shift brought new attitudes toward birds and bird-watching that played out in the park.[15]

The lives of human New Yorkers of all social classes and identities intertwined with those of nonhuman animals in the years before Central Park's establishment—and we have said little as yet about the food, fiber, muscle power, and companionship that animals also provided. Furthermore, human activities converted farmland and wildlife habitat into tenements and industry, streets and brownstones, mansions and office buildings. Health authorities deployed police power to drive urban animals out of downtown. It was no coincidence that the park's construction also became an opportunity to remake the place of animals in New York.

CHAPTER 1

Reassembling a Rural City

Many historians have told the story of human-animal life in central Manhattan right before the park, but it is worth revisiting this moment in time and space to set the scene. A lively multispecies neighborhood emerges from 1850s censuses and land sale records, plats and archaeology, and alternately sensational and snide accounts from media and the surveyors who helped lay out the park. Entering along a rocky pathway south and east of the current park's center, over a mile from the edge of the built-up city, we pass locals toting baskets of cabbages and potatoes or buckets of bones. Geese peck at the ground, catching worms among clusters of mulberry. Cows meander in pursuit of forage. A woman hangs laundry, a dog sleeping near her feet. Children play among the wooden homes, ostensibly supervising goats who climb on rock outcrops and root in refuse middens. Hogs jostle about in a pen behind a house constructed from the boards of an old dock. New Yorkers in adjacent areas called the main village "Pigtown" as a pejorative, and *Harper's* magazine cheekily captioned sketches of the animals as "remarkable zoological specimens" and the humans as "fashionable denizens."[1]

Urban livestock supplied food and livelihoods for many poor and immigrant New Yorkers. Authorities already attempted to limit livestock raising in the southern parts of the island, particularly practices that threatened human health and safety—the release of thousands of hogs downtown, the feeding of distillery waste to dairy cows.[2] Historians

Catherine McNeur and Ted Steinberg have called this process "taming Manhattan" and "the death of the organic city," respectively.[3] Still, north of the built-up city, farmers attempted to use open spaces as their forebears had in rural Ireland or Bavaria.

In the coming months and years, park authorities created and enforced new spatial boundaries that curtailed movement of the domestic animals in central Manhattan. The park also spurred rising real estate values on its borders, hastening the displacement of subsistence farming (some folks found other ways to keep goats, geese, and hogs). Yet commissioners, architects, and other powerful New Yorkers soon brought new domesticated creatures—majestic horses and renowned breeds of sheep and cows—into the park, embodying their vision of improved rural landscapes. Park authorities expected that encounters with these animals would promote health, education, agricultural progress, national character, and peaceful contemplation. Few acknowledged the tensions between displacing some humans and livestock in working relationships and putting other domestic animals on display. This chapter argues that while the park helped "tame" Manhattan, it also displaced one version of the more-than-human city and reassembled a rarefied facsimile of rural animal husbandry within its bounds. Here we will trace how park authorities and supporters reordered relationships between humans and domestic livestock, bringing animal spaces under municipal control and benefiting park patrons aligned with elite agricultural reform movements.

Domestic Animals and Manhattan Society before the Park

Since early colonial days, city dwellers in North America had used private, informal, and common land for raising livestock. Pastoralism (raising livestock for subsistence and livelihoods) persisted in East Coast cities well into the nineteenth century. From the 1600s, settlers enjoyed legal rights to graze cows or sheep on town commons, established through English law. In Boston, a cow tax supported a city cowherd and the purchase and upkeep of breeding bulls. As elite residents moved into adjacent neighborhoods, they demanded more exclusive access to the commons as recreational rather than productive space. Real estate interests seeking to increase property values campaigned against cows there, citing elite women's need for safer public spaces. The city finally closed the commons to grazing after a city referendum in 1830.[4]

For New Yorkers of this era, contact with domesticated animals remained part of daily life in public space. Livestock teemed in Lower Manhattan, but this was no grassy commons. Working-class New Yorkers had for decades released hogs—thousands of them—onto downtown streets to scavenge organic waste, becoming flesh food on the hoof. But hogs produced waste, too, and were strong and aggressive enough to trample children, knock human pedestrians into manure-caked streets, and topple an occasional horse cart. Control measures remained weak as lawmakers sympathized with the poor and recognized the need for cheap sanitation services.[5] The city's nascent health authorities seized upon the cholera pandemic that arrived in 1849 to decisively push for stronger regulation of street hogs. They deployed police to chase the feral herd toward suburban sections north of downtown.[6]

Reformers also argued that cities were unsuitable spaces for dairy production. In the 1840s, as many as eighteen thousand New York cows lived in narrow stalls, feeding on fermented grain mash discarded by distilleries. As historian Andrew Robichaud shows, these cows produced what reformers termed "swill milk," implicated in the deaths of hundreds of infants.[7] Tightly packed cows also became a ready metaphor for human city dwellers crowded into tenements with little fresh air to breathe or open space to exercise. By 1850, over a half-million humans lived in Manhattan, the vast majority south of Forty-Second Street.[8] Elites and reformers cited human health woes, rapid urban growth, and a lack of open space in their calls for the city to establish a public park.

In the early 1850s, authorities and property owners debated two possible sites for the park: a vast section in the middle of Manhattan or a private estate on the East River. The outcome would shape who had access to the park's amenities, who was displaced, who reaped the rewards of escalating property values nearby, and how and where human-animal relationships would be transformed.[9] The "central site" eventually spanned eight hundred–some acres running north from Fifty-Ninth Street between Fifth and Eighth Avenues. The long rectangle encompassed rolling hills, rocky outcrops, and wetlands; market gardens; military infrastructure; the city's reservoir; scattered businesses and estates; and some sixteen hundred humans and abundant nonhuman animals, domesticated and wild.

Like Lower Manhattan, the central site was a multispecies community, but here the buildings were smaller, with more rock outcrops and trees than streets. Spanning cross streets in the Eighties on the West Side, some two hundred humans called Seneca Village home—mostly Black, some Irish. Within and beyond this community, households gardened and kept livestock for subsistence.[10] Hundreds of families from Ireland and the German states re-created the rural landscapes of the old country there, and this included cohabiting with goats, hogs, geese, cows, horses, and dogs.[11] Pens connected to houses allowed pigs to move between indoor and outdoor spaces, and many livestock roved freely during the day.[12] When human mothers could not supply breast milk, babies likely suckled from goats, a common practice that avoided infections that could enter cow's milk in its travels from udder to bottle.[13] Some operated small-scale industries like bone boiling associated with animal by-products, smells, and nuisance. With industries and livestock banned from downtown, urban fringe spaces maintained immigrants' traditions and livelihoods. The census tract straddling Eighth Avenue and running south from Seneca Village was home to "135 horses, 196 cows and horned cattle, 655 swine, and $612 worth of poultry" in 1855, and this was but one section of the area that ultimately became Central Park.[14] Plans for the park reshaped Black and immigrant New Yorkers' place in the multispecies city.

The site selection process did not consider which animals and humans would be displaced; rather, it came down to a contest among powerful landowners and their political advocates. In 1854, a court judgment allowed the city to take land for the central site. Neighbors and park advocates cited the pastoralists' relationships with animals to argue that the city should seize and transform this land. As one landowner stated at a public hearing, "We want a park up town to remove the hog pens and filth that crowd people in the upper part of our city together."[15]

From Pigtown to Rus in Urbe

Indeed, while health authorities battled roving swine and swill milk dairies downtown, some commentators conflated all urban animal husbandry with these hazards. As topographic surveys for the park began in 1856 (delayed for years amid financial strains), the media published lurid portraits of the park-to-be. The *Times* described an Irish majority living in "rickety" shanties that housed "four or five persons, not including the pig and the goats; and indeed it would be a difficult task to distinguish the genus to which they severally belonged, so identified are they in the filth which is the garb alike of all."[16] In 1857, *Harper's* published its article about the park, including a famous sketch of Irish folks and their pig with the same round faces and squinting eyes.[17] Blurring the lines between hog and human seemed to bolster the case against the pastoralists' claims to urban space. As city workers surveyed the area, domestic animals resisted displacement. In September, "a large and exceedingly vicious billy-goat" threatened to charge a crew near the southwestern corner of the reservoir as they investigated a cave with evidence of recent human habitation. Human residents protested too—by staying in place until police forced them out and with demands for monetary compensation that could not begin to value the communities they had built with toil and care. Historian Alexander Manevitz argues that salacious reports about the goat and other animals in the park dehumanized Seneca Villagers and distracted from public interest in and memory of the human community.[18]

Meanwhile, park advocates began thinking of the area as a blank slate to reimagine and manipulate. In April 1857, the New York State Legislature had created the Board of Commissioners of Central Park and appointed eleven prominent men—not accountable to city voters—to exercise "exclusive control and management" over park elements such as its rules and design. The project's engineer-in-chief, Egbert Viele, had presented a plan addressing technical challenges and topography, but the board (goaded by young architect Calvert Vaux) tabled this proposal and solicited designs in a public competition. While would-be designers developed their plans, New Yorkers of all stripes debated what should be the character and features of the landscape. Working-class New Yorkers tended to favor attractions like zoological gardens and playgrounds, but elites urged more rural or wild scenery suitable for contemplative recreation, in hopes of educating the tastes of immigrants, workers, and city children.[19]

Horses were so indispensable to urban transport that their place in the future park went almost without saying. Many visions of the park favored the affluent who could afford to ride horse-drawn carriages and the elites who could afford to keep horses for leisure equestrianism. The *Times* pointed out that these users alone were insufficient for a properly democratic park, though: "The leading idea in the mind of almost any European would be to provide ample drives and rides for the upper classes, while here, on the contrary, it should be to provide not only for them, but more amply for the recreation and amusement of the laboring masses."[20] The competition wrote commercial use of horses into the plan by requiring passages for carts between Fifth and Eighth Avenues. Viele had assumed that these carts could drive directly through the park, affording working-class New Yorkers easy access.

The thirty-three entries for the design competition revealed how architects, artists, gardeners, and other New Yorkers envisioned public space, including places for animals there. No one mentioned grazing; urban greens no longer connoted a working agricultural commons. Still, Samuel Gustin, a horticulturalist working on the park, proposed a dairy for supplying fresh milk. A gardener who identified himself as J. Lachaume hoped to uphold places for livestock in the city. He proposed "agricultural depots," a kind of tasteful fairground along a picturesque lakeside walk where the city could display "fine specimens of horses, oxen, sheep, goats, &c." "No doubt," Lachaume wrote, "these would animate the scenery of the park, and give it a country-like air of which we citizens of this great metropolis are so fond, and most of the time deprived."[21] The term *rus in urbe*—the country in the town—described spaces that carried advantages of both rural scenery and cosmopolitan urbanism. Lachaume's plan embodied this idea while also promoting agricultural improvement, recalling the tradition of agricultural fairs that dated back to 1809 on the Pittsfield, Massachusetts, green. There a reformer named Elkanah Watson exhibited what he considered a superior sheep variety, the Spanish merino, to instruct local farmers in improved animal husbandry.[22] By midcentury, towns across the region held fairs on their commons, with hundreds of farmers displaying livestock and crops. Eventually, smaller towns followed Boston in marginalizing the grazing commons. But the idealized image of sheep dotting a sward was cemented in elites' popular iconography of the Northeast.[23] None of the commissioners voted for Lachaume's design, but his idea evoked interest in scientific agriculture and pastoral landscapes that was shared by urban gentlemen in New York and other cities. Lachaume claimed to be a "working man," but improvement of livestock, education of farmers, and nostalgia for the countryside were endemic among middle- and upper-class New Yorkers like Commissioner Andrew Haswell Green.

Like many clerks and educators, Andrew Haswell Green had come to the city from the rural Northeast, but Green rose in social and political stature to perform a leading role in shaping Central Park. He and his siblings had helped tend livestock on the family farm known as Green Hill in central Massachusetts. He arrived in New York at age fifteen to work in retail and trade but sought healing and comfort back at the family farm after the Panic of 1837 and his own long illness. He then spent months in Trinidad teaching and overseeing ostensibly free plantation workers. These experiences of Green's young adulthood presaged his lifelong dedication to rural landscapes and their use in educating and uplifting city dwellers. He returned to New York City, studied for the bar, became active in the Democratic Party, and funneled his savings back to Green Hill. Green promoted scientific farming both at Green Hill and as an officer in the American Agricultural Association. Earnest and studious, he rose to the presidency of New York's school board in the 1850s, tightly controlling the budget but also advocating for investments he saw as elevating city dwellers' education.[24] In Central Park, Green saw opportunities to turn fascination with animals into serious study of natural history and appreciation of rural and wild places.

Amid the planning process, the commissioners hired a park superintendent who also treasured rural landscapes and fervently promoted scientific agriculture. Frederick Law Olmsted came from an old, prosperous Connecticut family and spent much of his youth traipsing about the hinterlands of Hartford. He flitted from school, to trips in Europe and Mexico, to journalistic ventures, to a series of attempts at farming, funded by his patient and generous father. Most recently, he had restored an old farm on Staten Island. A reporting trip to the southern states in the 1850s inspired fervor for abolitionism in part because of the decrepit landscapes he saw on plantations and smaller farms. By contrast, he recalled the hills around Hartford (vistas surely dotted with sheep) and speculated about the effects of such landscapes "on the taste of a community—and through that on their hearts and lives."[25] He revered northeastern gentlemen farmers, such as his mentor George Geddes, an engineer and New York state senator whose fields and pastures composed open vistas of rolling topography stretching to the horizon. He found a similar sense of boundlessness hiking through the English countryside. Olmsted rarely centered animals in his writing, but a few were intimate companions; others populated the edges of his memoirs and shaped his experience of European and North American landscapes. He gazed out at flocks of sheep around Hartford as a boy, met shepherds tending flocks in the

English countryside, sheared Geddes's old merino ram, crossed Texas on horseback, and woke to singing sparrows at English country inns.[26]

Moonlighting amid his superintendent duties, Olmsted partnered with architect Calvert Vaux to develop their own proposal for the design competition. Vaux had come to the United States from his native London to become a junior partner in the design firm of Andrew Jackson Downing, who had proposed and promoted the idea for a grand park in New York. When Downing died suddenly, in 1852, Vaux inherited his portfolio of country home and garden projects and strived to fill Downing's role as leading tastemaker in American landscape design. Olmsted had written for Downing's *Horticulturist* magazine. He lacked Vaux's formal architectural training, but his writings reveal his sensitivity to the way landscapes affected him and a belief that his experience was universal. Together Vaux and Olmsted developed their design to shape visitors' aesthetic experiences, in contrast with proposals focused on technical problems like drainage or on attractions like zoo animals or formal gardens. They believed that the landscapes of rural New England and New York and the countrysides and parks of western Europe could condition viewers to cherish peaceful contemplation and immersion in nature. Their plan sought to improve upon and democratize European park models while providing respite from the restless change that, to their eyes, marked the urbanization of the United States.[27] Early in 1858, the majority of the Central Park board voted for Vaux and Olmsted's design, the Greensward plan.

Patrolling the Borders of Urban Animal Nature

Meanwhile, police and park staff finally forced some two hundred Seneca Village residents plus hundreds of pastoralists and market gardeners out of their homes.[28] Many pastoralists packed up their poultry and herded goats and hogs, cows and dogs, just a few blocks away outside the borders of what was now called Central Park. Developers were buying up adjacent lots; speculators and other property owners enjoyed hundredfold returns on their land investments, thanks to a burst of interest in park-side parcels.[29] Both within and outside its borders, the park reshaped life for goats and pastoralist households.[30]

Fire insurance maps from 1857 to 1862, before and shortly after the city evicted the last pre-park residents, show villages of wood frame structures east, west, and south of the park, not conforming to parcel lines. For example, west of the park, dozens of houses cluster near Ninth Avenue between Sixty-Fourth and Sixty-Ninth Streets.[31] Humans shared these spaces with goats and other agricultural animals. Over the next decade, investors purchased these lots, as predicted in the city's plans for the area surrounding the park. For example, former mayor Fernando Wood got a jump on buying up lots, taking ownership of about ten city blocks scattered along the West Side. But home construction was slower than expected; the people who could afford to build a mansion here were also likely to worry who would move in next-door.[32]

Those who built and resided there did so amid a multispecies neighborhood. Pastoralist children herded goats past a few homes now separating their homes from the park. Goats nibbled on shrubs along the way, while children watched out for new human neighbors who did not take kindly to them. Meanwhile, the park grew greener by the day as men planted black cherries, tulip poplars, sumac, honeysuckle, and other trees and shrubs. If left untethered and unattended, Billy and Nanny could make a feast of the developing understory and new, verdant shorelines along ponds and creeks. Olmsted later remembered that "the whole place was infested with goats, not dislodged like their former squatter owners."[33] Hooved herbivores spend many hours each day roaming and eating plants. While sheep *graze* by nibbling grasses and other short herbaceous plants, goats *browse*—stripping leaves from bushes or even low-hanging tree branches reached by walking their front hooves up the trunk. Sheep flock together while feeding, but goats often roam singly. Pastoralists valued goats for converting vegetation on marginal land into milk or meat, but goats disturbed park workers and the plants they tended, wandering far into the park.[34] Commissioners warned that "unless some measures are immediately taken, their depredations will be great and not easily reparable."[35] Park workers who happened upon goats faced tense confrontations. Domestic goats learn to recognize herd mates and human keepers, but an unfamiliar human approaching might register as a threat, prompting the goat to defend itself with loud bleats, pawing the ground, and even charging.[36]

The commissioners and other authorities enacted a series of escalating measures to bar these animals from the grounds. In 1857, workers erected a permanent barrier on Fifth Avenue and temporary fences around the rest of the park.[37] Fences could undermine a sense of boundlessness and immersion in nature, but Olmsted warned that the plantings "cannot be properly done until it is enclosed, so as to exclude the cattle, goats and swine that run at large in the neighborhood, the incursions of which are fatal to young trees."[38] The pastoralists and their animals defied the boundaries between this green oasis and the industrial and commercial city.[39] In 1858, Olmsted, now promoted to architect-in-chief, established two pounds within the park to remove "trespassing . . . animals found at large."[40] The commissioners set charges for keeping these beasts at fifty cents per day plus a two-dollar base fine for each horse, cow, or dog; twenty cents plus a two-dollar fine for each sheep, goat, or hog; and five cents plus a fine of a quarter for each goose. Commissioners also offered a one-dollar bounty for each goat captured in the park.[41] Yearly receipts from the pound averaged around two hundred dollars through its first two decades.[42]

These first rules did not explicitly forbid herders from guiding goats or swine to the park under supervision. So, in 1859, the commission banned domestic animals attended by their humans—a rule probably felt most directly by young goatherds—while also barring other common-resource land uses, such as firewood harvesting and berry picking (many species of fruiting shrubs and trees were planted, such as blackberries

and currants).[43] The ordinance exempted dogs on a leash and equestrians' horses, signaling changes in how human New Yorkers and their animals could use urban space. Dogs and horses—the latter usually fed hay or grain—presumably would not eat the vegetation. Only elites could afford horses for leisure riding; the exemption for leashed dogs signaled a shift toward their role as pets in a city where many canines had recently provided muscle power for small machines.[44]

Multispecies Labor Makes a Landscape

While Vaux and Olmsted largely omitted animals from their plan, they did include roads for horse-drawn carriages and equestrians and for commercial horse carts to cross the park. They planned to sink the roads to be used by commercial vehicles below the park's surface at intervals, preserving long, unbroken lines of vision, in contrast to Viele's proposal for above-ground transverse roads. The architects' main aim in sinking the transverse roads was artistic, but it had the effect of further separating commerce from leisure. Olmsted and Vaux had planned for leisure equestrians to share the same main drive around the park's perimeter with horse-drawn pleasure carriages and pedestrians. However, two commissioners who had voted against the Greensward plan, August Belmont and Robert Dillon, called for a separate bridle path to open up "miles and miles for the pleasure and benefit of manly and invigorating horsemanship."[45] Belmont was himself an equine enthusiast, later founder of the Belmont Stakes horse race, and one of the city's leading tastemakers. This change would protect the safety of riders and horses from carriages, but it also dedicated further city resources and park space for a rarefied group

OPPOSITE: D. E. Wyand's sketch *Squatters of New York—Scene near Central Park*, published in *Harper's Weekly* in 1869, shows the more-than-human communities that persisted just outside the park. Courtesy of the Library of Congress, Prints and Photographs Division.

of humans—those who could afford to keep a horse for leisure riding. Olmsted and Vaux revised the plans, and park workers—humans along with hired horses and oxen—toiled to pave six miles of isolated bridle path with a hoof-friendly surface, snaking near the edges of the park and looping around the reservoir.[46]

Visitors might assume that architects merely laid out paths and roads around existing forests, fields, and water bodies. But the picturesque and the pastoral had to be carved out with great effort by multispecies work crews from a patchy landscape of vegetable gardens, small industry and villages, wetlands and hills, pocked by granite and gneiss outcrops. Human and animal labor produced a varied, verdant environment for other New Yorkers to consume with their senses and navigate with their bodies. The work strained bodies and bombarded the senses—particularly the hearing—of all species of laborers. A worker played taps to announce shift changes and warn of impending explosions. Several times each day, workers set off charges to blast through rock and tree roots.[47] Horses possess keen senses and may respond acutely to being "spooked," to which a tethered horse might respond by shifting its feet or stamping. Horses may become conditioned to startling sights or sounds through repeated exposure, and some laboring equines in Manhattan may have brought such experience to their park work after hauling carts through busy streets in a city under constant construction. Some may even have been rendered deaf at worksites elsewhere in the city before arriving for this new assignment.[48]

Stumps of hundreds of trees, now out-of-place for the new plan, had to be uprooted and manure brought in to fertilize new plantings. Dozens of teams hauled in millions of cubic yards of manure, soil, stone, and vegetation by cart.[49] Some human crews blasted away outcroppings of granite and gneiss, producing crushed stone to fill the land here or pave paths there. Under human direction and alongside other human workers, horses and oxen provided the muscle to transform the landscape. Many humans lost limbs, fingers, and eyes, and a few lost their lives in the line of work, particularly when blasting rock. Park reports did not list injuries or deaths of horses as they do human workers; it is less likely that equines were nearby during a blast, but death from overwork was a common fate for many urban working horses.[50]

As the city emerged from the economic recession of the mid-1850s, thousands of men clamored for waged work opportunities in the park. Politicians often favored Irish workers for municipal jobs because of their political engagement. In this era, when horsepower ran the city, cartmen served key needs in the economy and in the creation of the park. Cartman jobs were coveted throughout the city. In the first half of the nineteenth century, they had been restricted to white men; recall that Irish Americans had seen to it that Black New Yorkers would not compete with them for work in this thriving trade.[51] Even when African Americans were allowed to participate in the horse-and-cart trade, they faced intense scrutiny. Elite horse owners often hired Black men as stable hands but refused to entrust them with sole charge of a powerful animal. As the humane movement emerged in the latter half of the nineteenth century, animal advocates often portrayed Black and Irish people as cruel and unfit handlers. Humans' exercise of power over animals was thus shaped by assertions of white, Anglo supremacy.[52]

Dynamics of class and wealth also marked equine labor in the construction and use of the park's bridle paths and carriage roads. Among the many tasks draft animals completed, horses' work paving carriage roads provides a poetic foil to the leisure experience of driving and riding on those roads after the park's completion. Engineers designed these drives and paths with several layers of stone and soil to ensure good drainage and absorb the impact of millions of hooves and wheels. This type of road would, according to engineers, offer the greatest comfort to horses and leisure riders and hired carriage drivers. Creating this comfort required great exertion. Working horse teams drew successive sets of rollers over every inch of road, packing down the gravel, and then pulled sprinklers over the soil layers to moisten them. A team of six horses drew a final roller

A horse pulls a cart with a human driver holding an irrigation tank used to water paths and turf; image is undated but likely from 1870s or 1880s. Courtesy of the New York Public Library Digital Collections.

weighing over six tons. Human laborers commanded the draft teams, and then a crew of men graded the roads' surfaces with rakes.[53] Horses laboring on the bridle paths and carriage drives helped elite and middle-class New Yorkers re-create rural modes of leisure mobility within the city, and thanks to Belmont and Dillon, equestrians and their horses would enjoy exclusive access to one segment of the park's landscape.

Reassembling the Rural

Within the park's first decade, authorities also brought in more creatures to reanimate its pastoral tableaux, even as Olmsted and landscaping crews battled encroaching goats. Olmsted and Vaux, the commissioners, and other park authorities and elites brought sheep, cows, and even some goats into the park to serve a variety of purposes. Some of these domesticated animals helped the park reproduce iconic vistas of western Europe and the northeastern United States, while also staking out the park's place in scientific movements to improve American livestock breeds. Along with their landscape function, park authorities also valued sheep and cows for the feelings they would help evoke; scholars now call this "encounter value."[54] Such animal encounters may divert attention from the more messy and violent aspects of the exploitation of nature. Some park leaders also hoped to generate financial value from domesticated animals to support the park's operating budget.

In 1859, the Finance Committee of the Board of Commissioners, led by the cosmopolitan August Belmont, explored several possible means of adding to the revenue side of the park's budget. Belmont exemplified elite New Yorkers who aspired to European standards of artistic taste, along with business interests' plans to generate financial value in the city. Born to a prosperous merchant family in the rural German Rhineland, Belmont had attended school in urban Frankfurt, where he admired wealthier classmates' elegant horses and carriages. As a young man, he developed his taste in urban architecture traveling as a secretary for distant relations in the Rothschild banking family. He arrived in New York as their agent in 1837 just as financial panic set in, becoming one of the few conduits for investment capital in the city. In addition to his access to finances, his knowledge of European culture soon endeared him to socialites hungry for continental cachet.[55]

Belmont and the Finance Committee drew their ideas in part from Paris's suburban Bois de Boulogne, a former royal hunting reserve recently made a public park as part of Napoleon III and Baron Haussmann's reconstruction plans. Following this example, park authorities could reap cash from the park's vast lawns. The committee asserted, "The grazing of the Park, by sheep, will be favorable to the ground, and afford some revenue" by converting grass into wool, meat, and manure. Furthermore, through the efforts of human and equine workers, "some hay may also be got from the lawns" to sell to farmers outside the city or stables within; "in the Bois de Boulogne the pasturage yields $4.57 per acre."[56] Two years earlier, this land had sustained goats and their humans; now commissioners hoped to help balance the park's budget via the bodies of other animals—whether in the park or elsewhere—amid soaring construction expenditures. Commissioners conceived the idea of raising sheep on the park on financial pretexts, but sheep soon came to embody other desires and contradictions related to urban nature.

Amid discussions about introducing sheep into the park, in 1859 the commissioners dispatched Olmsted on a tour of parks and zoological and botanical gardens in Brussels, London, and Dublin to gather ideas (and to ease Olmsted's present bout of melancholy). In addition to notes about these cities' zoos (to which we will return in chapter 3), Olmsted returned with a plan to reimagine cows and the commons. In London's St. James's Park, Olmsted saw girls and young women who brought in grazing cows from suburban farms. Parents and nursemaids paid the milkmaids a penny or so to express the cows' milk into tin cups for children's fresh consumption. Olmsted may have seen such scenes on earlier trips, too, and Vaux surely knew of St. James's Park from his youth in London.[57] Olmsted and Vaux had likely seen artistic renderings of these milkmaids and their cows too. One by American painter Benjamin West, from sixty years earlier, shows fashionable Londoners milling about as strong, tidy women kneel beside docile, clean cows to extract fresh milk. West's landscape centers on two cows bathed in sunlight, matching their cream- and snow-toned coats with the gowns of two ladies in the foreground, glorifying gentle bovines amid urban finery.[58] Ever attuned to the visual power of the rural tableau, Vaux and Olmsted devised a new interpretation of the urban dairy.

Olmsted shared their vision with the commissioners early in 1860:

> In a retired spot in the south-eastern part of the park, at the head of a glen formed by two large masses of rock, and looking over the lower lake, it is proposed to erect a small house, or chalet, of a rural or rustic character, and which may be called the Dairy. In front of it would be a hill of about five acres, which is nearly surrounded by water, and which can conveniently be fenced off as a pasture. Here it is proposed that several Alderney cows shall be kept, for the purpose of supplying, at certain hours in the morning and evening, milk fresh from the cow, as is done near the entrance of St. James' Park, London. At the dairy-house, light refreshments, especially such as are composed mainly of milk and cream, would be provided, and this establishment would be intended especially to afford a quiet place to which ladies and invalids might at any time resort with satisfaction.[59]

This vision replicated neither Boston's commons nor St. James's Park, which afforded grazing access to urban households or suburban farmers, respectively. The dairy would be a stripped-down and abstracted version of the commons. Here the city would own and control the land as well as the cows, and it would employ or contract with cowherds to tend the animals as well as with dairy businesses to process milk into refreshments. This was public land for recreation, education, and food consumption— but not for shared grazing rights. Furthermore, by specifying cow breeds, Olmsted and Vaux designated the animals' cultural referents. Alderneys hailed from the English Channel islands and were known for their small stature, brown coats, and rich, buttery milk. Olmsted and Vaux's vision for the dairy affirmed the park's enclosure against livestock from outside its borders, brought the functions of nutrition and health within park authorities' purview, and deployed cows and their milk as icons of rural European landscapes.[60]

Some authorities also hoped that cows and sheep could put Central Park on the map of movements to improve animal husbandry and breeding in the United States. Olmsted, Andrew Green, and other New Yorkers such as would-be park designer J. Lachaume sought to popularize scientific efforts to raise the productivity and reputation of American livestock. When he called for "fine specimens" of livestock to be displayed in the park, Lachaume spoke to gentlemen farmers' and elite and middle-class New Yorkers' desires to promote agricultural progress. Lachaume's vision for agricultural exhibits and Belmont's ideas about grazing sheep lay dormant until 1862, when a group of "gentlemen butchers"—as Andrew Green called them—appealed to the board of commissioners. Led by S. P. Patterson, William T. Warner, and James Nicholson, the butchers donated the skin of a "mammoth" ox named General Scott to illustrate that the United States produced "extraordinary" specimens of livestock worthy of promotion. Green agreed, leading the commissioners in a resolution to display "representations of the finest animals of the country, as a source of interest and attraction to the agriculturists and stock growers of the State."[61] General Scott's remains were only suitable for museum display—Green was also promoting a museum of natural history adjacent to the park grounds—but the gentlemen butchers also encouraged the board in its plans to obtain a sheep flock.

Threats to the park landscape provided the final push toward establishing the flock. As the Civil War began, military companies claimed the so-called parade ground for training. Olmsted and Vaux resented having to cede a lawn to this use; the exercises violated their vision of rural tranquility and also threatened the growing turf.[62] A flock of sheep would make these greens seem productive rather than empty for the taking. Even New Yorkers and military officials who preferred formal parade grounds over the greensward's pastoral aesthetic could appreciate the value of sheep for wool, meat, and manure. In 1862 and 1863, the park board spent one hundred dollars each year to purchase its first live sheep from the butcher Bryan Lawrence, who had also donated ox and sheep skins to the park for display.[63] Lawrence sold mutton to choosy New Yorkers at Manhattan's Centre Market; he also gained notoriety in the annals of American barbecue for 1860s Democratic Party cookout.[64] In the early 1860s, he diverted a few lambs from immediate slaughter to help turn the park into a new kind of city-owned farm. One hundred dollars likely bought seven to ten lambs each year based on contemporary auction prices.[65]

The commissioners chose to purchase sheep of the Southdown breed, expressing cultural and scientific aspirations while also connecting the park with rural England. As with Olmsted's vision of Alderney cows adorning park lawns, the park commissioners here selected a small breed connected with southern Britain and known for its flavorful products. Southdowns originated in the southeastern limestone hills of Sussex. There John Ellman had, in the late 1770s, selected the most compact individuals from the local type.[66] These short, stocky sheep rapidly converted native grasses and corn stubble into flesh and fleece, manuring crop fields as they grazed. They thrived even on poor soil, and their dense fleece, between "hairy" and "woolly" on the spectrum of textures, protected them from cold.[67] The classic type featured sturdy heads and thick necks; their broad muzzles seemed to bear perpetually pleasant smiles.[68]

Renowned for efficient grazing, flavorful meat, and serviceable wool, Southdowns became a favorite among British sheep farmers, including some aristocrats, and across English settler societies. American sheep breeders had been fascinated with Spanish merinos since the beginning of the century, but Southdowns gained popularity in the middle and later decades. American gentleman farmers promoted Southdowns as superior to sheep bred by yeomen.[69] Indeed, "high" farmers had for decades driven an organized movement to improve livestock breeds. Historian Eric Stoykovich describes these well-to-do livestock enthusiasts as "self-confident" in their knowledge of European breeds, assertive in their promotion of open trade policies to import pedigreed stock, and dedicated to a more productive agricultural modernity. Furthermore, as geographer Catherine Nash explains, connection with a particular place helped constitute the "breed wealth" associated with certain livestock varieties.[70] Though not a livestock breeder himself, Olmsted supported this movement as part of his devotion to causes—from abolitionism to agricultural reform—that he saw as improving American tastes, environments, and living conditions. Olmsted revered his farming mentor George Geddes, and his dispatches from the British Isles celebrated the livestock there. At one country estate, years before going to work on the park, he thrilled at walking among cows, sheep, and tame deer, observing that "the sheep and the cattle were of the most value for their effect on the landscape."[71] For Olmsted, animal husbandry and scientific progress dovetailed with pastoral aesthetics: placid sheep dotting rolling green hills inspired the kind of quiet contemplation city residents needed. Central Park's sheep flock embodied romantic agrarianism, the promise of progressive animal husbandry, and connection to European places that park leaders valued.

Furthermore, Southdown sheep produced flesh renowned among elite New Yorkers. By 1860, New York papers and the national agricultural press reported that Southdown mutton "always outsell[s] every other variety in New York to our first-class butchers." Supposedly, though, Southdown flesh was "not appreciated by the wholesale butchers, who are mostly Irish and Jews."[72] Lawrence, himself an Irish immigrant, belied this generalization meant to impugn ethnic butchers and consumers. August Belmont was Jewish but not from the working-class communities who purchased meat through the wholesale trade; he was known for personally selecting ingredients for his fashionable dinner parties and certainly would have chosen Southdown mutton. Agricultural and popular media celebrated the animals bred by farmers such as Samuel Thorne of Dutchess County, New York. Thorne supplied many of the sheep that Lawrence slaughtered for his shop at Manhattan's Centre Market, and his farm may have been a source of Central Park's original flock.[73]

The press covered sheep auctions as high society events, tracing lambs' lineage back to storied flocks of England and recounting the dear prices paid for imported breeding rams. For example, the *Times* lavished praise upon one J. C. Taylor of Holmdel, New Jersey, on the occasion of his annual auction in 1862, comparing his reputation to legendary English Southdown breeders. "From these choice importations," the reporter gushed about a thirteen hundred–dollar ram and other Southdowns purchased for kingly sums from England's Jonas Webb, "Mr. Taylor has succeeded in raising a flock which, for beauty of appearance, purity of blood, and general excellent qualities, is said, by good judges, to be unsurpassed, if it is equaled, by any flock of Southdowns, in England or elsewhere."[74] Park authorities aspired to make their mark on American agricultural progress as had gentleman sheep breeders such as Thorne and Taylor.

Park staff bred the lambs of 1862 as yearlings in 1863 and then again the next year, along with the up-and-coming yearlings. By day, the growing sheep grazed on meadows, starting at what had once been the "parade ground"; at night and in winter, they huddled in a barn awaiting plans and construction for a larger sheepfold building. A *Times* reporter, describing the park as it took shape, admired the flock, "black faced and fine wooled, always favorites in park scenery."[75] By 1864, the ewes had borne and nurtured enough lambs for park officials to boast of a flock over sixty strong. Someone—the records don't say who—sheared some of the sheep, and the wool sold for nearly $130.[76] On Christmas Eve 1864, Bryan Lawrence offered the "finest Southdown mutton, raised and fatted on the Central Park of this city," for sale at the Centre Market.[77] By the late 1860s, wool sales brought in about $200 each year, and young rams sold to butchers for slaughter added about $1,000 to the park's balance sheet annually—a small sum against a $1.5 million construction budget.[78] The flock's value went beyond sales, however.

Park visitors left behind the hoofbeats resounding from teams of horses on the streets, the din of new construction, the hum and clang of factories, the whirl of rapid motion and intense odors, the paved grayness of linear urbanization, to hear only "the bleating of the fold." Other "natural beauties . . . afford gratification of the senses," and the sheep flock, along with changing vegetation, immersed city dwellers in cyclical nature, "ever changing with the birth of each new season."[79] The park staff member now charged with guarding and guiding the sheep modeled how to experience this landscape. The art critic Clarence Cook—like Calvert Vaux, a protégé of Andrew Jackson Downing—found the shepherd "presenting an appearance of pastoral simplicity as he wanders after his nibbling charge," a scene that "carr[ied] the mind far enough away from the sights and sounds of the environing city." Cook wrote one of the leading guides to Central Park, in which he took the sheep as a cue to expound upon the pastoral verses of seventeenth-century English poet John Milton.[80] Elites saw sheep as inviting quiet delight and peaceful contemplation of the daily and annual rhythms of rural life, in contrast with the relentless bustle of city life.

While sheep converted grass into flesh, fiber, more lambs, and pastoral encounters along Eighth Avenue, the *Times* also predicted that the grass that would "maintain a good stock of milch cows" and yield "pure, wholesome and unadulterated milk" for children and ladies.[81] By 1864, Vaux designed the dairy building as a two-story facility that would house the cows in a stone-clad lower level below a cottage with a loggia, where visitors would purchase and eat their milk-based treats.[82] (Sources disagreed on whether to call the architectural style Tudor or Swiss; the flavor was certainly Old World.) But the dairy took years to complete amid a backlog of other construction needs on the park, many of them idled by the Civil War. In the meantime, patrons donated bovines that formed a small, motley herd housed in the basement of the Arsenal building along with many other animal gifts. Andrew Green donated two prizewinning Kerry cows from Green Hill. Kerry cattle are among the oldest breeds in Europe, small, sleek, and black, hailing from Ireland and well adapted to produce copious milk even from poor forage. The Alsops, a line of wealthy merchants and politicians from Connecticut, donated a "Flores bull" from the Azores—another compact, efficient breed from a tiny island.[83] Menagerie staff housed the Kerry and Azores cattle alongside a pair of what they called "Cape buffalo"—which usually refers to a wild and famously ornery

Members of the sheep flock graze near a pedestrian path, circa 1895. Courtesy of the Library of Congress, Prints and Photographs Division.

species of bovines. These were probably a domesticated breed from southern Africa. Union quartermaster-general Montgomery Meigs had seized this bull and cow—and another of their breed who may have died or been sold shortly thereafter—from the plantation of Confederate general Wade Hampton in 1865 in the common war-time practice of cattle raids. An agricultural journalist from upstate called the herd "peculiar" but praised the cattle's fine form and speculated that the cows would be outstanding producers of milk.[84] Milk production for public consumption remained a mere promise as construction delays on the dairy dragged on throughout the 1860s. The cattle did gain a little more room to move when staff tethered them outdoors on various lawns.

Green's cows now living in the park embodied his perpetual nostalgia for his family's farm, where he sought solace and healing in young adulthood and on frequent sojourns back to Massachusetts. Green was not the only New Yorker who longed for youthful hometowns and farms. Many of the clerks and managers who comprised Manhattan's middle class periodically flocked back for Old Home Week events. Small New England and Upstate New York towns hosted these community reunions, where urban transplants could see sheep and cows trotted out onto town greens.[85] Olmsted, too, recalled Hartford's hills dotted with gentle livestock. Olmsted and Green aimed to re-create the state of mind they associated with these places not only for other middle-class New Yorkers but also for the new immigrants who had never seen the places these Yankees considered the crucible of American values.

Of course, the park's greensward was more confined than the rolling hills of New England and Upstate New York. The shepherd kept the city's flock mostly within what was now called the Sheep Meadow, ushering them to other lawns later in the day. Cattle were confined to the old Arsenal building or tethered in a series of greens. Meanwhile, goats and other animals from nearby pastoralist villages continued to defy the park's borders. Goats browsed on young saplings, marring Vaux and Olmsted's intricate plan and threatening the park's maturing forests. In 1866, park

Olmsted and Vaux's plan for a working dairy that brought urban children together with the source of their milk did not come to fruition, but this photo, circa 1868, shows cattle donated to the park, tethered and grazing near the Arsenal building, where menagerie animals were housed. Courtesy of the New York Public Library Digital Collections.

authorities doubled the fee to retrieve an impounded goat to four dollars.[86] That same year, the city formed the New York Board of Health, an agency that would further limit urban animal husbandry.[87] While many elite New Yorkers valued the expansive feel of rural and wild spaces, concerns about health and the park landscape fed into policies that bounded human-animal relationships.

Working Animals, Leisure Landscapes, and Urban Children

Pastoralist children had formed relationships with goats—herding them and consuming their milk—and now some children consumed the services of goats for leisure entertainment. As park authorities made it harder for pastoralists to keep goats in Manhattan, they welcomed a new role for goats in 1869. That year, the commission approved a contract with an outside vendor who brought small goat-drawn carriages to the Mall. There children of affluent and middle-class visitors could ride around a track behind the Arsenal for a ten-cent fare. Other children gained a job managing the carriage goats; it was mostly youth who helped children into their seats and guided goats around the track.[88]

Administrators and patrons began to label this section in the park's southern half, around Sixty-Fourth to Sixty-Sixth Streets, as the "Children's District"—an area rich with engaging attractions, often featuring animals. Along with the goat carriages, there were the dairy, the sheep, the menagerie (to which we will return in chapter 3), and sometimes donkey rides.[89] Vaux and Olmsted resisted adding buildings that would interrupt scenic vistas, but the dairy and the sheep flock supported their vision by engaging children with lively animals evoking rural landscapes.

Construction on the much-delayed dairy building neared completion at the turn of the 1870s, soon to offer long-promised treats to children and their caregivers. But political events nixed Vaux and Olmsted's bucolic vision of city dwellers tasting dairy treats above the cows providing the milk. In 1870, Democrats in the legislature in Albany allowed New York City to adopt greater home rule. The new city charter dissolved Central Park's Board of Commissioners that had been accountable to the State of New York, replacing it with a Department of Public Parks whose new commissioners answered to the Tammany Hall bosses, most famously William Tweed, who controlled one wing of the Democratic Party (Green was a Democrat but not of the Tammany variety).[90] The new board, led by Tammany member Peter Sweeny, retained Olmsted and Vaux as advisors

Children ride in a goat carriage on Central Park's Mall, circa 1900, accompanied by adults and a young "charioteer." Courtesy of the Library of Congress, Prints and Photographs Division.

in name only. Under Tammany's management, the board turned the dairy into a restaurant, and staff stashed paint and other supplies in the stable at the bottom of the dairy building where Vaux had intended for cows to sleep and be milked. The *Times* spoke for infuriated Tammany opponents as it lamented the building's fate: "wrested from its original purpose and turned into a common eating-house" when it was supposed to be part of "the Children's District."[91] The Kerry cows and other bovines kept their sleeping quarters in the Arsenal basement along with other captive animals donated by park patrons. The park purchased the treats sold in the dairy from an outside supplier, breaking the connection between landscape, animals, and consumers. Vaux and Olmsted's vision came closer to fruition in Brooklyn's Prospect Park, where cows resided in the stone-clad lower level of a similar building and grazed and were milked each day before visitors' eyes.[92]

Amid the political turmoil, Vaux and Olmsted resigned their posts. Vaux's assistant Jacob Wrey Mould took on the architect position, overseeing design and construction of the Sheepfold building at the southwestern corner of the meadow, near Eighth Avenue. The enormous barn could accommodate hundreds of sheep. It also included living space for the chief shepherd, his family and assistants, and a sheepdog. Wings on either end of the dogleg-shaped building included galleries where the public could view the sheep along with educational exhibits intended to instill appreciation for improved sheep breeds and rural landscapes.[93] The building freed sheep from their cramped shed and even supported the goals of agricultural education and reform. In one interactive exhibit, visitors could view Southdown wool under a microscope. However, Olmsted, Vaux, and supporters of the Greensward plan and aesthetic bemoaned the twenty thousand–square–foot structure's disruptive location, along with its allegedly poor ventilation and drafts that chilled the sheep.[94]

In spite of the sheepfold's architectural offenses, park supporters celebrated the sheep flock for teaching urban children about rural landscapes. One children's book stands out for its translation of landscape ideas for young people, echoing Clarence Cook's guide. Under the pseudonym Francis Forrester, the Methodist minister Daniel Wise wrote his 1873 novel *Little Peachblossom; or, Rambles in Central Park* as a didactic children's guide to landscape appreciation. Wise, an Englishman who had immigrated to the United States in 1833, set up his narrative by creating a fictional family, the Birds, who move to New York City from their country home. Their kindly Uncle Nathan, a New Yorker, helps the four children adjust to city life by taking them on regular tours of Central Park. There he expounds upon the artistic and scientific value of the Greensward plan and casts aspersions on features, like the menagerie of caged animals, that deviated from the plan's emphasis on contemplation and recreation in nature.[95]

When the children see the sheep for the first time, Uncle Nathan explains at length: "Don't you think these broad acres of green are more pleasant to look upon dotted with sheep, as they are now, than they would be with no living creature upon them? . . . Besides, sheep do not hurt a green by feeding upon it. In point of fact they enrich the land. Moreover, by letting visitors from the country see those noble South Downs [*sic*], as this breed is named, farmers are led to see the folly of raising such scraggy little sheep as many of them keep on their own farms."[96] Uncle Nathan also approved of the goat carriages on the Mall, perhaps because they allowed children to imitate adults in horse carriages, gazing out on the landscape as in the original plan. In a footnote, Wise also revealed an odd fascination with the goat "charioteer," stating that he preferred to see Black boys in English livery managing the goats, rather than "white boys with no uniforms, except a sort of jockey cap." Wise, who had been an abolitionist in the decades before the Civil War, seemed to fetishize these costumed Black children, who he said "gave to the miniature turn-out a unique effect."[97]

Other memoirs and children's stories also interpreted small ungulates in the park through moral and aesthetic lenses. Annie Nathan Meyer, for example, a writer who helped found Barnard College and whose family spent summers upstate, felt at best ambivalent about animals who lived in cages or paddocks. But admiring the flock in Central Park's meadow, she fondly recalled her childhood traveling through the countryside, where cows waded in streams and vast lawns were dotted with "quiet sheep feed[ing] on the tender grass . . . until suddenly one overcome by the joy of life plunges them all into a wild gambol and frolic."[98] Meyer's admiration for the sheep grew out of both nostalgia—she spent her city months longing for the countryside—and their delightful, spontaneous behaviors.

A few New Yorkers were also growing nostalgic for the goats who, along with their human communities, were gradually being edged out by the construction of infrastructure and residences along the sides of the park. Some popular media coverage of the remaining villages mourned their passing while gently mocking residents' quaint ways. Mrs. C. W. Flanders wrote a romantic fictional story for the children's magazine *Youth's Companion* about a young German American goatherd with a heart of gold who lived in the middle of Manhattan before Central Park was built. Amid the girl's litany of arduous chores, she shared her goat's milk with a hungry and destitute stranger just before he died and was rewarded for her generosity.[99] In 1880, *Scribner's* reporter H. C. Bunner conducted an almost anthropological investigation of a "shantytown" whose location is somewhat obscured by a likely typographic error.[100] He mostly concluded that the residents' homes (at least the German Americans') were neat and well-kept in spite of their location on land that had yet to be graded and connected to any drainage system. In addition to raising goats, cows, and geese, they also produced vegetables for sale to downtown markets and ran various shops and small manufactures. Landlords who had bought property amid the real estate boom hiked up land rental prices, and each day more residents saw their homes condemned to make room for transportation infrastructure. Nearby "an American couple . . . cordially hated for a mile around" operated a pound where they held neighbors' goats and cows, turning them over to city officials for a cash bounty if their owners failed to show up first. Furthermore, "the dog is the goat's only rival as the typical animal of the colony," Bunner wrote, but geese were also notable "as a connecting link between the pets of Shantytown and its edible beasts and beasts of burden." Bunner called it a "peaceable and well-organized colony" but judged it doomed by the forward march of development.[101]

OPPOSITE: *Frank Leslie's Illustrated Newspaper* portrayed "building contrasts" between luxury homes and cottages of pastoralist communities near Central Park in 1889. This drawing was accompanied by a note expressing sympathy for farmers in "humble cottages" being displaced by luxury dwellings. Courtesy of HathiTrust.

CHAPTER I

German American and Irish American Manhattanites were losing spaces for raising domesticated animals in landscapes that resembled rural environments of the old country. At the same time, tenement dwellers found other ways to maintain livestock agriculture. City regulations prohibited keeping most farm animals indoors, but many tenement residents kept geese and even goats and pigs, practices that flew under the radar of the busy Sanitary Bureau. At least one immigrant attempted to gain permission for subsistence animal rearing for his community. In 1882, a New Yorker named Yein Fane applied on behalf of his neighbors in a Mott Street building, most of them Chinese immigrants, to keep "two dozen chickens or ducks" inside. The Sanitary Bureau denied his request, and the *Tribune* mocked him with anti-Asian prejudice characteristic of many white Americans: they implied that Fane's foreignness had led him to make an outlandish request, while marveling at his competent English skills.[102] Elite New Yorkers feeling nostalgic about urban subsistence agriculture might have looked indoors among the tenements as well as outdoors near Central Park. Fane and his neighbors were far from the only Manhattanites eager to raise livestock in apartment buildings.

Whose Urban Farm?

Meanwhile, life in and around the sheepfold resembled an orderly country estate, with its annual cycles of mating, gestation, birth, tail docking, shearing, and sales. Each spring, the sheepfold burst forth with dozens of new baby lambs who soon frolicked and gamboled to the delight of onlookers like Annie Nathan Meyer. Their lives marked the changing seasons, and their bodies and behaviors lent the park's lawns the sense of authenticity and rural simplicity that Olmsted and Green valued in the New England countryside of their youths. The sheep indeed appealed to "country gentlemen" who also valued fine horses for riding and racing. *Turf, Field, and Farm*, New York's leading journal for this crossover audience of sportsmen-farmers, lavished praise upon the "uncommonly large and gentle" specimens in the sheepfold whose fleece was "unsurpassed for texture and quantity."[103] Even visitors with no interest in purchasing and consuming the sheep enjoyed their antics. Perhaps unsurprisingly, slaughter was ill-suited to this context and took place beyond visitors' view, though many praised Southdown mutton.

The sheep's relationship with their herders and public space contrasted with that of the pastoralists' goats. Sheep and goats are closely related, but goats often take advantage of more marginal or varied environments, having evolved from montane offshoots of the caprine subfamily tree. Sheep more clearly connoted what English landscape gardeners like Lancelot "Capability" Brown had enshrined as pastoral aesthetics, flocking on greenswards rather than meandering through craggy hills and outcrops. Sheep's pastoral credentials extended to the religious sense of the word: they were vulnerable and docile, in need of tending and support like a flock of parishioners. Furthermore, scientific interest in sheep breeding dated to the early 1800s. The movement of gentlemen farmer reformers who promoted specific cow and sheep breeds showed little interest in goats until later in the century, and the goats roaming central Manhattan held little value for them as breeding stock.[104]

By the 1870s, William Conklin, head of the park's zoological department, oversaw management of the sheep flock. Like other early park leaders and visionaries, Conklin descended from old-line Anglo-Americans. His work in the park began in the modest position of property clerk, but he studied for a veterinary degree at Columbia and assisted the menagerie's first director, Dr. Albert Gallatin, as a keeper. Conklin succeeded Gallatin around the time of the Tammany takeover of the board. As menagerie director (a title sometimes used interchangeably with "zoological department director"), Conklin was committed to animating the landscape with lively creatures, regardless of their origin, to engage the interest of masses of park goers. He fashioned himself as a man of science and natural history, founding a scholarly journal of veterinary medicine and comparative anatomy in which he and other zoological professionals shared knowledge gained in the keeping of captive animals. This included many hard lessons drawn from autopsies of those who died at the menagerie and in the sheepfold. Conklin wrote with clinical concision, though sometimes affection, too, as in an article about lions who played with catnip.[105] Conklin was broad-minded in his dealings with people who could help him obtain animals to keep the zoological collection exciting and healthy. He and his staff managed a flow of thousands of living beings by communicating with animal handlers ranging from showman P. T. Barnum, to urban families who donated pets, to exotic animal traders, to British sheep breeders.

Among his many jobs, Conklin assisted with finding and purchasing new sheep to prevent deleterious inbreeding within the flock. Inbreeding itself was a contentious topic among agricultural reformers, who hoped to maintain the advantages of fine animal varieties while avoiding harmful traits. Gentlemen farmers had been breeding Southdowns in the United States for decades, importing rams from John Ellman's own flock in the 1820s to build "breed wealth."[106] The sheep that progressive farmers considered the finest and most needed in America had to make a long journey from the rural British Isles to New York. One such group of Southdowns, three rams intended to improve the breeding of Central Park's flock, boarded a train in Manchester, England, from there went to Liverpool, and then crossed the Atlantic aboard the Cunard steamer line, a trip that could take a week to ten days.[107] Sold from the park's flock, Southdowns could enrich other farms' bloodlines as Conklin oversaw their distribution to farmers across the region.

Park records and breed registries allow us to trace the journeys and families of precious few of the park's sheep. Southdown breeders had been organized in England for some time, but farmers in the United States only established their own breed-specific organization in 1882. When the American Southdown Association published its first pedigree book in 1884, Conklin registered a three-year-old named Dom Pedro, the offspring of two sheep in the famous flock of the sixth Baron Walsingham of

Norfolk, England. Among Dom Pedro's many offspring, in 1883 he sired a ram whom Conklin named Young Pedro with a ewe named only 106. Her forebears were imported from the flock of the legendary English sheep breeder Jonas Webb by L. G. Morris of Fordham, New York. Conklin sold Young Pedro to one Alfred Bonney of Dutchess County in Upstate New York.[108]

In 1885, Walsingham announced that he would sell off his Southdown sheep to clear room for a pheasant preserve—supplanting one animal with elite associations for another. By this time, the Board of Commissioners was headed by President John Crimmins, owner of one of the city's leading construction firms that frequently contracted services for Central Park—certainly a conflict of interest. Crimmins seized this rare opportunity to supply friends with some highly valuable sheep and used his connection with the park zoological department to ensure a place for them when they arrived. With Conklin's approval, Crimmins dispatched an agent to Walsingham's auction. There the agent mingled with representatives of several aristocratic families along with the agent of one well-heeled Upstate New York gentleman farmer—the president of the American Southdown Association and leading bidder. Crimmins's agent managed to purchase five rams and fifteen ewes for Crimmins, some of whom Crimmins would give to the park and others whom he would sell to friends. The *Times* reported fervently on Crimmins's purchase, cheekily calling the Southdowns "blue blooded" and wondering why the fifty dollars paid for each sheep's transatlantic steamer fare didn't purchase them a spot in the cabin rather than their wooden pens in steerage.[109] One fellow commissioner and a political opponent complained that Crimmins had "with a great flourish turned them loose in the Park to be fed and kept by the city . . . but never offered to pay anything for the care of the animals."[110] Over the next two years, municipal finance authorities launched an official audit to investigate this and other ways that Crimmins seemed to benefit from his position as parks board president and to use his office to support fellow Irish Americans.[111]

Crimmins and Conklin, in fact, used Crimmins's wealth and connections to enrich Central Park's flock greatly, perpetuating its value as a lively pastoral attraction on the greensward and the value of sheep for converting grass into income. The *Times* and investigators in the Tax and Assessment Department may have targeted Crimmins in part because of his Irish-Catholic identity. But as parks board president, Crimmins did not only promote elite interests; he also created jobs for working-class folks and increased Sunday programming in the park to provide access to workers on their only day off.[112] Investigators ultimately deemed Crimmins innocent of any graft, but he resigned anyway to avoid the appearance of impropriety as a prominent contractor on the Parks Department payroll.

While the Crimmins scandal was defused, the incident shone a light on the way in which urban land and domestic animals served vastly different kinds of economies and cultural meanings than they had just forty years earlier. The sheep exhibit did re-create rural rhythms, and people across many demographics seemed to delight in their presence. But alive or dead, improving their flocks or carved up on their plates, the sheep sold by the park enriched the lives of affluent farmers and consumers. The former accumulated wealth embodied in animals of storied lineage, while the latter feasted upon renowned flesh. Reformers like Green had hoped that yeoman farmers would gain greater access to what reformers saw as superior European breeds through Central Park's sheep exhibit. The park's flock was supposed to enhance the pedigrees of American stock and the quality of wool and mutton produced on American farms of all classes and sizes. But it was the class of gentleman farmers—much like Olmsted's mentor Geddes—who gained the most from this spirit of "improvement."

The Crimmins inquiry revealed other inner workings of the zoological department that surprised some New Yorkers. In his testimony about the role of sheep in Central Park, Conklin revealed that when sheep died before sale to butchers or farmers, keepers fed their carcasses to the menagerie's carnivorous animals. He also testified that "gentlemen whose horses had become unfit for their service turned them over to the department" for slaughter and feeding to zoo animals "in preference to selling them into a life of drudgery." The *Times*'s coverage of this revelation seemed squeamish about *other* animals eating urban livestock once kept for the benefit of humans.[113] Even when elites bought sheep to enrich their mutton production, revenues from selling the sheep in the 1890s were mostly cycled back into the zoological department—that is, sheep destined for human consumption also benefited the menagerie collection.[114]

The New Urban Farmland

In the second half of the nineteenth century, Central Park authorities, including the Board of Commissioners, zoological department head Conklin, and architects Olmsted and Vaux, began to manage the cycles of animal life and death over a large swath of Manhattan land and even bodies of animals beyond the borders of the park. The park and the real estate market surge it provoked helped displace informal livestock agriculture to Manhattan's margins. The park shifted who benefited from urban animal husbandry—whose interests and aesthetic ideals were sustained and elevated, whose livelihoods were allowed to wither, and what animals would be exploited and how. Middle- and upper-class New Yorkers claimed space, in part, via the bodies of livestock imported from the countryside around the city, from New England and the US South, and from select and precious points of origin in England and other parts of Europe.

By the end of this period, the rural landscapes that architects and authorities like Olmsted and Green intended to re-create in the park were themselves dwindling. Sheep raising in New England declined, and the center of US sheep agriculture shifted westward. As white settlers invaded the plains and railroads opened access to markets, wool and mutton production expanded into western territories with vastly different landscapes.[115] Meanwhile, Conklin and other authorities reshaped modes of raising domesticated animals in urban America. The state and elites appropriated, transformed, and manipulated the organic city's cycles of life and death—mostly hiding the death part from the public.

With its sheep breeding and raising operation, with its bridle paths, and even in the stunted effort to establish a herd of dairy cows, Central Park became a space for valuing animals in the city in new ways. Sheep, horses, and cows now represented a refined version of multispecies communities, most accessible and valuable to elite equestrians, gentleman farmers, gentleman butchers, and agriculture and education reformers. As Green and Belmont envisioned in the 1860s, the sheep did convert grass on the greensward into meat, fiber, and reproductive bodies that could be sold in a way that helped support the park. Receipts from sales of sheep and their products constituted only a drop in the bucket of the overall park budget but a respectable portion of the income that did not come from public funding from city and state tax revenues. The value of sheep, horses, and cows was not only or even mostly measured in money, however. According to art critics and visitors who embraced the pastoral aesthetic, the real value of these creatures lay in the encounter: horses carried riders through wooded paths where they could forget they were in the city, and hundreds of sheep and a few cows enlivened the greensward and showed city dwellers, particularly children, the rhythms of the country. Furthermore, the Parks Department, commissioners, patrons, and gentlemen farmers valued the flock for elevating Southdown culture in the United States and connecting American farms and New York itself to European spaces still considered the standard of livestock breeding. As Conklin retired in the mid-1890s, however, his successors sold off the last of the Southdowns, replacing them with Dorsets.[116]

Even in the closing years of the century, other farms persisted just blocks away from the thriving and quaint sheep farm that Central Park had created. "Found near Central Park in more than one place," in the shadow of luxury brownstones, pastoralists still maintained their cottages, flocks of geese, and herds of goats. One magazine asked in 1889, "Who shall say there is more happiness in the former [brownstones] than in the latter [cottages]?"[117] While park patrons celebrated the docile sheep who seemed to embody New England and old England, a few New Yorkers now mourned the dwindling of spaces where human families lived intimately with goats and geese, recalling other, less storied European places.

Few elites realized at the time, however, that tenement dwellers continued to live cheek by muzzle and bill with domesticated livestock and would do so into the next century. Those who paid attention to housing reform debates soon found out. A 1903 report by the New York State Tenement Commission noted, among other indoor multispecies living arrangements, "a number of goats solemnly parading up and down . . . beneath a crowded tenement house" on First Avenue. Not only that, but the proprietors of a small, adjacent macaroni factory used this same space to dry their noodles on rainy days, while "goats ke[pt] watch."[118] This scene seems particularly odd, but goats, geese, and swine were common sights (and smells and sounds) in New York tenements at the turn of the century, their human keepers of a range of racial and ethnic identities transgressing sanitary codes. We don't know whether Yein Fane's neighbors raised ducks indoors without permission, but others on the Lower East Side certainly did. Many neighbors also complained about the situation to the Tenement Commission. While the kinds of spaces that central Manhattan pastoralists once subsisted on dwindled, some city dwellers found other ways to uphold their own kind of rus in urbe.[119]

CHAPTER 2

Free Animals in a Changing Landscape

As goats "infested"—to use Olmsted's word—the park's shrubbery, other creatures even harder to keep out dined on the maturing tree canopy above. Some called it the spanworm, others the measuring worm or canker worm. Adults emerged from their metamorphosis as bright-white moths with fuzzy bodies and antennae, but it was the juvenile *Ennomus subsignaria* who devoured foliage, from apples to elms to maples as far west as Ohio. As of the 1860s, it did not spare Central Park's new forests. Like its inchworm cousins, it moved along the edge of leaves by "looping up and then straightening its body."[1] In preparation to pupate, it dropped from trees to the soil below on silken threads. To humans promenading along the Mall or exploring the Ramble, the brownish gray spanworm appeared like wiggly bird droppings sprinkling down upon them. The ornithologist George Lawrence called them a "horror of pedestrians" and reported that "a sensitive lady shrinks in disgust" from even a single worm. The *Times* claimed that most New Yorkers would fall victim to this "intolerable plague."[2]

In its early years as a public space, Central Park's varied landscapes matured into habitat and food resources that supported free-roaming creatures of many species. Park leaders were eager to populate the park with appealing creatures in lively abundance, preserve the tree canopy from "depredating worms," and shield visitors from unpleasant insect encounters.[3] Like farmers and gardeners across the spanworm's range of eastern North America, park authorities looked to a European bird, variously called the house, English, European, or German sparrow, to protect cultivated plants from a native herbivore—and to enliven the landscape. Central Park became one of many hubs for what the commissioners called "efforts to colonize this bird."[4]

House sparrows (to use Lawrence's preferred name) were one of several species of birds, most of European origin, that powerful New Yorkers set free in the park to shape visitors' experiences according to their own aesthetic values.[5] As with the sheep and cows in the park, authorities often selected types fraught with European cultural associations or exotic aesthetic effects. When authorities and elites claimed space with these animals' bodies, they could eclipse other possible meanings and uses for the landscape. Furthermore, authorities' attitudes and actions toward these animals were embedded in shifting ideas about what it meant to be native versus foreign and the value of beings from North America and elsewhere in the world.

The park's landscape grew to support other wildlife, some of whom found their way there themselves, others who had been released by officials. Fish were also introduced into the park's waters, some by conservationists but others furtively by visitors, in violation of park rules. Some creatures thrived as the city grew around them. This chapter argues that as wildlife made periodic or permanent homes in the park, naturalists came to value them for their role in encounters that might help city dwellers appreciate and learn about nature. Yet park leaders also found free animals challenging in their efforts to manipulate a seemingly "natural" landscape within a growing, industrializing city. Animals flying, swimming, or scurrying free brought animation and spontaneity, but authorities worried that some were too fragile for urban life. In spite of these worries, birds' and other wild animals' actions in using park resources, migrating to the park, and taking up residence—their own means of claiming space—changed the park in ways that its creators had never imagined.[6]

Worldly Swans and Manipulated Nature

In 1857, as laborers, oxen, and horses spread new topsoil over newly seized parkland, nursery staff planted the area with tens of thousands of trees, shrubs, and herbaceous plants, native and imported. The architects intended this vegetation to create varied scenery, shade, and fresh air for humans, but it also became habitat for wild animals. At the time, house sparrows, peafowl, guinea fowl, pheasants, and starlings, if present at all, remained a rare sight in Manhattan.[7] Over the next fifty years, park authorities and a few elite New Yorkers took advantage of the new park's features—water, vegetation, and food such as nectar, fruit, and nuts provided by trees and shrubs and abundant invertebrates at the next trophic level—to populate urban nature with birds that seemed useful and that evoked locales they considered worldly or exotic.

The story of Central Park's swans illustrates how manipulating animal life helped signal New York's rising role as a worldly metropolis. Park supporters in New York and patrons in Europe considered swans essential for any landscaped park. One entrant in the design competition imagined that waterfowl would help complete visitors' experience. He wrote that "to heighten the loveliness and animation of the whole ensemble, I would propose to stock the . . . lakes with swans and ducks, and to provide, too, breeding-places for them in the middle of the lakes. Picture to yourself the whole scene then: those birds sailing proudly, or sporting lustily in the sparkling waters" as human visitors rowed boats or looked on from the shore.[8] This would-be designer certainly had European urban landscapes in mind; his description evoked English estates such as the suburban London villa of the eighteenth-century poet Alexander Pope, celebrated in painting and literature.[9]

Hamburg's and London's traditions of using swans as living symbols in the urban landscape dated back centuries. Dozens of swans lived on Hamburg's Alster Lake, and the city had funded their feeding and protection since the 1600s. City leaders and residents claimed that the swans bestowed good luck upon Hamburg's economy so long as they were cared for and respected. Swan care included the annual ritual of transporting the birds to their winter quarters on a smaller suburban pond where pumps and the swans' own motion and warmth kept the water from freezing.[10] In London, two of the oldest livery companies divided ownership of the country's swans between themselves and the English Crown; by customary law, no others could own swans on open water. Chartered in 1363, the Worshipful Companies of Dyers and Vintners once harvested the city's swans for feasts, but over the centuries, traditional "swan-upping"— marking the animals for livery ownership—became at least as much a symbolic affair as an opportunity to gather food.[11] Swans from Hamburg and London carried their reputation for beauty and grace along with their association with European cities' cultural gravitas.

As park construction proceeded, dignitaries sent swans as tokens recognizing New York's emerging metropolitan status. The first group of swans departed Hamburg and arrived in New York with much ceremony. George Kunhardt, former president of the German-American Association and now consul to Hamburg, offered the twelve birds and shared a letter detailing their life history and care, including plans for nest boxes to be constructed and placed upon the Lake in Central Park. Municipal workers in Hamburg removed the swans from Alster Lake, and the birds cruised across the Atlantic on the steamship *Bavaria*. A temporary caretaker accompanied them on the two-week voyage, all paid for by the city of Hamburg. Kunhardt also relayed that "it is necessary, when the brood of the swans become about four or five weeks old, to cut the sinews of one of the wings, otherwise the birds would fly away in autumn."[12] The swans arrived in late May 1860, but nine died shortly afterward. No one seemed to question whether this was a harbinger of bad luck or an indication that the swans had been disrespected. Park authorities attributed their death to apoplexy, meaning that stress caused too much blood to flood the swans' brains.[13] Undiscouraged, Kunhardt's brother had staff in Hamburg capture and send ten more swans. Meanwhile, London's Worshipful

Company of Vintners and the Worshipful Company of Dyers, with logistical and financial sponsorship from a member of Parliament, sent twelve and thirteen breeding pairs, respectively, from the swans' home on the Thames. The swans from London anglicized the park's landscape, connecting New York to the Crown through the English trade guilds' allotment of birds. The surviving swans from London and Hamburg took up residence on the Lake.[14]

Swans also helped associate the park with European landscape architecture traditions. Architects Olmsted and Vaux were ever sensitive to the effect of changing vistas on park visitors, and the swans themselves conveyed different meanings depending on the place from which humans viewed them. The commissioners described them as sailing "proudly over the surface" of the Lake and under the bridge at the classically styled Mall. Especially during music concerts, they heightened the formal air of the landscape, reminiscent of geometric gardens in Versailles and Utrecht, with their pure whiteness and curved necks.[15] One guidebook gushed, "The swans moving so gently and so gallantly upon the quiet waters of the Lake never fail to awaken the most pleasurable feelings in all hearts."[16] The art critic and park guidebook author Clarence Cook admitted that birds associated with social hierarchy might seem out of place in a park that promised social leveling. He wrote in his guide to the park that "we may be encouraged to hope that these beautiful aristocrats have learned to accommodate themselves to our trying climate and our democratic institutions."[17]

When swans paddled into the Ramble's secluded inlets, their effect turned from the classical to the romantic.[18] A forty-acre district just north of the formal Mall and Terrace area, flanking the Lake, the Ramble epitomized the picturesque landscape tradition, with its dense and varied plantings in complex overstory and understory forest layers. Clarence Cook was particularly struck by the native honeysuckle and swamp magnolia and the wildflowers in the ground layer. Native blackberry and raspberry, tulip poplar, juneberry, locust, and many others grew there in the

An illustration from Clarence Cook's 1869 *Description of the New York Central Park* shows a human visitor in a rustic shelter in the Ramble meeting a swan on the Lake. The image suggests an intimate encounter, conveying quiet and stillness in a natural landscape.

park's first two decades.[19] The Ramble's paths wound up and down hills, around dramatic rock outcrops, and along the Lake's reticulated northern shores—organic lines and shapes contrasting with the rectilinear grid of avenues and streets that structured the rest of the city. Indeed, Olmsted and Vaux intended that visitors could forget they were in the middle of a growing city and that the park itself was a manipulated landscape. Streams meandered under rustic bridges and cascaded over rock formations. Visitors to the Ramble found quiet and stillness mere blocks from mushrooming neighborhoods and bustling streets.[20]

For human park goers, swans did not just animate the scenery from a distance; human visitors used landscape features in the Ramble to

A large group of children and youths pose with swans at the Lake's shore. Although the children are dressed in fine clothes, such large gatherings could become raucous. Swans accustomed to feeding by park goers might approach the group to seek food but might also take a defensive posture if children got too close. Courtesy of the New York Public Library Digital Collections.

pursue contact with swans. From shoreline shelters and boat landings in the Ramble, visitors "observ[ed] . . . the waterfowl in their playfulness" on the Lake.[21] Early photos and sketches portrayed children and adults approaching swans on land and in the water, sometimes offering food.[22] Human efforts to commune with these birds conflicted with swans' behaviors, however. Swans may have experienced humans as pervasive menaces, particularly excited children who tried to approach them. Swans respond to perceived threats by taking a defensive stance against seeming predators—the ill temper that many humans ascribe to them. During breeding season, swans become even more sensitive to potential predators as they guard nests, eggs, and hatchlings. Swans hiss and may even strike a perceived predator with wings strong enough to break bones—though there is no record of swan-related injuries to humans in the park.[23]

Mute swans can migrate but seldom do when supplied with ample food year-round in human settings like parks, country estates, and city lakes—as in London and Hamburg, where patrons, the Crown, or city coffers paid for their sustenance. They eat food provided directly by humans, along with aquatic vegetation like algae and larger freshwater plants, and may reshape pond ecologies by removing this vegetation. As visitors introduced fish into ponds and lakes in the park's early years, the swans surely made meals of their eggs and perhaps crustaceans and mollusks as well.[24] Many human visitors hand-fed swans cake from the shores of the Ramble; swans grew accustomed to this extra source of easy food and tolerated people who might provide a meal.[25] For human visitors, feeding swans was a relatively easy, if somewhat perilous, way to engage with a large, visually stunning animal. By feeding swans and watching them up close, human park goers of all ages brought these birds into greater dependence and control.[26]

Much as Olmsted and Vaux's design obscured the labor needed to construct the park, officials and workers carefully manipulated swans' habitats to make them appear natural and spontaneous. Mated swan pairs often work together gathering long, supple aquatic vegetation, which the female assembles into a nest as large as one and a half meters in diameter. She mounds these materials on or near the shore before laying up to ten eggs.[27] Yet design competition entrants, park patrons, and administrators worried about birds' survival in the urban environment and recommended constructing hidden platforms where waterfowl could reproduce, unthreatened by predators like cats and dogs that lurked throughout the city.[28] Nest boxes might make breeding season less stressful by shielding swans' view of human visitors, whom they perceived as threats. Based on two sets of designs sent along with the birds from Hamburg, zoological department workers constructed these boxes and concealed them near the Lake's shore. One set of designs from Hamburg resembled a small rowboat mounted on a platform that floated atop four logs chained to a pier, to be used "where the nests are exposed to waves." The other had an open framework, kept afloat by a log at either end, atop which swans could construct their own grass nests; park architects described these as "preferred by the swans" and of a more "natural character."[29] Landscape advocates and park architects preferred scenery in which animals could reproduce safely without the appearance of human intervention.

Other human elites sought to populate the park with birds appropriated into western European landscapes from Asia and Africa. In the early 1860s, patrons began to donate peafowl, particularly Henry Winthrop Sargent, an old friend of Andrew Jackson Downing who spent much of his life tending his estate along the Hudson River in Upstate New York.[30] The zoological department released them onto the lawns surrounding the Mall and the Ramble. Peacocks had long strutted about South Asian and Middle Eastern gardens, but in Europe, leading figures like British prime minister Benjamin Disraeli used them to express exotic opulence on landscaped lawns.[31] In describing the peacocks in his guide to the park, Clarence Cook promoted the bird as an orientalist icon, digressing at length about a "Mohammedan" version of the Garden of Eden story, in which a peacock is punished for his vanity and foolishness.[32]

Amid growing curiosity about guinea fowl among northern US gentlemen farmers, the board purchased several in 1864, and William Conklin and a New Yorker named Joshua Jones donated a few as well.[33] With their black-and-white speckled plumage and colorful, crowned heads (or their revered albino form), guinea fowl carried complicated cultural associations from across the Atlantic world. Communities across the African continent domesticated these plump birds for eggs and meat, and in the 1600s, traders imported them to western Europe, where elites used them to ornament pleasure gardens. Slave ships had also brought

Several guinea fowl strut and peck the ground for insects on a lawn in the Ramble. From Cook, *Description of the New York Central Park* (1869).

them to the Americas along with their human inmates; enslaved people had used them for sustenance and ritual, and enslaved chefs such as James Hemings cooked them for enslavers. Guinea fowl were also gaining renown as pest controllers on farms.[34] Like Cook's guide, Daniel Wise's *Little Peachblossom* remarked on the exotic and mysterious effects of peafowl and guinea fowl strutting about, pecking insects in the Ramble and on the lawns. Two of the park's most visible bird species served as living symbols of exoticism, empire, or enslavement translated through European optics, referencing places and cultures whose histories these birds embodied.[35]

In the 1860s, mute swans, peafowl, and guinea fowl in the park, about fifty of each species, quite visibly roamed the Lake, the Ramble, and adjacent greens, producing perhaps a dozen young per species each year.[36] They mostly stayed in the park, as feeding by visitors and staff cultivated dependency upon humans; staff also clipped the swans' wings.[37] (On one occasion, though, Conklin dispatched park police to fetch a peahen who had "strayed away to Harlem.")[38] Over the next decades, however, park officials joined in the growing acclimatization movement, using the park as a stage from which to release more birds who could populate surrounding areas. New York elites joined this empire-spanning movement that promoted new exchanges of animal life and deepened European influence in ecosystems and landscapes.

Acclimatization, House Sparrows, and "the Native"

The acclimatization movement originated with French naturalists in the early nineteenth century in part as a scientific counterpart to imperial ventures, aiming to test and observe how organisms changed when moved between European metropoles and far-flung colonies. Settlers across Britain's colonies and former colonies also pursued acclimatization, promising to "improve" landscapes with animals and plants they considered useful and attractive. Acclimatization societies in the British metropole and in Australia were more ambitious and long-lived than those in North America, but across all locations, their actions often muddled supposed utilitarian aims with shifting settler identities and scientific ambitions.[39] Of course, European invaders and settlers had been altering colonial ecosystems through the movement of animals, plants, and microbes across empires for centuries already. Acclimatizers cast this new wave of ecological imperialism in the trappings of science and economy—and in the case of Central Park, aesthetics and desire for encounter. Farmers, naturalists, and scientists across the United States imported cages full of *Passer domesticus*, the house sparrow, across the Atlantic for its utilitarian promise.[40] In New York City, amateur naturalists and zoological director William Conklin expressed a special need to bring birds from abroad to improve urban nature.[41]

Eugene Schieffelin was one such amateur naturalist, the seventh child in a family of lawyers and pharmaceutical wholesalers who traced their lineage to influential German Americans of the Revolutionary War era. By age twenty-three, he was a partner in the family business, moved in high society circles, and engaged in leisurely pursuit of natural history and genealogical knowledge.[42] An early proponent of acclimatizing European birds in New York, Schieffelin released about a dozen house sparrows each year at his father's Madison Square estate, beginning around 1860, in hopes they would devour the insects infesting shade trees.[43]

Paris, London, and Rome had all established acclimatization gardens for introducing organisms from the colonies to the metropole.[44] Conklin and the board were eager to use the park for a similar project, to "introduce some of the rapidly multiplying semi-domesticated birds of Europe" who would protect trees and enliven the landscape. They were aware that many European farmers had tried to kill off house sparrows for being "destructive to the grain fields." But house sparrows had proven themselves hardy and bold in Europe's industrial cities, able to share space with a thronging human populace. In 1863, the commissioners released house sparrows in the park for the first time—seven breeding pairs.[45] Within two years, park officials boasted that house sparrows—which they at first called by their French name *moineau*—had "increased in number and are quite tame, and will probably become domesticated."[46]

In the park, Manhattan, and beyond, house sparrows multiplied and thrived, and enthusiasm for them blossomed among some park visitors. House sparrow proponents celebrated both the promise of pest control and their endearing behaviors performed before human crowds. Daniel Wise and Clarence Cook delightedly anthropomorphized their antics in their books about the park. They imagined house sparrows as tiny Britons bickering, courting lovers, or holding a town meeting or May Day festival.[47] After another, larger release of house sparrows in Union Square Park, regular New Yorkers doted upon the gregarious birds, offering roosts at their homes along with additional food to satisfy their voracious appetites and promote their reproduction.[48] Park annual reports quoted observations by the ornithologist George Lawrence to trumpet the park's role in populating the region with bird life. In an 1866 speech to the Lyceum of Natural History, Lawrence remarked on local house sparrows' production of "two or more broods in a season."[49] His speech (which also enumerated 326 other bird species in the region—but park administrators were eager to take credit for this one) noted his own and other naturalists' observations of house sparrow colonies "in quite large numbers" as far away as "Jersey City, Hoboken, and Bergen Point."[50] In subsequent years, commissioners boasted that house sparrows were "exceedingly abundant" in the park, numbering in the thousands and breeding "under the eaves of buildings situated within a circuit often miles from it."[51]

Like Schieffelin but some twenty years his senior, Lawrence also belonged to an old, prosperous family in the pharmaceutical trade; birds and science were his passions. As a youth, he had identified and observed the birds that migrated through New York City, including thick flocks of passenger pigeons that once traversed Manhattan and much of the continent. As a young man, he began collecting bird specimens with a gun, as was common in that era of bird study. In 1860, while Schieffelin began introducing house sparrows as a young man, the middle-aged Lawrence left the drug business to dedicate himself full-time to ornithology. The two sometimes crossed paths while observing New York's birds. Over his lifetime, Lawrence belonged to the Lyceum and other learned societies, conducted ornithological expeditions to Central and South America and the Caribbean, and collected some eight thousand bird skins, which he donated to the American Museum of Natural History.[52]

Zoological director Conklin and other park supporters and officials cited Lawrence to contrast the house sparrow's easy success against what they saw as a relative dearth of native birds. They treasured native birds but doubted their sufficiency. Natives seemed too few to protect the park's trees and enliven the landscape for visitors, and besides, Conklin deemed natives timid and fragile. The commissioners claimed that "great pains [are] taken to secure . . . unmolested habitation" for native birds, which often meant that "artificial nesting places are provided."[53] Reports and guidebooks echoed this message about protecting native birds but, in the next breath, celebrated the prolific introduced sparrow, as if comparing a delicate, reserved younger child who had to be coaxed into public against an outgoing, ambitious elder sibling.[54] The 1866 edition of T. Addison Richards's guide to the park explained that officials endeavored to accommodate and preserve native birds but that "every effort will be made . . . to domesticate as far as possible the feathered songsters of all other climes."[55] The *Times* bluntly accused "the indigenous feathered ones" of having "naught to do with the unpleasant worms" that sent chills down the spines of park visitors.[56]

Expressions of disappointment with native birds and enthusiasm for those who were introduced came amid shifts in the meaning and valuation of the "native." Commentary on the seeming sparseness of native birds echoed settlers' representations of Indigenous Americans—tropes that helped justify seizure of land that, to imperial eyes, was unimproved and unpopulated or de-populated by disease and European settlement.[57] Acclimatization advocates imported organisms they expected to "go forth and multiply," fulfilling key roles in nature as they remade the Americas in Europe's image. Even pitying support expressed for native birds echoed nostalgic but fatalistic representations of dwindling American Indians across their homeland, such as by the contemporary painter George Catlin, who documented the Mandan, the Osage, and other Plains peoples.[58] In Central Park, acclimatization supporters saw imported sparrows as redeeming nature, animating an urbanized and manipulated landscape for the delight and edification of city dwellers, as native birds seemed to fade away.

As New York grew, native birds seemed too timid to enter built-up areas crowded with humans. The commissioners explained that these birds "leave on their annual migrations when the weather becomes too severe for them," depriving the park and its human visitors of their liveliness.[59] Officials quoted Lawrence's remarks on the hardiness of the house sparrows in New York's variable climate, even "after the extreme cold of January, 1866, when the thermometer marked ten degrees below zero, I noticed them in their usual quarters, apparently unharmed." Furthermore, Lawrence observed, they "were quite gentle and fearless" when approached

In the park's early decades, staff constructed and placed rustic bird shelters like this one in the Ramble in hopes of attracting and retaining more birds to animate the scenery. From Cook, *Description of the New York Central Park* (1869).

by humans.[60] To park authorities and patrons, these semi-domesticated foreigners seemed much better suited than native birds to populate the park to a pleasing, animated abundance. Conklin worked with other acclimatizers such as John Sutherland, who donated English blackbirds in 1865, and Joshua Jones, who released "six pairs of English skylarks" upon one of the park's meadows in 1867.[61] Acclimatizers successfully introduced insectivorous skylarks elsewhere in the British Empire, notably New Zealand and Australia, but they remained rare in the park.[62]

Acclimatizers pronounced house sparrows a hero in battles against the spanworm during the 1860s, boasting of their successes in improving nature. They also established local societies—including the group in New York, chartered as the American Acclimatization Society in 1871, with Eugene Schieffelin and Joshua Jones among its six founders. The society professed its aim to "introduce[e] and acclimatiz[e] . . . such foreign varieties of the animal and vegetable kingdoms as may be useful or interesting" and to discover and develop "valuable properties in species not hitherto brought into the service of man."[63]

Just as New York's acclimatization society was getting started, however, many naturalists began to question the benefits of house sparrows, casting them instead as foreign, unnatural villains. Sparrow critics attacked the characteristics that acclimatizers had celebrated: house sparrows were too numerous and bold, a danger to native species. Some of the contempt for house sparrows seemed to reflect their ubiquity in cities. Naturalist Thomas Gentry described the species as "noisy, familiar, impatient . . . one of those creatures that manifests a close attachment to man, and follows him wherever he goes."[64] While Schieffelin, Conklin, and others echoed discourse about disappearing Native Americans in their worries about native birds, sparrow critics equated introduced birds with the newest human immigrants. In these decades, the United States' foreign-born population grew rapidly, with a growing share of immigrants arriving from southern and eastern Europe and rural Ireland.[65] Many citizens of northern and western European heritage feared the growing social, cultural, and political influence of these human newcomers. Whites with some-what longer family histories in North America appropriated the identity of being native themselves. While acclimatizers—who included long-established Anglo- and German Americans like Conklin and Schieffelin, perching above the fray they helped create—imported house sparrows to replace or supplement the functions of native birds, nativist naturalists demanded protection for the birds they considered original to the continent. Critics lobbed insults and accusations amid the debate dubbed "the Sparrow Wars."[66] In urban areas, the vitriol against these teeming little brown birds echoed slurs against new human immigrants: filthy habitations, profligate copulation and reproduction, and their overall threat to native birds. Observers also expressed disgust when the introduced birds consumed undigested grain in horse dung in the streets. Some of the sparrows' most vocal detractors included conservationists, writers, and political figures who also called for human immigration restrictions, along with farmers who claimed the birds ate grain from their fields rather than protecting crops from insects.[67]

While the Sparrow Wars raged, house sparrows teemed, and skylarks struggled, the park board and the zoological department announced that "the number of native birds on the Park" had grown to a "considerable" size, although most species remained "rare." By 1868, George Lawrence turned his keen naturalist's gaze on the park and helped verify 129 bird species observed there—almost 200 fewer than the total number of birds he had identified in the New York region as a whole but still a promising picture of urban avian life. (And to be fair, many of those missing from Central Park's list were coastal residents on Long Island, unlikely to make homes in the park.) Their report included only three species introduced by European Americans—house sparrows, skylarks, and the canaries that sometimes escaped from houses in the surrounding neighborhoods. Notably, the list of free birds did not include the domestic pigeon, brought to North America by Europeans for utilitarian purposes, although several donors had given fancy pigeons to the menagerie. (Swans, guinea

An illustration from 1867 *Harper's Weekly* shows "Birds from the Central Park Collection," including a mix of species that would have arrived at the park on their own, some that were donated or released at the park, and some former pets that were kept in the menagerie. Courtesy of HathiTrust.

fowl, and peafowl appeared in a separate list of animals in captivity in the park.) Conklin also pointed out that the number of natives was "small in comparison with those that visit . . . during their spring and autumn migrations"—indicating that this unstable category of native did not include seasonal migrants.[68]

Animating the Park amid Urban Expansion

Various humans groups contested the categories of native, migratory, and foreign, but there was no doubt that New York's style of urbanization welcomed some animals to thrive while making others' lives difficult. Bold and adaptable house sparrows took advantage of sprouting neighborhoods and industrial sites, human crowds and their refuse. Many other species needed quieter shelters than construction sites, office and apartment buildings, and busy streets. Just a short flight away from the din, "numerous native birds . . . find home and refuge" in the growing and "varied foliage" of the park.[69]

Indeed, the 1868 list presents a lively picture of avian life in the park a decade after the city seized the land. Many birds found homes in forests and shorelines on their own, not only the "artificial roosts" offered by the zoological staff. The list counted species as "abundant," "common," or "rare," and many of the rarest resided or stopped over primarily in the Ramble. There were ruffed grouses and woodcocks; six pairs of the latter performed their dramatic mating ritual in the Ramble in 1868. Lawrence confirmed at least fifteen species of warblers who appeared in summer, most rarely so, and speculated that more stopped there without being observed. Large owls remained rare, except for one snowy owl in the Ramble, but three species of small owls were common, including one who stayed year-round and became abundant nesting "in the crevices of the rocks" there. Four types of woodpeckers appeared early in summer, "confine themselves to the Ramble, and leave very early in the season." Abundant and growing numbers of phoebes, flycatchers, and especially kingbirds bred in the eaves of rustic shelters built in the Ramble for humans to rest in. Wood thrushes, wrens, and titlarks (today usually known as pipits) also thrived, frequenting the shores of the Lake and also nesting in the park's meadows. Conklin was especially thrilled that a pair of belted kingfishers nested on the Terrace (not far from the Ramble) and reared a brood in early June 1868.[70]

Chipping sparrows and song sparrows, a few types of swallows, catbirds, purple martins, titmice, nuthatches, bluebirds, redstarts, red-winged blackbirds, ruby-throated hummingbirds, indigo buntings, and Baltimore orioles might stay in the park for the warmer part of the year, and many of them bred "abundantly" there, as did the "yellow-bird," today known as the goldfinch. Robins stayed year-round, as did crows; the latter were "exceedingly abundant," including in winter. Passenger pigeons "flock[ed] during their transmigrations in the spring and fall months" through the park. The "abundant," or "common," status of four hawks (Cooper's, sharp-shinned, red-tailed, and red-shouldered) suggests a wealth of smaller birds and other prey for these predators to subsist upon. A "bald-headed eagle" stayed "in the Deer Park for two months in the fall of 1866," but this species was seldom seen, although it sometimes frequented the more northern reaches of Manhattan, fishing in the Hudson. Some surprising species and groups remained less than abundant, such as blue jays, gulls, and cuckoos, but "cow blackbirds"—brood parasites today known as brown-headed cowbirds—were common. Mallards remained "not common," but "summer ducks"—today known as wood ducks—were common at the end of the season. Bitterns were common in summer, but green herons and night herons remained rare, and the report mentioned no great blue herons or egrets. There were no cardinals, or "red birds" (Lawrence had only ever seen one on all of Manhattan as of 1866), and the only mockingbird noted was thought to have escaped from a nearby home, where it had been kept as a pet.[71]

Other than the bird list and a study of the park's waters, lists of other types of creatures living at-large in the park—wild mammals, reptiles, amphibians, and the many invertebrates beyond the spanworm that made temporary or permanent homes there—were less systematic. Of course, an abundance of animal life had thrived on the Mannahatta of Lenapehoking before settlers seized it as New Amsterdam and then New York; settlers had hunted and fished here, decimating and displacing the island's Indigenous humans and many of its nonhuman animals.[72] One history recalled the early extermination of "bears, wolves, and other ferocious animals" who "abounded among the retreats afforded by the wilderness" and were "destructive to the cattle" on Harlem's commons. Later, "gentlemen coming from the city" hunted foxes and rabbits. Still, by the early 1800s, the future park "furnished ample extent for a full day's shooting" of small animals such as snipe, woodcock, and squirrels. Park proponents seldom acknowledged this former more-than-human world.[73]

Urban nature advocates had begun to introduce deer, peacocks, squirrels and other creatures in Philadelphia, Boston, and other cities to enliven public spaces, as historian Etienne Benson has shown.[74] At least one Central Park design competition entrant had assumed that deer would run at large in the park, necessitating a "light fence" around flower gardens to protect plants.[75] Given the troubles with goats, it is hard to imagine how this arrangement would have succeeded; Conklin placed donated deer, along with raccoons, in paddocks and cages. Conklin endeavored to enliven the landscape by setting birds and small mammals free in the park.[76] In the early 1870s, he released chipmunks, flying squirrels, and gray squirrels. As yet uncommon in US cities, some of these creatures were captured by park patrons and donated; others Conklin imported from Vermont (he also kept a few caged). In the same decade, other animals freed themselves: "several woodchucks escaped from their cage" in the menagerie and "increased in numbers" on the park; "European hares" and both domesticated and wild-type rabbits also thrived. In 1878, Conklin intentionally released a town of prairie dogs, who "after prospecting the grounds for several weeks finally settled" at the park's southeastern corner, "where they can be seen any clear day sitting up in front of their burrows."[77] Woodchucks and wild rabbits, common in the New York region, might seem better candidates for release than prairie dogs from western North America, but Conklin likely hoped to showcase the latter's appealing and visible behavior. The zoological director was motivated to ensure that visitors could see the park's animals.

The Ramble, designed immerse city dwellers in nature, created good conditions for city dwellers to encounter free animals, but staff also captured some native birds "specimens" to display in the menagerie. In 1868, for example, they confined a fish hawk, a night heron, a Virginia rail, and a mallard.[78] In spite of cramped and even dangerous conditions at the menagerie, Conklin used captivity to protect birds from perceived dangers and to ensure their visibility. Furthermore, few park visitors beyond expert ornithologists could find elusive birds in treetops, lakeshores, and shrubbery. Native birds who were donated to the park were often caged, much like abandoned pets such as parrots and canaries. Menagerie staff distributed some of the smaller birds in cages placed on pillars along the Mall, making them into ornaments.[79]

Migration seasons also aroused fear that birds might not find their way back as the city grew to engulf the park. Ornithologists were learning more about migration, but these movements remained a "mystery of mysteries," as one science writer noted. Naturalists were just beginning to understand that migration less as a direct response to cold itself and more as a survival strategy to take advantage of different locations amid seasonal, geographic shifts in food availability, particularly of insects and other invertebrates. With the solidification of evolutionary theory, naturalists surmised that migration instincts had emerged and become refined over geologic time. By the 1870s, a few began to appreciate that native birds or seasonal migrants were not somehow less hardy but, rather, were marvels of behavioral evolution compelled by as yet unknown forces to navigate between tropical and boreal latitudes.[80]

In spite of the Sparrow Wars and growing awareness that native birds were thriving in the park, Conklin remained wary about natives'

A woman attempts to feed a squirrel called "Bunny" in Central Park, circa 1900.
Courtesy of the Library of Congress, Prints and Photographs Division.

sufficiency. Throughout the 1870s, he welcomed European bird introductions. In 1876, he invited the Acclimatization Society to "set at liberty on the Park during the Summer a number of starlings." By fall, they flew to New Jersey, but Conklin expressed hope and confidence that they would return the next spring while casting doubt upon native birds' viability.[81] In 1877, Conklin addressed a society meeting, chaired by Eugene Schieffelin, boasting of the park's role in acclimatization experiments involving not just house sparrows, starlings, and skylarks but also English chaffinches,

CHAPTER 2

English blackbirds, and Java sparrows.[82] He appealed to Schieffelin and colleagues in that year's park report, stating that "it would be very desirable if the Society place other European species on the Park, as the number of native birds have been very much diminished in late years, owing no doubt to the rapid building up of the city around the Park."[83] Conklin recommended several other birds for acclimatization that would be "useful for farmers" and "contribute to the beauty of the groves and fields"—showing that his ambition to animate landscapes extended beyond the park.[84]

Amid successes with house sparrows, Conklin recognized that some acclimatized birds might struggle in the park. In addition to the skylarks who dispersed to New Jersey and the swans whose wings were clipped and nests carefully curated, he fretted that what he called "English pheasants" introduced in 1876 would not survive (their ancestors actually originated east of the Black Sea).[85] Pheasants hide in brush, shying from noises that might come from a hunting party, even in a place like Central Park with rules against hunting and off-leash dogs (these rules were often transgressed).[86] When donor John Sutherland released them in the Ramble that fall, "it was rather late in the season for them to breed," and the "great scarcity of underbrush" after the frost would put them at a disadvantage.[87] Pheasants were another example, like swans, peafowl, and guinea fowl, of European aesthetics and history imposed upon the landscape through birds linked to hierarchy and appropriation. Pheasants evoked aristocratic hunting grounds, recalling country estates across Britain designed by Capability Brown and Charles Bridgeman in the eighteenth and nineteenth centuries, where yeomen were prohibited from hunting.[88] Park visionaries promised to replace hierarchy with democracy when they imported European landscape idioms, but pheasants, like swans, could evoke aristocracy.

Stocking Central Park's Waters

While social class marked many birds' historical relationships with humans, some park patrons and visitors hoped that fish and fishing would be universally accessible for utilitarian purposes. Elites as well as regular New Yorkers attempted to introduce fish into the park's many water bodies. In 1857, at least four design entries proposed stocking ponds or lakes with fish. J. Lachaume, the pseudonymous entrant who also proposed "agricultural depots," suggested that fish would serve the enjoyment of working-class New Yorkers.[89] Upon the park's opening, administrators began to stock the park's waters in a haphazard, opportunistic way, beginning with one of the first animal donations—an unspecified number of goldfish offered by one William Murphy in 1860. Staff released these fish into one of the park's many fountains.[90] In 1869, Samuel Tilden, Andrew Green's dear friend and a leading New York politician (who later served as governor and ran for president), donated 568 trout to be released in the park's lakes and ponds.[91] New Yorkers' appetites for urban fishing exceeded even this large donation, however, and many took the matter of the park's aquatic life into their own hands. Anonymous visitors engaged in illicit, informal fish stocking, dropping pet fish along with wild species hooked elsewhere into constructed water bodies, including the Lake, Harlem Meer, the reservoir basins, and others. Park rules stated that both fishing and placing "any article or thing" in the waters were prohibited. This rule proved difficult to enforce, although frequently reprinted in newspapers and bulletins.[92] By supplementing formal stocking, New Yorkers introduced vernacular fish culture and new ecological implications into the park's waterscape.

Eels, catfish, perch, and other species also entered the park's waters through pipes installed to manage drainage and hydrology. These mingled with the formally and furtively stocked fish and other aquatic life in an environment marked by both technological interventions and elements that defied rational management.[93] The water in the park's two lakes (the larger adjacent to the Ramble, the smaller at the park's north end) "derived from the Croton and from the surface drainage of the surrounding slopes." Rain and irrigation water that fell on paved "roadways, drives, and footpaths . . . drained into underground pipes" that also connected with the Croton reservoir and fed into the lakes.[94] Fish released in one water body spread into others, along with mollusks, crustaceans, and microscopic rotifers and diatoms who might have been present in the fishes' water or on their skin. Gut flora from the feces of domesticated animals and wildlife infiltrated through the soil with precipitation and into these water bodies.[95] The park's waters thus connected with one another and the terrestrial landscape.

As aquatic life navigated the park's waters, with or without direct human intervention, some conservationists called for park officials to take a greater role in providing education and recreation related to fish. In 1870, Robert B. Roosevelt, uncle of future president Theodore, proposed using Central Park's waters as hatcheries to help stock the city and surrounding regions with fish for recreational, subsistence, and possibly commercial purposes. Roosevelt made this request on behalf of the New York State Fisheries Commission that he had founded three years earlier, suggesting that hatcheries for trout and perch would spark even greater interest than the menagerie and educate the public about fish culture.[96] Robert Roosevelt also appeared alongside William Conklin at an 1877 American Acclimatization Society meeting, emphasizing the usefulness of North American fish over those of other continents. Instead of introducing "foreign" fish, he encouraged efforts to "distribute the best of our fishes" such as shad, "landlocked salmon," "Oswego bass," and "California brook trout." Formal stocking occurred periodically, but true aquaculture remained elusive in the park, and a proposal for an aquarium there also languished.[97]

New Yorkers of all classes expressed fervent and visceral interest in connecting with nature through the park's fish.[98] These animals and the humans who cared about them exerted a growing influence on the waterscape, in spite of prohibitions and administrators' scattershot attention. Yet fishing could also be stripped of its productive functions and turned into a rarefied, elite pursuit. Rules against fishing did not apply to fly casting clubs, which practiced the rarefied sport without hooking fish—they even removed barbs from their hooks, though mostly to protect humans—and held regular tournaments in the park starting no later than 1887.[99]

Through the ecological relationships and lives of fish, official and informal fish stockers also changed the park environment in ways that affected visitors' and neighbors' health, sparking controversy. While some New Yorkers dropped fish in park lakes and reservoirs, others complained of the stench and sight of dead fish in these water bodies. In 1884, Conklin asked two naturalists, Louis Pope Gratacap and Anthony Woodward, to study the park's aquatic life. Gratacap and Woodward confirmed public complaints, declaring the Lake and the Harlem Meer "stagnant . . . foul and impotable." They also noted "unmistakable evidence of sewage contamination" such as vibrio microbes in these nascent days of bacteriology.[100] Miasma theories of disease persisted, too, and some city aldermen tried to pass a bill encouraging fishing to eliminate hazardous emanations that arose from excessive animal matter—and also for citizens' "amusement and recreation."[101] Fish in the reservoirs, for example, were growing to legendary sizes that attracted prospective anglers. A *Times* reporter gazed in awe and longed for a fishing rod when he glimpsed a "mammoth . . . bronze-backed bass" coursing through the water, seeking insects and smaller fish to prey upon.[102] Fish added to the multilayered ecological relationships developing in the park and inspired human visitors, but they could also contribute to sensory offenses and health problems for neighboring communities.

Bounded Nature and the Dangers of Freedom

Fish seemed to thrive in park waters, and since most humans saw them as a free source of amusement and food, few if any New Yorkers worried about these creatures' survival in the city—just their stench and health

CHAPTER 2

effects. Other free animals, particularly birds, remained a constant concern for those who perceived grave threats in the urban environment. These worries led Conklin and others to circumscribe some birds' lives, to ensure that they would continue to animate the landscape, even if that meant curtailing their freedom and compromising aesthetic ideals. Park authorities' treatment of birds reinscribed a tension in their spatial imagination of the park. Olmsted and Vaux intended landscapes such as the Ramble to immerse the human city dweller in nature. Authorities believed that strict boundaries between the park and the city were needed to maintain this sense of immersion and to protect delicate animals within.

In chapter 1, we saw how park authorities escalated efforts to control livestock who wandered into the park, erecting fences, upping fines, and ordering police to shoot goats who breached its boundaries. Along with wandering livestock who ate shrubbery and grass, cats and dogs also ranged into the park, sometimes preying upon animals there. In 1876, a year after the order to shoot goats, Conklin asked that "an officer be detailed to shoot cats, which infest Central Park in great numbers and destroy the birds."[103] As historian Katherine Grier has shown, before flea collars, kitty litter, and veterinary sterilization, families who kept dogs and cats often let them roam rather than allow pests, messes, and nonhuman sexuality indoors.[104] One outdoor magazine bemoaned the "prowling cats and the packs of wild dogs which infest the shrubbery at night," preventing ground-nesting birds from raising a successful brood in the park.[105] Dogs repeatedly attacked swans and penetrated menagerie cages. In 1877, Conklin ruefully reported that "fences have been placed around [the waterfowl nests] which are rather unsightly in appearance" to protect them from "destruction by dogs."[106] Fences detracted from the appearance that swans thrived without human aid. While reinforcing the park's perimeter against predators, Conklin also brought more birds into captivity in the menagerie—catbirds, bluebirds, goldfinches, crows, and owls.[107] The park's illusion of spontaneity and boundlessness was only possible if certain animals were controlled and bounded.

Humans could enter the park freely, and according to Conklin and some park patrons, some posed greater threats to wild birds than stray dogs and cats. While bemoaning the dog attacks, Conklin also lamented that "there could be found no means of protection . . . against visitors, who still continue to despoil the nests" so carefully co-constructed by swans and humans on the Lake.[108] Officials took the deadly behaviors of some human city dwellers as an indication of birds' and squirrels' vulnerability within the urban environment; similar tensions had been building for decades throughout the United States between hunters of different social classes. Elite sportsmen criticized "pothunters," who killed wildlife primarily for food or livelihood and who violated "the sporting ideals of restraint and fair play," as historian Adam Rome has described the discourse against working-class and poor hunters.[109] In the 1857 edition of his hunting guide, *The American Sportsman*, author Elisha J. Lewis disparaged them, saying that in winter, "every thoughtless and mercenary lounger in the country shoulders his rusty weapon and wanders lazily forth to kill and destroy whatever of animated nature may lucklessly cross his path."[110] Lewis distinguished his own class of hunters by their admiration of nature as a whole, in contrast to what he supposed was pothunters' predatory focus on bagging birds. He urged urban professionals such as physicians (he was a doctor himself) and lawyers to pursue hunting as physical recreation and a means of communing with nature.[111]

Human New Yorkers continued to hunt at the city's fringes and even close to the built-up districts. Elite commentators mocked those New Yorkers who rode the streetcar to Brooklyn in full hunting gear to bag small animals including robins, flickers, and other birds, as well as chipmunks, and blamed them for the decline of "songsters" who controlled insects in suburban farms and gardens. "The idea of any sane man attempting to find anything within the nature of *game* within fifty miles of City Hall is absurd," the *Times* remarked, joking ruefully that Union Square's sparrows would be their next target.[112] But not all New York hunters went to the suburbs to seek small "game," and authorities blamed them in part for the continuing dearth of birds in Central Park. Indeed, some subsistence hunters continued to see the park space as a source of wild food. Officials and patrons also complained of boys who killed small animals there. Commissioners promulgated an official park ordinance against "disturbing the birds." Yet "marauding Nimrods," as guidebook author T. Addison Richards put it (or "degenerate Nimrods" per the *Times*) continued to kill avian residents of the park and raid their nests.[113] These writers turned the name of the mighty hunter Nimrod of ancient Mesopotamian legend into a sardonic insult against hunters who killed indiscriminately, without what elite sportsmen considered art.[114] This slur often targeted immigrants—particularly Italians—who brought their homelands' food gathering traditions to the United States.[115]

In this era, people across ages, classes, nationalities, and urban and rural space hunted and killed small animals, for food, income, sport, science, or some combination thereof, but elites tended to justify their own hunting cultures. A young Teddy Roosevelt reported in his boyhood journal as early as 1869, at age eleven, that he snared robins and intentionally spilled clutches in his own backyard and on family vacations.[116] If anyone called the privileged Roosevelt a Nimrod, it was probably not ironically. Roosevelt also took part in a widespread "culture of collecting" in the nineteenth century. As historian Mark Barrow writes, Americans fascinated with nature brought materials and organisms into their homes and curio cabinets. Early ornithologists did their collecting with a gun.[117] George Lawrence recalled instances of bird hunting even in built-up sections of Manhattan, such as an incident in which a man shot a woodcock amid its mating dance in City Hall Park. He had also seen specimens of bald eagles shot on Long Island and sold at Fulton Market.[118] Hunters of various identities wiped out passenger pigeons and threatened egrets. While pothunters took just enough to feed their families, market hunters killed dozens or hundreds to sell to urban consumers. Historian Jenny Price has argued that conservationists who worried about declining bird populations across the United States largely overlooked elite consumers as drivers of endangerment.[119] Ornithologists collecting skins and elite sportsmen also escaped reproach thanks to their "restrained" ethos. Swans and pheasants gained their cultural cachet through histories of European royalty and aristocrats reserving access to them for hunting and feasting. In the United States, hunters and conservationists of many classes and cultures struggled over common access to space and wildlife. Acts of human violence against animals might be valorized or punished depending on the context and the hunters' identities.[120]

Some park visitors who witnessed cruelty to animals seized the opportunity to teach moral lessons. One Josephine Carter, writing for a religious and literary magazine in 1884, took the perspective of a fictional Central Park squirrel named Jack in a story that contrasted squirrels' gentleness against human boys who "can be so cruel and wicked when they have so many pleasures and blessings." Jack's wife, Brownie, had been sad and afraid since "we were first brought here from our mountain home" because of New York boys' callousness to animals and each other. At the end of Carter's story, Brownie avenged a mistreated younger boy by sneakily biting his brutal older brother.[121] "Animal-lovers" continued to observe abuse through the 1890s; "young vandals have infested the Park . . . stoning birds and squirrels," and men and older boys killed and brought home small animals, presumably for food. Etienne Benson argues that those who harmed small animals were seen as violating the trust of nonhuman urban citizens.[122]

Yet Conklin helped define where animals could and could not be killed, which animals were killable, and who was authorized to kill, for what purposes. In 1883, he hoped to have police shoot gray squirrels, a species he had released himself, when he deemed that their flourishing population had denuded the park's cedar trees. Protests from the American Society for the Prevention of Cruelty to Animals (ASPCA), led by formidable director Henry Bergh, restrained Conklin's plan that year. The *Times* also criticized the plan, citing "the balance of animals" that should not be tipped too far toward any one creature—including armed police officers.

Conklin got his way in 1886; the hunt yielded one hundred "fat squirrels," whose bodies were split among policemen, who took them home for pot pies, and lions and hyenas in the menagerie.[123] Conklin and many of his generation valued and managed animals in the park for their role in food webs and zoology lessons and their attractive liveliness. Many bird lovers and squirrel lovers, however, saw animals as teachers of heightened moral and affective sensibility.

Conservation and the Moral Standing of Urban Wildlife

Josephine Carter's story upholding squirrels' moral superiority over city boys belonged to a trend toward "sentimental" literature about animals, which emerged alongside women's involvement in ornithology and conservation. But earlier literature about the park often named animals as moral teachers in the city, much as Vaux and Olmsted saw the landscape itself as training New Yorkers in good taste and character. The most forward-thinking park leaders envisioned free-roaming animals as a "cheerful invitation to the enjoyment of its natural beauties" as tired city dwellers delighted in "the play of the water-fowl, the chirpings of the wren."[124] Guidebook author Clarence Cook suggested that songbirds could counteract the grind of factory and domestic labor: "The washerwoman going home . . . after a hard day's work over tub or ironing table; the sewing-girl shut up since early morning in a crowded room with the click of her sewing-machine in her ear for the oriole's song" could hear real birds in the park. There they could recoup "something of what has been lost in the wear and tear of the day," and birds could help provide that relief and recreation.[125]

Industrial capitalism wrought dramatic changes in city dwellers' lives, including those of women who had migrated from the American or European countryside for their own employment or with families. Many urban, working-class women felt alienated from rural temporalities and landscapes and sought out city parks and gardens to recapture something of what they had lost.[126] Urban visionaries, including Olmsted, believed that cities had much to offer women as well as men but expressed worries about the brutalities of urban life for working-class women especially. This did not lead such staid patricians to more radical stances for labor rights or housing reform, even as early labor leaders began organizing unions such as the Women's Typographical Union and the Central Labor Union. Indeed, sociologist Dorceta Taylor has argued that the park's founders hoped the landscape would pacify urban unrest.[127] Rather than support radical action, the park would provide salve for the spirit amid the "vital exhaustion, nervous irritation and constitutional depression" of city life, and wildlife offered examples of immersion in nature.[128] Cook envisioned that swan mothers could model for human mothers how to introduce their young to the beauty of natural landscapes. Watching the swans from one of his favorite sites in the Ramble, Cook related the exquisite care the mother provided her hatchlings: "The mother-bird assists the little blue-gray youngsters to mount her back" and from their perch upon their floating mother, he claimed, "the baby swans sit at their ease, or sleep, or look out upon the landscape, and, no doubt, think the most sweet and innocent thoughts."[129]

Similarly, in 1867, the board published an extended excerpt from writer and pacifist Elihu Burritt's account of an English "half-hermit" who tamed wild birds. The man was actually a landowner named Joshua Fox, famous for landscaping his grounds with dense plantings to nurture avian life and cultivating a patient and quiet demeanor around the birds. The Ramble closely resembled this picturesque, romantic vision. The commissioners hoped to convince readers that songbirds can become "attached to place and person" and that children could adopt Fox's gentle disposition, overcoming birds' timidity so they would alight on their hands.[130]

Ideas that birds (and squirrels) held moral wisdom for humans gained favor among a small but growing movement who claimed bird-watching and nature study as pastimes and cultivated affective qualities that allowed them to observe birds in nature. The park's first half-century coincided with the spread of interest in bird study from a few professionals—including those such as George Lawrence who transformed pastimes into careers—to a segment of middle-class and elite Americans, many of whom also sympathized with an emerging conservation movement. The establishment of the Linnaean Society of New York by amateur and professional naturalists marked the growing interest in bird study beyond institutions like the Lyceum of Natural History.[131] Professional ornithologists were changing too; Frank Chapman, for example, belonged to a new generation who gradually set aside collecting by gun in favor of live viewing and field identification (though skins collected by the likes of Lawrence remained important for learning to identify species). Chapman shot many birds as a young banker who pursued ornithology before and after work; he eventually left the bank to become an assistant curator of birds at the American Museum of Natural History, located adjacent to the park. In 1894, he compiled a guide to specimens in the museum collection that noted species found in Central Park, encouraging visitors to cross Eighth Avenue and observe living birds in the park after viewing stuffed ones in the museum.[132]

In the 1890s, bird lovers began to form state Audubon societies, beginning with Massachusetts' society established by two upper-class women, Harriet Hemenway and Minna Hall, in 1896. From their parlors in Boston, Hemenway and Hall staked affluent women's cultural claims to bird conservation, shaming other socialites into eschewing hats adorned by dead birds and enlisting prominent men to lead the political charge for bird protection laws. In the field and in moralizing books and magazines, the gun-free bird-watching trend and a sentimental style of writing about nature became marked as feminine and elite.[133]

New York State's Audubon Society formed in 1898 and lobbied for what it called "Bird Day." Society members promoted this occasion for schoolteachers to inoculate children against temptations to injure animals—whether hunting like "marauding Nimrods" or purchasing hats topped with birds. The Bird Day campaign argued that children could be steered toward lives of protecting nature instead. Theodore Roosevelt was in the New York Governor's Mansion; his childhood marauding had transitioned into a robust, masculine conservationism. He famously remained a hunter and criticized moralistic nature tales as "nature faking," but with Roosevelt's support, New York established Bird Day in 1899. The national society published curriculum suggestions in the Audubon magazine, *Bird-Lore*, bemoaning the difficulties of exposing "city children, especially those of the poorer classes," to ornithology. Contributor Isabel Eaton lamented that city children "have seen no birds but English Sparrows and caged Canaries and Parrots, few of them know the Robin, they practically never go to the country, and many of them never even go to the parks." New York City teachers settled for indoor guessing games and art projects and then a visit to the American Museum of Natural History rather than venturing into the Ramble to glimpse live birds.[134] Audubon Society and park leaders insisted upon the educational benefits of direct contact with birds, but many teachers failed to use Central Park as the pedagogical landscape that committed bird lovers hoped for.

As editor of *Bird-Lore*, Frank Chapman also promoted replacement of sportsmen's traditional Christmas Day "side hunts"—competitions to kill as many birds as possible—with the Christmas Bird Census, along with advocacy for wildlife conservation laws.[135] Central Park was among the earliest sites where bird lovers watched and counted birds to report back to *Bird-Lore*. The Christmas census and other activities in the Ramble helped build community among New York's bird lovers and gather information about local bird populations.[136]

Bird and squirrel lovers seemed ever eager to convert more city dwellers, particularly children, to pursue contemplative communion with nature. However, compared with watching a swan gliding on the lake, finding small, timid birds required greater skill and persistence. *Forest and Stream* magazine urged readers to "quietly use [their] powers of observation," describing the birds who could "be enjoyed by anyone not too oblivious."[137] Olive Thorne Miller (the pseudonym of Harriet Mann Miller), prolific nature writer and bird advocate, explained in the *Christian Union* when to expect song sparrows, robins, and bluebirds in the park, how to identify them, and the delights of hearing their songs and watching their behaviors. She focused on these highly recognizable species, insisting that "every city child should know them well"—and perhaps they might be a gateway to learning more.[138] Some children readily took to bird-watching, such as one Floyd Noble, whose prizewinning account of birds in Central Park was published in *Bird-Lore*.[139] But many lovers of wild nature found teaching this ethos to urban youth to be an uphill battle. Mary Allaire wrote in *The Outlook*, the *Christian Union*'s successor publication, about an encounter with a band of "ragged, dirty boys" attempting to catch a squirrel in the park. Allaire tried to convince them to stay quiet and still so that the shy squirrel would approach and explained how a friend would wear a hat covered in twigs and leaves to put wildlife at ease. Eventually, though, she "walked on, disappointed, for I wanted them to have a friend in the Park . . . but they would not be polite in the squirrel's way."[140] For bird lovers like Miller and Allaire, birds and squirrels exemplified a quiet, patient way of being in nature that contrasted with the volume and speed of the city.

Bird-Lore encouraged readers to offer hazelnut crumbs to chickadees and nuthatches by hand in the Ramble. Anne Crolius was one of the first to document encounters with chickadees there, observing individual personalities and bestowing names upon them. Frank Chapman often took his lunch with the birds in a "retired nook" of the Ramble, where, "as always happens when birds learn that they will not be harmed, they become remarkably tame." These accounts mixed anthropomorphism, affection, and joy at interspecies contact. According to Crolius, those who tamed chickadees in the park were "thrilled through and through with the sensation" of touching and feeding birds and with "the perfect trustfulness of the little creature."[141]

Bird lovers cherished the discipline and rewards of communion with chickadees and complained about the noisy, obtrusive manner of the house sparrow. Bemoaning their "incessant chatter" in the park, a writer for *Forest and Stream* stated that "to the casual observer it would appear as though there were no other members of the feathered tribe to be seen beside these persistent little fiends."[142] Frank Chapman noted with "mixed humor and regret" the story of "English" sparrows' introduction in New York, lamenting "the discordant notes of these ubiquitous little pests constantly in our ears."[143] Olive Thorne Miller began a bit more gently but eventually skewered the species as she described seasonal transitions in Central Park's bird life: "All winter . . . one sees hardly anything but the English sparrow—noisy, sharp-witted little rogue that he is." As the song sparrow emerged, "if we do not look carefully, we might think him one of the English sparrows we have seen all winter . . . but he doesn't act like the saucy foreigner; he never squawks, he doesn't seek his food in the dirty streets, he is trim and neat in looks."[144] Part of what these bird lovers valued about rarer birds was their rarity, timidity, and vulnerability and the disposition required to commune with them. In contrast, it is notable that one native bird that fascinated Eugene Schieffelin was the kingbird, which remained prolific in rapidly urbanizing New York both within and outside the park. Schieffelin once pointed out to George Lawrence that an old remnant sycamore tree on Broadway in the heart of downtown Manhattan hosted a teeming family of kingbirds, "unmindful of the noise and confusion below."[145]

Birds, squirrels, and fish, of course, had no intention to inspire humans with their liveliness, vulnerability, trustfulness, boldness, or abundance. For Audubon members, fisherfolk, acclimatizers, children, and other park goers, wildlife imparted meaning to urban spaces while pursuing their own bodily needs—for food, mating territories, weather conditions, and safety.[146] Amid the many human and nonhuman threats to the park's free animals, authorities and patrons hoped that these creatures could help cultivate more humane feelings, a love of nature and landscape, and quiet contemplation among human New Yorkers they deemed worn down and alienated from nature. They claimed the Ramble as a space where, they hoped, a broader range of New Yorkers might connect with wildlife.

Sketch of vernacular birdhouse architecture accompanying an 1880 article about immigrant and pastoralist communities near Central Park, which faced displacement by real estate and infrastructure development. These birdhouses suggest love for and engagement with bird life among communities marginalized by the park and urban growth. Courtesy of HathiTrust.

Meanwhile, other New Yorkers expressed their own kind of bird love elsewhere. In *Scribner's* reporter H. C. Bunner's account of the community of German and Irish pastoralists who clung to the land near the park in 1880, residents constructed whimsical birdhouses attached to the eaves of their own homes. "The poor always love birds," Bunner explained, at once romantic and patronizing. Some birdhouses were simply tomato cans nailed up on a post, but others were "curiously ornate, testifying to the industrious leisure of some ingenious, bird-loving shanty-dweller." Natives and newcomers mingled here peaceably, at least according to the reporter: "the rare, old wild birds that you never see nowadays in the city squares, share with the noisy English immigrants the larger domiciles."[147]

Starlings and Other Boundary Crossers

Amid the rise of bird love and bird conservation politics among middle- and upper-class urbanites in the waning years of the nineteenth century, Eugene Schieffelin continued to introduce birds in New York, sometimes in Central Park and with Conklin's enthusiastic approval. On March 25, 1890, Schieffelin "set at liberty" eighty more starlings into the park, the act for which he is now most notorious. Conklin reported that the starlings, as well as the chaffinches that Schieffelin released the following month, "remained about the grounds of the Menagerie for some days and then scattered themselves throughout the Park."[148] Recent popular narratives about this release claim that Schieffelin was motivated to introduce all of the birds who appear in the writings of William Shakespeare into the United States, but evidence points to a much later invention of this part of the story.[149] Schieffelin's motivation to introduce these birds combined pseudoscientific experimentation, Eurocentrism, and aesthetic whimsy. He was eager to manipulate nature and encourage life—any life—in the city. Like the animal husbandry reformers in chapter 1, Schieffelin, Conklin, and other acclimatizers seemed to self-confidently promote the ecological Europeanization of North America. Most of their experiments failed: skylarks flew away; chaffinches, pheasants, and even the previous release of starlings faded. There was no reason to assume the 1890s release of starlings would succeed.

The house sparrow critics who emerged in the 1870s used nativist tropes against introduced birds; their anti-immigrant sentiment does not, however, render acclimatizers like Schieffelin and allies like Conklin innocent. By importing swans, peafowl, guinea fowl, sparrows, and starlings—and their unsuccessful counterparts—acclimatizers within and outside the park claimed space and manipulated the more-than-human world according to European aesthetic tropes. Even when those animals were not originally European, such as peafowl and guinea fowl, they were interpreted through western and northern European lenses. The belief that native birds were dwindling, inadequate for utilitarian needs and lively animal encounters in Central Park, undergirded Conklin's support for acclimatization. This belief echoed other tropes about the decline of Indigenous humans of North America and their replacement by white settlers. House sparrow critics turned that trope on its head when they ignored their own complicity in the erasure of Indigenous people, lambasting new immigrant humans and introduced birds alike. Both stances on bird introductions upheld northwestern Europeans' domination of aesthetics and the more-than-human world.

Furthermore, wild animals' vulnerability justified their elite and middle-class advocates' claims that they were best suited to govern spaces like the Ramble. Professional ornithologists like Frank Chapman and dedicated bird lovers like Anne Crolius did important work helping document birds in Central Park and became fierce conservationists protecting spaces like the Ramble. Park patrons and a growing culture of bird lovers valued birds in part *because* of their supposed helplessness and timidness, the need to cultivate quiet appreciation to see and make contact with them. They hoped to instill this way of being in nature in city dwellers across genders, nationalities, and classes, through the park landscape. Earlier landscape advocates like Olmsted and Cook focused on similar feelings as a salve against urban unrest. Late-nineteenth-century bird lovers did not necessarily intend to control the mass of city dwellers but, rather, seemed intent on refining how individuals perceived and encountered nature.[150]

But there remained a tension between, on the one hand, the boundary making that park officials thought necessary for protecting vulnerable animals in the city and the boundlessness that characterized both the artistic aim of the architects and the regular spatial behavior of wildlife and humans who cared for them. Aquatic life flowed through conduits designed by park engineers to carry water, and children and adults furtively added fish to lakes, streams, and ponds. Birds found this green patch amid the burgeoning city, and dozens of migrant species, particularly the perching songbirds, returned reliably each year, connecting this space to far-flung breeding and wintering territories, as far north and south as Canada and northern South America, respectively.[151] Squirrels multiplied beyond all expectations and dispersed into the city at large—although sometimes city dwellers embarked on wild chases to put them back, as in 1904, when boys chased one squirrel from a stable to an office building and across a residential block, before finally returning it to the park.[152] In a landscape where humans initially valued wild animals for their practical utility, their connections to European environmental aesthetics, and their simple liveliness, free animals persisted and helped reshape urban space— inside and outside the park.

CHAPTER 3

Captive in the City

As we have seen so far, Central Park leaders along with elite and middle-class supporters attempted to shape city dwellers' experiences of nature by curating encounters with animals in designed spaces. Sheep grazing on the meadow and chickadees chirping in the Ramble were supposed to encourage quiet contemplation in settings quite different from the bustling city. Leaders such as park comptroller Andrew Green and the first menagerie director, Dr. Albert Gallatin, also hoped to enlighten New Yorkers about the nation's rural and wild landscapes by establishing a zoological garden. Gallatin published a list of the vertebrates of North America, hoping to confer natural history knowledge. Green wrote in a report that "the forests of the country with their magnificent beauties, the growth of centuries, are being swept away rapidly and wastefully, and the beasts and the birds that live in their shelter are becoming extinct for want of an intelligent appreciation of their value, both to the present and coming generations."[1] Green was delighted when the park received the gift of an "American buffalo" in 1868—the second of its kind given to the park.[2] The country's remaining bison—called "buffalo" by their tribal kin—were associated more with prairies than forests, but they were surely among the endangered beasts to which Green and Gallatin wished to expose city dwellers and immigrants.

The buffalo who arrived in New York, however, embodied jarring contradictions about sustaining American landscapes and cultures, particularly because it was sent by "the Officers of the Seventh U.S. Cavalry from their headquarters in Fort Leavenworth, Kansas," as the park annual report detailed.[3] The Seventh Cavalry dispatched the creature as its troops patrolled the Great Plains, executing the federal government's plans to control and remove Indigenous communities such as the Cheyenne, Kiowa, Arapaho, Comanche, and Pawnee. The cavalry's actions, far from "intelligently appreciating" buffalo, helped facilitate its slaughter and further undermine the basis of many Indigenous cultures' livelihoods and spirituality, clearing the way for white settlement and the replacement of buffalo by cattle for market production.[4]

Incorporated into the menagerie's collection, this buffalo also became entangled in tensions spanning the rest of the century over this feature's purpose, design, and accessibility. Vaux and Olmsted omitted a zoological garden from the original Greensward plan, and they feared how such a feature would affect visitors' experience of the carefully designed landscape. Thus, as unsolicited patrons both local and distant began to donate animals to the park, authorities scrambled to provide minimal housing and care for a motley population that quickly numbered in the hundreds. Soon thousands of human New Yorkers, many from the city's more crowded, poor, and immigrant neighborhoods, lined up every weekend to view these caged creatures. On multiple occasions, park authorities or neighbors attempted to move the menagerie from cramped, often makeshift quarters at the southeastern corner of the park, to a site more distant from Manhattan's current population center. Menagerie fans sometimes protested their possible alienation from the animals, expressing affectionate attachments and a sense of public ownership of these creatures. Elite New Yorkers living near zoo sites, both current and proposed, protested the sounds, smells, sights, and social classes they expected to come with the attraction.

These local, city-bound debates about the menagerie's function may seem separate from the mass slaughter that the Seventh Cavalry facilitated. However, western invasion and settlement were connected to the expansion of New York City's urban footprint, a process that encroached on wildlife and space for domestic animals locally. This chapter argues that we can understand the menagerie better by connecting it with urban processes at many scales.[5] Within the menagerie itself, mass audiences, including many poor and working-class New Yorkers, gained free access to exotic animals in public spaces with a character quite different from other animal features of the park. At the scale of Manhattan and the urbanizing region around it, many donors saw the park as a kind of refuge or curiosity cabinet for animals (domesticated and wild) displaced amid the city's expansion. And at a broader scale, animals embodied geopolitical and economic connections between New York and places like Kansas, where industry converted other buffalo into hides and even more abstract capital flows, severed from their habitats and their human kin. Some, like Green and Gallatin, thought across these scales, but the menagerie was no panacea for urban and ecological ills. Their vision for a zoological garden to promote conservation and education jostled awkwardly with the development of Greater New York that the park and Green himself helped drive. Rather than focus on the more exotic animals at the menagerie, this chapter visits with creatures representing local urban change, regional connections with New York, and the United States' overland empire.

Zoological Display in New York before the Park

As with the choice of livestock and birds to ornament the park, the conception of the zoological garden shaped both which human New Yorkers could access this public space and its meanings for them. In turn, debates about how to display captive animals grew out of a long history of zoological exhibits. Many European zoos (as well as those on other continents) began as royal collections that embodied courtly opulence and the monarch's imperial might. In the nineteenth century, science and nationalism gave rise to new pretexts for displaying animals from worldwide empires.[6] The Garden of the Zoological Society of London inherited its animal exhibits from the royal menagerie of the Tower of London in the early 1830s and eventually collected animals from around the globe—flesh, fur, and feathers embodying the British Empire. European zoos also expressed power by controlling who could encounter animals in a scientific setting. Although no longer the monarch's possession—like swans transferred to livery companies in London—British subscription gardens continued to limit access to these living symbols; well into the nineteenth century, only wealthy patrons were admitted.[7]

Early visions of a zoological garden in New York's grand park echoed the prevailing theme of imitating but democratizing their European counterparts. Elite Americans often gained familiarity with zoological exhibits in urban parks while traveling in such cities as London, Paris, and Vienna. Andrew Jackson Downing had called for a zoological garden in his first proposals for a city park in the 1840s. Influenced by English gardens, Downing hoped the new park would reference the design of exclusive, landscaped estates but would welcome people of all classes. Downing expected animals to teach Americans about nature and nation, and the zoological garden should exceed the standards of European science. Yet Downing seemed complacent about elitism creeping into his imagined park. "Zoological gardens, like those of London and Paris," he predicted, "would gradually be formed by private subscription or public funds," although subscription fees might exclude many potential zoo goers.[8]

By the time of Downing's writing, many Americans already enjoyed private animal exhibits of a different character from European zoological gardens. Since colonial days, itinerant menageries had traveled the countryside, stopping in towns to display bears, elephants, leopards, and monkeys in tents on village greens. Many evolved into circuses.[9] Some recent zoo critics have argued that zoos were primarily urban phenomena that emerged to replace intimate contact between humans and animals as farms and wildlife habitat were converted to towns and cities.[10] Yet these traveling exhibits visited rural areas, feeding appetites to encounter exotic and thrilling animals foreign to daily agricultural life. Besides, as we have seen, city dwellers still had plenty of access to animals: hunting and fishing, at the slaughterhouse, in the tenement, or in the Ramble.

In larger cities, national companies, such as Isaac Van Amburgh's and P. T. Barnum's, established permanent menageries. Barnum's animal exhibit aimed to make displays of human curiosities more respectable to old-line New York elites and religious types.[11] Van Amburgh's charged twenty-five cents for admission, which included a show of elephants, "trained but not tamed" lions, and "educated ponies, monkeys, and mules." The *Times*, known for skewering anything below its standards of taste, wrote approvingly of Van Amburgh's menagerie.[12] Barnum fashioned himself as a benefactor of natural history, but he displayed his wonders in spectacular, commercial contexts that many considered "artificial" and antithetical to the appreciation of genuine nature. Some cultural historians have argued that his later three-ring circus exemplified the emerging modern, urban condition of distraction and divided attention—so unlike the Ramble, where stillness and patience were required to attract a chickadee to one's hand.[13] Others compare Barnum's ambition to democratize culture and natural history with Downing's original aims for the park. Downing believed that "subscription gardens" would become so popular that urbanites would turn away from Barnum's.[14] Next to favored European examples, itinerant menageries and the American Museum appeared coarse, hardly befitting a country that aspired to become a world power.

Animal exhibits in the United States were not always accessible; some reinscribed the country's social hierarchies and racial oppressions by controlling access to captive animals.[15] In the 1830s, the New York Zoological Institute on the Bowery (which later became Van Amburgh's) maintained a race-based admission policy: "The proprietors wish it to be understood that PEOPLE OF COLOR are not permitted to enter EXCEPT WHEN IN ATTENDANCE UPON CHILDREN OR FAMILIES."[16] Black people were only allowed in to serve the convenience of white enslavers or employers. Slavery had been outlawed in New York since 1827, but white visitors from slave states might bring enslaved caregivers, and free Blacks from free states might come as part of an employer's retinue. In 1837, the Anti-Slavery Society's newspaper, *The Emancipator*, called on allies in New York and visitors from abroad to boycott what they termed "the Slaveholder's Zoological Institute." A prominent Black leader, Thomas Van Rensselaer, challenged the policy by attempting to gain admission for his family. Private security officers physically assaulted him as he attempted to purchase tickets.[17] Van Rensselaer and Anti-Slavery Society agent H. C. Wright seized the moment to show how the policy made a sharp statement about Black peoples' personhood. Part of what the institute guarded jealously was the ostensibly superior ontological position that a zoological exhibit affords the human visitor who gazes upon caged beings. In other words, if the zoo positioned *white* humans as controlling nonhumans, nonwhite people viewing the animals subverted the racist hierarchy. Wright and Van Rensselaer compared the proprietors unfavorably with the creatures on display, proclaiming "savage beasts are not only to be seen within, but" those "more savage than all the rest, keep the door."[18]

Other circuses and museums promoted certain humans as oddities alongside exotic animals, but elites rebuked them mostly for their breaches of taste and truth. Barnum's American Museum at Broadway and Ann Street in Lower Manhattan exhibited seals, otters, kangaroos, and fifty other examples of "animated nature" along with human performers, including the "Lilliputian King," a girl named Anna Swan who Barnum said was over eight feet tall, a family of people with albinism, and "a splendid company of Indian warriors." His first exhibit at a Broadway theater featured an elderly Black woman named Joice Heth whom he had purchased and billed as George Washington's impossibly old nursemaid.[19] By the early 1860s, as many as 1.25 million visitors paid fifteen to thirty cents to see Barnum's exhibits and shows each year. *Scientific American* called Barnum "indefatigable" in keeping New Yorkers entertained: "If the whale dies the hippopotamus who won't die takes his place."[20] Meanwhile, critics in religious and high-culture communities lambasted him as a "distraction," a "quack," and a "humbug" (he embraced the latter epithet) who extracted wealth by deceiving the public with false claims about the beings on display (never minding the racist and ableist implications of exhibiting these humans).[21]

Between reliance on European models of zoological gardens and some elites' disdain for sensational shows, discussions about captive animal displays in the new park were from the start freighted with tensions of social class and culture. Leisure attractions in American cities seemed to diverge into two camps: public landscapes designed by elites to convey virtues of genteel nature appreciation and private spaces where entrepreneurs appealed to paying mass audiences.[22] Animals could be exploited by either type of establishment to capture city dwellers' leisure time—whether they promised wholesome edification or thrilling spectacle.

Few New Yorkers, other than the emerging humane movement, asked whether animals belonged in captivity at all. Most simply assumed that US cities, as they grew in size and economic and geopolitical prowess, would offer access to captive animals, whether for purposes of entertainment, natural history research and education, or conveying personal, civic, or national power. After all, major cities in Europe (and worldwide) displayed animals, and New York boosters intended that their city would match and exceed these models of urban culture and bearing. Furthermore, by 1860, Philadelphia, New York's chief rival for the role of the United States' cultural and intellectual capital, already had its own zoological society and plans to construct a zoological garden.[23]

Olmsted and Vaux's original Greensward plan omitted any zoological garden. A zoo would have cluttered the landscape, breaking their carefully designed sight lines and emphasizing spectacular entertainment over peaceful contemplation. Even relatively naturalistic enclosure designs like some proposed in other plans would "be a major . . . attack on the integrity of the park landscape," as Olmsted later explained.[24] Yet fourteen of the other thirty-two entrants in the 1857 design competition proposed or mentioned a zoological garden, reflecting many New Yorkers' hopes to establish animal displays distinct from Barnum's.[25] Some entrants based their designs on traditional English deer parks, where gentry reserved deer for pleasure hunting and to distribute venison to subjects as a display of largesse.[26] Others envisioned ditches, screens of vegetation, artfully placed rocks, or subtle fencing to contain animals while retaining a sense of open landscape.[27] Some proposals blended natural and human-made materials as an alternative to the artificiality connoted by bars separating humans from other-than-humans in many European zoological gardens, which were well funded but spatially constrained.[28]

Demands from across New York's social spectrum for a captive animal collection proved irresistible, though the design, location, and character of the eventual menagerie were never inevitable. Many hoped that a zoological garden would help put New York on the global map in terms of its support for science and learning. Even commissioners who shared Vaux and Olmsted's commitments to natural design found these educational and geopolitical goals worth compromising the landscape somewhat. The board (probably Green) wrote that zoological gardens give "a character to the city and the intelligence of its government, that [to] visitors and travelers from our own and other lands, make it more distinctly the acknowledged seat of wealth and power," marking the city's "liberal foundation and generous management."[29] As demands from the board and the public gained momentum, August Belmont spearheaded a subcommittee to investigate. Olmsted, in his role as park architect, agreed to add a zoological garden to the park while insisting on control over the design. As mentioned in chapter 1, the board sent Olmsted on a European tour in 1859 amid its deliberations about developing a zoological garden. The subcommittee also gathered reports from ministers in London, Paris, Brussels, The Hague, and Amsterdam about those cities' zoological gardens.[30] There remained financial questions about how the city could manage such an institution, and the subcommittee determined that a private entity could operate a zoological garden in the park. So, in 1859, Belmont and others petitioned the State of New York to charter a private zoological society.[31]

Claiming Space and Animal Bodies

The New York State Legislature named Belmont (along with two other commissioners and Olmsted, though these may have been a matter of formality and courtesy) among the forty-some founders and associates of the American Botanical and Zoological Society in April 1860.[32] Belmont served on the Central Park Board for just a few years in the early 1860s amid his multifaceted career in finance, local and national politics, and horse racing, but he had hoped for New York to establish a zoological and botanical garden in the park even before the city seized the central site, when he was also considering building his estate adjacent to the park. He had urged his father-in-law, Commodore Matthew Perry, to help organize a company to manage an exclusive subscription garden, but Perry passed away in 1858, and Belmont ultimately established his home far to the south of the park. Still, Belmont hoped to create an attraction where cultured families could enjoy the refined atmosphere of European zoos, one that would be sustained by private rather than public resources.[33] Belmont socialized with P. T. Barnum and many of the people who performed for raucous crowds at his museum, yet he saw a need for a natural history institution befitting more refined tastes.[34]

The act establishing the society specified that its garden would be closed to nonmembers on Sundays and that the society and the park board could together decide upon rules for admission.[35] Society members set a lifetime subscription fee at one hundred dollars, or five dollars annually.[36] These machinations did not go unnoticed by the larger public. Working folks found it especially flagrant that on many workers' only day off, access to the zoo animals would be open only to paid subscribers. A *Herald* editorial protested that "the Park is public property, and no portion of it must be diverted to uses in which all classes . . . will not be allowed to participate."[37] *Scientific American* magazine lauded Belmont and the other "wealthy and influential gentlemen" who were developing the garden. But it also praised those European gardens that offered admission free of charge and called upon New Yorkers "who have the power" to "manifest their public spirit" by supporting an attraction worthy of the nation and city.[38] These debates made access to animals a matter of democratic principle.

Belmont soon rolled off the Park Board; meanwhile, the Zoological Society did nothing to advance the creation of an animal exhibit, and Green emerged as a leading voice in planning the proposed garden. Green envisioned an accessible animal exhibit; he pointed out the challenge of fencing off a zoological garden for exclusivity "without injuring landscape effect" and that gardens in Paris and Kew offered "free public access."[39] He also expected that bison and mountain goats, bears and monkeys, would enlighten New York's children, in keeping with his lifelong dedication to education for public uplift.[40] Green noted, "The subject of zoology has been too long neglected in our common and public schools."[41] Botanical and zoological gardens could become "valuable auxiliaries of that great free public educational system, which is already the pride of the city, as well as the source of useful practical information to agriculturalists, merchants, and manufacturers through the land."[42] For Green, such education was vital not only for developing children's and adults' knowledge but also for molding a public that would take pride in American landscapes and species and demand their conservation. Zoos today continue to make similar claims that exposure to animal exhibits can promote environmental causes. Like other conservationists and advocates for zoological parks in the United States in coming decades, Green believed that a well-planned zoo could shape national character and identity, forming citizens who appreciate rural and wild landscapes, even if from afar, and exposing urban youth and foreign newcomers to what they considered America's unique nature.[43]

In 1859, donors began to introduce living animals into the contradictory vision formed by Belmont's refined and exclusive tastes, Green's educational and conservation aims, and Vaux and Olmsted's dedication to naturalistic landscape art. Park authorities had yet to create a space for these creatures. Longtime zookeeper Philip Holmes later remembered a trained bear dropped off at the gate in 1859, but the park board reports only began cataloging donations the next year.[44] G. Granville White, a fur importer living in Brooklyn, donated several foreign animals over the next few years—musk deer (a fanged gazelle relative from Asia, whose glands were used in perfumery), a peacock, and two "Syrian gazelles"— as well as domestic "trumpet cranes" (likely sandhill cranes). All but the peacock died shortly thereafter. Others donated white-tailed deer, some goldfish, ducks and geese, foxes, a ring-tailed monkey, and an "American Eagle." The eagle came from the Washington Market Social Club, a group of growth-minded grocers seeking to promote New York and the market.[45] Recall that ornithologist George Lawrence rarely saw wild eagles in Manhattan but did find them sold in public markets, brought from Long Island. The park's gardener, Ignaz Pilat, gave the first raccoon.[46] As we saw in chapter 2, park officials released some donated animals into spaces such as the Ramble and confined others in cages all about the southern end of the park. The park board lamented that it was "forced to provide . . . facilities for the preservation of the animals presented, and unless they are conceived upon some convenient plan, they must of necessity be incomplete and unsatisfactory." As construction proceeded from Fifty-Ninth Street northward, the board, in agreement with Vaux and Olmsted, "reserved from operations" a section of land between Seventy-Second and Eighty-Sixth Streets along Fifth Avenue for a possible zoological or botanical garden—the first of several proposed zoo sites that never came to fruition.[47]

While the first caged animals awaited more permanent quarters, human visitors enjoyed what the *Times* in 1863 called a "nucleus of a zoological collection." Despite these cramped, impromptu shelters, "the deer on the Park, the foxes, the peacocks, the cranes, pelicans, gazelles, eagles, storks, and swans"—some of whom roamed at large in the park—"are already sources of constant interest and pleasure to very large numbers of visitors."[48] On a typical weekend day, children crowded around a wire paddock that held a small herd of deer—two fawns, three does, and a buck. The paddock could be moved about the park's lawns, and on the day the reporter visited, it was between the Sheep Meadow and the Mall. The raccoon seemed to languish in its wire enclosure adjacent to the Arsenal building—the *Times* said he was "disconsolate"—and three bald eagles shared a "cramped iron-roofed cage" nearby. Many humans stopped before a cage fronting the walkway to watch three monkeys catch and eat insects and cavort as much as possible about their small quarters. The *Times's* account of these caged animals suggests such encounters sparked a variety of emotions. The fawns melted hearts, the monkeys inspired hearty laughter, and the eagles and raccoon evoked tinges of regret. Whether the spectacle of caged animals was attractive or pitiful, the reporter and other visitors seemed unable to look away.[49]

While media and other visitors remarked on the caged animals displayed in the park, attractions like Van Amburgh's continued to draw more attention for their larger collection. The *Times* noted their "fine" specimens and clean conditions, regardless of their commercial flavor.[50] The Zoological Society took no action to claim the sixty acres in the park allocated by state law.[51] For the time being, the park board maintained plans for a more permanent zoological garden in the Seventies and Eighties on Fifth Avenue, but this site later became the Conservatory Lake and the Metropolitan Museum of Art.[52] In the meantime, park authorities placed many donated animals in cages, either inside or just west of the Arsenal building at Sixty-Fourth Street and Fifth Avenue.[53] The Gothic structure contained three main floors, a basement, and towers flanking the entryway; it had housed the New York State militia and its armaments for just a few years before park authorities annexed it.

The board insisted that the quarters in and around the Arsenal were temporary, but more and more animals spent long stretches of their lives there. Patrons donated several creatures each month who were clearly unsuitable for wild release into the park, further crowding the facilities. These included pets such as parakeets, guinea pigs, and white rabbits,

White-tailed deer, donated to the park by patrons, stand within a paddock on a park lawn. Deer in paddocks were a popular attraction in the park's early decades; they may have experienced fear from having limited access to deep woods but may also have become tame as humans offered them food through the fence. Courtesy of the Library of Congress, Prints and Photographs Division.

small monkeys, and a "prairie wolf" and a black bear.[54] Staff freed some donated animals such as owls, hawks, and turtles in the park, and they crammed many more into the Arsenal site. Those who were confined spent their days with paws, hooves, or talons on hard floors, in spare wire or iron cages, some indoors and some outdoors, with nowhere to flee from the humans who now dominated their environment. A larger "dove-cote" was less cramped but held birds that might have been released into

A mixed crowd of human visitors views harpy eagles, monkeys, and fox squirrel in indoor cages at the Arsenal, as sketched by Stanley Fox for *Harper's Weekly* in 1867. Courtesy of HathiTrust.

the park and the city. Thousands of people passed by on any weekend day, talking, shouting, laughing, a few of them throwing food or reaching between the bars.

Some animal donations might seem bizarre from our contemporary perspective. G. Granville White's donations were likely "bycatch" animals from his work in the fur trade—those caught or killed incidentally amid trapping efforts—intended to represent exotic lands and given rather carelessly based on their poor condition. But why did donors and park workers put foxes, raccoons, and eagles on display? The "culture of collecting" mentioned in chapter 2 helps explain why New Yorkers captured and donated animals that once roamed free about the city. Middle- and upper-class hobbyists engaged in the growing craze for outdoor recreation also collected items to admire and continue their nature study at home. They filled curio cabinets with living and deceased organisms, parts such as bones and leaves as well as rocks and minerals. While excitement about exotic big cats and pachyderms in traveling exhibits was widespread in both rural and urban areas, the culture of collecting seemed to take on particular significance as cities expanded. Outdoor enthusiasts in cities likely felt that their finds connected them with undeveloped spaces that felt ever more distant. Furthermore, as awareness spread of the decline of creatures like buffalo and passenger pigeons, many city dwellers along with western settlers and soldiers shared Green's sense that New Yorkers needed greater exposure to wildlife, especially dwindling American species.[55] For collectors in and around New York, Central Park became an outlet for sharing living specimens.

From the Great Plains to the Arsenal to Manhattan Square

In 1864, as patrons continued to deliver pets and wild animals for exhibit at the Arsenal building, park authorities moved toward relocating the zoological collection to more permanent, architecturally significant, and exclusive quarters. That year, the state legislature allowed the board to annex a nineteen-acre area known as Manhattan Square, located just west of the park between Eighth and Ninth Avenues, bounded to the south and north by Seventy-Seventh and Eighty-First Streets, respectively.[56] The law permitted the park board to establish a zoological garden there, and the board asked Olmsted and Vaux to develop a plan for the site. Placing the zoo west of Eighth Avenue would help preserve the architects' vision of unbroken greensward within the park itself.[57] Olmsted and Vaux intended for visitors to encounter creatures in an open, naturalistic landscape. The plan laid out an exercise yard for each animal, which the five-acre Arsenal site could not accommodate. Olmsted and Vaux believed that these design features would provide the most enriching experience for visitors and also ensure the animals' health.[58]

With the annexation of Manhattan Square into the park board's purview, along with new responsibilities for laying out streets and other public areas, Green expressed growing foresight about how green spaces beyond Central Park would be important for the city's future. He believed that a zoological garden could promote natural history education and species conservation and still preserve the park's intended landscape function. In coming years, he also pragmatically balanced priorities as he envisioned New York City's development. Green at once accepted the juggernaut of New York's growth *and* sought to preserve green spaces for the benefit of humans and nature, within narrow limits of what he considered politically practicable. As the city's growth converted agricultural and undeveloped land across the region, Green believed that government could act as a mild check on unbridled capitalist expansion, preserving "scenic beauties" for city dwellers—and perhaps for wildlife who survived nearby.[59] Of course, pastoralists also continued to live on the ungraded land west of the park, many of them paying rent to private owners who had purchased parcels but had yet to build on them. Some pastoralists lived on land like Manhattan Square held by the Corporation of New York, and Green would be responsible for evicting them and their numerous goats, dogs, and other domesticated creatures.[60] There were no plans to preserve pastoralists' mode of more-than-human city life.

Moving the captive animal collection to Manhattan Square might have somewhat curtailed working-class and poor New Yorkers' access to large and exotic animals, but according to Green, the architects, and others, it would be better for the captive creatures themselves and would also elevate New Yorkers' experience of nature there. The square was about a mile northwest of the Arsenal, where working-class New Yorkers living on the Lower East Side already had to walk or take the streetcar dozens of blocks to visit the animals.[61] The board also hoped to charge a small

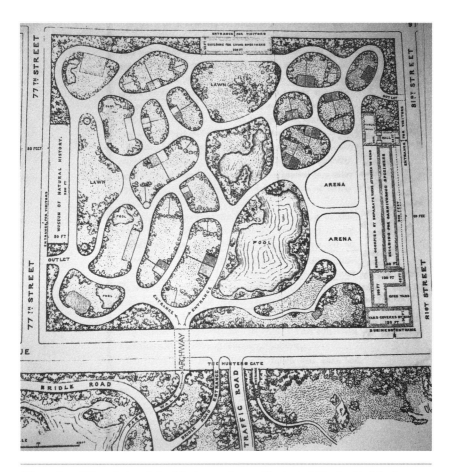

Olmsted and Vaux designed the Manhattan Square Zoological Garden for Manhattan Square in 1866 in hopes of providing more space for human visitors and captive zoo animals. Courtesy of New York City Municipal Archives.

entrance fee for buildings containing popular animals such as big cats, to limit traffic.[62] They echoed Downing's earlier predictions, arguing that "taste grows by what it feeds on," and thus "habitual visits to the city Park" would foster New Yorkers' "undeveloped capacity for enjoyment of broad, simple, natural lines, forms and colors."[63] In other words, although the menagerie animals already drew crowds, the board believed that New Yorkers were learning to appreciate the natural environs they experienced in the Ramble, the Sheep Meadow, and other, greener parts of the park. By this line of reasoning, New Yorkers would soon prefer that the zoological collection inhabit a more naturalistic landscape and even gradually abandon attractions like Van Amburgh's or Barnum's (whose American Museum had burned down in 1865). Furthermore, the board heightened its scientific and educational ambitions, hiring the polymath Albert Horatio Gallatin, a medical doctor and member of the Lyceum of Natural History, as curator of the zoological garden. Gallatin stayed in this office for only a short stint before Conklin succeeded him, but during his time there, he compiled for the board a list of North American vertebrate animals to guide efforts to represent the continent's fauna.[64]

As the board prepared to build the new zoo, the buffalo arrived from Kansas, a fleshy, woolly representative of not just a species but a more-than-human landscape, both of which were gravely threatened by the United States' imperial expansion. The Seventh Cavalry that donated the buffalo ranged throughout Kansas and the Great Plains after the Civil War as part of the federal government's efforts to remove Indigenous communities. The market for buffalo hides and the general incursion of Euro-Americans had already wrought social and ecological dislocation upon Plains people. As the species dwindled after decades of onslaught by settlers and corporations such as the American Fur Company, the army failed to uphold treaty provisions that promised to protect buffalo from white market hunters. On the contrary, Seventh Cavalry members encouraged hunters and sometimes even challenged one another to petty buffalo killing contests. Overall, the army helped clear a path for white settlement through direct violence against Indigenous people and by protecting enterprises, namely commercial buffalo hunting and railway expansion, that destroyed the basis of Plains societies' livelihoods and spirituality.[65] Bison were also the basis of some Plains peoples' claims to the land based on treaties that held "so long as the buffalo may range thereon in such numbers as to justify the chase."[66] The Seventh Cavalry helped sever connections among buffalo, the plains, and Plains peoples such as the Kiowa and Lakota, who considered buffalo to be blood relatives.[67]

On the surface, the buffalo on display seemed to uphold Green's pedagogical goal of sparking appreciation for the disappearing western wilderness. Spared from slaughter on the plains, perhaps this animal could help to educate, entertain, and inspire compassion among New Yorkers.[68] Yet an enlarged and entangled story of buffalo in Central Park connects to multispecies communities and multiple sites of economic activity. Historian Katherine Grier observes that there is a limit to how ethical and compassionate conduct toward animals can be within broader structures of exploitation.[69] Indeed, as historian Andrew Isenberg has documented, heavy belts made of buffalo hides, less expensive than cowhide, "were the sinews of nineteenth-century industrial production." A "spasm of industrial expansion" spurred further slaughter even as buffalo herds dwindled into the 1870s and 1880s. Companies consolidated tanning facilities near hemlock forests, such as in New York's Adirondack region, which supplied tannins for processing the hides. Not only were forests decimated, but chemical and organic by-products coursed into waterways. By 1864, the conservationist George Perkins Marsh already recognized that timber harvest in the Adirondacks could have devastating effects on soils and waterways, as in the montane forests of Europe.[70] The belts cut from tanned hides turned wheels and gears in mills that ground grain, cut timber, and wove textiles. Capital for these industries and their material products flowed through New York's own financial district, fueling the city's growth.

In the years surrounding the Seventh Cavalry's buffalo donation, other agents of empire and extraction sent additional "specimens" from the threatened West. Thomas C. Durant helped finance the Union Pacific Railroad as it split the plains (including buffalo habitat) and enabled the subjugation of Plains peoples and the transport of millions of buffalo hides to markets and factories in the East. The same year as the Seventh Cavalry's buffalo arrived, Durant sent a grizzly bear captured from along the Pecos River in the Rocky Mountains; the bear went on to delight visitors with his playful antics. Elias Hicks Durfee operated some of the leading trading posts in Kansas and Montana that helped enroll Indigenous hunters in the fur trade. Durfee donated a black bear the same year, which joined others of its species from across the northeastern and midwestern United States.[71] General George Custer of the Seventh Cavalry (who was likely on leave when his regiment sent the buffalo in 1868) soon sent badgers, porcupines, marsh hawks, and several rattlesnakes between battles against Indigenous nations resisting conquest.[72] Others donated pronghorn antelope and additional buffalo, some of whom went on to breed in the park. Animal donors such as Custer and the Seventh Cavalry, Durant, and Durfee connected the West with Central Park via the bodies of animals and also through capital that flowed between New York City and investments upstate and out West, funding urban expansion that would eventually engulf the park.

Valuing Land, Landscape, and Animal Habitations

For the time being, however, actual construction along the park's west and east borders proceeded slowly. As we have seen, speculators purchased land around the park, and the value of these parcels generally increased. But villages of pastoralists persisted on ungraded and unbuilt lots, sometimes paying rent while landowners bided their time for the construction of more permanent roads and complete sewers and through periodic economic downturns. Meanwhile, construction of the zoological garden also began on ungraded land. The park board budgeted "for draining the ground, and for constant cleanliness in every department" in order to make the garden "unobjectionable to the neighborhood."[73] By 1869, aquatic habitations for a polar bear, seals, a walrus, capybara, and beaver "that will conduce their healthfulness" were underway. Builders had almost completed the foundation for the outer wall and began excavations for the buildings to house the bears, including those donated by Durant and Durfee.[74] Amid the construction, ungulates such as deer, "Indian cows," and the buffalo found themselves in scattered pens or tethered periodically in both "sylvan groves and grassy lawns."[75]

Shortly after work began, however, the Tweed ring took control of the park board, installing Tammany henchman Peter Sweeny as president, and announced their plans to move the zoological garden to a more northern section of the park. The new board was renamed the commissioners of the Department of Public Parks to encompass the expanded responsibility for public spaces throughout the city. Sweeny's board claimed that the former board's reports about work on Manhattan Square were overstated and that the site's geology, drainage, and lack of sewerage made the project impossible.[76] It predicted that offensive odors would "depreciate the value of the surrounding property" and that visitors would find transportation access difficult.[77] This was surely a disappointment for Green, who, besides advocating for the zoo's educational and conservation benefits, also deplored the corrupt Sweeny board. But after that board's brief tenure, he was happy to see a natural history museum developed there—another opportunity to promote public education. Donors and staff were already assembling animal models and stuffed specimens at the Arsenal by 1870.[78]

Storage and temporary display of specimens for the natural history museum crowded with the living animals at the Arsenal. Donors had delivered more live creatures each week, about 230 new mammals, birds, and reptiles in 1869 alone (the year before the Sweeny board took over), although 40 of them died before the park board published that year's annual report.[79] In 1870, while construction on the planned menagerie north of the upper reservoir began, the board had workers rapidly construct new but ostensibly temporary buildings behind the Arsenal. This allowed birds and monkeys, carnivora and camels, to move outside and alleviate the stench of concentrated animal excretions before the summer heat peaked. Builders converted an old dovecote that had held donated birds into an aviary for birds of prey, and erected two eleven hundred–foot frame structures lined with iron cages for carnivores and monkeys, lit by clerestory windows. A stable included cage stalls for large "ruminantia"

Human visitors view bears and cats at the new carnivore house constructed under the Tammany board, from *Appleton's Journal* in 1872. Courtesy of HathiTrust.

such as elephants and buffalo. Visitors would walk down a central aisle in these buildings, separated from cage fronts by a rope.[80] Conklin, now in his role as menagerie superintendent, declared that "the animals have been benefited greatly by their removal to the buildings recently constructed." He was also proud to exhibit nineteen mammal species new to the menagerie, including zebra, rhinoceros, and two types of kangaroos.[81]

On a spring day in 1871, the *Times* complimented the clean cages and new buildings while also noting the "uncomfortable density" of the human crowds gathered around the bear cages to gape at a mother grizzly tussling with her cub. Menagerie visitors seemed to feel a bottomless hunger for beastly encounters, but they may have absorbed less knowledge about the animal kingdom than Andrew Green hoped. The throngs that gathered to see the rhinoceros had to line up single- file and enjoy only a glance as they passed by. To round out the animal collection, the park now arranged with Barnum and other private animal shows and traders in the city to temporarily exhibit certain animals free of charge. In April 1871, Barnum (now in the circus business) loaned out five lions and a baby elephant. These, along with the buffalo from Kansas and a black bear, "demanded so much attention that shutting-up time finds the crowd about the cages as numerous as ever, and hundreds were forced to depart with their taste for zoological information still unsatisfied."[82]

The new administration promised even better times ahead for the animals with their long-range plans to build on forty-eight acres on the park's North Meadows, above Ninety-Seventh Street. The northern site more than doubled the area proposed for the Manhattan Square zoological garden, allowing room for still more animals. But Olmsted and Vaux were aghast at the plans, which they only learned of through public documents. As construction began, they protested to the Sweeny board, "These meadows constitute the only broad space of quiet rural ground on the island which has been left undisturbed by artificial objects, and much labor has been expended" toward the "preservation of their present general character" with artful "masses of rock" and "indigenous trees." While defending Manhattan Square as a worthy site, if one requiring some work, they also suggested that the expanded purview of the Department of Public Parks might include other properties that could house a proper zoological garden.[83] The board gave no response, but the whole affair was moot by late 1871, when the *Times* exposed the Tweed ring's misuse of public funds. The Sweeny board fell, and a new board with members sympathetic to Vaux and Olmsted's landscape aims took office.[84]

In retrospect, Manhattan Square was one of the best chances to include a landscaped zoological garden near the park that others considered worthy of the name, without compromising the Greensward plan. Olmsted later estimated that there were a dozen different attempts at creating a zoo over the course of the park's first four decades.[85] A growing number of captive animals remained confined to a crowded corner of the park, where they performed their curtailed bear-ness, elk-ness, and buffalo-ness for throngs of human visitors, also remarkably crowded. The Sweeny board

Crowds view a parade of elephants at the menagerie, circa 1890. The Arsenal building is shown covered in ivy in the background. Courtesy of the Museum of the City of New York.

had purchased a few animals, but the collection remained haphazard, dependent on donations, loans, and the availability of animals. In 1874, the Philadelphia Zoological Society finally opened its zoo in Fairmount Park after years of delay, claiming to be the first true zoological park in the United States because of its more systematic collection and landscaped character. Unlike Central Park's menagerie, Philadelphia's was governed by a private society with its own budget for acquiring animals. However, scholar Lisa Uddin argues that advocates for "zoological parks" or "zoological gardens" used such terms to create "a virtuous point of origin" for

American zoos, distinct from European imperial zoos, museums like Barnum's, and mere "menageries." Indeed, Philadelphia's zoo and others that opened in the 1870s also received and displayed donated pets and what historian Elizabeth Hanson calls "random, accidental finds made by chance sportsmen." Those who attempted to create a zoological garden in Central Park sought to separate their exhibit from animal displays that many considered sordid. The similarities between Central Park's menagerie and Philadelphia's zoo create an uncomfortable fuzzy area that calls into question that virtuous point of origin and the lofty aims of zoos.[86] Examining the lives of creatures brought into the zoo collection can help place this transition in the context of urban history as well.

The Churn of Life in the Menagerie

As thousands of curious humans flowed through the menagerie each weekend, the flow of other-than-human lives through the menagerie also never ended. With a new veterinary degree from Columbia and the title of zoological director, William Conklin managed animals entering and exiting the facility along with a budget of fifteen thousand to eighteen thousand dollars for personnel, animal feeding, and a precious few new animal purchases. For much of the period after 1870, animals temporarily "placed on exhibition" by circuses and traders constituted the majority of new mammals in the menagerie and an even greater percentage of the large, exotic ones. In 1875, for example, about 150 new mammals were placed on exhibition, out of about 250 new mammals altogether.[87] It was common for zoos of this period to house large animals such as elephants, rhinos, lions, seals, and zebras for animal traders and circus businesses, paying for their care and feeding while attracting interest among zoo go-ers. Conklin frequently accepted animals for exhibition from prominent German American traders such as the Reiche brothers and then Louis Ruhe while they awaited permanent buyers for creatures imported from locations around the world. Circuses such as Barnum's also deposited animals during pauses in touring.[88] Conklin endeavored to keep the exhibit exciting and accessible, the animals healthy and fresh looking, while also accepting donated creatures who did little to enhance the collection's scientific value.

Donations remained common after 1870, slowing only somewhat as some would-be donors seemed to understand that temporary exhibitions filled the need for large animals. Contemporary pet keeping practices along with accelerating urban growth help explain continuing donations of many smaller creatures. Especially given the new menagerie buildings constructed in 1870, some city dwellers continued to see the park as a better alternative than simply releasing tame animals in the city or death by drowning, which was a common means of disposing of surplus pets.[89] Families such as the O'Sheas of 1414 Broadway, between Thirty-Ninth and Fortieth Streets several blocks south of the park, disposed of series of pets that they were no longer willing or able to keep. In May 1876, Miss Mary and Master Arthur O'Shea were listed as the donors of guinea pigs, a guinea fowl, and a "yellow bird." The true reasons for the O'Sheas' gifts are lost to history, but they may have related to urban expansion. On the O'Sheas' block and others, builders were carving Manhattan's residential zones into ever smaller dwelling units, expanding northward and subdividing the sky with apartment buildings—leaving little room for family pets at a time when animal traders were nonetheless promoting conventional dogs, cats, rabbits, and small birds and rodents, along with foreign curiosities as household companions. Some families also had few options for caring for a sick pet or injured wild animal found about the city. Conklin's terse notes leave few clues about these animals' stories, but Mary O'Shea's yellow bird may have arrived in poor condition, as it died within a week or so.[90]

Other donated creatures represented wild species that roamed Manhattan and surrounding hinterlands and waters, whose ranges increasingly overlapped with human residential and business spaces. As residential development and extractive activities converted nonhuman habitats, human New Yorkers crossed paths with deer and bears, owls and turtles. A man on West Twenty-Ninth Street brought in a rail (a small wading bird) that had flown into his window, for example.[91] By 1875, there were nineteen bald eagles on display, several from military or government officials, captured in New York locales or as far away as Florida or Texas.[92] Occasionally, fishers brought the odd aquatic specimen to the Fulton Fish Market, and Eugene Blackford, a renowned fish merchant and later state commissioner of fisheries, came calling at Conklin's office with the bycatch, including loggerhead and green sea turtles dropped off in 1878. Dozens of New Yorkers seemed to think that rabbits, raccoons, and opossums appearing in their yard belonged at the menagerie instead. Grover Cleveland, living in New York between his two presidential terms, brought in a raccoon two weeks after he won the election of 1892.[93] As the city's economic and urban growth edged or careened into wild animal populations, New Yorkers felt urges to collect and display, snagging creatures in the net of captivity, forever altering and curtailing their lives.[94] The zoo ledgers also record the ebb and flow of ill-advised fads for bringing home souvenir baby alligators from Florida.[95] In the mid-1870s, an adolescent Teddy Roosevelt sent an alligator and woodchuck he had obtained, who joined twenty-three and eight of their kinds, respectively.[96]

Conklin's reports often pointedly noted insufficient spaces for exhibiting animals or justified occasional new buildings by claiming that animals there were healthier. In 1875, he announced a "marked decrease in mortality" thanks to a new building for herbivorous animals. Yet just a year later, he lamented that staff had to crowd new animals into existing paddocks, at one time holding twenty-six deer and guanacos in one 130-foot diameter area.[97] Henry Bergh, the formidable leader of the American Society for the Prevention of Cruelty to Animals, frequented the menagerie and wrote letters to the commissioners demanding better care for the animals.[98] Sometimes staff killed creatures when they had no room or perceived that they were suffering. Conklin selected animals who went blind or were injured for early culling as directors considered them unsuited

Several bald eagles share a cage near the menagerie, circa 1865. A *Times* reporter called the cage "cramped." Many park patrons from around the United States donated eagles. Courtesy of the New York Public Library Digital Collections.

for display or in need of relief from pain. Conklin's successor, explaining his job in a children's magazine in 1903, clinically described the process as "chloroforming."[99] Animals who belonged to Barnum, animal importing companies, the Fairmount Park Zoo in Philadelphia, or other animal exhibitors and dealers could be cycled in and out of the menagerie space to refresh the collection when Conklin perceived that the public craved new creatures to gaze upon. But no one would take back relinquished pets or small wildlife deemed out of place in urban residential neighborhoods. Thus, Conklin ordered the killing of a domestic dog "for want of room and food." The following week, staff "killed five raccoons having too

A mixed crowd of human visitors views alligators of many different ages
by their water tank at the menagerie. Courtesy of the Library of Congress,
Prints and Photographs Division.

many on hand and [they] cost too much to keep"—and four days later,
a resident of East Twenty-Ninth Street captured yet another raccoon to
present to menagerie staff.[100] So much did New Yorkers believe that such
raccoons did not belong at large in the city (they surely thrived on growing flows of organic waste) that visitors killed those who escaped from
the menagerie. A similar fate befell foxes released by a group of prankster
boys from well-to-do families who vandalized the zoo in 1892.[101]

Captivity differed from life in the wild not only because it confined animals to tight spaces and exposed them to the vagaries of zoo
life. Captive animals also lost their ecological connections, including

intraspecific interactions from mating to parenting to communication; interspecific communities with predators, prey, and symbiotes; and links to specific resources. In their wild existence, buffalo bred in huge congregations. White encroachment on the plains had already diminished such group behaviors as hunting reduced herds. Mating and the rearing of young would also be completely different in a paddock in Manhattan.[102] From the times when buffalo numbered in the tens of millions, cultures such as the Lakota connected with the Great Spirit through their relatives the buffalo, as leader Black Elk explained in the early twentieth century.[103] Wild buffalo also wallowed in mud or water in late spring or early summer to shed their winter pelts. In New York, they would need help from a keeper with a hose or shears or perhaps could just rub on a beam of the herbivore stable; they somehow managed it, as Conklin noted in May 1877. Again, his notes don't say how the buffalo shed its pelt, but the sheep were shorn the next day, and it is easy to imagine menagerie staff getting out the shears early for this rather more perilous task.[104] In spite of Green's hopes in the early days, buffalo in a paddock in Central Park represented their wild fellows in only the most tenuous sense.

It took some effort to keep buffalo on display. After the Seventh Cavalry and another donor sent buffalo to Central Park in the 1860s, Conklin briefly exhibited an additional buffalo placed in the menagerie by an animal trader. In 1876, he tried to obtain an American buffalo cow, most likely for breeding, by trading a Cape buffalo (probably born at the menagerie) to a botanical garden and farm in St. Louis, Missouri, through the Reiche brothers' agent. However, bison disappear from the menagerie's records until 1878, when Conklin was able to set aside more funds and purchased a cow from a dealer in New Jersey. Across the 1880s, she gave birth to and nursed three calves who survived into the next decade.[105] While other animals such as elephants, rhinos, and tigers drew greater attention in the press, Conklin still endeavored to represent this species amid the slaughter of its fellows on the plains. Buffalo in New

York certainly represented the changing relationship of animal life to urbanization and overland empire, if not the species' wild behavior and more-than-human connections.

Claiming Space and Captive Animals in Manhattan

While managing the flows and keeping of other-than-humans in the menagerie, Conklin was also responsible for entertaining the park's largest flows of human visitors. In 1888, he boasted that the crowds increased each year, with the number "sometimes reaching 100,000" on Sundays.[106] Samuel Parsons, Olmsted's successor as architect, insisted that "no greater crowds gathered anywhere in New York."[107] Such entertainment constituted an awkward job within the park under a board of commissioners with renewed commitment to the Greensward plan after 1871. Elites surely resented that amid the quiet, romantic beauty of the rest of the park, the mass of Manhattanites flocked to the menagerie.[108] Still, Olmsted credited Conklin for his "sincere devotion and rare discretion" and being "responsible for almost everything in the whole history of the affair that is not to be regretted."[109] The board, composed of elites, surely knew that these crowds helped politically justify the park's existence. And perhaps the working-class New Yorkers who came for the rhinos and bears would stay for an invigorating stroll in the Ramble or a refreshing picnic in the meadow.

Park leaders and patrons noticed that the mix of people who visited the menagerie differed visibly and in their language, accents, and conduct from those who dominated other sites in the park.[110] Residents of Lower Manhattan, including many immigrants, visited frequently and in large numbers. A longtime keeper and later successor to Conklin in the director's position, John Smith, remarked especially on the engagement of Chinese, Black, and Italian New Yorkers. Many Chinese men, living in a bachelor society limited by racist immigration restrictions, spent leisure hours studying anteaters and badgers. New Yorkers in one of the city's largest Black neighborhoods at the time, San Juan Hill, would have had a relatively short walk to the menagerie—a few blocks from Tenth Avenue to Eighth, then across the width of the park. Smith noticed groups of Italian American laborers on the way home from work on weekdays: they "do not make a casual visit of, say, fifteen or twenty minutes, but examine and talk interestedly in front of each cage."[111] The city had no other public space like the menagerie; for no admission fee, New Yorkers could socialize with compatriots while engaging (however problematically) with other living beings, objects of curiosity and fascination.

New Yorkers like Olmsted and Andrew Green believed that captive animals should enlighten human city dwellers, but poor and working-class visitors may have sought other kinds of feelings there. Historian Kathy Peiss emphasizes that unmarried women from low-income and immigrant families claimed public spaces like the menagerie to resist patriarchal family structures. Many such young women lived with parents and siblings and were expected to support their families with both unpaid family labor and income from work—in the sweatshop, the streets, or elite women's houses. In their leisure, these women made places for themselves at the many "cheap amusements" New York had to offer.[112] Those who saw only confinement failed to account for the ways the poor, laboring women, and minoritized people, made their own kind of freedom at the menagerie. The exhibit curtailed the lives of its captives, but people who often met with sexism, racism, and labor exploitation in other spaces found a kind of community and entertainment there. Together, members of menagerie crowds claimed urban space.

The menagerie was one space where a different aesthetic and audience dominated over those that defined much of the rest of the park. To elites, in addition to the size and character of the crowds, the menagerie and its attendees too closely resembled the circuses or sideshows elsewhere in the city to belong in a landscape intended to cultivate good taste.[113] In the case of Thomas Van Rensselaer, the New York Zoological Institute tried

Women and girls and one man get close to a male lion caged at the menagerie, circa 1900. City dwellers who experienced exclusion on the basis of their sex and/or race claimed public space in the menagerie and at other park attractions. Courtesy of the Library of Congress, Prints and Photographs Division.

to exclude and marginalize racialized human spectators, to deprive them of access to the superior position afforded by looking at caged, dominated animals.[114] Now that poor and immigrant spectators dominated the landscape at the Central Park Menagerie, elites dismissed and insulted their way of looking at caged animals. Keepers gave one of the menagerie's most beloved animals, a chimpanzee from Liberia, the very Irish name Mike Crowley, which some Hibernians took as an insult. The whole exhibit was derided as "poor man's monkeys," as Rosenzweig and Blackmar note.[115] Daniel Wise had his tasteful protagonist Uncle Nathan in *Little Peachblossom* divert his nieces' and nephews' paths away from the menagerie when the saintly youngest child got a headache from all the sights, sounds, and smells. The naughty brother remained preoccupied with the monkeys, whom Uncle Nathan described as "dirty little caricatures of men and women," referring to what some considered uncomfortable implications of Darwinian theory.[116]

Critics further conflated the nonhumans in the cages with their most devoted human fans, accusing menagerie visitors of re-creating the worst conditions of city life within a corner of the park. Humans crowded together looking at formerly free and wild beings who were trapped and crowded together themselves. As Olmsted and Vaux repeatedly reminded the board and the public, the point of the park was to be different from the rest of the city, including in its population density. In 1873, the architects had even suggested dispersing the animal exhibits around the park, to avoid what they considered uncomfortable and unhealthy crowding of both human visitors and other-than-humans on display and also to limit disruptions to scenic views.[117] That year, a map of the park represented the menagerie with dashed lines to indicate that its location was temporary. In 1876, the menagerie was nearly starved out of existence; it closed for several days in mid-November, when its budget appropriation ran out, only to open again amid protests.[118] In 1878, Vaux published a long letter to the *Times* suggesting, among other things, that charging admission fees on some days would help disperse the crowds.[119]

Soon wealthy and white New Yorkers more assertively claimed space in the residential neighborhood right across Fifth Avenue. Residents of this now-posh neighborhood protested the popular, free menagerie at a park board meeting and in the editorial pages in 1883. The *Times*, echoing menagerie neighbors who circulated a petition, declared it a "howling nuisance" that "poison[ed] the air" and should be removed as a matter of city health regulations. Another letter accused the menagerie of causing malaria and "marring the outlook of the residences on the avenue adjoining." Residents declined an offer from the park board that invited them to pay for the menagerie's removal to the North Meadow, but Vaux and Olmsted were poised to defend the scenery, again, if they had accepted the deal.[120] Fans of the menagerie in its perpetual location, who usually had limited say in the machinations of urban planning, kept a prized public space thanks to the opposed positions of certain very wealthy Manhattanites and stalwart supporters of the Greensward plan.

Crowds continued to both justify the menagerie's existence and vex landscape advocates. Asked by the commissioners in 1890 whether the crowds, particularly large numbers of children, indicated the menagerie was a worthy part of the park, Olmsted answered tartly that minstrel shows were more crowded and audiences found Punch-and-Judy performances more amusing. This answer came amid a lengthy and often sardonic "catechism" that Olmsted delivered in response to the latest flare-up of ideas for expanding the menagerie.[121] Meanwhile, a writer to a magazine, "one of the people" who "must get their recreation cheap or go without," argued that keeping a little space for this "most delightful and innocent of gratifications" would counterbalance the great expense of the drives that only the wealthy could access. Furthermore, "what more reasonable than that these people (not being aesthetes and content to gaze forever at the grass) should wish to see some of the remarkable creatures that they have heard about?"[122] The following year, the city's lawyers drafted a bill that would have moved the menagerie to land north of the park in Harlem—to no effect.[123]

The decades-long debate about the location and character of the zoo-logical garden for the city was finally resolved in the final five years of the nineteenth century, when a new New York Zoological Society was chartered, with Andrew Green becoming its first president in 1895.[124] Green had long ago left his post as comptroller of the Central Park Board, serving as comptroller of the whole city after the Tweed ring was toppled. He pursued several other scenic preservation and urban planning efforts in the city and beyond and finally got to oversee his early vision for a zoological park that served pedagogical and conservation aims. Most of the other founders were outdoorsmen and hunters of the state's Boone and Crockett Club, including Theodore Roosevelt, former donor to the Central Park Menagerie. The New York Zoological Park, or Bronx Zoo as it is known today, would be located an hour by train from City Hall in Manhattan. The first director, the crusading naturalist William Temple Hornaday, timed the trip and believed the zoo would be sufficiently accessible to the expanded city's population center.[125] The Bronx Zoo (a name that Hornaday hated) surpassed every zoological collection in the world in terms of both the size and the naturalism of its landscape.[126] It separated human visitors from nonhuman animals, and sometimes predators from prey, with moats and barely visible wire fences rather than iron bars and occupied 265 acres in the Bronx Park. While insisting upon accessibility for city dwellers, Hornaday also impugned entire ethnic and racial groups in his conservation publications for their role in wildlife hunting—Black hunters, Italians, and Indigenous Americans particularly. He complained that Italian Americans attempted to hunt songbirds at the zoo. Hornaday also helped exhibit a Mbuti man from Central Africa, Ota Benga, in the zoo, sparking protests from Black activists. In spite of his disdain for unscientific animal collections and the hunting of threatened animals, Hornaday embodied many of their contradictions. He killed thousands of animals, including buffalo, and deemed destruction of wildlife and development of the West an inevitability necessitating intervention by white conservationists.[127]

The Zoological Society through the New York State Legislature nearly deprived Manhattan's crowds of their free and easy contact with exotic animals. The bill to create the society and grant it space in Bronx Park also provided for the transfer of animals from the menagerie to the society. The new zoological park would be less accessible to Lower East Siders than the menagerie, but the society and its supporters believed that the animals would live in better, more natural conditions on the new site.[128] This plan created an immediate tension between animals' living conditions and access for working-class New Yorkers, who visited the menagerie frequently. One New York doctor articulated a particularly misanthropic feeling in support of the plan: "I am very fond of animals—they are better than men. Please relieve the Central Park innocent victims as soon as you can."[129] Residents of the city's poorest districts acted through their alders to vanquish the society's plans "to deprive boys and girls and their parents from coming over a few blocks from the east side to enjoy cheaply and quickly the attractions of the Menagerie."[130]

Buffalo in Manhattan and the Bronx

In late June 1899, a few months before the New York Zoological Park in the Bronx opened its gates, one captive animal from Central Park seized a morning's worth of relative freedom. On this early summer day, a buffalo cow escaped from within one of the fenced yards on the park and spent much of her time swimming in the Lake and dodging human pedestrians, equestrians, a bicyclist, a shepherd dog, the sheep flock, and a trolley. She caused only mild injury to her keeper, Phil Holmes, as she gently butted him aside while exiting the paddock, and to the cyclist who collided with her. Some might be tempted to say that she was performing her natural running and swimming behaviors, but Manhattan was a very different nature from that of her ancestors. This cow lived with just three others of her species, unlike her forebears, who had roamed in herds of thousands, encountering communities of human hunters. Now high densities of urban human visitors overwhelmed Central Park's buffalo every day. Although constantly exposed to human contact, the cow was startled by children shouting and dashed from the lawn where she had settled down to graze. As she took her second swim of the morning—perhaps a "wallow" to cool down and shed some wool—a keeper finally lassoed her, dragged her ashore, and stilled her with the help of some twenty men. The *Times* quipped, "It only needed some cowboy costumes to make the thing a very good imitation of a buffalo hunt on the Western Plains"—a joke whose humor falls flat against the realities facing the buffalo's kin on the plains. Wild herds in the United States by that point numbered under one thousand, and white settlers raised cattle on allotments in their former habitat.[131]

Meanwhile, at the Bronx Zoo, buffalo lived in a "range" rather than in a paddock. Furthermore, Hornaday took Green's vision of conservation further, attempting to replenish decimated wildlife populations. Indeed, in 1907, society members celebrated the successful release of buffalo from their breeding program into preserves throughout the northern plains.[132] Of course, Indigenous tribes had already been engaged in deliberate conservation, protecting kernels of herds that seeded today's returning buffalo populations. As Indigenous feminist scholar Lindsey Schneider points out, conservationists like Hornaday and Roosevelt "saw the enclosure of the prairie and the replacement of buffalo with cattle as inevitable but nonetheless wanted to ensure that buffalo were preserved as a species that symbolized what once had been."[133]

Green's role in helping establish a zoo in what was then a growing suburb presaged his next feat. His foresight about the growth of New York came to fruition under his own direction: after leading the New York Zoological Society for two years, he oversaw the consolidation of the five boroughs into one municipality. The two efforts may seem disconnected, but they should remind us of the tensions between conservation and capitalist urbanization. New York's footprint continued to grow, fed by its investments throughout the economy. This urban agglomeration eventually merged with neighboring cities via sprawling suburbs.

Park visitors, seemingly all men, look on as cow bison Kittie nurses her calf, Black Diamond Jr., in 1914. They are in a pen, not a movable paddock as was used when a bison escaped in 1898. Kittie's fleece appears to be shedding—a normal process that would have been more difficult in the city than in a wild bison's natural habitat. Courtesy of New York City Municipal Archives.

By viewing the Central Park Menagerie through creatures such as buffalo, eagles, and raccoons, we find a tangled and telescoping story about the growth of a city and claims to animals there. Working-class visitors to the menagerie ultimately retained their access, claiming public recreational space and animals as emotional resources. But New York City as an economic juggernaut also encroached upon wildlife habitats at multiple scales, and park patrons and visitors of many classes saw the menagerie as a space of last resort for raccoons and eagles, rabbits and rails, opossums and owls, who came into the city's orbit. Furthermore, the financial resources that fueled the growth of Manhattan and its urbanizing region derived in part from the United States' overland empire, extracted through white settlement and conversion of plains ecologies for market production. Perhaps the most poetic example of the mingling of money, land, and animals across history was embodied in a house constructed from 1894 to 1896, just across from the menagerie. Heirs to the Astor family fortune, accumulated through the fur trade, including John Jacob Astor IV, moved into the largest mansion on the avenue in 1896. The first John Jacob Astor had invested much of his wealth in Manhattan real estate after selling the American Fur Company, which took devastating tolls on buffalo populations in the 1830s and also spread smallpox among Plains peoples.[134]

So, some of the wealthiest people in the United States lived within olfactory and auditory range of an animal exhibit their neighbors considered rickety, malodorous, and malarious. The much-maligned attraction remained popular, perhaps mostly due to its accessibility to Manhattan's laboring classes and for frequent, short visits but perhaps also because the island's residents remained loyal to the animals nearby, often looking forward to encountering particular individuals. In 1903, three years after the park in the Bronx opened, menagerie officials reported that in the previous year, three million people had visited its 381 mammals, 498 birds, and 59 reptiles, including a new prairie dog den and other expanded and "more humane" cages.[135] With 938 individual creatures, the menagerie held an enormous density of animals compared with the park in the Bronx, which opened with only 843 creatures. The former seemed a city for animals, the latter, lying across the East River from Manhattan's human densities, much like the suburb of the Bronx itself. Hornaday thought of Central Park's animal exhibit as a "menagerie slum," an epithet against its human attendees, captive animals, and physical structures.[136]

Recent critics of zoos have argued that the experience of seeing animals in captivity does not teach appreciation of nature or increase the likelihood that zoo visitors will support conservation, contrary to Andrew Green's hopes back in the 1860s—hopes that persist in some form to the

CHAPTER 3

present.[137] Critics charge that zoos instead reinforce human dominion over nature by exposing visitors to animals in controlled, curtailed environments, turning them into spectacles to be consumed. It is easy to dismiss zoo audiences as consumers of cruelty, rather than reflecting upon their efforts to claim space and connect with animated nature within a city rife with power struggles that mostly deprived them of such opportunities. Certainly, millions of human park visitors enjoyed the spectacle of domination inherent in caging wild beasts. Visitors' appetites and actions took place within larger power struggles in which elites expanded control over animals, humans, and land in growing empires beyond the city and over private real estate and the use of public resources within the city.

PART 2

Human and Animal Claims on a Plural Park

IT IS TEMPTING to think of a seemingly natural landscape like Central Park's as self-sustaining. By the start of the twentieth century, however, the decades-old park was in need of physical maintenance to meet the needs and desires of its increasing and diversifying constituents. Park administrators mostly thought of these constituents as human New Yorkers, though as we will see, some human constituents prioritized other species too. Important park features had not seen adequate investment in years, and "restoration" was a constant theme in Parks Department reports. In 1912, there was enough money to address "poor lawns and plantations" along with "the roadway question" (the latter were crumbling) and obsolete drainage pipes under much of the park.[1] In 1927, Commissioner Walter Herrick reported that "due to many years of insufficient appropriation and surrounding conditions" the park "had deteriorated to such an extent that great remedial work was necessitated." The city allocated a million dollars for "rehabilitation." Every corner needed investment of material and labor, from the zoo (they gradually dropped the term *menagerie*) to the bridle path. A thousand of the park's largest trees needed new soil to cover roots exposed by the eroding action of rainfall and foot traffic; hard, packed soil needed aeration and fertilizer. Outbreaks of fungal disease and boring insects had killed off hundreds of trees; living trees had branches that needed trimming, and many shrubs, vines, and herbaceous plants needed outright replacement. Damage from deliberate human activities also marred some sections of the park, from vandalism that destroyed trees to messes left by the crews constructing the subway stations nearby.[2]

The human population of Manhattan alone had nearly tripled in the years since the park was created, yet the city cut the parks budget in the 1910s. Manhattan's human population was not only growing; it was shifting culturally and spatially. In the 1910s and 1920s, commissioners noted a desperate need for more playgrounds throughout the borough to serve the city's youth population—even before the midcentury baby boom.[3] As European immigration peaked shortly after the turn of the century, dominated at that point by southern and eastern Europeans, Black folks arrived in growing numbers from the US South, fleeing violence, oppression, and material deprivation. Like the city population as a whole, the center of Black population shifted northward as it grew, from west of the park to America's new "Black Mecca" emerging in the old Dutch village of Harlem to the north. Italian Americans also migrated toward Harlem, mostly on the east side. Immigrants from the West Indies joined Black Americans in Harlem, followed by Puerto Ricans newly granted US citizenship. Restrictive policies limited immigrants from much of Asia, but Chinese communities exceeded ten thousand people by the 1900s, with smaller numbers of Japanese and Filipinos. Mohawk Indians settled in Brooklyn to take jobs in the construction industry, but many looked down at the park from Manhattan's rising skyscrapers and surely walked through it after work.[4]

New York State received the greatest number of new Black residents of any state during the Great Migration—nearly 75,000 souls in the 1920s and 150,000 in the 1930s, most of them moving to New York City from Virginia, the Carolinas, and Georgia.[5] The Puerto Rican population of the state, again mostly in the city, with some also identifying as Black, exceeded 300,000 by the mid-1950s. Other Caribbean populations grew by tens of thousands each decade.[6] These new Manhattanites of color joined New York–born African Americans of all social classes, making community and their own form of thriving in segregated neighborhoods.

Working-class New Yorkers eked out homes in an increasingly expensive island—or moved out to other boroughs and beyond—while elite and established families enjoyed the fruits of growth in real estate and other sectors. These changes in the economic and cultural geography of New York altered conditions for human park goers and nonhumans around the entire city. High-rises lined the park's east and west sides, where tenants gained immediate access to the park in exchange for high prices per square foot of indoor living space. Meanwhile, Black and Puerto Rican Harlem residents gained access from the north end of the park but often felt unwelcome. Human New Yorkers rode the new subway system to all parts of the park, but space and access around the park became more limited for many other species. Land claimed for real estate, streets, and other spaces of commerce overtook green space, leaving little room for common companions like dogs and horses and for aquatic life in streams buried in the paving of the city. The expanding northeastern megalopolis overall left fewer green spaces for birds migrating down and up the Atlantic flyway. Beyond Central Park, New York and the surrounding region were changing in ways that also reshaped animal life, particularly in the conversion of wildlife habitat and farmland to urban and suburban developments.[7] Thus, the twentieth century brought new struggles for quality and accessible green space and the freedom to take up those spaces as powerful elites sought to police the borders of who could use the park, how, and who got to speak for and associate with animals there. In this context, Central Park became an ever more important resource for New Yorkers of many human identities and nonhuman species.

Discourse about Central Park's condition fixated on "deterioration," and many elite and middle-class New Yorkers drew parallels (sometimes contradictory) between physical degradation, moral and social erosion, and deviation from the original landscape and purpose of the park. Part of the problem, for Greensward purists, was that the Department of Public Parks increasingly diverted parts of the park to recreational programs serving diverse constituencies, including children deemed in need of more play spaces. In one year, programs ranged from a miniature airplane activity on the Sheep Meadow to canoe regattas on the Lake to roller-skating on the Mall.[8] In the 1920s, several years after Olmsted's death, his son Frederick Law Olmsted Jr. worked with architectural historian Theodora Kimball to publish Olmsted Sr.'s papers, hoping to inspire renewed dedication to the original spirit of the park landscape. In the preface to their second volume, dedicated to the Central Park years, they lamented the "deteriorating effects of neglect and misuse which [the park] has suffered during the last few decades."[9]

In spite of the growth of people of color populations and the needs of the urban poor and working-class folks, park administrators and other municipal officials were eager to satisfy and retain the city's white middle class. The million dollars allocated for rehabilitation only went so far to address deferred maintenance needs, and a shabby park could not compete with the beckoning suburbs. As the Great Depression wore on and the proportion of New Yorkers who were white declined, a new Parks Department head took office in 1934 with an ambition to leverage federal work-relief funds to remake the city's entire landscape. Robert Moses reshaped New York in ways he hoped would appeal to those New Yorkers desired as workers and consumers by the city's business community and growing service sector. With a political science doctorate and an inherited family fortune, Moses accepted a very modest salary and served in leading positions across several city agencies and commissions: the Parks Department, the Bridge and Tunnel Authority, and the Planning Commission, where in the post–World War II era he controlled the city's Title I urban renewal funds. Moses professed an intention to use government funds and the vast power of his many offices to improve the lives and character of all New Yorkers.[10]

In the early years of his tenure in the Parks Department, many New Yorkers viewed Moses as incorruptible and a blessing to the entire city. He answered the discourse about Central Park's deterioration with promises of a modern, orderly renewal that expanded access to good, squeaky-clean fun, such as in the Central Park Zoo. However, as his administration continued, it became clear that Moses's Parks Department often prioritized other concerns over the Greensward plan and many of the creatures living in it and that his visions of order and wholesome recreation were not for everyone—human or otherwise. Moses earned a reputation for racism, particularly in housing and urban renewal activities, though recent research has called into question some accusations related to his recreation work. Furthermore, Moses did not work alone. As political scientist Joel Schwartz argues, Moses could not have accomplished such acts of displacement and exclusion without the support of liberal agency staff and power transfers by politicians, which helped his administration conceal his schemes under a facade of good government.[11]

This second part of the book includes the period before 1934 as well as Moses's tenure, the longest of any New York Parks commissioner. Several trends and forces shaped how more-than-human communities fared: a growing human population and demands on the park, a deferred maintenance backlog, the city's interest in holding onto a lucrative segment of the population, the development of the built environment around the park, and Moses's dedication to modernization. New Yorkers staked new claims to spaces in Central Park, many of them focused on features and activities associated with specific animals. As ever, equestrians and their horses traversed the bridle paths, and vast numbers of visitors still crowded the zoo. But the new century brought greater numbers and varieties of human New Yorkers seeking space to congregate, to be outdoors, to cross Manhattan, to see and be seen—with or without animals. Bicyclists and joggers wanted to exercise on the bridle paths; birders and queer communities occupied the Ramble. Children played and fished in streams, dog owners sought places to exercise their canines, and a few people still loved to see sheep on the green. Such claims to park space may seem compatible, but they played out in a context of competing assertions over who spoke for urban animals. Furthermore, park authorities, some environmentalists, and other powerful New Yorkers treated maintenance funding and the park itself as scarce resources, limiting and even policing certain uses based on tight budgets, tradition, and fears about landscape and moral degradation in a plural city.

Authorities maintained a tone of scarcity in the way they allocated resources, rendering Manhattan's growing population and varied communities into competing constituencies to sustain their corner of the park. On many occasions, environmentalists have represented animals in public space as weak and vulnerable, needing exclusive access and greater resources. By aligning themselves with these nonhumans, affluent and elite people have bolstered their claims to political rightness and space in the city, sometimes neglecting the needs of marginalized human communities or even threatening them with policing. Central Park remained an animated landscape within the built-up city, but many humans and animals struggled to claim this space.

CHAPTER 4

Freedom, Joy, and Privilege in Multispecies Spaces

In the fall of 1923, six women from Harlem took advantage of a stretch of beautiful fall weather to enjoy a part of Central Park with which many of them had had little experience: the bridle path.[1] That fall, and for several subsequent seasons, they and other members of Harlem's Young Women's Christian Association took equestrian courses sponsored by the YWCA and the Hauter Riding Academy. An unnamed equestrian who advertised the spring 1926 course in the *New York Amsterdam News* felt thrilled with a sense of freedom and contact with nature when experiencing the park on horseback. "Horseback riding in Central Park! Imagine it!" she wrote. "Imagine cantering along Central Park West, past the lakes, the reservoir, and Fifth avenue; amidst the birds and blossoms in the balmy spring weather. Try this thrilling exercise in the beautiful out of doors for health and happiness." Furthermore, horseback riding was a chance to "don your chic riding habit"—to not just enjoy nature but to do so in style.[2]

Central Park's bridle paths had long been elite spaces for exercise, nature enjoyment, and fashionable display, accessible to a narrow set of white New Yorkers and visitors who could afford not just the time and money to learn the skill in the first place but also the cost of either hiring a horse or—much pricier—owning, feeding, and stabling one themselves. Park regulations restricted carts crossing Central Park on business to the sunken arteries, leaving the bridle paths to leisure riders and their mounts. For Black New Yorkers in earlier decades, horses were mostly a source of income and not leisure in a city run on horsepower—that is, when the city wasn't denying licenses to Black would-be cartmen. Middle- and lower-income whites, too, had little access to the bridle paths. But in the 1920s, more Black women from Harlem's middle and upper classes gained access to this world. The repeated command to "imagine it" suggests the service that horses provided in opening up public space and nature to them. Horses offered Black women more than access to physical space and its resources; they also provided a sense of safety, a new vantage point on the world, and a chance to flaunt their own style just as white women always had. In the 1920s, many women New Yorkers of all colors approached Central Park with trepidation given the rumors and reality of sexual violence and harassment there.[3] Many men indeed targeted unaccompanied women in public space with unwanted stares, jeers, and often much worse, and Black women endured more of this harassment than their white counterparts.[4] From atop a tall, powerful equine, perhaps Black women might rise above the fray, all while expressing their sense of style and feeling joy in the more-than-human park.

Black women equestrians were one group of New Yorkers who claimed access to nature and public space in Central Park through their associations with animals. This chapter argues that multispecies place-making could be an avenue to joy, but that more privileged New Yorkers also sometimes asserted special claims to the park based on their advocacy for animals they deemed vulnerable.[5] Such claims were wrapped up in park users' identities, including personal styles and ways of being in public space; recall the quiet, contemplative manner that bird lovers attempted to inculcate in other human visitors to the Ramble.[6] Claims to park spaces became ever more fraught within discourse about erosion in the physical and moral landscape, as many park users argued that their activities and spaces deserved more municipal resources for maintenance and good health. It was true that heavy use of many park spaces led to soil compaction, erosion of slopes, and even death of sensitive vegetation.[7] Claims of erosion and the need to protect vulnerable animals who relied on these spaces also coincided with neglect or stigma toward marginalized human park users. Queer folks, for example, had created community and found joy in the Ramble, which was also the park's most inviting habitat for birds. While bird lovers cited native avian beings' vulnerability in bolstering calls to protect the Ramble, gay men also faced violence from police and civilian bashers who feared the erosion of normative genders and sexualities. Greater attention to nonhuman animals need not have detracted from the struggles of marginalized humans who sought pleasure, respite, safety, and belonging in the park, but the latter were often far less visible.

"A Rendez-vous for Bird-Lovers": Birders Claim the Ramble

Perhaps the clearest example of a group claiming space through animal affiliation were the bird enthusiasts who gathered in the Ramble. By the late nineteenth century, New York's Linnaean Society, a natural history organization, and later the local Audubon Society knew that the Ramble sheltered extraordinary bird diversity, and bird lovers (as many called themselves at the time) were beginning to claim this space. At that time, a boy named Ludlow Griscom, the scion of a wealthy and powerful but also eccentric white family, got his start in ornithology. His stories of this time period show how birders' style of nature enjoyment became accepted in the park. As a ten-year-old child in 1900, Griscom took part in a growing but still small group of bird lovers who gazed into the Ramble's dense forest with opera glasses and, increasingly, new and accessible types of binoculars, scouring the brush for warblers and woodcocks. As a teen, he joined New York's Linnaean Society.[8] Griscom's recollections might not be entirely reliable; in addition to being very young as a new era of ornithology emerged, he was also reputed to bear a perpetual chip on his shoulder about the outsider status of bird lovers and his own stature within the ornithological community.[9]

According to Griscom's telling, urban bird-watching had become popular in Boston before New York, so the New Yorkers who tried to bring the same practices to Central Park around 1900 felt conspicuous and strange in spite of their privileged social position and secure sense of belonging in public space overall. In New York and beyond, the birding pastime underwent a generational transition as the glass replaced the gun as the primary means of collecting birds. Griscom was instrumental in this transition, confirming with his own skill that birds could be identified by sight alone, without needing to shoot the individual for verification.[10] Griscom's own publications helped subsequent birders hone such skills that, in addition to birding by ear, remain essential for birders today. The new birders kept life lists of birds they had spied, often vouched for by companions and verified with reference to skins collected by George Lawrence's generation and housed at institutions like the American Museum of Natural History, just across Central Park West from the Ramble.

It took time for other Central Park visitors to understand and accept these bird lovers peering into the shrubbery. In 1926, Griscom recalled that in the early days, "we were quite eccentric and barely respectable . . . . I can remember the astonishment of people at seeing us gaze steadily through a glass into the treetops and the shamefaced way in which most of us used to do it."[11] Griscom's later recollections of early birding in New York became even more harrowing. Biographer William Davis quotes the "dean of birdwatchers" as claiming in a 1952 speech that around 1900 "you could hunt and shoot birds, but you couldn't ogle birds with a glass. Many is the time a derisive and unfriendly crowd has run me out of Central Park."[12] Griscom was sensitive to ornithologists' styles of occupying space and enjoying nature. Hunting birds with a gun could come off as robust, masculine, and decisive, but birding with the eyes seemed effete, refined, and introspective. Griscom, ever proud of his physical prowess but also dedicated to this new mode of birding, likely exaggerated the marginalization of his early birding companions. Clearly, though, some birders felt awkward in the park.[13]

Perhaps Griscom's childhood isolation accounts in part for his early feelings of outsider status. Though privileged by material resources and family connections, along with race and gender, Griscom experienced an unusual upbringing. His parents were descended from respected military generals and successful merchants, inherited abundant fortunes, and continued to build wealth through investments and businesses. His mother, Genevieve Ludlow Griscom, led a secretive religious sect, splintered off from the Theosophists, whose inner circle sequestered itself at the Griscoms' suburban New York estate. Ludlow Griscom himself enjoyed little contact with peers or even affection from his austere family as a child; he filled lonely days honing his skills in ornithology, foreign languages, and classical piano.[14]

By the 1920s, Griscom was a rising star in American ornithology and an assistant curator at the American Museum of Natural History, and his generation of birders had developed much greater comfort and security in their claims to space. Griscom referred to the Ramble as a "rendez-vous for bird-lovers" and the Central Park birders collectively as a "clan." The camaraderie of this community was vital for its members' growth as naturalists and conservationists. Reflecting on growing public acceptance of birders, he reported that "now we are entirely sane and normal." Members of this cultish group of "physicians, tired businessmen, authors, schoolboys, teachers"—largely middle- and upper-class white men and boys—helped each other discover the Ramble's great avian diversity. Griscom claimed credit for establishing "the underground railroad of the fraternity," which involved stashing a note in a hollow stump listing the species he had seen that morning for birders who arrived later.[15] In likening birders to people escaping enslavement, Griscom probably intended to compare the groups' use of secret signs in the landscape. However, the metaphor also aggrandized the mild discomfort of mostly white nature lovers who felt like lonely eggheads, suggesting a casual insensitivity to those who faced true physical danger and exclusion. By 1926, birders' claims to space were even supported by law enforcement. Certain police officers aided the "fraternity," passing tips for finding shy birds between members recognizable by their binoculars.[16] Although some of Griscom's writings focused on men and boys among the birding "clan," he also praised women birders such as Anne Crolius, who "visited the Park more than 250 times annually between 1895 and 1915, a record of consistent observation probably unequalled in this country." Women such as Gladys Fry led the Museum of Natural History's birding tours. Griscom's own knowledge of the Ramble was exemplary too; he birded there daily during spring migration from age fourteen until he left New York for a curatorial job at Harvard.[17] These birders had claimed the space of the Ramble, in spite of what was initially a strange and even suspicious style of being in public, by virtue of their affiliation with birds—and their identities.

Queer Desire, Community, and Identity in the Ramble

For humans who, like most of Griscom's fraternity, enjoy ample access to and control over their own private spaces, public space can be a site for exercise, fresh air, and contact with more-than-human nature. It can also be a site of expressing identity, of gathering and display, settings in which to see and be seen and to demand recognition as part of the polity.[18] Elite white women and men flocked to Central Park's bridle paths for such functions when these routes opened in the 1860s. Urban development, however, has often constrained some humans' access to space—any space—leaving them to fulfill functions considered "private" in public. Particularly during economic downturns, many New Yorkers lost access to the private space of their own homes. Those unhoused by the stock market crash of 1929 and other people who had drifted to New York in search of work sought shelter in Central Park. Those who made a temporary home there slept, washed, and performed other bodily functions in this public space, arousing controversy and joining the other-than-human creatures who used the park as a home or way station.[19]

Whether or not they had a house to call home, many New Yorkers also looked to Central Park as an alternative private space for romantic and sexual encounters. The art critic Clarence Cook in the 1860s wrote affectionately of young couples stealing an embrace in a secluded spot within the Ramble.[20] He did not mention their identities, but a sketch in his book and other images show white heterosexual couples. A growing city and more park visitors in general meant more lovers in search of such hideouts. Youth from the Upper West Side or Harlem might find a sheltered cul-de-sac off a path in the North Woods to meet a lover beyond family members' watchful eyes. Men seeking companionship or sex with other men found one another in the Ramble and adjacent spaces.[21] The Ramble's cave had long provided a thrilling and mysterious setting for romantic encounters, although some men used it as a hiding spot from which to prey upon women. Indeed, many women, including birders, were wary of attack and molestation in the park and particularly in the Ramble; over three hundred men were arrested for such crimes in 1929.[22] For consenting adults (along with would-be molesters and trysting youth), the Ramble offered "vast stretches of unsupervised wooded land" full of "secluded spots," as historian George Chauncey explains.[23] Such trysts brought humans more deeply into the same spaces as non-human animals who also found seclusion in Central Park. The same park features made these spaces attractive for birds and therefore bird-watchers; dense foliage, for instance, sheltered lovers and warblers from prying eyes or predators.[24] Birders and cruisers alike were also often lone men sending messages to each other in the landscape. Lovers in the Ramble could use nature appreciation as their cover—and surely many did enjoy nature there.

Chauncey relates a report by a physician in 1895 of "a young man who . . . by his manner and gestures [seemed] affected with sexual abnormity . . . arrested in the Central Park for masquerading in feminine dress." The physician revealed that the young person had been sent to "the

This 1899 photo of a man and a woman in the Ramble, entitled *A Romantic Spot*, suggests that this section was recognized as a place for lovers from the park's early days. Courtesy of the Library of Congress, Prints and Photographs Division.

Psychopathic Ward" for treatment of the supposed "abnormity."[25] This arrest and forced psychiatric treatment represented one example of how a person's identity, style, and appearance could attract unwanted attention in the park and other public spaces in the city. But this arrest in 1895 was an outlier in the timeline of New York's regulation of queer folks. During the first decades of the twentieth century, moral crusaders focused mostly on curbing cisgender women sex workers—who sometimes plied their trade in Central Park and also faced arrest and violence throughout the twentieth century. In the meantime, queer men formed community and found companionship and fulfillment in the Ramble as well as certain cafés, clubs, enclaves, and other urban spaces, often with little intervention by vice squads. Indeed, as Chauncey shows, laws punishing homosexual acts and styles "were enforced only irregularly"; "gay men had to take precautions, but, like other marginalized peoples, they were able to construct spheres of relative cultural autonomy in the interstices of a city governed by hostile powers."[26] The Ramble and other outdoor cruising spots were not merely bedrooms of last resort. People who sought romantic and sexual encounters outdoors in this period did so not *only* (or in many cases, not at all) because they could not do so in the privacy of a home or hotel but also, often, to enjoy the thrill of transgression and perhaps to subvert categories of public and private.[27]

Over the decades, however, and particularly after World War II, authorities in New York gradually shifted law enforcement practices to erase queer people from public space, expanding policing and arrests in Central Park. Chauncey explains that "New York City's police and courts construed the disorderly-conduct statute to mandate a much broader ban on gay cultural practices" than simply prohibiting gay sex in public. Rather, "they regularly used the statute to criminalize the assembly of gay men in a public place or their adoption of specific cultural styles, from camp behavior to dancing with people of the same gender or wearing clothes assigned to the other gender."[28] Men need not have been caught in a sex act together, say, in the bushes of the Ramble to face arrest. Simply appearing on the Ramble's paths and displaying queer affect or sitting on a rock too close to another man could draw the attention of police. Police enjoyed wide latitude to detain and courts wide latitude to sentence. Women and Black folks—queer or otherwise—might face even greater limitations on their public and even private sexuality.[29] Gay style and assembly increasingly became grounds for arrest, whereas bird lovers' assembly in public space did not. In addition to the threat of arrest and psychiatric treatment, queer people in Central Park faced violent beatings by police or gangs of civilians.

The most violent of these incidents in the park occurred in the same year when Ludlow Griscom published his memories of birders coming to belong in the Ramble. In the summer of 1926, the young heartthrob actor Rudolph Valentino died suddenly. Thousands of mostly young, white women thronged to his funeral bier at a church just west of the park on Sixty-Sixth Street. Mounted police assembled to control the crowd, and the police horses trampled several women, some of whom had to be hospitalized.[30] The police likely still felt tense that evening around the time when a Black vaudeville and drag performer from Harlem, Clinton DeForest, paid respects at Valentino's bier. DeForest called Valentino a friend and was surely distraught by the loss and shaken by these clashes while walking back from the memorial. Crossing into the park just to the southwest of the Ramble, DeForest encountered a white police officer named Joseph Higgins. Higgins beat DeForest's face and head with his fists and then moved his broken body to the opposite side of the park.[31]

Queer people in the park were often accused of crimes such as robbery and obscenity. A white woman journalist later claimed that women and couples had reported DeForest. Higgins said that DeForest was acting suspiciously and disobeyed police and that Higgins was attempting to arrest him or chase DeForest out of the park. DeForest died in the hospital a few days later, and Higgins was convicted of manslaughter. New York governor Franklin Roosevelt commuted Higgins's sentence before he had served three years.[32] Higgins's contradictory, vague story, paired with the vicious beating, suggest that he was reacting to DeForest's gender presentation and race in this attack.[33]

Clinton DeForest's story is an important one too little told in the history of Central Park, but Black and queer New Yorkers were not merely victims in Central Park. Black folks, queer folks, women, and other marginalized identities that could intersect in an individual all faced oppression *and* claimed space and made place for themselves. As one frequent Ramble visitor, a gay white man, later explained, "I always went there to relax, meet other gay people, talk"; he also met his eventual partner there.[34] For those who did and do have sex there, the setting alongside the entire process of cruising may have been part of the appeal—hiding in shrubs and behind boulders, noticing birds, insects, plants, or beautiful tableaux. Nature appreciation and the picturesque aesthetic that Olmsted and Vaux imported from English landscape architecture took on new layers of meaning amid the thrill of transgressing norms. As the natural historian Louis Peet wrote of the Ramble in 1903, its beauty, "set[s] free the swift, aspiring thoughts in new flights, like the rush of birds skyward."[35] For many queer folks, the Ramble offered this same kind of freedom.

Authorities and privileged members of the public had long used visible markers of identity and style to delineate belonging in Central Park—as we saw when elites disparaged ethnically diverse and boisterous crowds at the menagerie. Birders in Central Park once seemed like shifty or ambiguous characters. Sneaking about with opera glasses and peering into the treetops, they could easily be mistaken for peeping Toms. At the least, they looked like out-of-touch eggheads.[36] Yet for many, appearing white and acting straight shielded them from suspicion and eventually ensured them a place for fellowship and connecting with nature.

In the coming years, other humans who visited Central Park struggled to find belonging there, and declining physical environmental conditions brought scrutiny to growing crowds and those who strayed from official paths. Soils suffered erosion and compaction from foot traffic, and poor soil conditions rendered trees more vulnerable to herbivorous insects and pathogens. As trees died from poor soil, infections, infestations, and even some vandalism and paths crumbled, park supporters demanded that authorities more strictly regulate the use of sensitive spaces and also provide greater public investment in upkeep.[37]

More-than-Human Public Spaces and the Dangers of Erosion

While humans exerted power through physical and social control of public space, the social-ecological lives of animals in the Ramble were also complex in their own ways—some similar to humans' lives, others less so. Whether seeking opportunities to see and be seen by others of one's species, to claim shelter or belonging, or to find a safe route home, humans and animals often occupied the same spaces and used them for comparable purposes.[38] Spaces like the Ramble are home to ever-shifting temporal and geographical complexities for birds and other creatures. Avian migrants from the Caribbean and Central and South America cross paths here in April and May and again (though to a lesser extent) on the way back south in October. The conversion of habitat around the metropolis further complicated birds' lives. Griscom explained that a bird's "world has changed, its landscape is inconceivably altered, it is surrounded by the incomprehensible hum of human activity, yet [it] clings grimly to its ancestral home." In the spaces left for birds, dozens of species sort out territories and food sources with one another; the air fills with songs whose full meanings humans will never know; residents choose some mates and reject others; brood parasites take advantage of other bird families to raise their eggs and chicks.[39] Bird lovers and queer human New Yorkers made a place rich with community meaning alongside these multilayered avian dynamics.

In addition to their role as places where beings connect with one another and claim belonging in the polity, public spaces also provide conduits for movement of humans and other animals. As Manhattan's human population shifted northward, residents inhabiting the island's edges around the park increasingly crossed this space in directions unanticipated by the original design. Whether heading to work, play, school, home, or a social visit, New Yorkers of all identities chose routes through Central Park to get to their destinations. In 1919, parks commissioner Francis Gallatin noted the need "to lay out proper paths" as walkers seeking the shortest route wore lines through swaths of green.[40] Wildlife, too, often require safe and expedient corridors to move between different activities—seeking shelter or building nests, mating, gathering food, or moving to and from warmer locales with the seasons. Wildlife face many dangers as they navigate the city: predators of many species, automobiles, glass windows that an unwitting bird may strike in flight, to name a few. Humans, too, navigate spaces to avoid real and perceived threats, and for some humans, those threats have a greater likelihood of bringing actual harm. Humans and wildlife all sought safe and expedient routes that they could use to pass through space unmolested.

In a 1923 report for the Linnaean Society and the Museum of Natural History, Griscom stated that the park was "an ideal station for studying the migration of birds and is unquestionably the best place for insectivorous transients in the region." Bird lovers had observed avian diversity thriving in the Ramble for decades, but Griscom still felt it necessary to acknowledge that this claim was "astonishing"—revealing, perhaps, a bias against urban environments among natural historians. He explained that the park was "an oasis in a vast desert of city roofs, in which the tired hosts must alight to rest as the day breaks, and where the great variety of shrubbery and trees affords an ample food supply and shelter."[41] He estimated that 100 species appeared during the peak months of April and May alone. Of 192 species documented in the metro region by 1926, birders had by now spotted 163 in the Ramble, up from 129 confirmed in the park by George Lawrence in 1868. The diverse plant community formed multiple layers, providing fruits and nesting sites as well as habitat for myriad invertebrates that some birds fed upon. It was not only the bird species that made the Ramble extraordinary; it was the web of plants, insects, and other creatures that constituted this urban haven.[42]

Subtle and not-so-subtle differences in human uses and management of the park could affect vegetation, animals, populations, or communities of several different species. Griscom noted that "many trees and shrubs have died" in recent years, "reducing the available cover" that many resident birds had relied upon. Millions of human feet, walking on and off trails, compacted the soil, often endangering trees. Trees and shrubs withered and died, often from exposure and damage to their roots, fungal infection, or herbivorous insect predation; soils that once had their roots held in place might crumble. Soil washed away from slopes in hilly areas like the Ramble. Indeed, Griscom also noted "the great increase in the number of people using the Park." He recalled that "ten years ago one could spend an entire morning in the Ramble and scarcely see a soul. Now it is certain to be full of people by 10 o'clock, except in bad weather."[43]

As early as 1919, administrators such as borough commissioner Francis Gallatin contemplated more protective fencing in the Ramble.[44] Growing crowds disrupted habitats that birds had once perceived as quiet and un-threatening. Most of the bird species that appeared in the Ramble were "transients"—seasonal migrants that might be spotted mostly in May and to a lesser extent in October. Griscom believed that the crowds did not trouble these species much during their brief touchdowns. The reduced vegetative cover through tree and shrub deaths and the growing human crowds most seriously affected the species that lived in the area year-round, and Griscom noted the decline in the number of such species nesting there.[45] The Ramble, along with other parts of the park, was de-grading noticeably for plants, insects, birds, and humans.

In the early twentieth century, growing numbers of human visitors came to Central Park at the same time as city budgets for this and all New York City parks were stagnant and sometimes even in decline. Conditions were already strained by 1912, when the Parks Department report for Manhattan noted many instances of "damage and abuse."[46] The park was sixty years old, and the population of Manhattan alone (not counting the other boroughs that were incorporated in 1898, or the growing suburbs beyond, and steady streams of tourists) had risen from about 800,000 at the time of the park's construction to over 2.2 million by 1920. In the mid-1910s, as effects of the Great War in Europe cascaded into New York's globally linked economy, the city reduced budgets for Manhattan parks by half, allowing little funding to address deferred maintenance or increased pressure from users.[47]

Meanwhile, the Parks Department allocated a growing slice of its budget for "recreation"—organized activities for New Yorkers, often children, including a wide range of games, sports, dance performances, folk festivals, and even vegetable gardens. Events in Central Park brought hundreds of visitors trampling out onto the Sheep Meadow and other greens. After the war and under new city leadership, budgets increased, but the Parks Department had to use much of the higher allocation to raise wages at pace with inflation.[48] In its report for 1926, the Manhattan section of the Parks Department lamented, "The park, due to many years of insufficient appropriation and surrounding conditions, had deteriorated to such an extent that great remedial work was necessitated." The department hired a consultant to assess the landscape and recommend where to focus resources and effort, and the city dramatically increased funding for the following two years. The Ramble needed replanting to replace damaged shrubs and trees, and several other spots needed rehabilitation after years of degradation.[49]

Speaking for Horses and Claiming the Bridle Paths

One such feature was the bridle paths, whose four-plus-mile loop had a small but growing and vocal constituency. At the park's origins, equestrians had been a privileged class, those able to keep a horse in the city. Leisure riders exercised disproportionate power over the park landscape. The trail required frequent, specialized, and expensive maintenance yet served a tiny fraction of the city population.

As urban development filled Manhattan, space for horses was now at a premium at stables and clubs often to the west and east of the park.[50] By the 1920s, automobiles had thoroughly replaced horses as the main mode of transport in the city; for equestrians, this gave their sport and their horses greater meaning as a way of connecting with nature and enjoying special access to sections of the park. The segment of New Yorkers who could afford to ride was expanding, however, posing challenges for stabling horses in the city. The Metropolitan Riding Club, whose membership included the mayor and other officials, finalized plans for a new site at Central Park West and 100th Street just two weeks after the 1929 stock market crash. Riders were clamoring for space, and according to a piece in *The Spur* in November 1929, "the overcrowding of existing clubs has long been obvious."[51]

Over time, it became more difficult for Manhattan's equestrians to make the case for spending on trails exclusively for horses. In the first two decades of the twentieth century, runners and bicyclists increasingly demanded space and time on the trails, and mayors and park authorities responded by restricting equestrians' access in the evenings in favor of much more affordable recreations. In 1923, for example, Mayor John Hylan closed the paths to riders and their horses on some evenings, prompting protests from equestrians, some of whom were "riding under the doctor's orders" and could not ride during the day because of their work schedules. Parks commissioner Francis Gallatin also explained that "riding masters claim that their business has been injured" and that horses themselves would not get enough exercise. Equestrians felt that they and the rising numbers of runners "would not interfere with each other," asserting that horses would not be troubled by different kinds of moving beings alongside them. Furthermore, Gallatin took pains to emphasize that the equestrians' complaints came "from all classes of our population"—assuring the mayor that he was not merely favoring the elites known for their assertiveness in demanding city services.[52]

Amid competing uses of the bridle paths, consultants in 1926 found "that the bridle paths in Central Park had been deteriorating for many years . . . numerous complaints were received from riders." In fact, the grading of the paths was so worn and uneven as to endanger riders and horses. Thus, "the paths were reconstructed for the first time since originally laid out."[53] Periodic regrading was not the only need, however; more frequent effort—many times each year—was needed to keep down dust as the surface of the paths became compacted and horses' hooves pounded the gravel. Sprinkling with water, used motor oil, or other fluids required labor, supplies, and specialized equipment.[54] After a burst of investment in the late 1920s—sixty thousand dollars for resurfacing and grading— equestrians complimented the Parks Department for better riding conditions than they had seen in years.[55]

For several reasons, however, the improved conditions were short-lived. First, the paths needed more frequent oiling or watering than the Parks Department allocated effort and resources for, at a time when expensive equipment was worn-out and malfunctioning. Second, the Depression cut into the parks budget just a few years after the city first increased spending to make up for its maintenance backlog. And third, it was not only human runners and cyclists who seemed to be making increasing demands on the bridle paths; it was also a growing *number* of riders. Some equestrians claimed more horse-rider dyads took to the trails than ever before; the available data renders reliable comparisons difficult, but the sheer numbers of riders seemed to have exploded.[56]

In 1930, a coalition of several riding clubs, the ASPCA, the Women's League for Animals, and the Parks Association, a private advocacy group, banded together under their shared identity as "lovers of horses" to demand another complete rehabilitation of the trail. They sought to prove that it was not only privileged humans who would benefit from better maintenance for the bridle paths. In a 1930 survey of thousands of New York horse riders, Parks Association president Nathan Straus Jr. found

Equestrians used the bridle paths as a multispecies social space and for gaining access to secluded natural areas while atop powerful animals. Paths required careful and costly maintenance to remain gentle on horses' hooves and to prevent the surface from becoming muddy or dusty. Courtesy of the Library of Congress, Prints and Photographs Division.

that only 15 percent of equestrians in city parks owned their own horses; the rest hired them from a stable.[57] Stables that hired horses to the public made riding more accessible and expanded the number of bridle path users, but hourly rates to hire a horse still remained beyond the means of many New Yorkers and were certainly more expensive than running or even bicycling. The group asked for $125,000 to $150,000 to be allocated for repair and maintenance of the paths.[58]

This group cited grave dangers to both horses and human riders. When authorities last repaved the road, they had introduced crushed stone, but horses and this paving material were mutually destructive. The stones' sharp edges at first cut into the soft, spongy tissue within the horses' hooves, causing many to become lame. Eventually, the constant trampling reduced the stones to powder, which became "a sea of mud" after rainstorms. During dry spells, the dust became airborne. Many complained of the ill effects and dangers of the often-degraded and dusty bridle path, relaying doctors' warnings that the particles could cause conjunctivitis and sinus problems—not to mention the effects on horses of a dusty working environment. Dust covered riders and horses from head to foot, and the clouds drifted beyond the park into adjacent neighborhoods, where luxury apartment managers complained it endangered their tenants.[59]

Equestrians voiced these concerns first to Parks Department borough commissioner Walter Herrick and then to Robert Moses and his staff during Moses's early years as parks commissioner. When Moses took office, his administration typically responded that there was simply insufficient money and resources to maintain a part of the park that served so few elites.[60] In response to this constant refrain from park authorities, a group of riders formed the "Early Risers Club," claiming to stand for "democratizing the bridle paths." Chaired by prominent attorney Bernard Sandler, the Early Risers endeavored to increase ridership, make the city "horse-conscious," and overcome the bad optics of solitary riders or small groups and the perception that they were all "ritzy riders or millionaires" by gathering huge throngs of horse people for morning rides.[61] When slow progress on bridle path repairs kept a portion of the trail barricaded to riders, riding academies "reported [to the ASPCA] sickness among their horses" because of "lack of exercise."[62] The Early Risers threatened to have a "society woman" from the group crash the barrier on her horse to get herself arrested and generate publicity. In April 1936, when the paths were open again, the Early Risers organized an equestrian day designed to raise New Yorkers' awareness of horses. One hundred human-horse dyads simulated a hunting party without the hunt on a chilly Sunday morning, parading with top-hatted officials and a brass band. The ride ended with lunch accompanied by hot toddies and prizes for the best riders at the Tavern on the Green restaurant.[63] It is unclear whether the cheekily Anglophilic flavor of the ride helped attract riders or detracted from the Early Risers' rhetoric about democratizing riding in the park.

In 1939, conditions for horses, riders, and nearby park goers got even worse when the park's secondhand sprinkling equipment conked out and the city budget director denied Moses's request for funding to acquire a new sprinkler and the proper kind of oil for the job. Stable owners and powerful equestrians—lawyers, business leaders, clergy, even the lieutenant governor—flooded park administrators with letters and joined the Early Risers in a protest at the Tavern on the Green on May 8.[64] Prominent lawyer, former judge, and political advisor Joseph Proskauer, a friend of Moses and enthusiastic rider, attempted to start a committee to raise private funds to pay for the needed maintenance, but other equestrians refused, insisting it was the city's responsibility. Moses wrote, "If we must choose between the poor and the well-to-do, I am for the poor, but after all, the well-to-do pay taxes and there is nothing wrong with riding horseback on bridle paths provided by the city for that purpose."[65] Moses finally scraped together the resources to oil the whole trail over the course of months, all the while pelted with complaints that horses, riders, and passersby were breathing unhealthy trail dust.[66]

For parts of the 1910s, 1920s, and 1930s—and indeed for much of the twentieth century—the Parks Department operated under fiscal austerity

Large crowd of white equestrians gathers at a corner of Central Park for a collective ride, 1927. In the 1920s and 1930s, equestrians organized group rides to gain visibility for horse culture and make the case for better maintenance of the bridal path. Courtesy of the Library of Congress, Prints and Photographs Division.

or conditions approaching it. The department's limited budget allocations made it difficult to address the needs and desires of all human and other-than-human New Yorkers, particularly for the city's oldest and largest park, with its many diverse features, at a time when the department was also trying to create additional smaller parks and playgrounds. Indeed, equestrians from Harlem also complained that Colonial Park north of 145th Street (now Jackie Robinson Park) was not only bereft of a bridle path but was also still being refurbished as of 1935.[67] This narrow park took up ten blocks between two major thoroughfares and provided an important retreat for Harlemites who lived farther from Central Park as well as for those who resided closer to Central Park but found Colonial Park more welcoming and less racially hostile.

In the clamor for more funding for parks, many constituencies with assorted interests called for attention and funding for their desires, and they could bolster their pleas by invoking the inherent value or uniqueness of a particular park feature, by citing the number of human users or their needs or by appealing to pity or sympathy for animals. Equestrians and birders called upon all of these justifications to demand support and preservation for the bridle paths and the Ramble, respectively. The latter rhetorical move, citing animal welfare, could be jarring at a time when other, marginalized humans—Black and queer New Yorkers—who used the same park features received little support themselves.[68]

"Imagine It": Horses, Black Women's Styles, and Access to Nature

The Great Migration brought a growing and diverse constituency of Black New Yorkers into debates about recreational space and access to nature. Scholar Saidiya Hartman called the movement an en masse "refusal of the plantation regime," a system that depended on oppressed labor and the denial of political rights to African Americans in the South.[69] Arrival in northern industrial cities immersed Black Americans in a new physical environment but an unfortunately familiar racial hierarchy—not encoded in the same kinds of laws as in the Jim Crow South but still violent and degrading. As historian Brian McCammack shows, parks and other outdoor recreation areas were important landscapes for migrants to connect with each other, with rural traditions, and with nature as they moved from farms in the south to northern cities.[70] In New York, as early as the 1910s, park commissioners noted the disparity of funding and attention to parks in Harlem versus the more southerly parts of Manhattan; even the northern end of Central Park received poorer care than its southern reaches.[71]

When they were available, public spaces could also be hazardous. Black women in New York during the early twentieth century, regardless of their socioeconomic status, faced frequent harassment simply for being present in public space; police often assumed that they were sex workers, and men of any race assumed that they were sexually available. Hartman observed, "For black women, there was no path through the city where they might avoid insult or obscene proposition." A moral panic arose over young, single women hailing from the rural South, whom many white Manhattanites and some elite Black Harlemites believed were either too naive or too sexually loose for the city. So, on top of the harassment, Black women felt pressure to regulate themselves and each other, including their use of space.[72] Women varied in the degree to which they despaired from or coped with the challenges of urban life, but the Black press often represented women as vulnerable, both physically and emotionally. An editorial in the *New York Age* in 1925 observed a rash of incidents in which men harassed, groped, and attempted to entrap Black women, including many who arrived in New York from smaller cities, rural areas, and the Caribbean. And of course, there was the constant grind of racial animus from whites. One woman who had recently arrived attempted to drown herself in Central Park's Harlem Meer, explaining upon her rescue that life in New York "was just like being in a den of beasts."[73] Often alone, afraid, and strapped for cash, working-class women new to the city likely faced the worst of the beasts. Harlem women of all classes endeavored to make safe and fulfilling places for themselves in the city where they could feel autonomy and control.

As historian Judith Weisenfeld argues, the Harlem YWCA attempted to create a safe space for single Black women who arrived in New York amid the Great Migration, and the institution also gave middle-class and affluent Black women an outlet for activism and a chance to help newcomers.[74] As we have seen, the Black women who first took equestrian classes with the Harlem YWCA in the 1920s enjoyed the park from a special and privileged vantage point atop a horse—and within Harlem society. At the same time, they also knew the potential risks of claiming space in ways that racist white park users and authorities found jarring. Clinton DeForest was known to Harlem YWCA women; he had sometimes performed drag shows for YW events, and his violent death was surely devastating for them, making the park seem all the more threatening. But many of these women were privileged in other ways, as neither newcomers nor poor women struggling with racist and brutal markets for jobs and housing. Few such women could have afforded lessons, even at the reduced price. Group lessons helped the YW reduce the price to one-quarter that of private lessons, but enrollment still came at a steep price that may have put them beyond the reach of many Harlem women.[75] At fifteen dollars for ten lessons, safety and exercise in the saddle would have been a luxury for all but Harlem's elite, unless those elites provided scholarships.[76] In 1925, *New York Age* reported typical incomes of twenty-five dollars per week among Harlem residents.[77]

Oscar Hauter operated the riding school on West Sixty-Sixth Street, from which the Harlem YW women would ride horses such as Glenarm and Sultan to the park. We know little about these horses themselves, but they were likely among those whom Hauter showed in New York and other cities. Hauter was one of many stable owners who actively pressed park administrators for better conditions on the bridle paths. He took intense interest in the paths and surrounding architecture, meticulously seeking out and addressing hazards that might harm his own or other owners' animals. His letters also reveal a generous and inviting if somewhat eccentric manner; in long, elegantly handwritten letters, he invited the park superintendent and, by the late 1930s, Robert Moses himself to visit his stable or join him for a ride. Hauter also complained about steep real estate assessments on the West Side.[78] In spite of the costs of maintaining the stable, Hauter's generosity also extended to the YWCA women, for whom he offered discounted riding prices.

The YWCA riding class enrolled such notable figures as Escobeda Sarreals, a Black YW leader, and Dr. Gertrude Curtis, New York's first

Black woman dentist and a patron of Black show business.[79] The first Black women riders from Harlem enjoyed the freedom of riding horses through the park, and equestrianism gradually gained popularity among Harlem elites and some middle-class residents over the next decade. As New York's Black elite class grew, more members of Harlem society sought the chance to ride in the park.

Over the next decade, some white stable owners and park users sought to exclude Black riders from the bridle paths. As an anonymous "socialite" wrote to the *Amsterdam News* in 1935, "There appears to exist an unwritten agreement between the various riding academies to have their steeds always conveniently engaged or not available when Harlemites apply for mounts."[80] From enslavement to more recent labor practices, white supremacy has long confined African Americans' relationships with horses.[81] Enslaved people trying to escape were pursued by mercenaries on horseback; some enslavers had Black boys race horses for their amusement, a practice that evolved into the sport of horse racing, which up until the twentieth century included many Black jockeys. As we have seen, in the early nineteenth century, New York City barred Black people from operating horse-and-cart businesses, but whites often employed Black boys and men as stable hands such as groomsmen caring for horses.[82] For some white New Yorkers, Black people riding horses for leisure were almost unheard of, and many surely found it even stranger to see Black women in the saddle. For some Harlem residents, this history of subordination through horses inspired an even greater desire to claim fulfilling relationships with horses. Furthermore, Harlemites showed renewed determination to enjoy public space after a civil uprising against over-policing heightened Black-white tensions in the spring of 1935.[83]

At least one Harlem entrepreneur saw an opportunity for business in this struggle over public space and nature. Frank Tucker, who grew up riding horses on his family's Virginia farm and spent part of the Great War training horses and riders in the mounted cavalry, catered to prominent Harlem physicians, journalists, restaurateurs, performing artists, and businesspeople. Frank Tucker's Riding Academy stabled "four spirited but well-trained thoroughbreds" named Rushing Nola, Lady Connie, Silver Queen, and Snoopy, eventually locating at West Sixty-Third Street—far from Harlem but still popular among residents of that neighborhood.[84]

Black women on horseback enjoyed connections with individual animals along with greater access to nature, healthy exercise, and a sense of freedom and autonomy. Women riders such as Barbara Deas, a millinery entrepreneur and designer, felt particularly drawn to Tucker's horse Snoopy. Snoopy had a special and curious endowment: she was said to be a "five-gait" horse, meaning she could go at a pace between a walk and a canter. Tucker also recommended Snoopy as the best mannered of his stable and therefore good for beginning riders like socialite Binga Dismond, who appreciated that Snoopy made it easier not to fall off. Dismond's clumsy early attempts on horseback earned her much teasing among friends. Other of Tucker's patrons, such as salon owner Joyce Robinson, were drawn to the tall, dark, handsome Rushing Nola.[85]

Few documents remain to help us understand these individual horses' experiences, but we have some clues to their temperaments and the environments that they learned to live and work in. Each had their own talents and personalities. Snoopy was gentle and tolerant, while Silver Queen could be "fiery" but was an award-winning prancer when Tucker showed her.[86] With a small stable, a lifetime of experience working with horses, and a strong interest in their continued well-being, Tucker surely formed close bonds with his animals and spent considerable time training them. Furthermore, the horses accommodated a rotation of different riders with varied skill levels and temperaments themselves, and they seemed to do so with affection toward the humans who hired them. Harlem socialites rode them in their leisure, but these were disciplined, working horses, who had to be trained to endure work in the city, an environment full of startling noises and sights, particularly in the age of automobiles. From Tucker's eventual location on the West Side, they had to cross busy Eighth Avenue to arrive at the park. Within the park, they learned to navigate the bridle path and endured its ever-changing, often degraded conditions: first the crumbling trail, then the sharp rocks, then the alternating mud and dust.[87]

Much like their white counterparts, Black equestrians and the media that covered them embraced the fashionable aspects of horse culture. They also relished upsetting whites' expectations about Black people and horses. The socialite who wrote anonymously for the *Amsterdam News* explained that the horseback riding "craze made its way up the seaboard from the nation's capital," where fashionable Black residents could be found "cantering along the banks of the Potomac to the dismay of a southern congressman." Like the writer who urged YW riders to "don your chic riding habit," the *Amsterdam News* writer shared sartorial advice from a Harlem sporting goods seller, which included, among other things, "a bowler hat, shirt and tie, or lightweight turtleneck-sweater" for ladies and a "soft hat, shirt and tie, and V-neck sweater" for gentlemen.[88] The anonymous socialite was likely either Maurice Dancer or Bessie Augusta, two of Harlem's most active and visible equestrians. Dancer, a controversial gossip columnist who directed Harlem's Turf Hunt Club, appeared in the social pages of the *Amsterdam News* himself with several women on horseback together on the trails. Bessie Augusta was bookkeeper of the Turf Hunt Club and a constant fixture on the bridle paths who also competed and performed in shows and promoted horse riding among her Harlem social circle.[89]

While the YW, Frank Tucker, Bessie Augusta, and Maurice Dancer helped open up the bridle paths as spaces for nature enjoyment, companionship, and fashionable display for relatively affluent Black Harlemites, some whites continued to seek out ways to keep equestrianism exclusive and claim the paths as a whites-only space. In June 1937, Pittsburgh's Black newspaper, the *Courier*, reported that "the bridle path in Central Park, New York, is luring a greater number of Harlem equestrians every week. Their presence has resulted in protests by whites."[90] Such protests might seem counterproductive for the efforts of other white Manhattan riders to show that equestrianism was an accessible sport suitable for public expenditure. However, inclusion of Black riders may not have helped riders' case either, as racist conditions in city politics would not have favored integration.

Those white riders who tried to edge out Black riders sometimes used style and appearance to exclude them. Not all riders from Harlem projected a preppy, conservative style in the park. The world-renowned performer Ethel Waters brought her own style to the bridle paths—joking, chatty, and flamboyant. A Harlem resident since 1919, Waters had toured in white and Black vaudeville circuits as a highly versatile performer. She sang jazz and the blues on Broadway, and her acting credits included stage and screen roles. She recorded dozens of singles in the 1920s and 1930s, becoming one of the most popular singers of those decades. By the mid-1930s, Waters was the star attraction at Harlem's Cotton Club. In 1937, the Cotton Club reopened in a new Midtown location, and Waters took up riding in Central Park, along with the chorus girls who performed with her nightly that spring. Waters and her fellow performers rode to let off steam and build camaraderie, exercising in nature between strenuous performances. She recalled to her biographer Donald Bogle that they laughed and talked loudly on the trail. She surely would have been one of the most recognizable equestrians in the park. When Waters and her fellow performing women first rode horses in Central Park, white riders and passersby gawked at them—which perhaps would have been the case regardless of their color on account of Waters's fame.[91] But fame does not explain the escalation of some white riders' efforts to force Waters and her colleagues off the bridle paths.

The Cotton Club had for much of its history allowed only white audiences to enjoy glamorous shows by Black musicians and dancers. Waters and her colleagues attempted to perform their own versions of sexuality onstage and in their private lives. Waters was bisexual and had performed in drag during her vaudeville days. White patrons took the Cotton Club's exotic staging, decor, and costumes as cues to sexualize Black women, affecting their ability to move through public space and define their sexuality and personhood for themselves offstage. Theater scholar James F. Wilson argues' that white audiences enjoyed a privileged vantage from which to "gawk" at Black performers of this era, "but they were not compelled to come into contact with them from their unobstructed and comfortable positions" in the social hierarchy.[92]

Wilson's observation helps explain what happened to Waters when she and her companions dared to take up space on the bridle path. In 1937, a group of unidentified white riders confronted Waters and her party along the path. When Waters refused to quit riding, the white riders sought to convince West Side Manhattan stables to deny Waters a horse and also asked the park police to detain her and her entourage. The park police answered that they needed proof of disorderly conduct to take action against the riders. Then the group announced a plan to boycott the Cotton Club if Waters did not cease to use the bridle paths, calling itself the Equestrian Club and claiming the same address as a West Side riding academy. The *Pittsburgh Courier*'s New York correspondent could not track down the conspirators against Waters; the riding academy's spokesman claimed they had used his institution's address without permission. Undeterred, Waters continued to ride and enjoy the bridle paths.[93]

"The Battle for the Ramble"

Black equestrians on the bridle paths connected with equine nature and the park landscape, sometimes enduring racist and often (hetero)sexist threats. Meanwhile, amid the Ramble's forest and birdsong, conditions for queer men were becoming more difficult. Increasingly, authorities framed homosexuality as a subversive threat to society and queer people as "perverts," as menacing as Communists. After World War II, a "Lavender Scare" accompanied the better-known Red Scare, in which members of Congress made a show of exposing suspected Communists and homosexuals, purging them from government agency staffs. Accusers often identified potential "subversives" by their appearance at known gay cruising sites and suspected them of being vulnerable to blackmail by foreign operatives.[94]

The purge's perpetrators framed queerness as undermining the moral order of postwar America. The 1948 Kinsey Institute report *Sexual Behavior in the Human Male* found evidence of widespread homosexuality and bisexuality among American men. Rather than allow these findings to normalize sexual variation, many in politics and media portrayed same-sex attraction as a weakness or temptation lurking around every corner, to be feared and resisted. In the early 1950s, the Eisenhower administration vowed to purge civil servants considered to be security risks, "cleaning house" by firing over two thousand "subversives."[95] Ludlow Griscom noted that his "clan" of birders had become "sane and normal" by the 1920s, enjoying help from the police and recognition for their birding prowess. By contrast, in the following decades, queer visitors faced shame, violence, threats of arrest, and even loss of livelihood and alienation from family just for appearing in the Ramble.

Civil service purges of gay men and lesbians began among Washington, DC–based State Department employees, but hostility to queer folks was growing in other cities such as New York with thriving queer communities. Vice squads squashed queer men's freedom in several New York public spaces, but plans to limit queer gathering in Central Park began more subtly. In 1955, Commissioner Robert Moses and Iphigene Ochs Sulzberger, philanthropist, civic activist, and a matriarch in the *New York Times* publishing dynasty, conceived an idea to welcome an often-forgotten population in the park while also imposing moral order in a landscape suffering physical decay.[96] The connection between physical and moral erosion was easy to make: lovers straying from the trail for a secluded tryst might trample herbaceous plants; the soil might become more compacted and delicate slopes more degraded with every rendezvous.

Amid heightened attention to children's spaces in New York City parks, some felt that elders were neglected. Sulzberger, Moses's friend and supporter who was active in the Central Park Association that also advocated support for the bridle paths, encouraged philanthropist Loula Lasker to help support the construction of a senior center in the Ramble. Lasker agreed to donate $250,000 from her sister's memorial foundation for the construction of the center, to be named the Florina Lasker Recreation Center. The Parks Department planned to supply additional funds for needs such as lighting, new access paths, and fencing. The plans would dramatically remake the environment of the Ramble for wildlife and all humans—queer folks, birders, queer birders, or more casual visitors—accustomed to using it. The plan would introduce a building on the site and a parking lot to serve it, along with recreational facilities such as croquet courses and a shuffleboard court. Outdoor tables would dot the area, and all of these facilities would necessitate clearing considerable vegetative cover from the Ramble.[97]

The Parks Department released plans for the Lasker Center in May 1955 to a swift and vociferous outcry from birders. Many affirmed that the there was much illegal activity in the area, including dangers for birders themselves, but emphasized the negative effects the development would likely have on birds. Indeed, plans show that considerable shelter and habitat would have been removed, resources that were important for species such as warblers and wood thrushes. By the 1950s, professional ornithologists and dedicated birders together had compiled several decades of systematic knowledge, passed down through generations, about the Ramble's importance for birds. As sociologist Elizabeth Cherry notes, birders employ their "naturalist gaze" to observe birds' behavior and use of habitat, which in turn informs conservation stances.[98] In the Lasker Center plans, New York birders saw an irrevocable loss for birds who require dense forest habitats. Birds that have limited sheltering requirements such as robins, mockingbirds, catbirds, and cardinals, who could already thrive in the park's meadows and groves with less understory vegetation, may have found it easy to take over the reordered niches of the space. Migrants may have spent less time there and been forced to seek

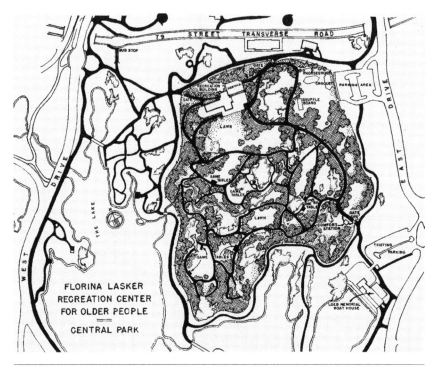

This proposed plan for the Florina Lasker Recreation Center would have placed features such as shuffleboard courts and picnic tables in the prime bird habitat of the Ramble, where bird lovers and lovers also gathered. The plan was released and also abandoned in 1955. Courtesy of the New York City Municipal Archives.

other stopovers; birds who nested there may have been more subject to brood parasitism by species such as cowbirds. Data collection about migrating birds would have been disrupted permanently. The Lasker Center likely would not have eliminated all birds from the area but would certainly have made it a more impoverished and unwelcoming environment for birds with few other options for stopover and nesting habitat. Birds that already had many places to rest and nest may have improved their lot, as the Lasker Center would have made the Ramble like other green but humanized landscapes that are already widespread enough to sustain these adaptable species—meadows, playgrounds, and maybe even the zoo within the park itself and farms, college campuses, and golf courses beyond it.[99]

Birders recognized the threat of Moses's plans to the unique avian community and also that their treasured recreation area would be destroyed. The plans threatened to end free access. A statement meant to reassure the bird-watching community explained that "serious bird watchers will be admitted at early hours of the morning during the migration periods and all orderly adults will be admitted at all times," but this was only more worrisome because it conveyed the degree to which the space would be policed.[100] Linnaean Society leaders met with Moses's deputy to attempt to negotiate a compromise plan for the center and the Ramble that would protect birds themselves along with birders' access.[101]

Moses's response that summer made clear that his plans were intended in part to exclude unwanted users. In a public statement designed to calm birders' worries, Moses explained that "the fencing, additional lighting and regular use of this part of Central Park as a recreation center for older people will make the Ramble, which has been the scene of muggings, acts of vandalism and other nuisances, once again a safe and pleasant place available to the public for the purpose for which it was originally intended." Birders criticized the fencing plan, and Sulzberger urged Moses to limit "interference with the . . . bird sanctuary." Moses answered that fences were "absolutely essential if the reconstructed area is to be maintained as a quite [*sic*] area for passive recreation, and if the conditions which originally made it attractive to birds are to be restored and preserved." Moses framed the senior center project as necessary to maintain the Ramble's physical and ecological integrity, including the birds whom the birding community was fighting for. He promised to "resist any improper invasion or misuse of the area" as it was "being eroded at an alarming rate" in the absence of city resources to replace damaged vegetation.[102]

If we consider this framing in the context of intensified crackdowns against queer men's use of public space and queer men's continued resistance and defiance of disorderly conduct policies that excluded them, notions of physical and ecological integrity take on new meanings. Moses's language is coded, but he hinted at whom he considered undesirable. Some New Yorkers were less circumspect in explaining why the renovation was needed. One rare birder who supported the plan wrote to Moses: "The Ramble used to be a delightful and safe area for nature lovers including bird watchers—much needed by those of us who must live in midtown Manhattan year round. During the past three or four years, however, this area has become more and more a hangout for bums, degenerates and sex perverts. . . . Few male bird watchers now dare venture into the Ramble in early morning, which is the time most birds go through."[103] This writer's focus on male birders was notable, as discourse had often focused on women's vulnerability to crime in the Ramble. For those who kept their language subtle, "erosion" of the Ramble was not only a geological process but also a social one. Indeed, one New Yorker who wrote to Moses in support of the Lasker Center testified that the plan would make the "moral environment cleaner."[104] For many supporters of the Lasker Center, queer enjoyment of the landscape in Central Park violated the idea of pure "natural" spaces, where humans could admire nature but not pursue other desires.[105]

Moses also defended his record as a supporter of avian life in the city against birders who claimed park space through their defense of birds. Early in his administration, Moses had used New Deal funding to create three small bird sanctuaries in Central Park as well as a larger preserve for birds on Staten Island. Moses touted these pro-bird achievements, stating that "the Department of Parks has demonstrated many times its concern for the preservation of areas attractive to birds and other wild life."[106] That Moses felt the need to prove himself an ally of birds showed the power of birders and other environmentalists to command attention; they had become a formidable constituency of middle- and upper-class New Yorkers. These humans claimed to speak for birds in their fight against Moses's plans; preservationist groups as far away as Massachusetts and Pennsylvania even joined the call to stop the Lasker Center. One letter from a former New

CHAPTER 4

York birder explained at length that while she and fellow birders would also lose out, birds deserved the greatest mercy. "I still have friends in New York whose soul saving recreation is birdwatching in the Ramble," she pleaded. "If you have no pity on the humans who crave and need more such space—not less—have pity on God's feathered friends." Kathleen Skelton of the Linnaean Society even lobbied the mayor to intervene on behalf of the birds.[107]

The *Times* dubbed the entire affair "the battle of the Ramble," and the birders won just before ground was to be broken in late November 1955.[108] Queer Ramble visitors might have won too. They would not have to see a cherished gathering place cleared of sheltering vegetation, flooded with nighttime lighting, and replaced by horseshoe pits—though perhaps these new obstacles may have made cruising there an even more thrilling sport. With their outcry against Moses's plans, the Central Park birders inadvertently protected gay men's access to the space from what would have been an immediate and forceful curtailment of territory. However, gay men's lot declined in other ways. Some birders and landscape advocates called for more policing, an ongoing threat to gay men's safety and peace in the park. The Garden Club recognized that the Lasker Center was designed in part to make the area feel safer and specifically endorsed heightened policing: "A compromise on this question is easily available—namely, use a fraction of the funds needed for the fence to assign special guards to the Ramble."[109] Indeed, in subsequent months, park authorities launched more forceful efforts to expel queer men from the Ramble. By July 1956, the *Times* reported on aggressive new policing activities directed at "homosexuals" in this section of the park.[110] Rape and theft did happen in the park, including the Ramble, but the *Times*, park authorities, and police profiled queer men as dangerous criminals. In reality, crime rates in the park only picked up in the following decade, but homophobia and perceptions of crime empowered park police under Moses to take a hard line on surveillance of behaviors and people deemed out of place.[111]

Children feed ducks in one of the nature sanctuaries created by Robert Moses's parks administration, 1942. This sanctuary is in the southeastern portion of the park. Courtesy of the Museum of the City of New York.

Reports on the crackdown in Central Park emphasized the wild land-scape of the Ramble and other locales and police officers' need for horses to help root out criminals. The *Times* reported: "The police patrolled wooded areas so dense they are known as 'jungles,' they climbed steep hills, circled rocky crags and trudged along open meadows. Sections too deep to be traveled on foot were patrolled by ten mounted policemen." Moses fixated on the difficulties of controlling human activities in this wild landscape to achieve standards of moral and physical cleanliness. He told the *Times*: "The remote and interior regions of our larger parks are not safe at night. Some are even unsafe in daytime."[112]

Gay men continued to frequent the Ramble, but the heightened po-licing around this and other gay gathering spots in the 1950s, coincid-ing with the peak of the Lavender Scare, suppressed the community's visibility. Yet at the same time, groups such as the Mattachine Society organized as a political voice for queer people, challenging authorities' attempts to exclude them from the public sphere. Such organizations also challenged the stereotype that gay men were lonely and isolated, without community.[113] The Ramble remained an important place to uphold that community, in a setting that also gave queer folks special access to birds, picturesque landscapes, and other nature lovers.

Expanding the Park's More-than-Human Publics

The Ramble is far from the only urban public space whose seclusion has invited wildlife *and* romantic trysts. Geographer Matthew Gandy has explored a more recent case in London's Abney Park Cemetery, where vegetation grew wild after the owners abandoned it. Birders, butterfly watchers, and other wildlife advocates came to know the space as a haven for many species otherwise rare in the city. Meanwhile, men seeking com-panionship and sex with men—particularly older men, immigrants, and others who felt excluded from London's gay club scene—could also find secluded meeting spaces. According to Gandy, these two groups have, since the 1990s, formed a sense of alliance and shared purpose around the preservation of the cemetery's dense shrubbery and minimally disturbed, unsurveilled landscape, a rare such space in a city where much vegetation has been removed to open unobstructed views for security cameras.[114]

There is little evidence that Central Park's birding community formed such an alliance with the community of gay and bisexual men who met in and around the Ramble during the twentieth century. Some visitors to the Ramble, though, embodied multiple identities. Christian Cooper calls himself a Black, queer "bird nerd," though he prefers not to cruise where he birds.[115] Queer and Black New Yorkers seized park spaces to claim their joy and sense of belonging in public and in nature, but Central Park's administrators, the city government that allocated its budget, and visitors committed to their own style of park use curtailed pluralistic and open uses of public space. At a moment of increasingly visible human difference in the park, animal spaces became battlegrounds where white supremacist and heteronormative users attempted to maintain hegemony over the landscape. But urban public spaces served vital and diverse functions for humans and other creatures, including a sense of freedom and belonging. Limiting access and funding to maintain these spaces for plural publics carried dire costs for society and ecology—Black New Yorkers' and queer New Yorkers' claims to space. Many scholars and writers have called for a "queer ecology" movement that extends radical empathy to counter rigid ideas of who and what belongs in natural landscapes.[116] Similarly, Black ecology scholars criticize white supremacists' hierarchy of being and call for its abolition in favor "a deep sense of commonality and even comradeship" among humans and across species, to quote ecocritic Joshua Bennett.[117] Perhaps Harlem equestrians and Frank Tucker felt this sense while playing and working with horses. The bridle paths and the Ramble show there is much room to expand imaginations of urban nature and who belongs there—birds and horses who were unusual in the big city, along with humans whose styles, affects, and identities did not match those of dominant nature lovers.

CHAPTER 4

The struggle for the bridle paths and the battle of the Ramble are two relatively brief moments that tell us much about how animal lovers seized power in struggles for public space. White, (presumably) straight protesters raised loud voices for themselves and for animals, and although it took months of resistance, their demands were eventually heard, in part because they knew and cared for animals considered vulnerable in the city. Black equestrians like Bessie Augusta and Ethel Waters and hundreds of gay men who faced dire threats in the Ramble had to struggle for their own recognition as members of the polity.[118] For these New Yorkers, simply occupying public space was a kind of protest in itself that required sustained bravery in the face of exclusion and aggression. They were not (only) studious birders staring into the trees or horse riders in English costume; they brought to the park their own styles that were often too flamboyant or just "other"—the wrong color, the wrong sexuality in a space conceived as mostly white and straight.

While humans who have been marginalized from public spaces demand radical empathy, these stories also point to the ways nonhumans—both animals and the physical environment—may be affected by park management practices that are austere or ignore ecology. Horses felt the stab of gravel in their feet and the sting of dust in their noses, throats, and lungs, the discomfort of being unable to exercise. City budgets had neglected the places where horses worked, much as the parks budget neglected Harlem overall. Birds like warblers and wood thrushes never suffered the effects of the Lasker Center, but they might have lost the important sheltering acres of the Ramble or reduced ability to seek food and nesting territory had the Ramble been gutted. Many birds' embodied energy budgets operate on thin margins, and any increased energy spent seeking food or shelter may reduce their fitness. Furthermore, it was not just Manhattan's increased population but also reduced budgets that deprived the park environment of needed maintenance. Soils held and nourished plants' roots and were the medium for rainfall infiltration; soils also required fertilizers and aeration to maintain their condition amid increased human use. In turn, plants, dependent upon soils for their health, formed the basis of urban food webs that fed birds and other wildlife. Queer and Black folks demanded space in the city, while communities of nonhumans—horses, birds, trees, and even soil—became visible parts of the urban polity, hailing the city to make space and care for all.

CHAPTER 5

Modern Childhood and Modern Captivity

On December 2, 1934, park superintendent W. Earle Andrews and Mayor Fiorello LaGuardia officially opened a new zoo on the site of Central Park's original menagerie. Some twelve hundred guests, most of them children, crowded into the site, while several thousand other humans stood outside the gate, all shepherded by two hundred police officers. They witnessed a boisterous and eclectic ceremony. Former governor Al Smith, renowned for his love of animals, was named honorary night superintendent of the zoo, a position he could easily fulfill from his home just across Fifth Avenue. A New Deal official praised the swift efforts of the Works Progress Administration (WPA) employees who brought the zoo into being. A boy presented a turkey to the mayor. The welfare commissioner sang an energetic rendition of "The Animal Fair," and Superintendent Andrews's young daughter rode up in a miniature carriage drawn by a pony to deliver an oversized, engraved key to the mayor. LaGuardia unlocked the picture book–shaped doors of the zoo; children and adults spilled in. Smith and his grandchildren fed the buffalo; the mayor and his family clamored toward the monkey house. Robert Moses missed celebrating the crowning achievement of his first year as parks commissioner, confined at home with a cold, but his hopes for a squeaky-clean, family-friendly attraction set the stage.[1]

The event was so whimsical and fun, one could almost forget the suffering and sacrifices the Great Depression had wrought on American children. Indeed, that was part of the point: New Deal spending promised to resume the advances begun in Progressive era children's programs, allowing more children to "have a childhood," to quote a maxim dating to Victorian era child welfare institutions.[2] The Depression had interrupted this seeming progress; at its nadir, one in five children in New York City were malnourished.[3] The new zoo was one of Moses's many answers to the perils of childhood in New York, designed to leverage public resources to create spaces for good, clean fun.[4] In this case, the Parks Department employed exotic animals to transport children into a fanciful story land designed by architect Aymar Embury II. They even claimed the title of "zoo," at last shedding the "menagerie" epithet that had long cast the exhibit into a category beneath those in the Bronx and Philadelphia.

The version of happy childhood offered by the new zoo depended upon animals' liveliness, which often conflicted with other concerns in the city. Reveling in his honorary position during the opening ceremony, former governor Smith proclaimed: "If you people hear any roaring in the zoo at night that sounds like lions and tigers, you needn't be afraid. It'll just mean that I'm on the job talkin' to 'em."[5] Smith was joking, but within a year, he fielded complaints from neighbors about sea lions barking throughout the night. Zoo authorities scrambled to ask their peers across North America whether surgery could quiet them. The sea lions were likely voicing their hunger, but authorities' impulse to surgically alter them showed their willingness to manipulate animals to keep humans both entertained and comfortable in a dense urban environment.[6]

In addition to its promises for children, the New Deal funded work-relief agencies to improve the landscape of animal captivity in Central Park and other zoological collections across the country.[7] The picture-book zoo, so called because of its book-shaped gates, aligned with changes that Moses planned throughout the parks system and New York in general. Like his playgrounds and pools, the aesthetic emphasized cleanliness and sound management. Moses was determined to expand access to new spaces for recreation that would cement playfulness as a quality of modern, urban childhood. This chapter argues that adults designed and managed a zoo that celebrated the thrill of encountering exotic animals in large part to advance a liberal vision of a smoothly functioning and prosperous city, the kind of place where middle-class parents would want to raise kids. However, like many of Moses's urban planning schemes, the clean and appealing surface concealed a degree of manipulation that would later horrify some members of the public. And like other examples of zoo reform, it was rapidly followed by new ideas about how animals ought to be displayed.[8]

A Crumbling but Popular Menagerie amid Urban Change

To appreciate the changes that New Deal funding brought to captive animals in the park, it will help to review the state of the exhibit in the first three decades of the twentieth century. These decades show the ways the Central Park Menagerie embodied urban change, both in its physical condition and in the way varied urban human constituencies thought about it.[9] As we have seen, from the first days of Central Park, the menagerie in and surrounding the old Arsenal building had been a makeshift affair but one beloved by the multitudes, including many poor and working-class immigrants. After repeated failures to construct a zoological garden more aligned with scientific ambitions and Central Park's landscape design, the Bronx Zoo finally achieved these loftier visions at the turn of the twentieth century. Attention to and investment in captive animals from scientists, conservationists, and more elite audiences shifted to the Bronx in 1899 with funding from a new New York Zoological Society.[10] New York City itself was growing, incorporating boroughs including the Bronx. For the Parks Department, this necessitated a more complex structure and distributed budgets for managing public green space.

The Central Park Zoo was left as ever in perpetual decay. The buildings themselves were falling apart, and authorities were painfully aware of how the exhibit paled in comparison to the Bronx Zoo just a train ride, but also an admissions fee, away. In 1919, the parks director for the Borough of Manhattan, Francis Gallatin, pleaded with the mayor for funding to fix the animals' accommodations. For example, "one side of the lion's cages was in such a condition that an animal might easily have . . . broken through," Gallatin lamented, detailing repairs intended to shore up the big cats' cages along with the elephant house. Furthermore, he explained, "the collection of animals had fallen below par. I have by trading, by sale, and by purchase increased the variety. . . . When they [arrive], the collection will be very creditable though not, of course, comparable with the collections of the great Zoological gardens."[11] Gallatin got the new animals and the repairs, but as with other aspects of park rehabilitation, new investments barely kept pace with decades of deferred maintenance.

Gallatin's repairs sought primarily to protect the public from escaping animals, rather than improving animals' comfort; keepers still stashed guns nearby in case of a breakout. Animals themselves repeatedly drew attention to dire safety breaches, as when honking geese warned keepers of a fire in the bison barn in 1926.[12] That year, a consultant called for increased funding for the zoo, praising its "many valuable specimens" but warning that the buildings "constitute a fire hazard and should be removed and be replaced by buildings of stone or concrete of a sanitary type."[13] Such descriptions were reminiscent of the Tenement Commission's warnings about human habitations in New York some twenty years earlier. Indeed, working-class and poor New Yorkers still struggled to afford adequate housing, while growing communities of Black New Yorkers faced the brunt of a segregated housing market.[14]

In addition to the monetary and geographic accessibility of the menagerie, its landscape and design also differed from those of the new Bronx Zoo, in ways parallel to differences between central city and suburban housing for humans. Automobiles were starting to open up suburbs beyond even New York's new boroughs, with dramatically lower densities and more private green space than the city proper.[15] As we have seen, the Bronx Zoo defined the ideal of zoological parks; its 250 acres featured many "habitats," not the small, simple cages that dominated the menagerie. On the other hand, the menagerie fit with Central Park's growing emphasis on recreational activities in the park overall, although these brought more wear-and-tear on the landscape and objections from supporters of the Greensward plan's naturalism.[16] Small cages brought human crowds and other-than-human captives into stark proximity, where the latter performed their hippo-ness or monkey-ness right before spectators' eyes, ears, and noses.[17] Meanwhile, in the Bronx, zoological director William Hornaday insisted on the collection's educational and conservation value. Hornaday believed that zoo spaces should be big enough that "the sense of confinement is either lost or greatly diminished, yet at the same time sufficiently limited that the animals are not inaccessible or invisible to the visitor."[18]

Animals at the menagerie remained objects of a degree of public adoration that contrasted with the dangerous, curtailed conditions to which such affection confined them. Menagerie animals became familiar cultural touchstones for New Yorkers, living symbols animating humor and pathos, tragedy and struggle, gender and race. Births became opportunities to marvel at the virtues of motherhood, as when the *Times* cooed over hippo Fatima's new calf; successful hippo births in captivity were rare.[19] Illness and death could bring a shared sense of loss to city dwellers who seemed to empathize more with charismatic nonhuman beings than with human New Yorkers. Gallatin noted after the death in 1922 of Hattie the elephant—to whom keepers administered a daily "medicinal" quart of whiskey during the early Prohibition years—that "few men can hope that their illness will excite so general an interest."[20]

The occasional escaped animal (so long as it was not dangerous) provoked comical chases as media conjured absurd contrasts between wildness and the urban landscape, as in 1932 when a fox leaped a fence only to be chased down by keepers and equestrians, who seized the rare chance to cheer "tally-ho!"[21] The growing public transit system eased movement across Greater New York, allowing visitors to return frequently for the free attraction. One early-twentieth-century menagerie director observed that some New Yorkers visited "almost every day for years"—suggesting a great attachment to and curiosity about the animals, in spite of the shabby conditions in which they were kept.[22] With their constant presence, visitors who felt attached to these animals ensured that public and donor funding would continue at some level, although less than what was needed to keep the facilities in good shape.

Black media, like its white counterparts, used zoo stories for colorful filler and often drew parallels between familiar experiences of discrimination or marginalization and the lives of caged animals. In 1924, for example, the *New York Age* reported the birth of a baby monkey but lamented that keepers separated the baby from its father. According to the reporter, the father paced his enclosure cradling an armful of straw instead of his infant.[23] The reporter surely saw in this monkey's response parallels to the scourge of family separation among African Americans under historic enslavement and contemporary incarceration.[24] The menagerie was not only an allegory for human struggles, however; Harlem Renaissance authors also associated it with fun, leisure, and human-animal attachments. Later, in his semiautobiographical novel *Go Tell It on the Mountain*, James Baldwin imagined his fictionalized parents traveling from Harlem to the menagerie to feed peanuts to the elephants in the early 1920s.[25] Harlem's *Amsterdam News* also used menagerie creatures as symbols of wildness and other characteristics, showing that this attraction over fifty blocks to the south of the city's Black mecca held wide cultural currency.[26]

However, a few years before Moses took the helm of the park system, Black media and activists responded very differently from white media and park staff when the menagerie allowed the young African employees of two famous animal collectors to live on-site. Known in the media by just one name each, Aussayne and Manuelli, from Uganda and Kenya, respectively, accompanied Martin and Osa Johnson from Nairobi to New York in the summer of 1931.[27] The Johnsons were an American celebrity couple, global adventurers who brought locations from the Solomon

Islands to the Serengeti to American audiences via films, photography, children's books, and other media, combining exoticism and sensationalism with a touch of natural history. They also acquired both live animals for sale to zoos and skins to display at the American Museum of Natural History, where curator Carl Akeley was one of their patrons.[28] On a sojourn in New York to promote their upcoming film, *Congorilla*, Aussayne and Manuelli accompanied the Johnsons as caregivers for eight live animals they had acquired in Central and East Africa and planned to sell stateside—two adult gorillas, one infant gorilla, two chimps, two monkeys, and a cheetah.[29] The Central Park Menagerie housed this small group of animals for a few months, and caregivers Aussayne and Manuelli ended up sleeping in the apes' pen, across from Chang the elephant, while the Johnsons stayed at the Moritz Hotel.[30] Twenty-five years earlier, Black activists had protested the exhibition of a Mbuti (pygmy) man named Ota Benga by the Bronx Zoo under William Hornaday. To journalists in Harlem as well as other Black New Yorkers, Aussayne and Manuelli's situation looked all too similar.[31]

In New York, Aussayne and Manuelli navigated an urban world of stark racial hierarchy with some commonalities and some differences from the racism they knew as subjects of empire in East Africa. Patronizing and infantilizing language was one commonality. We have no knowledge of how Aussayne and Manuelli defined themselves with reference to Euro-American constructs of childhood and adulthood. Whites applied such ideas inconsistently across race and empire. White media and the Johnsons often referred to them as "boys," which was how Martin Johnson addressed any group of Black males, such as the many Kenyan and Ugandan men who schlepped equipment and tended to their retinue's campsites. Some whites accused the Johnsons of treating Africans too liberally, but films such as *Congorilla*, which featured an extended sequence in the Ituri forest with a Mbuti community, portrayed Indigenous people as backward curiosities.[32] Martin called the Mbuti "little guys" and asserted that their intellectual and physical development halted at age ten.[33] An *Amsterdam News* reporter, Henry Lee Moon, helped connect Aussayne and Manuelli with Pan-African activists in Harlem who helped them demand better wages and homestay housing outside the menagerie. Martin Johnson believed they were being led astray; he enlisted a Central Park food vendor and a police officer to keep his employees from visiting Harlem again.[34] Scoping out their work situation, a concerned reader of the *Amsterdam News* reported that crowds of white visitors paid more attention to Aussayne and Manuelli than to the gorillas they cared for, gawking at and mocking them "as if they had never seen a Negro before."[35]

Officials took great pains to keep Aussayne and Manuelli, during their brief stay in New York, near the menagerie in their role as spectacularly entrapped workers, limiting their exposure to Harlem's crucible of Black liberation and anti-racist, anti-colonial activism. The men returned to East Africa in October of that year.[36] Assisted by their advocates in Harlem, they tried to visit the Black Mecca one last time the day they departed; their minders appointed by Johnson attempted to restrain them, an incident the *Times* used for comic filler. Months later, the *Times* also reported that they had cursed their police minder's dog.[37] White people portrayed the young men as childlike and backward as justification for denying them access to critiques of the city's racial and spatial hierarchy. As for the apes the two men had tended, Osa Johnson reported that they went on to live happy lives at zoos in Florida and California.[38]

Children, Animals, and the New Deal

Martin Johnson tried to limit Aussayne and Manuelli to the role of workers and exhibits, but park authorities and patrons had long centered children (perhaps mostly white children) in their visions of animated urban landscapes. From the park's origins, advocates for the virtues of the Greensward plan touted the healthful and educational benefits of contact with wild animals, complained that the makeshift menagerie sapped its

CHAPTER 5

inmates of their wildness, and promised a better zoo, someday, as an educational institution in conjunction with the public schools.[39] When the New York Zoological Society finally established its park in the Bronx, zoo advocates remained focused on natural history education.[40] Yet the Parks Department emphasized play with actual playgrounds as well as festivals encroaching on the Sheep Meadow and other Central Park features. Robert Moses used New Deal funding to further entrench this trend by shaping a playful environment for children around animals.

In the early 1930s, when President Roosevelt's New Deal paid millions of workers to rebuild urban landscapes across the United States, distinct ideals shaped zoo architecture in the dozens of American menageries that were rebuilt or constructed from scratch. Those who imagined, designed, and ran the new zoos still focused on children, but ideas about what zoo animals could and should provide for children had shifted. The new Central Park Zoo exemplified these trends, offering a seemingly endless series of ways for children to engage with animals but few of the lessons in natural history, taxonomy, and biogeography promised at the origins of Central Park or carried out in the actual Bronx Zoo. Ideas about presenting animals in a natural or scientific context were set aside for the pure thrill of close contact with wild beasts.[41] Park administrators seemed to finally accept the types of animal encounters the menagerie had always hosted, and that many New Yorkers seemed to want, but supplied cleaner, modern buildings for this purpose.

Exotic thrills and raucous hilarity marked New Deal–era zoo projects' appeal for their youthful intended audience. Historian Daniel Bender argues that zoos of this era competed with other ways of displaying wildlife, such as circuses and staged adventure films like the Johnsons' *Congorilla*, which were often made by the same people who collected animals from around the world to place on display in America. For people like the Johnsons who dealt in small numbers of animals, animal collection was a losing business because of the high monetary (not to mention moral) costs of wresting creatures like gorillas, rhinos, and tigers from their homes and keeping them alive until their sale to buyers such as zoos. Instead, the Johnsons banked on endorsements, traveling exhibits, and films; the latter two offered audiences spectacular and comical animal sights in settings of staged exoticism. The new urban zoos also promised exoticism and animal comedy along with constant, proximate access to animals in hopes of winning back visitors (and, in zoos that charged admission, revenues) from movie houses and circuses.[42] Furthermore, with New Deal funding, the architecture and animals themselves embodied the power and resources of a strong federal welfare state, making cities sites of free leisure consumption.

As of 1934, Moses insisted that he have charge of parks across the boroughs. Indeed, his Parks Department hoped to offer an animal exhibit in every borough—Moses counted the Zoological Society's semipublic Bronx Zoo—putting thousands of unemployed men to work and creating new habitats that would need to be filled with animals. By late 1934, Central Park's new zoo opened its picture book–shaped gates, and Prospect Park's zoo welcomed its first guests in 1935. Staten Island's Barrett Park Zoo was run under different management, and plans for a zoo in Queens went on hold until the 1960s. Thus, Moses fell short of his aim of having a zoo in each borough, but he brought many New Yorkers of all ages closer to nonhuman animals to whom they otherwise would have had little access, under conditions that looked and smelled much better, and were likely safer for humans, than the shabby old menagerie.

Moses, New Deal officials, and the media trumpeted that a team of architects and draftsmen, employed by the Works Progress Administration, conceived and designed the new Central Park Zoo in just fourteen days. All the while, zoo officials emptied the menagerie's cages, sometimes by temporary or permanent "disposal"—seeking new homes for the animals, whether at the Bronx Zoo or in private collections—or by "destruction," killing the animals. Hundreds more workers tore down existing cages and built new ones. The zoo architecture and aesthetic were modern; animal sculptures echoed the glorious human forms gracing other New Deal creations, like the *Winged Figures of the Republic* on the Hoover Dam. Concrete blocks housed each animal grouping, with iron bars enclosing cages for the larger animals within each house and wire enclosures for the smaller creatures. Like the many zoos that received New Deal funding in the mid-1930s, the Central Park Zoo became a space where hundreds of unemployed men earned wages for several months drafting designs, demolishing old buildings, moving earth, pouring concrete, aligning bars, chiseling monkeys in limestone, paving paths, and planting shrubbery in preparation for the nonhumans and humans to come.[43]

By employing adult men in construction and providing leisure entertainment for children and families, the new zoo seemed to restore a trend in American imaginations of childhood. The United States was imagined to guarantee heightened states of innocence and leisure for children in ever-upwardly-mobile families. In spite of such optimistic projections of the American dream onto childhood, inequality among families and children persisted. Furthermore, the state, rather than some invisible hand of the market, was responsible for driving those improvements that did come to fruition.[44] Generations of New York children had worked to support themselves and their families. Former governor Al Smith, for example, had dropped out of school after eighth grade and his father's death and worked at the Fulton Fish Market. Motivated in part by his personal history, Smith promoted policies to improve children's lives and expand access to an array of public services.[45] His protégé Moses joined him in promoting progressive reforms and good government during Smith's gubernatorial administration in the 1920s. Rising consumerism and standards of living had facilitated cultural beliefs that childhood should be a special time of life protected from the cares of the world, but the Depression had exposed even many affluent children to hardship and want. Of course, working-class children had long needed wages to support themselves and their families, and now they could not find work.[46]

The Depression deprived adults of waged work and thus deprived young people of the promise of easier childhoods; lack of work for children also worsened family hardship. Childhood hunger soared, particularly among the working class and children of color, and many families broke up as members, including young people, went on the road in search of wages.[47] The New Deal remade the public sphere as a source of meaningful waged work for adults *and* supplied funding to create shared spaces where children could enjoy leisure. Federal programs and an emboldened labor movement reduced youth competition for positions with their elders, as federal law restricted child labor in public contracts and the private sector in the 1930s; more jurisdictions also mandated school attendance.[48] Entertainment businesses clamored to capture the emerging youth market, absorbing children's leisure with inexpensive comic books and matinee shows. The New Deal promised that this generation of children would become leisured consumers, and exotic zoo animals joined the many public goods marshaled by an amalgam of the state, workers, and business.[49]

In New York, Moses expanded publicly funded recreation as part of this leisure turn. In addition to the new zoo, the Parks Department built twenty-two new playgrounds in Central Park by the end of the decade, where there had been just a few before. Moses also oversaw the construction of hundreds of other playgrounds outside of Central Park and public pools throughout New York City, and his administration offered myriad programs to help families and children enjoy these new public spaces.[50] While recent scholarship has questioned stories of Moses's discrimination against Black New Yorkers in recreation settings, Moses did displace and marginalize Black communities in the realms of housing and development as part of his broader aim to impose order and harmony through top-down city planning. He was certainly aware that the city was becoming proportionately more Black and less white and that perceptions (often racist) of crime and disorder might lead white middle-class New Yorkers to leave for the suburbs. These race- and class-based visions of the city help explain the kind of atmosphere he established in the zoo.[51]

As Moses tapped into WPA funding in the 1930s, he was inspired by his mentor Smith's love of zoo creatures, along with Smith's commitment to giving more New Yorkers immediate access to animals.[52] These ambitions for Central Park's zoo were not unique. New zoos across the country offered up-close and immediate visual pleasures. At the Central Park Zoo, railings separated spectators from the animals' cages, but curious children and adults could lean over or hang from bars nearly face-to-face with monkeys, llamas, and bison. Inside the cages, lions, bears, and elephants found little space to hide. Keepers could close the doors to the inner chamber of these large creatures' cages, leaving the animals to spend their days on concrete floors, perhaps lined with straw, in plain sight of thousands of humans who filed through the buildings each day.[53] Other animal features of New York parks were far less accessible to the casual visitor. During the Bronx Zoo's first few decades, brochures, guides, architecture, and animal groupings asked visitors of all ages to learn about the geography and natural history of the animal world.[54] A child such as the young Ludlow Griscom—who enjoyed ample leisure time and familial resources—might take years to learn to distinguish trills or color markings to identify bird species in the Ramble.[55] The reconstituted Central Park Zoo contrasted with the trend toward scientific zoos (including not only the Bronx Zoo but also the National Zoo in Washington, DC) and other animal-related leisure pursuits in the park in the extreme ease of access to exotic creatures. Once the picture-book gates opened, all were welcome to take in the sights. The new zoo placed animals in an easily comprehensible world constructed to delight and entertain children so strained by the Depression, and it asked little of children in return.

Filling the Cages

Amid the upheaval of the old menagerie's demolition and the new zoo's construction, the Parks Department began to rebuild its animal collection—and to build a following of youthful animal enthusiasts, sometimes one child at a time. For weeks that early spring of 1934, Tommy Sarnoff, age seven, had been reading up on wallabies in anticipation of a gift from an overseas associate of his father. Media mogul David Sarnoff, president of the Radio Corporation of America and television pioneer, arranged for his Australian colleague's gift to arrive at Central Park, "for reasons obvious to any urban family," the *Times* explained.[56] Namely, urban families mostly lacked the outdoor space to satisfy any pet, particularly ones so ill-suited to domestication. The elder Sarnoff had himself worked his way up through media businesses, starting as a newspaperboy, to support his immigrant family in New York—and now his youngest son enjoyed a very different sort of childhood. Not everyone could achieve the Sarnoffs' social standing and wealth, but their upward mobility reiterated an increasingly familiar story about the lives parents hoped to give to their children.[57]

A wallaby pair had traveled across the Pacific in a crate, landing in Los Angeles, where the female was rumored to have given birth before their transcontinental journey to Manhattan. When the pair finally arrived in early April, the new zoological consultant and a keeper released the two adult marsupials into a cage within the Lion House, across from a black bear named Maggie. (Some early buildings were already finished; the architect's daughter, six-year-old Judith Embury, had laid the first cornerstone.) Upon hearing of the wallabies' arrival, the youngest Sarnoff demanded to see them. Tommy was allowed inside the cage, but the wallabies refused the carrots he offered. Meanwhile, onlookers wondered where the baby was. The zoological consultant insisted that the joey must be in the female's pouch but that no one should disturb her until she had acclimated to her new surroundings. Tommy promised to return frequently and teach the wallabies tricks once they settled in, even though they seemed to ignore him on his first visit. No one reminded Tommy Sarnoff—who may have known from his books already—or *Times* readers that marsupials are born smaller than a worm and use only their tiny front leg buds to crawl from the mother's cloaca into her pouch to find warmth and milk. The moment seemed ripe for some natural history education,

This pair of wallabies traveled from Australia to New York as a gift for a media executive's child; the family gave them to the new Central Park Zoo in 1934. © Wildlife Conservation Society. Reproduced by permission of the WCS.

but the *Times* instead focused its story on Tommy Sarnoff's breathless excitement and the oddity of a child interacting with wallabies.[58]

The consultant who deflected calls to inspect the female wallaby's pouch was Captain Ronald Cheyne-Stout. Born in Maine in 1895, Cheyne-Stout had commanded a squadron in the British Royal Air Force in India during the Great War, gaining international experience that informed his later work gathering animals from around the world for exhibit by New York's Parks Department.[59] Moses first appointed

Cheyne-Stout as zoological consultant for the department in 1934 during the early phases of the zoo-building program and then promoted him to director of menageries for Central and Prospect Parks later that year. If Tommy Sarnoff's antics with the wallabies epitomized the new zoo's idealization of close encounters between children and animal, then Cheyne-Stout embodied the sleight-of-hand required to conjure animal spectacles while concealing the perils of zoo keeping from youthful audiences. Such acts of concealment were central to the job of zoo management and, in some ways, planning the city itself. The baby wallaby might have been in its mother's pouch, but if it was not, Tommy and the *Times* reporter would have witnessed a sad indicator of the stress of global travel for animals.

In his tenure as director of menageries, Cheyne-Stout moved living creatures around the world and among New York's zoos (especially Central and Prospect Parks and to some extent the Bronx Zoo) and numerous other public and private collections. He was driven by similar imperatives and attitudes toward animals as his peers at zoos across the United States and around the world. Zoo directors worked daily to coax from their charges the liveliness they believed audiences expected while also enforcing the life-altering experience of captivity. Like the wallabies, many zoo animals traveled in confinement for weeks to creep cautiously into a world of concrete and iron, isolated from their wild communities and surrounded by unfamiliar creatures.

Contemporary zookeepers and zoo advocates insisted that captivity was a safer and more salubrious condition than wildness. Dr. Edward Hindle of the Zoological Society of London wrote of his experiences at the Regent Park Zoo in the 1940s: "Some extremists regard even the most up to date zoological gardens as little better than prison establishments. This view completely ignores the fact that the great majority of these animals are far healthier and better fed than those in the wild, and also have a longer average life."[60] In addition to the consistent feeding long provided by menageries and zoos, the growth of veterinary medicine meant that zoos could increasingly offer antibiotic treatment and sanitation to clear parasites and prevent reinfection. Furthermore, zoologists such as Hindle argued that individual animals' ranges were far smaller than zoo critics might assume and that even those "such as elephants, larger ungulates, and birds of prey" with vast wild ranges "are among the easiest to keep in menageries and generally live to a ripe old age." Once they arrived in the zoo, "fear of man is a far more important factor" than habitat size in captive nonhumans' lives, "but fortunately most animals gradually overcome this fear and eventually seem to take an interest in the spectators."[61] This quality of taking interest in human visitors was exactly what keepers like Cheyne-Stout hoped for—that visitors and other-than-human beings would form a sense of mutual connection. Zoo professionals' views of both the benefits of captivity for animals and the ability of creatures to overcome fear and engage with humans justified incorporating animals into urban life for children's enjoyment.

These creatures arrived there through myriad kinds of journeys, sometimes bizarre and meandering but always breaking their ties to places and their wild communities. The collectors, importers, merchants, and zoo directors that comprised the animal trade extracted value from the people and landscapes of global empires and postcolonial states while also isolating creatures from ecologies and conspecific social groups as well as any material or spiritual value they held for local human communities.[62] Collectors like the Johnsons sometimes led expeditions employing dozens of Indigenous men, often denied access to guns and game by colonial rulers such as Belgium or Britain, to track down and entrap large beasts capable of injuring humans. Bycatch animals fed families who had few other sources of meat. Collectors also purchased village children's pets or haggled with traders in urban markets who had set up shop to meet rising demand from paying foreigners.[63] The growth of zoos helped fuel expansion of trading dynamics such as these, and trade networks penetrated deep into parts of the world with access to creatures considered exotic and desirable.

The economy of animal trading included small as well as large play-ers, reliant upon ocean liners to connect sources of animals—often Asia, Africa, and Latin America—with buyers mostly in wealthy countries. The Johnsons returned from East and Central Africa on a passenger line with just a few especially elusive animals and sold or donated them individually. Major importers like Louis Ruhe—with whom the Parks Department often did business—collected and sold hundreds of small monkeys, wad-ing birds and songbirds, and small cats from the tropics, sometimes to zoos and other exhibits, sometimes to private buyers for personal me-nageries.[64] Cheyne-Stout himself planned to take leave in 1939 for an expedition to Colombia with Louis Kasin, another frequent dealer with the Parks Department, to bring back leopards, anteaters, monkeys, and more.[65] This venture was planned to benefit the zoos Cheyne-Stout di-rected but also to enrich himself through sales to other buyers. Large creatures who exerted powerful resistance to capture and transport, like elephants or hippos, could fetch thousands of dollars from well-endowed zoos or private collectors. On the other end of the price scale, colorful singing finches might cost a few dollars at a pet shop.[66]

Moses, Cheyne-Stout, and other parks officials were eager to fill the zoo's cages, but given their limited budgets, this often meant haggling for animal donations and seeking out trades and cast-offs. In April 1935, Moses attempted to twist the arm of Bronx Zoo director Dr. W. Reid Blair, demanding that he furnish the Central and Prospect Park Zoos with surplus animals from his collection. Moses reminded Blair that the latter's institution "is a quasi-public agency, and the City contrib-utes a considerable amount toward its upkeep." "We are very short of animals, having weeded out those in Central Park and Brooklyn which were old and decrepit," Moses explained; "we have not succeeded in fill-ing the Central Park cages, and we are in desperate shape for exhibits in Brooklyn."[67] Blair promised a number of ungulates: pairs of aoudads (Barbary sheep) and Himalayan tahr and a European red deer. He assured Moses that he would always pass along unneeded donations to the city park system's zoos but that clades such as "monkeys, large carnivores, birds or small mammals" would be hard to come by.[68] That month, Cheyne-Stout jumped at the chance to trade a bison calf conceived by a daughter-father coupling in Central Park for a pair of demoiselle cranes from a leading animal dealer. Cheyne-Stout valued the calf at only twenty-five dollars because it was "inbred" and would be short in stature, but the dealer, Elias Joseph, was willing to make an even trade for the graceful Eurasian wading birds valued at seventy-five dollars—"a corking good bargain," in Cheyne-Stout's estimation.[69]

Cheyne-Stout also jumped at opportunities to acquire animals that would be novel to New York audiences, sometimes leveraging monetary donations when city funds were scarce. In 1938, for example, Cheyne-Stout was excited to learn that Germany's Dresden Zoo planned to sell its tiglon—a rare tiger-lion hybrid—at a deep discount because its encounter value had expired. Cheyne-Stout explained, "The people [in Dresden] have seen this animal and therefore it is no longer a great attraction." The Parks Department lacked even the funds to match what Dresden was asking for a depreciated tiglon. So, Cheyne-Stout solicited one of a number of large animal donations from the industrialist and philanthropist Emil Schwartzhaupt, whose foundation also promoted public participation among immigrant communities.[70] The zoo's animal trades, gifts, and purchases moved living creatures not just from distant landscapes of empire but also among different spaces of captivity, locally and internationally, according to what zoo directors and traders believed to be the public's tastes and desires.[71]

The exotic animal trade commodified the thrill of meeting or even sharing a home with the furry, the feathered, and the scaly along with their often fantastic (but also often somewhat disappointing, as in the wallabies' case) variety of other-than-human behaviors. As we have seen, private human homes and businesses that displayed exotic creatures often turned out to be temporary way stations before animals moved on to a public zoo. As in the nineteenth century, every year dozens of park supporters near and far still wrote to the zoo to offer animals they could no longer handle or off of whom they hoped to make a little money. Most offers were tropical birds, which were largely accepted until the birdhouse filled; later, though, a macaw got a privileged space because it could talk. Suburban New Jersey households pleaded with the zoo to take their pet monkeys, but the monkey house, too, had filled, and Cheyne-Stout feared that the tame pets would be defenseless against territorial attackers. Some animal offers revealed bizarre pet relationships: a New Jersey silk dealer hoped to trade in his emu for some pheasants and swans (which the park no longer had); a Manhattan mechanic hoped to unload his young niece's town of prairie dogs; an apartment building superintendent on the West Side wanted a better home for two "tame" alligators and several turtles. Exotic creatures like ocelots came from private homes, as did more typical northeastern suburban denizens like raccoons and even two black bears from different hinterland towns.[72] Many who had purchased exotic pets or adopted young wildlife decided that Central or Prospect Park was a better place for such creatures than their apartment or backyard, becoming links in the chain of dislocated animal lives.

When animals arrived directly from the wild to zoos like Central Park's, the experience could be taxing and even deadly—and zookeepers knew it. Swiss zoologist Heini Hediger, who gained a global following in the 1940s for applying the growing science of animal behavior to zoo keeping, wrote that acclimating wild animals into zoo life "is very often possible only at the expense of serious losses."[73] When Edward Hindle claimed that captivity benefited animals, he was referring to those individuals who survived the initial transition from the wild. Those who made it found themselves in a world dominated by new sets of sights, sounds, smells, weather, living quarters, and fellow beings whom they would have to adjust to.

Animals as Children's Entertainment and At-Risk Travelers

The hundreds of animals Cheyne-Stout assembled, many of them new to the city, along with the modern, lively look of the exhibits attracted a new upwelling of visitors. In under eighteen months, by April 1936, six million humans had flowed through the picture-book gates to tour the new Central Park Zoo, taking in lions and elephants, bears and talking parrots, bison and cranes, on its six acres. The new zoo buildings centered around a glistening pool in which three young California sea lions, named Barker, Water Lilly, and Flappy, cavorted on an abstract sculptural island visible from all sides. Other New Deal zoos featured monkey islands as their centerpiece, so the seals made Central Park's unique. Dealer Louis Ruhe had supplied the pinnipeds and transported them across the country, and philanthropist Emil Schwartzhaupt had donated $135 to purchase each animal.[74]

The six millionth visitor, a five-year-old named Cynthia Cogswell, got a behind-the-scenes tour and lunch at Kelly's with the charming Cheyne-Stout; Cynthia professed to being most drawn to the small monkeys.[75] Parents, too, were delighted by the zoo's cleanliness and modernity, a welcome change from the old, motley group of cages arrayed around the Arsenal building. While other New Deal–funded zoo renovations removed the bars and transitioned animals into more capacious habitats, the limited footprint of Central Park's zoo meant that many animals remained in cages, but now more were open to the air rather than crowded into buildings. Zoo goers visited cages from a paved outdoor path rather than entering dank buildings to view the animals. The crisp, neatly arranged animal houses echoed the tall office buildings now sprouting from the avenues south of the park. Radio reporter Dorothy Thompson lavished praise upon Moses in a broadcast testimonial for his role in fixing up Central Park and ensuring she and her young son could enjoy such features as the "open-air zoo where the seals disport themselves against a background of skyscrapers." "Thank heaven for Bob Moses," she repeated

Crowds view the new seals at the Central Park Zoo whose water feature formed the central attraction of the renovated zoo, 1944. Courtesy of the Museum of the City of New York.

with a litany of the child-friendly improvements to the park and the rest of the city provided by "America's public servant number one."[76]

The picture-book zoo offered myriad diversions for its presumed audience of youngsters, and Cheyne-Stout worked the press to advertise every new animal addition to the collection, every special feature, and every event where children could celebrate the animated city. As before, peanuts were available for purchase to feed to monkeys, elephants, parrots, and others, allowing children the feeling of connecting with animals over food. For ten cents, a child could ride in a cart drawn by a pony on the track next to the park, much like the goat rides a half-century earlier.[77] Cheyne-Stout also initiated contests and public votes to name new animal arrivals, hoping to maintain excitement about the collection and heighten the animals' charisma. Once the names were selected, schoolchildren were invited to come to the zoo to celebrate the "baptism"; there youngsters stretched over railings that barely separated them from llamas and zebras.[78]

Even with such constant activity, children and even adults seemed to bore easily—or perhaps they just preferred a different kind of interaction. The *Times* wryly lamented in 1938 that voting for the latest round of animal names had dropped off and that children's ideas for names "lacked originality"—"Blackie" for a new black bear, "Leo" for a new lion.[79] Still, Cheyne-Stout loved bringing children into contact with animals and seemed to genuinely feel close affinity for them himself, as shown in intimate photos of a Congo porcupine gifted to him by an animal dealer. Too small to stay in any zoo cages, the tiny porcupine lived in Cheyne-Stout's office in Central Park.[80]

Cheyne-Stout also worked with other agencies and civic groups in the city to organize and support family-friendly spectacles that brought children into close contact with animals. In May 1935, he hosted at the alligators' winter quarters one hundred frogs flown in from Louisiana by the Boys' Club of New York and the Mark Twain Centennial Committee, to re-create a "big town version" of the "frog-jumping contest

Zoo director Ronald Cheyne-Stout cuddles a porcupine given to him as a gift, which he kept in his office at Central Park. © Wildlife Conservation Society. Reproduced by permission of the wcs.

immortalized by Mark Twain." Al Smith was master of ceremonies, and James Mulholland, director of recreation for the Parks Department, oversaw the contest. Children from around the city raced the frogs in five arenas on the Central Park Mall, but leading up to the ceremony, the frogs seemed "desultory" in their way station.[81] On other occasions, Cheyne-Stout enlisted the public library to hold book fairs among the cages and brought a book into the lion cage to read to children assembled outside—but he mostly told tales of his own prowess training big cats.[82]

Cheyne-Stout felt that even unique creatures like Dresden's tiglon could become humdrum to audiences hungry for the latest thrill. Once the animal collection came closer to filling the cages, Moses and Cheyne-Stout strived to maintain the animal exhibits' lively appearance. Cheyne-Stout himself insisted that animals imported directly from the wild were preferable to those bred in captivity because of their greater vitality. This imperative extended even to killing animals who no longer upheld the appearance of vigorous wildness in order to make space for younger creatures. In 1937, the newspaper magnate William Randolph Hearst donated three young felids to the zoo, two female lions and a male leopard. To make room for these fresh new charges, Cheyne-Stout "destroyed" four

CHAPTER 5

female lions already on display, "which were either old or infirm or had some specific deformity." Moses and Cheyne-Stout insisted that only the "best specimens" should be displayed, and sometimes there was not another home for creatures no longer useful to the zoo.[83] Injury and deformity could be part of animals' wild lives, but zoo life could also bring additional behavioral and physical changes to individual animals, and many keepers believed these rendered animals unfit for display.[84]

Cheyne-Stout prided himself on maintaining a lively set of animals, but his ambitions ultimately exceeded his ability to physically, financially, and logistically manage the collection. Most spectacularly, in late July 1936, a lioness named Curley pounced on Cheyne-Stout as he showed her off to America's most famous animal collector, the swashbuckling Frank Buck, and the director of the Berlin Zoo, who was visiting New York.[85] Cheyne-Stout entered Curley's cage in near-total darkness after boasting about his "pet's" comfort with him; the unusual nighttime visit likely startled her. He was hospitalized for weeks, and he professed to never fully recovering from the mauling. Cheyne-Stout reported more nips from lions and bears in the coming years—claims perhaps designed to exact sympathy, as publicity stunts, or both.[86]

As Cheyne-Stout eased back into work, Moses and Manhattan Borough director Harry Sweeny learned that he had overextended his animal budget. They received complaints from a bird dealer that Cheyne-Stout had never paid for a pair of cranes delivered to the zoo the previous year.[87] Cheyne-Stout seemed to have signed some false affidavits when receiving animal shipments at the New York Customs Office, later claiming ignorance that certain animals were actually still alive. Animals that died on board or that were destined for a public zoo were subject to no customs duties; Cheyne-Stout most likely took advantage of this allowance to sell small animals to private buyers for personal gain, having reported them dead.[88] Cheyne-Stout dug himself into more trouble when he pleaded with Benjamin Lepow and his brother Raymond, leading leopard skin importers, for Benjamin to acquire more animals for the Central and Prospect Park Zoos on his upcoming trip to Kenya. Cheyne-Stout promised to pay for the capture, care, and shipment of any live animals the Lepows' "native" staff of some three thousand Kenyans could catch while hunting for leopards to kill and skin. The Lepows' staff proved remarkably effective, and in June 1937, an astounding shipment of dozens of mammals large and small, hundreds of birds, and a few reptiles landed in New York. After distributing most of them between the zoos he managed, Cheyne-Stout brokered sales of others to the Smithsonian Zoo and the Chicago Zoological Society. But Cheyne-Stout's share of the bill still exceeded his budget by thousands of dollars. As the Lepows threatened to sue and as the British government denied Cheyne-Stout's appeals for new animal trapping permits throughout its empire, Cheyne-Stout scrambled to sell off more animals, further breaching customs rules.[89]

Moses learned of these and other lapses, which violated his principles of clean and well-managed public works, and fired Cheyne-Stout in March 1939.[90] No one charged Cheyne-Stout with greed for trying to extract too many animals from foreign lands or with subjecting these beings to stressful forced movement and confinement. The practice of killing off old and infirm animals was widely understood among zoo professionals as part of doing business.[91] Cheyne-Stout's case underscored how death was unremarkable among imported creatures; no one questioned his claims that creatures had died en route, allowing him to conceal animal side sales. Routine zoo operations turned animals into movable, fungible objects of entertainment for children and other spectators. After a two-year court battle, a New York court found inadequate evidence that Cheyne-Stout had abused his position and reinstated him, much to Moses's fury. Cheyne-Stout promptly retired, citing continued pain from Curley's attack, working just long enough to earn his city pension.[92]

Innocence Lost and New Attitudes toward Zoo Animals

After Cheyne-Stout's embarrassing departure, the picture-book zoo lost its flamboyant showman, but New Yorkers still expressed attachment to the city's animals and often took a proprietary attitude toward them. Some responded vehemently to fragile relationships between mother and baby animals. These responses seemed to signal a tarnish on the zoo's reputation and perhaps Moses's as well. If the zoo was supposed to show that New York was a good place for children, what did it mean when baby animals suffered quite publicly?

Two hippos named Rose exemplified troubling cases of shattered maternal bonds, and mothers who lived near the zoo expressed particular concern for the urban condition in which these creatures had to raise their youth. Hippo mothers kept in zoos in this era regularly killed their babies. Human observers often found such incidents disturbing; for hippos, this behavior might represent a kind of resistance to captivity. In a scrapbook dedicated to memories of his zoo director days, Cheyne-Stout wrote that "Rosie" was a mother of fourteen babies, although the veterinary records do not record each birth.[93] In 1955, "Rose II" gave birth to a baby described as healthy and became the first zoo mother in fifty years whom zoo officials could recall having nursed her young. Rose II had arrived from "East Africa" just a year earlier, and her mate, Falstaff, had been at the zoo since 1951.[94] Whether hippo calves lived or died, they did not stay with their mothers; even if they survived, Central Park lacked sufficient space to keep a growing baby hippo. In spite of a promising beginning, Rose II's first baby, a son, died within a few days. In 1961, Rose II's first daughter was sold to Ringling Brothers Circus, and another baby died. Rose II gave birth to nine babies over twenty years at the zoo. Her last baby, Daisy, was born in 1973 and traded through an animal agency for two sea lions for the collection.[95]

The birth of a baby animal was often an anticipated and publicized event and a source of pride for zoo authorities. Authorities trumpeted

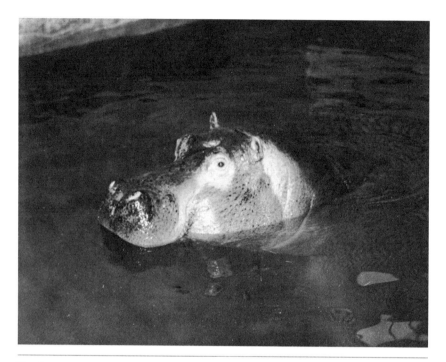

This hippo was one of two named Rose, or Rosie, who lived in the Central Park Zoo in the early to middle twentieth century. Both hippo cows struggled to successfully raise their calves. © Wildlife Conservation Society. Reproduced by permission of the wcs.

reproduction as a sign that animals were "acclimated" and well cared for, and human crowds lined up to see new babies. Newspapers covered the death or sale of those babies, sometimes sparking allegations of poor treatment. Such outcries revealed how some humans believed that even in the curtailed environment of the zoo, bonds between mothers and children remained sacred. Zoo goers were particularly incensed at the sale of Rose II's daughter to the circus.[96]

Other zoo goers protested the conditions under which another baby, who died in infancy, was exhibited. A mother named Theresa Robinson who lived a few blocks southeast of the zoo threatened to involve the AS-PCA. Although her family had taken "a real rooting interest in this young thing born in captivity," she now charged that zoo officials had failed to protect the hippos' privacy when the baby became ill, causing Rose II to become "distressed by the relentless attention of the bystanders." "To expose suffering animals to the inhuman curiosity of the mob constitutes an act of extreme cruelty," Robinson concluded. Zoo officials assured Robinson that they had taken all precautions to protect Rose II and her baby and that the cause of death was congenital deformities, as seen in a number of Rose II's calves. Another neighbor of the zoo, who identified herself as Halle December, charged that the zoo had left Rose II and her baby exposed in order to appease the public's demands to see the infant hippo and that the mother had injured her baby in attempting to hide it from human crowds.[97] It is perhaps unsurprising that the two most pointed letters about conditions for zoo mothers came from women, who have long dominated the membership, even if not the leadership, of humane organizations and who likely felt they understood the perils of being a caregiver in the city (though it is unclear whether December was a mother). Zoo visitors believed they could understand animals' feelings about life in captivity and felt informed and empowered to demand different treatment by zoo staff.

Meanwhile, changes were underway in the profession and scholarship of zoo keeping. Heini Hediger, the Swiss zoologist, began to develop the field of zoo biology, which upheld with science the idea that animals could thrive in the small space of a zoo facility, so long as keepers administered proper training and stimulation. Ideas about conditioning and animal psychology were already spreading with the work of such behaviorists as Konrad Lorenz and the scholar of animals' perceptual environments, Jakob von Uexküll. Translated into English in 1950, Hediger's textbook, *Wild Animals in Captivity*, applied these ideas to the management of zoo creatures, expanding on other scholars' theoretical underpinnings and providing practical instructions. According to Hediger, zookeepers must redirect wild animals' fearful behavioral response to humans, help the zoo captive reestablish a sense of its territory, and provide occupational training to manipulate and play with objects in that territory.[98]

Hediger, along with Hindle of the London Zoological Society, believed that captivity was no hindrance to animal well-being and asserted that successful breeding in captivity was the "one criterion" for judging that a zoo provided "suitable biological conditions" for animals.[99] Hippos, of course, were a hard case, both shy and territorial, with a long history of difficulties reproducing in captivity. But Hediger seemed unconcerned about mothers' responses to crowds when caring for a newborn. Perhaps Robinson and December had a point about the need for more special and discreet treatment of zoo mothers and babies—and they likely knew that cities could be better designed for human mothers and infants too.

Newly informed by animal behaviorism and psychology, Hediger and others also placed renewed emphasis on zoos as educational institutions that must play a role in conservation. While justifying captivity, Hediger insisted that zoos must not traffic only in amusement. He explained that zoo audiences' interest in "the active animal rather than one at rest" was proper "but for the wrong reasons." Rather than distract zoo visitors with the "intensity" or "unusualness" of animals' behaviors, they must be educated to understand why animals do what they do and to appreciate that animals would not always perform the entertaining antics humans had been conditioned to expect.[100] These precepts contradicted the design and programming of many New Deal zoos, including Central Park's, less than two decades after their reconstruction.

To some, zoos still symbolized childhood wonder and even innocence, but there were hints of disappointment in midcentury writing about the Central Park Zoo. Literary works published as Hediger's zoo reforms were taking hold present feelings and meanings that redesigned animal encounters evoked for zoo goers. J. D. Salinger's 1951 book, *The Catcher in the Rye*, has disaffected teenaged narrator Holden Caulfield take his sister, Phoebe, to the Central Park Zoo as he attempts to protect her innocence and renew his own lost joy. For many, the animal world contained in a zoo could still capture the imagination and inspire thoughts of all that is strange and different about humans' relatives who seemed so physically close and yet so ontologically far away. Ultimately, though, Holden and Phoebe spend hardly any time at the zoo because "there wasn't much to watch" other than the sea lions and the polar bear on a slushy December day. The brown bear was in the cave, and "all you could see was his rear end." A little boy nearby demanded of his father, "Make him come out, Daddy," completing the scene of dissatisfaction in Holden's narration.[101] At least on that winter's day, the animals proved insufficient to rekindle Holden's lost childhood wonder, in spite of his longing, and they didn't inspire Phoebe much either.

Literary scholar Randy Malamud argues that while zoo proponents used children's need for education and connection with nature as a justification for animal captivity, children do not actually like zoos. To support this argument, he draws upon works of fiction that discuss zoos and children. In spite of Holden Caulfield's example, however, the unhappy young zoo goer may be more interesting as a trope than as truth.[102] Instead, we can examine New Deal zoos as part of a strategy for remaking older industrial cities as family-friendly sites of consumerism and leisure and how varied publics—parents and animal advocates, particularly—responded when the moral costs of zoos were revealed.

Indeed, at least one author of children's literature acknowledged the thrill of seeing animals at zoos but also anticipated the moral costs and, from this point of tension, imagined different kinds of more-than-human spaces. Poet Countee Cullen reports frequent forays from Harlem to the zoo in his 1940 children's book, *The Lost Zoo*, which lists Cullen's tabby cat Christopher as coauthor. Cullen explains the joy he took in watching animals: "They always astonish me. I am never sure of what they are going to do." Early in the book, Cullen reflects on zoo animals' conditions through a conversation with Christopher after a particularly exciting visit during which "all the animals at whose cages I had stopped had behaved just as if they were doing a circus act for me alone." Christopher is not impressed; rather, he expresses pity for "all those poor animals," to which Cullen responds that "we couldn't very well have them walking up and down the

Poet and author Countee Cullen sits for a portrait in Central Park
with photographer Carl Van Vechten. With his cat Christopher,
Cullen published *The Lost Zoo*, which envisions a more-than-
human city that liberates its animals. © Van Vechten Trust.

street rubbing elbows with people, could we?" Christopher contradicts him, retorting that "if people didn't annoy *them,* I am sure *they* would be very polite, and that all of them would mind their own affairs, and the world would be much more interesting than it is now." In Christopher Cat's voice, Cullen appeals to young readers to imagine a different kind of city, open to the free movement of beings of all species—and presumably all colors of humans too. But *Lost Zoo* is not simply a didactic argument against captivity and species segregation. The clever Christopher goes on to one-up Cullen's zoo anecdotes with his own fantastical story about creatures who didn't make it onto Noah's Ark, such as the shy and timid Squililigee.[103] Cullen imagines that other-than-human beings like Christopher held vast knowledge of worlds as yet beyond humans' understanding, and these worlds could hold promise for marginalized humans as well. Literary scholar Joshua Bennett argues that as part of the "black aesthetic tradition," Cullen "provides us with the tools needed to conceive of interspecies relationships anew."[104] The "lost zoo" of the title evoked wonder but also sadness at animals sacrificed for (some) humans' sins, never to thrive upon the earth again, and the possibility that humans and animals might learn from their loss to share a world together in radical kinship.[105]

New Models of Zoos and Childhood

Robert Moses's zoo renewal (presaging his other urban renewal activities in the city at large) cleared away the dank and dark sheds and opened the cages to cleansing light to replace the misery of the Depression and the crumbling menagerie with a sense of celebration. At a precarious moment in the history of American childhood, New Deal funding enabled Moses to remake the Central Park Menagerie in line with other family-friendly spaces he was creating across New York. The new Central Park Zoo centered children's presumed fantasies about encountering wild animals, promoting fun and leisure. In addition to playgrounds and pools, Moses used new zoos as demonstrations of what good government could do for urban families. Furthermore, zoo authorities, particularly Ronald Cheyne-Stout, employed animals' bodies and liveliness to create spaces for children that exuded pleasure and thrills.

Ideals of childhood and of animal captivity changed rapidly, however, rendering the picture-book zoo obsolete within a human generation. Moses's tenure as parks commissioner ended amid mounting criticism of zoo conditions—and his other urban renewal activities—and was followed shortly by the construction of the Lehman Children's Zoo adjacent to the picture-book zoo. The picture-book zoo may have brought children and adults into close contact with exotic animals, but the public seemed to tire of merely looking at animals reduced to objects, even if few understood the extent to which animals suffered for humans' entertainment. In 1960, former New York governor Herbert Lehman and First Lady Edith Lehman offered yet another alternative. The Lehmans donated $500,000 to turn an acre of open land just to the north of the existing zoo into a playground mixed with a petting zoo, where children could climb into sculpted features like a whale's mouth and a rabbit hole and feed tame llamas and lambs.[106]

The Children's Zoo embodied one of a few trends in American zoo programming and architecture during the 1960s and 1970s, alongside several naturalistic renewals.[107] In contrast to the emphasis on entertainment in Cheyne-Stout's menagerie in the 1930s, the Children's Zoo envisioned a tamer, gentler version of childhood that, like some of the park's original pastoral features, evoked an imagined rural past.[108] Like the new naturalistic zoos, children's zoos removed the bars, but the latter allowed more intimate and tactile contact because the creatures were young, tame, and nearly harmless. The animals seemed almost free and as cuddly as pets—though we must recall that many zoo donations were once cuddly young pet monkeys purchased from exotic animal traders. And Lehman and Children's Zoo administrators made sure that the "three little pigs" and other baby animals stayed little through a deal with a New Jersey farm. The farm sent animals as soon as they could be separated from their mothers, and the zoo sent them back to become real farm animals again once they passed the cute and docile stage—in exchange for another batch of youngsters.[109]

In 1963, Little Golden Books published *A Visit to the Children's Zoo*, using Central Park's Children's Zoo as its model, preserving a sense of what the new feature felt like to its first visitors. In contrast with Cheyne-Stout reading books in the lion's cage, flirting with a mauling, here the atmosphere of the Children's Zoo feels gentle, safe, and domestic. The mother of the two child protagonists, Susie and Ned, lets her children explore the one-acre space on their own while she waits outside the gates; most of the adults in the book are keepers who help supervise the rabbits and goats.[110] Indeed, in real life, Central Park's first two female keepers joined the zoo staff, lending what administrators surely considered a more maternal air to the Children's Zoo, nurturing the young humans and nonhumans there.[111]

To the south of the Children's Zoo, the picture-book zoo remained as it was for another two decades as public zoos across the country removed their bars and placed animals in landscapes crafted to conjure—at least for human visitors—their native habitats. In what may be an apocryphal story, in the late 1970s, the young daughter of New York's first African American parks commissioner, Gordon Davis, begged her father to never again take her to the Central Park Zoo after her first visit.[112] Regardless of what Lizzy Cooper-Davis actually thought of the zoo, her father would help initiate the handover of the southeastern corner of the park to the New York Zoological Society for yet another round of zoo renewal.

CHAPTER 6

Animals Out and In

As park authorities and New Yorkers generally clamored for more activities and space for children in the early twentieth century, new proposals increasingly threatened to edge out the park's sheep. Some regarded the sheep as occupying potential play spaces. Former park board president John D. Crimmins got caught up in the frenzy of recreational additions to the park in the early decades of the twentieth century. As we have seen, Crimmins was briefly accused of conflicts of interest when some sheep whom he purchased for a friend sojourned on the Central Park lawns in the late 1880s (he was exonerated but resigned from the board to avoid the appearance of graft).[1] Well-known for heading one of the city's largest construction companies, his charitable works, Catholic faith, and active role in the Democratic Party, Crimmins pointed out the competition between sheep and children when he proposed sweeping changes to the park landscape in 1909. He explained: "The children are very much crowded on the North Meadow, and the South Meadow is often held in reserve. Sheep graze on the lawns."[2] At that time, Crimmins proposed that the old reservoir be capped to create more space for children's recreational activities, leaving the meadows and sheep intact.

Within three years, however, Crimmins could not ignore how the changing city and growing demand for park space were affecting the sheep. In 1912, amid a controversy about the fate of an architecturally significant private building, the Lenox Library at Fifth Avenue and

Seventieth Street, Crimmins proposed moving the building to the site of the sheepfold. The Lenox Library controversy revealed rifts among the city's wealthiest families—the demolition eventually made way for the Frick Museum—and raised concerns about the threat to the park's landscape, but Crimmins's suggestion also contained a prescient statement about sheep in Manhattan. The sheepfold's "full purpose has long since passed in its present location." He continued, "There is practically no pasturage, and we see [the flock] driven from the meadow to make way for children's play. Whether or not my suggestion for the location of the [Lenox Library] be adopted, the sheep should be removed to Bronx Park, where there are abundant pasturage and ideal conditions."[3]

It took over two decades for park authorities to implement Crimmins's suggestion to move the sheep out of Manhattan. Some more recent narratives of their relocation have cited the concern that the sheep were "malformed" from generations of inbreeding.[4] Crimmins observed other dynamics that placed pressure on some of the most visible remaining agricultural animals in Manhattan and eclipsed their former role in generating value from the park landscape.[5] (As we saw at the end of chapter 1, there were still livestock in the city, sequestered in tenements and slaughterhouses.) Crimmins's foresight about the sheep flock's fate illustrates a tension between his roles in New York City. As a former parks board president who had purchased fine Southdowns to enrich the flock, Crimmins appreciated the historic value of sheep in the landscape. But considering his life's work in building the city, physically and financially, it also becomes clear that Crimmins had helped sow the seeds for their displacement.

Urban development placed new demands on the park landscape in the first half of the twentieth century, amplifying pressures on human-animal relationships that relied upon those spaces. The growth of businesses, neighborhoods, and infrastructure along Manhattan's length that helped displace the sheep was not simply a natural process. Rather, urbanization was marked by deployments of wealth and power and shaped by identity and difference. Park authorities resigned themselves to the loss of spaces for sheep in Manhattan, asserting that a more suburban location would be better for them. Furthermore, the usual means of controlling the sheep—their shepherd and his dog—were insufficient to keep them safe as the city changed.

While the sheep lost their place in the park, at least for the time being, human relationships with other animals, such as fish and dogs, were transformed rather than displaced. In spite of these different outcomes, this chapter argues that similar dynamics shaped changing relationships and multispecies spaces involving sheep, fish, and dogs. Animals could be redefined as belonging in public space or not based on pressures related to urban development and ideas of modernization, the power and identity of animals' human advocates, the availability of alternative spaces for them, and changing means of control over these creatures.

Suburbanizing Sheep, Modernizing the Park

In 1901, a park employee explained Sheep Meadow dynamics to the *Tribune*, showing that sheep and children need not have competed for space. The twenty-acre site was "always a playground. On every day but Saturday, the sheep own it, but once a week, the children are the bosses." Park staff also maintained that adults benefited as originally intended back in the 1850s: "Country people pass by the museum and the menagerie, the flowers and the statuary, to see the sheep, and many city people who play at farming a few months of the year come here and look wise while they examine our sheep."[6] As of the early twentieth century, the sheepfold upheld daily and yearly cycles of pastoralism, even as sheep agriculture waned in the northeastern United States. Sheep departed the sheepfold in the morning, grazed the meadows, and returned each evening; over the course of the year, sheep bred and gave birth to lambs, then the lambs were docked and sheep shorn and sold at auction. From the flock's origins, park administrators and boosters had asserted that the sheep were also good for children, though often from a rather didactic perspective, teaching urban youth to appreciate an idealized (but now transformed and westward shifting) American countryside. In the early twentieth century, park lovers still took joy in the encounter, claiming that the sheep "furnish unlimited amusement to children of all ages"—not just lessons and quiet contemplation but actual fun.[7]

John Crimmins saw another dynamic gaining momentum, however. In spite of his dedication to philanthropy for city green spaces and the poor, his position in city development and finance gave him a different viewpoint. Crimmins carried out the expansion of key pieces of New York's urban infrastructure and financed many other elements of the growing city that over time hemmed in the park. This expansion set up some of the conditions that edged out Central Park's sheep. Taking the helm of the family construction business in 1873, Crimmins employed tens of thousands of New Yorkers in constructing railways and streets, "putting up dwellings and skyscrapers." He invested his wealth not only in charitable causes but also in the businesses that filled the island. Although he "possessed a passion for flowers and for landscape gardening" both in New York parks and at his Connecticut estate, the former occupied increasingly confined spaces within the United States' capital of finance and trade.[8] And construction and infrastructure workers needed homes, too, and many of them had children who needed spaces in which to play. Such urban growth was not simply a natural process but was fueled and carried out by powerful individuals and corporations like the Crimmins company, with support from city government, and embodied in families who flocked to the city from the rural United States and from abroad seeking livelihoods.[9]

The City of New York did little if anything to carve out space for animal husbandry amid all this growth, although slaughterhouses and farms still clung to Manhattan's edges, and many tenement dwellers kept geese and pigs inside their buildings.[10] Internal combustion engines and other means of generating power also reduced the need for horses (as we have seen, leisure equestrians still valued them), but Central Park remained an island for visible animal agriculture. In 1912, the year Crimmins called for sheep to be moved out, the Parks Department auctioned off fifty-three Dorset sheep, including twenty-one ram lambs, and 813 pounds of wool. With fewer sheep than in the 1800s, park staff also began to convert part of the sheepfold to a stable for housing the Parks Department's horses. Furthermore, other types of children's activities had begun to eclipse urban animal husbandry. There were day-to-day play needs as well as special events, such as a children's folk dance festival on the south meadow and an extravagant "Fairy-Land" pageant at the sheepfold, attended by five thousand children.[11]

By the 1920s, the remaining sheep looked quaint grazing between streams of motorized traffic on Central Park West and the West Drive. The longtime shepherd Thomas Hoey (and his family, until his children grew up and his wife passed away) and the sheepdog still lived in an apartment on the second floor. Part of the sheepfold now served as a base for the "motorcycle-mounted members of Traffic I," the police who enforced transportation rules throughout the park—signaling a beginning of a shift away from horse-mounted police, although they still patrolled many park spaces. In 1926, Hoey acted out for a reporter what had once been the sheep's routine during the warmer months of the year. The flock departed the sheepfold early in the morning to graze on five acres just outside. By late morning, Hoey and the sheepdog—at that point a collie named Gunther, the only dog allowed in the park unmuzzled and unleashed—led the flock east to frolic and graze in the broader pasture known then and today as the Sheep Meadow. The journey required the sheep to cross West Drive, and their agitated bleating seemed to indicate a great deal of stress. Hoey "whistle[d] with a peculiar trill that [was] obeyed by his wards with alacrity," and Gunther yelped and nipped at their heels to urge them forward.[12] Once they arrived, green grass and space to roam about were much more plentiful.

In 1927, however, the *Times* captured a more typical day for the flock, showing what Crimmins meant by "lack of pasturage." Hoey limited the sheep's perambulations to very early in the morning. He boasted to have

Central Park shepherd Thomas Hoey poses by the sheepfold with some of the park's Dorset sheep in 1913. Courtesy of the New York City Municipal Archives.

never lost a member of the flock to traffic, but he and Gunther herded sheep across West Drive at 5:00 a.m. to avoid rush hour. The sheep now spent most of their day at the sheepfold rather than wandering about the park and thus had fewer encounters with park visitors, who tended to arrive a bit later in the day.[13] This timing cut into what Hoey considered the most valuable part of his work: exposing city dwellers, especially children, to the sheep. Hoey still asserted that city children needed these animals to learn about the countryside and where products such as mutton and wool came from. In the days when sheep roamed more, children would approach him to ask what the animals were, and Hoey planned the schedule of sheepshearing in the spring around school visits, prolonging the shearing season as long as possible to allow greater numbers of schools to participate. Hoey shared early administrators' concern that city dwellers were losing their connection to nonhuman life, particularly the rhythms of animal agriculture. The sheep flock's curtailed existence further limited opportunities to connect.[14]

Along with the burgeoning automobile traffic, other hazards of city life troubled the sheep. Human park goers sometimes left food and wrappers out on the meadow, and some sheep ate too much or the wrong kind of leftovers there. Once, some thirty sheep fell ill from eating human leftovers, and a few died in spite of the veterinarian's efforts.[15] Consistent sanitation was necessary to protect the flock's health in this space shared by humans, who could be careless about refuse. While litter was a hazard to sheep, wandering off and theft were rarely a problem. Indeed, the only recorded incident of sheep theft was quickly reported when loud bleating disturbed neighbors in Vincent Buenroste's West Harlem apartment building in October 1928. Buenroste, a young immigrant man, got help from two friends boosting the lamb and bringing it home to his unit on 118th Street. As the lamb cried out, Buenroste attempted to quiet it with a bowl of milk in his kitchen. The mother ewe back at the park alerted Hoey with loud bleats for her missing baby.[16] Buenroste's reasons for taking the lamb are lost to history; it may have been a prank, or he may have wanted a pet or future dinner (for many humans, those two are not mutually exclusive).[17] He may have been asserting a claim to the lamb as a common city resource. Lack of opportunity rather than lack of motivation likely prevented further thefts; the sheep were well guarded.

Constant supervision by Hoey and Gunther (and after Gunther passed on, Zen) of course cost the park salary, space, and resources, but park administrators and city residents varied in the degree to which they valued these investments in the flock. The auction was one indication of their monetary value, apart from the educational value so important to Hoey. The sheep (along with their wool) were among many animals auctioned off by the park each year in late spring or early summer. By the early 1920s, buyers bid up to twenty dollars for mature ewes, which some used to begin their own flocks or enrich the breeding stock of existing flocks. Wool from each sheep fetched between twenty and fifty dollars at auction. From the auction at the sheepfold, lambs commonly traveled to butchering facilities within New York and ewes to estates in hinterland towns in New York, Connecticut, and New Jersey.[18]

Within just a few years, interest in Central Park's sheep dropped off drastically. At the 1927 sale, longtime auctioneer Edwin McDonald settled for five dollars per lamb if bidders bought several at once.[19] The sheep that Buenroste lifted that year may have been worth very little money to the city anyway. A *Tribune* article openly disdained the 1928 auction and the animals for sale. The reporter covering the event called the bidders "two hundred New Yorkers who don't know anything about zoology" and described the ewes as "insipid" and "lacking intelligence, wit, and vivacity." Reporters made no mention of inbreeding, but they implied the flock was doomed for lack of new blood.[20]

Hoey and others insisted that the dwindling flock still enriched the park. Landscapers considered sheep manure the best fertilizer to leaven the soil and nourish the many new trees that would be planted to rejuvenate the park. The sheep provided a ready supply, along with that from horses in the park's stables and the zoo captives. Landscapers used fifty tons of sheep manure in 1927.[21] However, Central Park's sheep could not make enough, so the Parks Department contracted with suppliers outside the city.[22] Throughout their daily travels, sheep also fertilized the lawns they visited with their dung, as did the Jersey cow who was penned on one of the lawns and whom Hoey was also responsible for milking. Along with these material ways the park valued the sheep, media representations were not all as negative as the *Tribune*'s auction report. In the two months before the 1928 auction, two other *Tribune* correspondents wrote fondly of that year's spring lambs, unlike their sardonic colleague.[23]

A few years later, Moses's Parks Department removed the sheep to Prospect Park, where they joined the flock already living in Brooklyn's largest public green space. In March 1934, fifty-nine sheep, including many pregnant ewes a few weeks from giving birth, boarded a truck to cross the East River. Hoey was reassigned to care for the lions at the zoo amid its New Deal makeover.[24] New Deal workers converted the old sheepfold into a restaurant envisioned by Moses, the Tavern on the Green. Moses promised that New Yorkers, even during the Depression, could afford to eat there, but some complained that meals were beyond their reach.[25] Many found that this space in the middle southwest portion of the park was never for them—but the meals were certainly more accessible than the hoity-toity auctions. The menu offered many entrees based on animals Manhattanites would seldom see alive—lamb only sometimes appeared on the menu, but there was always the flesh of cows, chickens, turkeys, and various crustaceans.[26] Replacing a sheep flock with a restaurant continued trends in which modern cities displaced livestock production beyond the sight of most consumers, making it easy to ignore the conditions that produced flesh food, milk, eggs, and fiber.[27]

The sheep flock's departure also fit within Moses's overall drive to modernize the park, although the Tavern on the Green bore a traditional English flavor. The flock's move seemed justified on the basis of changing conditions inside and surrounding Central Park that curtailed their lives. Life in Brooklyn was a bit slower paced than in the middle of Manhattan, and the sheep would have more time and space to roam and fewer risky and startling encounters with motorcar traffic. The existing flock in Prospect Park, managed by head zookeeper John O'Brien, spent almost their entire day outdoors, returning to their sheepfold only once in the middle of the day to drink from their troughs, in contrast to foreshortened grazing time in Manhattan.[28] In his first year as commissioner of New York's consolidated Parks Department, Moses also ended the use of horse-powered equipment in the park, calling the horses "decrepit." Since the 1850s, horses had provided much of the park's power for construction and maintenance, alongside the mowing and manuring services provided by the sheep. Now Moses had his Parks Department replace the horses with motorized equipment.[29]

A few New Yorkers felt a sense of loss for the sheep.[30] In 1938, the *Times* editors published a remembrance of the sheep that blended nostalgia with arch wit. "There is not even one in the Menagerie to teach the stay-at-homes what a sheep looks like," they lamented, referring to families who did not go to the country for vacation. They reflected on the social symbolism of the sheep in the era of New Deal welfare programs: "Sheep have qualities that are more than ever admired. They flock together."[31]

Ultimately, inbreeding is only a partial explanation for the flock's displacement. Throughout the nineteenth century, park officials had purchased new sheep to limit inbreeding, and they might have done so again if they saw a future for sheep in Manhattan. Parks officials and city planners might also have chosen to protect spaces for urban pastoralism. Instead, they allowed development to run a course that conflicted with this more-than-human space. With a ready space in still-suburban Brooklyn where sheep could go and a sense of resignation among most of their human advocates, an emerging vision of the modern city drove the flock away.

Real and Abstract Fish in City Waterscapes

Urban development was also encroaching upon fish and human Manhattanites' relationships with them, at least relationships of the sporting kind. A Harlem old-timer told an outdoor magazine in 1907 about "Gold Fish Pond" just north of the park, where local children used to play and fish. "There were many other ponds and streams north of Central Park which have now disappeared," he explained, "the ponds having presumably been filled up and the streams turned into sewers."[32] Fishing in Central Park in the twentieth century helped replace historical fishing practices around Manhattan as development marched northward, filling these waters or channeling them underground. Fishers in the park of all ages and ethnic and racial identities knew the city's waters and its creatures in ways that few others did.[33]

Still, the filthy conditions of waters inside the park, considered a threat to human and nonhuman health since the 1880s, persisted into the twentieth century. In 1903, the Health Department reported rampant mosquito breeding, noisome rotting vegetation, and extensive rat burrows along shorelines and in puddles all around the park. Sewage pipes fed into the park, forming foul pools. A joint effort led by the Parks Department's entomologist, Dr. E. B. Southwick, and Dr. William Berkeley of the Health Department refurbished the park's waterscape from 1903 to 1904. The Parks Department lacked the budget to remedy all problems, but its crew removed two thousand cartloads of rotted aquatic vegetation along with debris washed in from the trails and bridle paths. They also paved the shorelines with copious amounts of gravel and cement. Southwick and Berkeley claimed to have constructed a "clean and continuous border over which fish can feed and keep down all [mosquito] larvae that might be there." To help perform this role, "fishes which once were scattered unevenly have been distributed so that they abound everywhere."[34] Even in this paved waterscape, parks administrators relied on fish to help maintain health and cleanliness.

As waters outside the park became inaccessible and conditions within the park improved, Manhattan fishing enthusiasts of all ages and social positions sought out new sporting sites. But the place of fish and fishing in Central Park had been ambiguous for decades. Fishing officially violated park ordinance number 22, as did placing any item in the waters of the park.[35] Since the park's early days, however, New Yorkers had deposited pet fish in the ponds, lakes, and the reservoir, hoping to later reap the pleasures of fishing—and for many, fish flesh—by stocking the waters illicitly. Conservation organizations and other donors had also deposited larger numbers of fish to help keep aquatic environments clean as well as lively; eels, perch, sunfish, and goldfish had also found their way in via the drainage system.[36]

Some fishing clubs were allowed to hold regular fly casting tournaments, but this sport engaged with fish in a mostly abstracted way.[37]

Elite and middle-class fishing enthusiasts connected with the waters and aquatic life of Central Park to hone their angling skills and create a community of like-minded sportsmen.[38] In 1905, two Manhattan-based editors of the magazine *Field and Stream*, Edward Cave and Perry Fraser, conceived of "a social organization of gentleman anglers" that would bring together sportsmen with similar interests and hold public fly and bait casting tournaments in New York.[39] Not only the term *gentleman* but also *anglers* conveyed the self-identified stature of the founders of the Anglers' Club of New York (it began admitting women in 1931). More than *fishing*, *angling* implied for many a practiced technique that was as much about contemplation, skill, and style as about catching fish themselves. As the club grew to its self-imposed limit of 250 members in the coming decades, its rolls included writers, merchants, physicians, druggists, and lawyers who lived in the city and could afford not only club dues but also occasional club outings upstate and even across the country to try their hand in new waters.[40] The club also lobbied the New York State Legislature for laws and funding that were advantageous for fishing, from anti-pollution regulations to fish-stocking projects.[41] Many anglers cited the seventeenth-century British writer Izaak Walton to elevate the contemplative ethos of the sport. A national group founded in 1922 and named for Walton had long lobbied for wildlife conservation and clean water regulations as well as promoting fishing as a social pastime. The Anglers' Club of New York formed over a decade before the national Izaak Walton League and anticipated many of its social and political styles, although the latter attracted more working-class members.[42]

The Anglers' Club started out eager to use the waters of the city for recreation, although its members seemed resigned to limited access to fish. Indeed, although Central Park prohibited fishing, Parks Department Manhattan borough commissioner Moses Herrmann accommodated the club for related activities. One of the club's first acts upon forming was to seek out water for regular fly casting practice and a convenient space to stash tackle and relax together afterward. Fly casting is a kind of rarefied version of the fishing tournament, abstracted even from the fish itself. Contestants in other fishing tournaments compete to catch the longest or heaviest fish of many types, but fly casters compete for the most accurate or longest cast, throwing fishing line from rod and reel toward a target or across long distances.[43] Members Gonzalo Poey and George LaBranche gained permission from Herrmann to construct a platform on the pool near Eighth Avenue and 101st Street. However, "members were not to enjoy their practice in perfect peace" for "many 'public spirited citizens' . . . when asked to step back from the platform . . . demanded to know why a club claimed rights in a public park." This challenge to the club's exclusive access spoke to New Yorkers' sense of ownership of park space and desire to connect with water and fish. Herrmann was willing to afford the club more secluded, secure quarters, though: "The Park Department built another platform on the big lake near the West Seventy-second Street entrance, and enclosed it with a high wire fence and gate."[44]

While park goers questioned the club's exclusive access to space, they also showed strong interest in its activities. On October 12–13, 1906, the Anglers' Club hosted its first fly casting tournament, on the Harlem Meer instead of the lake farther south in order to accommodate spectators. Club historian Fraser recalled, "It is doubted whether an affair of this sort ever drew a larger throng than the one that milled about the Mere [sic] on Saturday afternoon." The spectators included thousands of "humble denizens of what is now the preferred residential section of Manhattan"—"East Siders, for the most part." Fraser thought that these spectators assumed they were "fishing for the little goldfish that could be seen in the shallow water near the walks."[45] Although the crowd of onlookers was dominated by "humble" East Siders, rarefied out-of-towners competed and took home the sizable purse, with an Irish fishing rod maker named John Enright taking the top prize.[46] Club member George LaBranche also used Central Park's waters to teach casting to Boy Scouts through the 1920s.[47]

The Anglers' Club's ties to the park waned in the 1920s as changing modes of city life for comfortable middle- and upper-class families gave them greater access to waters with more and bigger fish, not just fly casting. Most members lived in the city, but affordable automobiles and shorter workweeks—particularly the elimination of half-day work on Saturdays—eased weekend trips upstate. Some members moved to the suburbs. Fly casting practice in the park dwindled in popularity, and they "gave up our platform. The Parks Department was already eyeing dubiously a facility from which the public was excluded."[48] The Depression years saw a renaissance in urban casting, when another fishing club applied for a more accessible platform in Central Park, and sponsors such as Macy's Department Store and Abercrombie & Fitch Outfitters supported tournaments on the Conservatory Lake.[49] The Anglers' Club coalesced a network of privileged urban fishing enthusiasts and leveraged political voices for conservation, but the club's connection to urban fish was brief, abstracted, and exclusive.

Abstracted fishing earned the endorsement of the Parks Department, merchants, and clubmen, but fishing for real fish remained illicit, though sometimes law enforcement looked the other way. A photo from 1939 shows white-presenting children fishing openly in an area where law enforcement surely would have seen them. Many Manhattanites less able than Anglers' Club members to leave the city, especially children, seemed more determined than ever to encounter fish there, even if it was only goldfish. The ban on fishing was felt keenly by children for whom the ponds provided recreation and, for some, sustenance. One of the jobs of police stationed in the park was to monitor the water bodies for so-called poachers, including young people who made their own fishing poles and hooked fish with bent pins. Adults also entered the park before sunrise to "haul fish out of the park lakes and out of the Reservoir"; some constructed makeshift tackle with dead branches and string, using breadcrumbs for bait. Those caught by police might be fined a dollar.[50]

Recreational and subsistence fishing have long been associated with cultural identity, as communities develop their own fishing practices and foodways.[51] The privileged members of the Anglers' Club seemed most interested in trout and perch in streams near New York City and larger fish elsewhere. Anthropologist and writer Zora Neale Hurston, who moved to Harlem from Florida for her studies, insisted on the continued importance of southern Black culture amid the Great Migration, including fishing. In other destination cities of the Great Migration, Black migrants also connected with nature through fishing, including during the Depression, when this activity provided recreation, subsistence, and community building.[52] More privileged neighbors often saw catfish as trash animals. Indeed, "muddy" flavors in catfish flesh came from its ecological niche, feeding on the bottom of ponds, lakes, and streams.[53] Harlem residents, including both new migrants and their children, helped transform the waterscape of the park's northern end by releasing and fishing for catfish, one of the most common types of fish there alongside closely related goldfish.[54]

Indeed, the *Times* reported that one of the most popular spots for children—boys and girls—to fish was in the streams connecting the ponds and the Harlem Meer at the northern end of the park. These children likely hailed from Italian, Caribbean (including Puerto Rican), and African American families in neighboring residential areas, and they believed that the fish in their part of the park were the best. "The fish grow larger there. There are also more fish; they are fat and sleek," the *Times* explained. Regular reporting on the young Harlem fisherfolk was part winking, part romantic in tone, and white *Times* readers would have recognized the wistful portrayal as part of the paper's almost anthropological

OPPOSITE: In spite of rules against fishing often enforced by police during the 1930s, a group of children and adults fish openly in this 1939 photo. Police enforcement seems to have been uneven by this time. Courtesy of the Museum of the City of New York.

reporting on the multiethnic community north of the park.[55] Summer was peak fishing season, and the culture of youth fishing had developed a number of innovations and customs. Expert fishers brought bent pins and string instead of formal, purchased tackle equipment; dug worms for bait in the park; placed caught fish in jars; and kept their shoes on in the stream, ready to outrun police through the woods. Goldfish went through the opposite trajectory of feral animals—first domesticated, they were then released, then captured again. A few children "lobstered" for crayfish around the Harlem Meer, but it was hard to catch one of these creatures from under its rock without either getting pinched by its claws or surprised by a cop from behind.[56] Fishing children experienced the landscape in a visceral way: they stood in streams, feeling the water on their feet, waiting for goldfish and minnows to find breadcrumbs or worms on their hooks, and also knew the surrounding forest well enough to flee law enforcement. This type of leisure and contact with animated nature was distinct from that promoted at the new Central Park Zoo. These children also flew below the radar of reformers promoting supervised playgrounds elsewhere in the city, making their own spaces for play.[57]

Park authorities sought to control not only fishers but also fish themselves, mostly for the same health reasons as in the nineteenth century, although bacteriological explanations replaced older miasma theories that blamed vapors from rotting animal matter for illness. In the 1920s, Mayor Hylan had city workers fire guns near the reservoir to scare away circling gulls; others objected that the gulls were actually keeping the water cleaner by eating garbage and excess fish.[58] In 1926, a debate among the State Health Department, the city Department of Water Supply, and the private Central Park Association led to calls to drain the upper reservoir entirely because of the fish corpses and garbage that accumulated there, threatening the safety of water still used by many city residents.[59] The upper reservoir remained in place but with new access restrictions. In 1930, the Parks Department drained the lower reservoir, eliminating the rumored habitat of salmon of legendary size.[60] As John Crimmins

Two children play in a stream near the north end of the park in this photo from 1937.
Courtesy of the Museum of the City of New York and the Carl Van Vechten Trust.
© Van Vechten Trust.

had urged many years earlier, the Parks Department converted the thirty-five acres to playgrounds. The Southern New York Fish and Game Commission removed an estimated ten thousand fish from the lower reservoir, including a four-foot eel and many small-mouth bass, perch, and sunfish, and trucked them to "new abodes in reservoirs and lakes of Westchester County," where anglers would now have access to them. The draining and seining took several days' work, and park employees suspected that so-called poachers absconded with the largest fish before they were loaded into trucks, having gained easy access to the water after workers left for the night.[61]

In 1948, the Parks Department abruptly announced the end of its ban on fishing in Central Park but only on the largest lake, far south of Harlem, where *Times* reporters had documented a thriving culture of youth fishing. Only people younger than sixteen could fish; the official rules called for real tackle, but bent pins remained popular.[62] A Parks Department spokesman explained the change in policy, stating "We and the police got tired of chasing the kids," but it is unclear whether children continued to fish on the sly in Harlem.[63] The following year, the State Conservation Department brought hundreds of perch, sunfish, and bullheads from the Cold Spring Harbor hatchery on Long Island to stock the Lake.[64] Authorities gave no explanation for their omission of the Harlem Meer, and therefore Manhattan's largest Black neighborhood, also home to large Caribbean and Italian communities. Many have accused Robert Moses and his Parks Department of excluding Black New Yorkers from recreation programs alongside his well-documented and larger-scale demolition and displacement of Black communities. Although other historians have called into question evidence for several of those slights, this may be a genuine instance of racist neglect and exclusion.[65]

As in the case of sheep, urban development threatened to deprive fishing enthusiasts of space in Manhattan in the first half of the twentieth century. Unlike sheep, though, plural human-fish relationships maintained and even gained greater space in Central Park, thanks in large part to children who claimed their piece of nature and persisted in violating park rules. And while authorities simply moved sheep to Brooklyn, fish flowed—by their own and human efforts—both into and out of Central Park as part of efforts to control the health of the park's aquatic environments and to satisfy urban fishing enthusiasts.

City Dogs as Leashed Citizens

Central Park has for its entire history been an important space for the shifting belonging of dogs in the city. When the park first opened, dogs were often impounded for running at large. As we have seen, loose dogs were destructive to wildlife in the park, particularly waterfowl and other ground-nesting birds. But dogs and horses were the only domesticated creatures from outside the park allowed in at all (dogs had to be on a leash no longer than five feet). Meanwhile, pet keeping grew in popularity from the nineteenth century into the twentieth, and Manhattan dogs and their humans came to rely on the park even more as real estate development filled up spaces where they might have exercised and roamed.[66] The cultural geography of dogs and dog people in Central Park was in flux; fewer dogs entered unaccompanied by a human, and more humans gained access for their dogs by attaching them to leashes.[67]

It wasn't only strays who ran loose, though; many pet people still had trouble controlling their animals. Even the pooches of the rich and famous sometimes escaped in the park while out for an "airing" with the servants, such as the Vanderbilts' terrier Spot and opera star Emma Calvé's collie Jacque.[68] Strays and pampered dogs alike faced risks if unaccompanied, in part because they threatened other animals. As of the 1910s, a National Guardsman was posted in the park to shoot dogs and other potential predators of vulnerable and desired creatures such as sheep, swans, and ducks.[69] Coming years brought new developments in dog training and dog health, and affluent dog owners sought to open up spaces in Central Park to themselves and their animals. Still, many dogs roamed the park, and city authorities—police, the ASPCA, health officials, and Parks Department leaders—tried to bring dogs of all kinds under control.[70]

The threat of rabies continued to shape urban canine-human relationships at the turn of the twentieth century. Vaccination was available, but few dog people got it for their pets because of the expense of early versions of the inoculation and suspicion about its effectiveness, necessity, and value. New York's urban animal populations saw periodic, terrifying outbreaks, but many pet people believed that better control of dogs was the answer, not mandatory vaccination.[71] New York City's Health Department expanded its capacity to monitor and control animals' health with the addition of veterinarians to its staff; the Health Department and a private laboratory also offered treatment to humans bitten by suspicious animals.[72] Meanwhile, the Health Department challenged the ASPCA's role in enforcing dog laws, which it had held since the 1890s, because the ASPCA opposed muzzling as cruel.[73]

During the 1930s, even upper-crust New Yorkers found themselves affected by the Great Depression, and dog keeping practices became one expression of the downturn. The *Times* reported that there were more dogs than usual in the wealthier sections of the city as many affluent New Yorkers let go of their country homes, where their dogs once spent much of their time. For dogs, life must have felt even more constrained as they moved permanently from rural estates to townhomes and apartments that were relatively cramped for them, although lavish for humans, on the Upper East and West Sides. Privileged dog people, reduced somewhat in their wealth and luxury, lobbied for better conditions for dog walking, resulting in slightly relaxed city rules in early 1935: dogs walking outside the parks no longer needed to wear a muzzle, only a leash.[74]

The rules remained stricter on Parks Department property, where administrators "lean to the side of caution, because of the very mixed company they entertain."[75] In other words, the mix of many different kinds of dogs, dog people, and non–dog people increased the chances of

A person in a chauffeur uniform walks a dachshund on a park path in the early 1940s. Photo by Marjory Collins, courtesy of the Library of Congress, Prints and Photographs Division.

encounters that could be nerve-racking and potentially dangerous—for humans or canines. Many still perceived dogs as aggressive, unpredictable, and potentially diseased. The deadly threat of rabies remained fresh in many New Yorkers' memories; human deaths had been reported in 1926, 1927, and 1928. But New Yorkers disagreed about whether this meant rabies was too close for comfort or "hysteria" about it was blown out of proportion.[76]

Dog training as popularized in books such as Dr. James Kinney's *How to Raise a Dog* was beginning to help some dog people mold their pets' behavior.[77] Kinney asserted that trained dogs would behave in a controlled, predictable way in urban and suburban settings, and in time, this would normalize dogs even for city dwellers who encountered them on sidewalks or park paths but did not keep them as pets themselves. Pet people, such as Mrs. A. Cooper of the Hampshire House high-rise co-op on Central Park South, cited Kinney's book and her interpretation of those ambivalent rabies records in appealing directly to Robert Moses for the park to set aside space for dogs to run free. Cooper argued that the current policy deprived the dogs of "necessary exercise and pleasure" and their owners of "the pleasure of watching them run about," but an enclosed yard in the park would gratify "hundreds of dog-lovers."[78] Staff gave Cooper the "usual reply" to the question "we have wrestled with" since Moses took office, that such proposals were impractical.[79]

Rabies was not the only concern of health officials, park authorities, and residents considering the place of dogs in Central Park. As in the case of fish released into the park, water quality was also a serious concern. The city health code prohibited dogs from the remaining reservoir path because of the risk that feces could taint the water supply, even though other water sources had become more important for New York.[80] Dogs still defecated elsewhere in the park, though. Mothers expressed gratitude for Robert Moses's improvements to the parks but complained of the high risk that toddlers would pick up a handful of dirt contaminated with dog feces.[81] A park engineer replied that "there are not sufficient policemen to serve summonses against all those who refuse to curb their dogs"—that is, having dogs defecate along curblines where their feces would be washed into sewers, rather than on grass or soil.[82]

If the *Times* was correct about the increased number of dogs and sensitivity to dog-related rules in the city's wealthier sections, perhaps this helps explain an outburst of protests against rules restricting dog walking within the park. Most notably, in 1939, Dorothy Forbes gathered signatures from over thirty neighbors around the Upper East Side demanding access to "part of the area between the reservoir cinder path and the bridle path" for "responsible" dog people. Forbes argued that "dog owners" such as herself and her neighbors suffered from an "inequality of privilege" because pedestrians without dogs and equestrians each enjoyed access to a nearby trail for their exclusive use.[83] Dog people hailing from the moneyed east, south, and west perimeters of the park claimed that their dogs were healthy and well-behaved, undeserving of these limitations in the parks.[84] Kinney's book helped support the position that cities could be good places for dogs; he dedicated an entire chapter to refuting the popular assertion that "it is cruel to keep a dog in the city."[85] Many dog people claimed to train their pets in the "good city manners" Kinney described and thus demanded more freedom in the park.

Park administrators grew weary of such demands while standing firm in denying further freedom for dogs within the park. Moses's deputies frequently rejected calls for fenced dog runs.[86] Meanwhile, violations for dog rules were the most common reasons park police issued summonses.[87] Judges remained strict in assessing fines against people who unleashed their dogs, particularly for the affluent. One judge who heard many leash law violation cases charged owners of purebred dogs twice the fines for owners of mutts (two dollars versus one dollar forty-four and twenty-two dollars, respectively, in 2024 currency), on the theory that New Yorkers who could afford a pedigreed animal needed a steeper deterrent against doing what they thought was best for their dogs.[88] Affluent New Yorkers pushed back with protests and even occasional force, as when one woman slapped a police officer who issued her a summons for setting her collie free in Central Park's Heckscher Playground.[89] The actor Victor Moore quipped after paying his fine that the squirrels in Central Park should be muzzled based on the rule applied to his wee Pomeranian. Indeed, available muzzles were ill fitting for small breeds with short snouts—increasingly popular during this era and in a neighborhood of tiny apartments.[90]

There remained a sizable stray dog population in the city—as of 1908, one estimate stood at 150,000—many of whom frequented Central Park in spite of the police scouring the area.[91] Historian Fred Brown has aptly referred to urban spaces where canines roam free as "dog commons."[92] Pet dogs at large in the park were at risk of joining the city's stray population, whose health was suspect; indeed, many pets went missing when their people let them off leash. In 1935, ASPCA agent Martha Kobbe knew of five dogs lost in Central Park on a single Sunday, pleading for dog owners to comply with the leash law and not assume that their pets would return.[93] As had been the case since the park's origins, police often used deadly force against domestic animals who appeared without a human. Soon dogs would be even more tightly managed by the state, by leashes, guns, and other tools.

Some New Yorkers in the 1930s thought rabies a thing of the past, but the disease had not completely disappeared from the city. In the 1940s, an outbreak of rabies led health authorities to impose dog quarantines first on individual boroughs and then citywide in late 1944, banning transport of dogs across borough borders.[94] Regardless of a borough's quarantine status at any time, people caught letting their dogs off leash would now be fined three dollars and required to have their dog tested for rabies within twenty-four hours—as many violators of the leash law found out when issued a summons in Central Park, one of the most popular spaces for illicit leash-free dog running.[95] After over a decade with no cases of dog-to-human rabies transmission, in 1944 a human New Yorker died of rabies contracted from a dog bite.[96] Thousands of dogs died either of the disease itself or at the hands of humans who killed them because they could not verify that the canines were disease free. Many New Yorkers, including some veterinarians, resisted compulsory rabies vaccination in favor of higher fines for dog people who unleashed their dogs in public. Compulsory vaccination was finally adopted amid a series of debates in 1946–47, dramatically altering the ecology of rabies and dogs in the city.[97] In 1949, "no case of animal rabies was reported" for the first time in the Health Department's history.[98]

Dog Runs and Dogs on the Run

Even while rabies remained a threat, some humans attempted to establish relationships with stray dogs by leaving food for specific animals who frequented known locations within the park. Starting in the mid-1930s, the opera singer Frieda Hempel watched a free-ranging dog from her high-rise window overlooking the park and also tracked him on foot with treats. A police officer helped with the tracking, ignoring the command to shoot strays. In her biography, Hempel praised what she saw as the dog's ingenuity in making a living in the park—for example, he evaded capture by police and, Hempel said, cooperated with a black cat who helped protect his food from rats. "This wild dog commanded all my respect, and I wanted to help him," Hempel later recalled.[99] She eventually found the dog's hiding spot, named him Brownie, and for five years left packets of meat in a hiding spot near his territory in the park. In 1942, Hempel finally enlisted the help of the ASPCA in capturing and adopting the dog.[100]

Publicity around Hempel's dog led other New Yorkers to share their own stories about feeding strays in the park. Helen Balfour Adams empathetically explained the behavior of creatures like Brownie: "Many a lost dog, frightened by the streets, chased by cruel people, has found refuge in the Park."[101] Adams gave much of her wealth to animal welfare causes such as the Women's League for Animals and worked at New York's most prestigious animal hospital. For animal welfare advocates and health and park authorities alike, Hempel's adoption of Brownie helped reduce a population viewed as both dangerous and vulnerable. The *Times* captured this attitude as it explained that "measures must be taken to regulate Brownie's status and make him a member of society."[102] In other words, dogs in the city would have to conform to human ways of living. Brownie would now spend his days in an apartment on Central Park West with Hempel's other dog and henceforth only enter Central Park leashed, muzzled, and accompanied by a human.

Hempel's latest adoptee experienced two very different types of dog life in Manhattan—first, that of the roving stray subject to impoundment and even killing by law enforcement authorities, and then that of a contained and law-abiding companion of a privileged human New Yorker. For animal welfare advocates like Hempel and the ASPCA, Brownie's story was one of redemption, the kind of happy ending that they hoped for. But this story did not account for the lives of all dogs and their humans in Manhattan and Central Park. The park continued to provide an attractive environment for two very different kinds of canine lives: it was a convenient spatial niche, full of hiding places for stray urban dogs, and also an appealing landscape where dog people could exercise their (presumably) trained and well-behaved canines. Both individually and collectively, New York dogs crossed many boundaries of "canine citizenship," to borrow a term from visual studies scholar Lisa Uddin. Uddin argues that thinking of dogs as a kind of innocent, vulnerable citizen "mobilizes human beings to act like concerned citizens toward nonhuman beings."[103] Like the bird-watchers and equestrians of chapter 4, Hempel and her ASPCA supporters fortified their own citizenship by caring for vulnerable creatures. Laws defined acceptable practices for dog people, but power and social difference could make some off-leash dogs more acceptable than others. Meanwhile, dogs' citizenship was judged according to their conformity to human ways of life, not their distinctly canine ways of relating to public space and other species.

Thomas Hoving's brief stint as parks commissioner in 1966–67 brought new ways to hone canine citizenship in Central Park by bringing dogs further into the human social sphere. In his bid to expand park attendance, Hoving conceived a motley profusion of new activities, several of them relating to dogs. Zookeeper Louis Ciccia had long dreamed of offering free dog obedience training courses in the park, and Hoving finally green-lit the project. Ciccia emphasized topics such as "city manners— like curbing" that were as much about training humans as their dogs. By offering the course free of charge, Ciccia hoped to benefit children in families with dogs, blind New Yorkers interested in dog guides, and lower-income New Yorkers who were reputed to exert less control over their dogs. But early classes attracted mostly sighted "adults from the nearby high-rent district" across Fifth Avenue from Seventy-Ninth Street, where classes took place.[104]

Dogs were still required to stay on leash elsewhere in the park and throughout the city, but Hoving created two fenced dog runs in Central Park that remained beyond his tenure. One stood near Eighty-Sixth Street and Central Park West, and a *Times* reporter investigating dog walking practices found that fenced-in space empty, with a number of park goers letting their dogs off leash just outside. The other run served the long-standing enclave of dog people on the Upper East Side—from the neighborhood where Dorothy Forbes, nearly thirty years earlier, had organized her neighbors to petition for more dog walking space. Dog people remained dissatisfied with the space allocated for them, observing that the fenced-off area was paved and no larger than their own apartments. "I've never seen a dog in there," snarled a human resident of nearby Eighty-Third Street who visited the park with her Irish setter. Like many of her neighbors, she illicitly ran her dog on a spot within the park called Cedar Hill, snapping on the leash only when police officers were spotted nearby. The police only caught about thirty dog people violating the leash law in the park each year. The largely white and affluent dog people on Cedar Hill represented themselves as a community capable of controlling their dogs: "Everybody here knows everybody else, and the dogs get along well." They asked authorities to designate the whole of Cedar Hill as a dog run, and they justified their use of the space as a response to conditions that were unfair to nonhuman citizens who needed exercise outside cramped New York apartments.[105]

The dog people of Cedar Hill presented themselves as a responsible, functioning polity of dog-human dyads who deserved leisure space in the park. Meanwhile, many white New Yorkers, whether or not they lived with a dog, increasingly imagined a more menacing and also racialized canine geography of the city. Whites associated Black and brown New Yorkers with increasing reports of crime in the city at large and Central Park particularly. As part of his effort to expand park attendance, Hoving proposed having the police department instate dog patrols in Central Park; he hoped the presence of police dogs would deter crime and reassure visitors that the park was safe.[106] Hoving's suggestion was soon rejected, but New Yorkers of many racial identities had become interested in large dog breeds with martial associations. Police sometimes even told crime victims to purchase a big dog to protect themselves.[107] These trends brought shifts in New York's dog population and that of cities across the United States. German shepherds replaced small breeds like the miniature poodle as the breed most sought for adoption in cities, and the ASPCA noted that larger dogs were filling up obedience classes.[108] Dog owners who received summonses for unleashing their dogs complained that the police should pay more attention to muggings and assaults.[109] Those who kept big dogs were keen to give their companions space to run in the city's largest park. But city dwellers who were not part of this trend feared that bigger dogs brought more aggression and powerful bites, greater need for space, and higher volumes of feces.

Many commentators framed the situation as a conflict between dogs and children—particularly children's health, safety, and access to play spaces. "New York is going to the dogs at the expense of its children," warned writer and parent Claire Berman in 1970, citing diseases spread in ubiquitous dog feces and growing numbers of large and aggressive dogs that children encountered at every turn. Children were a leading concern at a series of "speak-outs" and workshops held by park officials and community in 1978 aimed at opening dialogue among New Yorkers with competing claims on Central Park. Sessions focused on dogs in the park seemed to find no middle ground between children's health advocates, who warned of dog bites and contamination by dog feces, and those who longed to set their dogs free off leash. In response to the question of whether there was a place for dogs in Central Park, dog opponents such as pediatricians and child health advocacy groups insisted that the city should look into vacant lots instead—a space where dogs could be separate from children.[110] A 1973 survey found that 15 percent of Manhattanites wanted to see more dogs in the park, but 37 percent wanted fewer dogs.[111]

Once widely viewed as marauding, potentially rabid curs, dogs attained a tentative and fragile status of acceptance over the first two-thirds of the twentieth century. As it was with both sheep and fish, urban development limited dogs' access to space—and in the case of dogs, this trend proceeded in tandem with the spread of dog ownership among New Yorkers. When the Depression confined many wealthy New Yorkers' dogs to the city, those owners mobilized to demand their due as supposedly responsible citizens. Restrictions on dogs in the park remained for years, even after rabies vaccines and obedience training afforded greater control over them. It is perhaps a mark of the ambivalence city dwellers feel for dogs that nearly thirty years elapsed between the upwelling of petitions from well-heeled (no pun intended) park neighbors and Hoving granting their requests. Over time, dogs gained more diverse human constituencies, but Black and brown folks with dogs, and dogs roaming near Black and brown neighborhoods, felt even less respect.

More-than-Human Pluralities

By the 1960s and 1970s, the status of sheep, fish, and dogs in Central Park continued to change as Central Park hosted a growing variety of activities in which humans and nonhumans interacted. Of course, the Lehman Children's Zoo opened in 1961 and included a few lambs to pet but too few to flock; on just one acre, they had too little room to wander and graze anyway. Three lambs died within the first month of operation at the Children's Zoo. "This may have been due to overfeeding," speculated

A dog wanders near human sunbathers by the Turtle Pond and Belvedere Castle in the 1970s. Off-leash dogs have been a topic of frequent controversy in the park. Courtesy of the Museum of the City of New York.

the Manhattan parks director, "or it might have been due to some physical defect or a combination of both."[112] Visitors to the small attraction could purchase Ry-Krisp crackers from a vending machine and feed them to the animals, and in the feature's early days, the keepers had yet to figure out how to limit animals' cracker intake. Unable to flock and fed by children rather than through their own grazing actions, sheep in the 1960s lived very different kinds of lives and served very different functions within the park than on the farm.[113]

The Central Park Children's Zoo, like others across the United States, offered a comforting facsimile of human relationships with livestock, contrasting with the violent reality of animal husbandry and slaughter that provided many New Yorkers with the animal products that they consumed. On the other hand, creators of children's zoos seemed to be reviving a stylized version of what park authorities imagined for the Children's District in the 1860s, included the dairy and the sheepfold, where children were expected to encounter the simple pleasures of rural life. In children's zoos, lambs and piglets embodied a pastoral fantasyland for urban children. This was how agricultural animals fit in the park as of the 1960s: as gentle babies cycled back to the farm before they matured to sizes and temperaments that would become less manageable.

While baby sheep came back in limited form, support for access to fish expanded. In 1969, twenty years after the Seventy-Second Street Lake was opened, the Harlem Meer again became the site of fishing contests, now with thousands of real fish stocked there thanks to donations by the Schaefer Brewing Company, and targeted specifically to Harlem youth. Schaefer distributed free fishing kits, and the *Amsterdam News* helped sponsor prizes for participating youth. Contest officials set up access for children using wheelchairs and other mobility aids on a section of the shore. Thousands of children from Harlem participated each year.[114] Of course, Harlem children had expressed their knowledge of and connections with fish for decades.

Harlem residents' connections with dogs and the park saw more ambivalent changes. Authorities and many New Yorkers from all neighborhoods perceived that free-ranging dog packs at the north of the park were growing. A deputy parks commissioner pronounced in 1972 that "they are starting to run in packs more than before." The ASPCA attempted to control these animals by chasing individuals out of the park, where it became easier to corner them on city streets.[115] As Brownie knew almost forty years earlier, the park was full of places to hide from humans they knew might chase them. It was also full of other dogs with whom they could form relationships. In domestic multispecies families, dogs performed such relational behaviors with the humans and other pets.[116] Stories about these dogs gathering in public spaces beyond human control evoked a racial geography of Manhattan. It was no coincidence that dog packs at the north of the park got the most attention, as this area was closest to the borough's largest concentration of Black and Latino New Yorkers. Not only in New York but in cities across the United States, officials blamed Black residents for controlling their dogs poorly while conflating packs of dogs with gangs of humans that whites feared—and which motivated some whites to buy large dogs for themselves. Alan Beck of New York's Bureau of Animal Affairs had published his doctoral thesis on similar struggles in Baltimore in the 1960s and 1970s and warned of an epidemic of dog bites and dog-borne parasitic illness.[117] In many US cities at that time, dogs embodied and also extended social conflicts and racialized representations of crime and safety concerns.[118]

Since the park's origins, park authorities and other New Yorkers have grappled with questions about which animals belonged in the park and in the city. As we have seen, these questions are also in part about the belonging of different groups of people in the city as well as the meanings and uses of urban nature. Park goers' neighborhood identities and social positions marked their sense of entitlement to animals and to public spaces. We must not ignore, however, the way development outside the park shaped the needs of New York's more-than-human polity for open space within the park. Business, residential, and infrastructure development around the park limited spaces that sheep, fish, and dogs might share with humans. Meanwhile, animals and their plural human partisans experienced different opportunities to move such relationships to suburban, rural, or wild spaces beyond the city. Finally, these creatures experienced changing means of human control over them and the possible risks of animal life within New York. Overall, many groups of humans and nonhumans helped reshape whether and how these more-than-human relationships still belonged in an urban park.

Conclusion

In August 2013, some five hundred human New Yorkers poured into Central Park over one twenty-four-hour period in an attempt to identify and record all fauna and flora living there. Called the "BioBlitz," this event seemed high-tech. As a cosponsor of the event, Google provided Google Glasses with which participating City University students could instantly photograph plants and animals that they found. Yet some of the language used by the organizers recalled bird lovers' ideas from around 1900 about connecting human city dwellers with each other and the creatures in the park. "These students are having a chance to use the city as their classroom," explained a CUNY dean. Another cosponsor, the Central Park Conservancy, the private organization that now operates the park, cited its preservation work in ensuring that "millions of people get to enjoy the outdoors in the heart of Manhattan." But whereas early park supporters mostly saw select animals as serving humans by "animating" the landscape and "elevating" the tastes and knowledge of New Yorkers confined to the city, events like the BioBlitz help reveal the park's importance for other creatures' lives. According to organizers and participants, the park and its supporters give "countless species [. . .] a place to call home."[1]

Promoters of the BioBlitz and other participatory ecology activities celebrate the benefits of urban green space for humans and wild species.

The green gem of Central Park seems perhaps more precious than ever. The urban growth predicted by Frederick Law Olmsted, shaped and implemented by Andrew Haswell Green and John Crimmins, and reasserted by Robert Moses continues: the paved, fast-paced, and inequitable city has engulfed the park. Not only that, but Greater New York now joins a contiguous urban agglomeration stretching from Maine to Virginia, in which development has converted habitat and farmland into cities and suburbs, industry and infrastructure. In a world where there is less space for animals to move and more people living in urbanized spaces, we ask much of Central Park's animated landscapes and those of other green spaces in New York and beyond.[2]

The same themes that marked Central Park's first one hundred–some years as an animated landscape have persisted over the past fifty. Real estate markets and social oppression in Manhattan continue to displace some humans and nonhumans whose access to the park becomes more attenuated. New Yorkers still make claims to space in the park through their affiliation with animals, sometimes for the good of multispecies communities and sometimes in ways that may be self-serving. Park authorities and users continue to articulate values related to urban animals, often translating long-standing ideals in new language and programming. Animals still connect the park with other spaces as land conversion, species loss, and climate injustice alter more-than-human geographies near and distant.

Some persistent challenges that we have seen throughout this story have culminated in decisive changes in the way the park manages animal spaces. Most notably, after more than a century of suggestions that a private organization should operate the captive animal display, starting with August Belmont and continuing as the original architects repeatedly urged such an arrangement, the New York Zoological Society (NYZS) assumed control of the Central Park Zoo, in addition to its existing portfolio that included the Bronx Zoo. Multiple park boards, Olmsted and Vaux themselves, master planner Moses, master showman Ronald

Cheyne-Stout, and the Lehmans had all endeavored to remake the attraction. Under parks commissioner Gordon Davis, whose daughter was reputed to have begged not to go back to the zoo, the NYZS took it over in 1983 amid yet another round of protests about the conditions there.[3] The project drastically exceeded its timeline and budget for renovating the attraction, reopening finally in 1988.[4] The zoo is no longer a public space for casual weekly visits; admission fees support the facility, and there are no free days as Vaux and others had once recommended.

Accredited zoos promise to leave behind retrograde standards of animal captivity in favor of modern conditions, including more environmentalist values.[5] Indeed, the NYZS changed its own name to the Wildlife Conservation Society (WCS) in 1993 and attempted to rebrand its urban animal displays as "Wildlife Conservation Parks" (it manages three others in New York besides the Bronx Zoo and Central Park Zoo).[6] As we know, park administrators have valued captive urban animals as conservation ambassadors since Andrew Haswell Green promised to spark appreciation for American wildlife with a zoological garden. While *menagerie* was certainly a pejorative term when Central Park authorities attempted to improve its animal collection, conservationists as early as William Hornaday even attempted to abandon the term *zoo* as well. Now animals are no longer taken from the wild; captive breeding has replaced animal collection. The Central Park Zoo mostly displays small animals, keeping larger animals at other WCS facilities. However, other flows tie the zoo to distant social, ecological struggles. Admission revenues at the zoo, and the workings of the institution itself, materially connect visitors with the WCS's projects all over the world and thereby both wildlife populations and the human communities who live near them. This connection may seem to fulfill the long-standing conservation promises of zoos, but it also ties the exhibits to continuing concerns about the marginalization and displacement of Indigenous communities by wildlife "protected areas." In the 1800s, buffalo on display in Central Park (and later the Bronx Zoo) embodied contradictions between New

York's financial role in the United States' overland empire and the liberal conservation rhetoric of zoo advocates. Now zoo visitors become entangled in accusations that WCS's "fortress conservation" approaches violate human rights of communities who had long lived in spatially fluid arrangements with wildlife in places such as the Democratic Republic of Congo.[7] In some ways, the hard borders of protected areas reflected sharp boundaries of parks like Central Park too.

The shift to private management of the zoo has proceeded in tandem with the creation of the Central Park Conservancy and the movement toward private maintenance of the park as a whole. The Conservancy formed in the 1970s in cooperation with the city and Commissioner Davis's administration, as concerns spanning the twentieth century about the deterioration of the park became heightened amid New York City's financial crisis. As has been the case for all of the park's history, conditions in environment and society around the park could not be separated from the space within. Global economic shocks, deindustrialization, and suburbanization hit New York hard, especially given its relatively generous public programs (although park administrators and patrons have long argued that budgets were too austere). To protect the park from fiscal conditions in the city, the Conservancy, a nonprofit organization, raised money, enlisting a slew of wealthy donors. Rehabilitation efforts took over a decade, and the Conservancy contractually assumed most operating functions of the park as a whole in 1998.[8] Led by urban planner Elizabeth Barlow Rogers, the Conservancy also attempted to balance the Greensward plan's landscape principles with recreation demands.

Besides global fiscal crisis and deindustrialization, another urban condition that pervaded the park was the city's bias against Harlem, which remains a thriving neighborhood of Black and Latino New Yorkers, although it is threatened with gentrification. A study by Columbia University urban affairs faculty in 1973, the *Savas Report*, showed that New Yorkers from the northern end of Manhattan were far less likely to visit the park and that the park's northern end was the most likely section to be avoided by other park visitors.[9] Rehabilitation activities had been slow to reach the park's northern end, and some activists from Harlem worried that placing the park in private hands would sharpen the divide as features close to privileged white and affluent areas could receive priority. As we have seen, Harlem residents had experienced exclusion from animal relationships in the park as early as the 1930s, whether on the bridle paths or when the Harlem Meer remained closed to fishing. Discourse about urban dogs in the 1970s also blamed Harlem for canines billed as dangerous.

Media and prosecutors used animalistic representations of Harlem park goers in much more dire ways in the case of five Black and Latino boys wrongly accused in 1989 of raping Trisha Meili in Central Park. In the rush to charge someone for this terrible harm, media, police, and prosecutors conjured images of an animalistic culture at the park's north end. They referred to the boys' activities in the park as "wilding," Harlem as a "jungle," and the boys themselves as "animals" or "wolves." The persecution and imprisonment of Antron McCray, Kevin Richardson, Yusef Salaam, Raymond Santana, and Korey Wise, who were exonerated and freed after spending between five and thirteen years in prison, communicated to Harlem's Black and brown communities that they did not belong in the park, casting them lower on a hierarchy of being alongside nonhuman predators. Authorities sharpened policing at the boundaries of spatial and ontological belonging where the park met the neighborhood.[10] This major incident but also many day-to-day incidents, dating back to the harassment of Black riders on the bridle path in the 1930s, have led some Harlem residents to frequent other parks, limiting the kinds of human-animal relationships that can form at Central Park's northern end. Meanwhile, gentrification amid the park's rehabilitation further threatens this historic neighborhood's connection to these animated landscapes, although an entrance renamed the "Gate of the Exonerated" for McCray, Richardson, Salaam, Santana, and Wise seeks to welcome Harlemites to the park.[11] Black New Yorkers more recently have looked beyond Manhattan to uphold relationships with horses. For example, the Federation of Black Cowboys has partnered with a city park in Queens to stable horses, operate youth programs, and preserve the history of Black cowboy culture.[12]

Equestrian trails and carriage roads were so essential to elites' hopes for the park in 1858 that their inclusion in park plans was taken for granted. It has proven difficult, expensive, and controversial, however, to maintain space for horse-human relationships in the park and Manhattan in general. After decades of waxing and waning conditions on the bridle paths, equestrianism disappeared from the trails for a number of years after the city's longest-operating stable, the Claremont Riding Academy, shut down in 2007. The owner and patrons blamed the costs of operating the stable, declining profitability because of poor bridle path conditions, and a hot real estate market as factors in the closure—troubles that Oscar Hauter had written about in the 1930s. Other stables eventually opened to take its place, but it is clear that human-horse relationships in the city have become even more difficult to sustain.[13] Other working horses pull carriages, but starting in 2014, Mayor Bill DeBlasio sought to ban these vehicles, claiming that the urban environment, with its hard pavement and high heat, is detrimental to horses' health. Sheep had also faced threats from an urbanizing environment in the early twentieth century, but they had only a small constituency that spoke for them. In the more recent debate over horses, a group calling itself New Yorkers for Clean, Livable, and Safe Streets, along with animal welfare organizations, supported DeBlasio's efforts, but stable owners and carriage drivers argued that the horses live in healthy and supportive conditions. The debate has often pivoted upon competing claims about who knows horses best.[14] Some animal geographers argue that "letting go of attachments" to certain species is the most just way of sharing space, while others point to the depth of entanglements between humans and species like horses. The latter position argues that humans and horses have coevolved, and continue to do so, as companion species.[15]

As with horses, the park has been vital to defining and redefining the place of raccoons in the city. Both in the 1860s, with the park's establishment, and when the Central Park Zoo reopened in 1934 after its New Deal renewal, raccoons were among the creatures that many donors gave to the attraction. As we saw, donors seemed to believe that captivity in the park was a preferable condition for raccoons as the city expanded. Furthermore, in 1961, raccoons were among the animals the Lehmans carefully selected for the Children's Zoo, meant to offer close contact with animals for young New Yorkers. The raccoons were housed in a deep pit to prevent them from escaping into the wilds of the park.[16] While many New York dogs gained tentative acceptance in the park (depending on location) as rabies came under control, urban growth has left raccoons perpetually in potential conflict with humans. Furthermore, in 2010, the Department of Health found dozens of rabid raccoons in and around Central Park, and signs around the border of the park warn visitors about possible disease and the risks of transmission.[17]

While raccoons have exercised their own mobility and behaviors to make their way in Central Park and New York City, red-eared sliders, a species of turtle, have mostly arrived in the park through direct human manipulation, similar to house sparrows introduced by acclimatizers, informally stocked goldfish, or the baby alligators that children acquired as souvenirs in the nineteenth and early twentieth centuries. This species is the most popular type of turtle taken as a pet today, and although they originate from the southeastern United States and are farmed there, the species is considered invasive and a public health threat in the Northeast. Increasingly, farms in China also produce baby red-eared sliders for global trade. The baby turtles often carry salmonella on their skin, and the fast-growing adults can produce more young than species native to the Northeast. While many of these turtles are exported abroad, within the United States their sale is illegal; some shops in New York's Chinatown do a brisk underground business in the babies, often selling to parents whose children are charmed by their tiny features. Later, families become overwhelmed when turtles grow to need a twenty-gallon tank. As ubiqui-tous captive animals, red-eared sliders have also become a popular choice among New York Buddhists seeking to practice "release life" ceremonies that improve karma during difficult times such as illness. Former pets and ceremonial turtles alike are often released into Central Park's Turtle Pond near Seventy-Ninth Street in the middle of the park, where some die from cold and others reproduce prolifically, depending on the season. Valued ceremonially and for their appealing looks, these turtles connect the park with distant landscapes where they are bred but may also dis-place vulnerable species when humans claim Central Park as an outlet for these creatures.[18]

Many early bird and squirrel lovers considered wild animals vulner-able and valued them for teaching urban humans patience, quiet, and gentleness. Now the BioBlitz seems to marvel at the resilience and po-tential of urban animals. Urban ecology still entails intense study, but accessible technologies and environmental education programs promise to include more city dwellers. Some urban environmental advocates even value cities as potential corridors or refugia, including for species shifting their ranges with climate change. As we have seen, birds migrating on the Atlantic flyway have relied upon the park as a vital stopover.[19] During the first two decades of the twenty-first century, scientists discovered new species of frog and centipede in the park. Olmsted, Vaux, and bird lovers like Frank Chapman, Anne Crolius, and Ludlow Griscom would surely approve of the deep immersion practiced by professional ecologists and citizen-scientists to find and identify these creatures.[20] Furthermore, even outside of formal ecological studies, urban parks like Central Park foster encounters with wildlife that many humans find inspiring and rejuvenat-ing. From longtime expert birders like Christian Cooper to newcomers to the pastime such as birding podcaster Tenijah Hamilton or even the casual park visitor, human city dwellers value these creatures as indica-tors of resilience and the role cities can play in conservation. Around 1900, Bird Day and Christmas Bird Count activities were adopted to help spread natural history knowledge. Today participatory science and even individual wild animals like the longtime Central Park neighbor Pale Male, a beloved red-tailed hawk, connect city people to one another and to the ecologies in their backyards.[21] Birders and naturalist organizations continue to serve as forces for conservation, whether focused on spaces within the park or distant but connected locales such as the wintering and breeding grounds of visiting warblers.[22]

Such connections should remind us that urban parks are vital but insufficient for preserving wildlife and addressing the injustices of urban life for humans, in spite of hopes of the park's founders. Central Park and other urban parks are important for wildlife, but threats to wildlife outside them are grave beyond the scale of these patches of green and blue, however beloved. Bird populations across North America have declined precipitously since the 1970s, exemplifying threats to biodiversity that urban green spaces cannot by themselves undo. Meanwhile, access to planning processes for urban green spaces remains limited for communities of color amid gentrification, entrenched power structures in city planning and conservation organizations, and tight budgets for parks and recreation.[23] Community-managed green spaces do not enjoy the same resources and protection afforded by municipal government or major conservation organizations.[24] Wildlife experts such as Corina Newsome argue that investing money in green space and infrastructure in Black, brown, and Indigenous communities for their health and climate resilience will benefit birds and other creatures too.[25] Urban communities who have faced segregation and disinvestment find hope and fellowship stewarding grassroots green spaces, including opportunities to connect with wildlife or raise domestic animals there. Yet even if communities who manage their own green spaces can withstand urban development pressures and local environmental threats like soil lead levels and water access, the pressures of climate change and the loss of migratory habitats elsewhere lie far beyond the community or urban scale. Public green spaces do serve as "lungs for the city," retreats from urban clamor, and refugia for wildlife. But the design, rules, and norms of public spaces still reflect the values and power hierarchies of the larger society. And however much the tired human laborer or the migrant warbler find refreshment there, the sanctified space of the park can only do so much to change the world beyond.[26]

Public space can be an arena for challenging the status quo and for any member of more-than-human society, of any species, to achieve visibility. In the late nineteenth and early twentieth centuries, animal advocates such as Henry Bergh and Olive Thorne Miller afforded nonhumans in Central Park a certain kind of membership in the polity, but animal advocacy was often based on assumptions of animals' vulnerability and that privileged human New Yorkers would protect them. Environmental justice activists and other minoritized communities champion green spaces and ecosystems but receive too little credit and support from the best-endowed environmental groups. Indeed, Indigenous Americans have led buffalo conservation since the late 1800s in spite of domination by wildlife advocates like William Hornaday; today the Intertribal Buffalo Council has become a force for rebuilding plains ecosystems.[27] Descendants of displaced Lenape people are reclaiming visibility as longtime stewards of Manhattan's cultural and ecological heritage.[28] And birders, ecologists, and other naturalists of color show how communities of color share ecosystems with wildlife—and did so even before Christian Cooper so powerfully brought inequities in conservation to light in 2020. The organization Black AF in STEM founded Black Birders Week in response to Cooper's experience and emphasizes the ways the health and land issues connect movements for environmental justice and wildlife preservation.[29]

The history of Central Park as an animated landscape shows that elites and privileged city dwellers have asserted their power to shape green spaces and animal life but that other communities, human and more-than-human, have also made places that are socially and ecologically consequential. The mid-1800s was a time of grand park building across the eastern United States, when elites with access to land and power seemed able to reorder city fauna to their aesthetic tastes. But their power was not absolute, and both nonhumans and marginalized people pushed back by taking up space and seeking opportunities to thrive. The twentieth century was a time of park decay as cities like New York rolled back investments in shared green space. Humans and nonhumans who used— and often *needed*—these spaces struggled to maintain health and culture there, denied the resources sent to more affluent areas. If current trends toward property abandonment in some postindustrial cities, from Detroit to Philadelphia to Baltimore, continue, the twenty-first century might be a new era of park building and otherwise reordering of urban space. In cities that now have tens of thousands of vacant lots, city planners, communities, farmers, land trusts, and other organizations are turning these places into green space, including urban forests and buffers that might ease local effects of climate change and invite and support wildlife much as Central Park's Ramble has. Some of these spaces have already become attractive for species from butterflies to bats, and public partici- patory science activities like the BioBlitz bring residents into such spaces and reveal how rich are the habitats cities can provide.[30] These efforts are fraught with tension, as many, if not most, of the vacant lots were aban- doned as a legacy of racist planning policies dating back a century and are located in neighborhoods where Black communities have watched the city neglect infrastructure and environmental conditions for decades.

Countee Cullen (and Christopher Cat, of course) seemed to under- stand a similar situation back when they wrote *The Lost Zoo*. Within the world of that book, many animals were lost forever, and many descendants of the survivors lived in cages. In the real city and country where Cullen lived and wrote, racist policies segregated Black people from other com- munities and resources in the city. Harlem Renaissance artists like Cullen imagined other possible multispecies worlds. More recently, author Teju Cole wrote about racial and national identity, social dislocation, and his- tory in New York in his 2011 novel *Open City*. Cole's novel is also richly populated with nonhumans, particularly migratory birds with whom the narrator, a young Nigerian German doctor named Julius, identifies, and other birds who animate his walks through New York. Cullen finds joy with Christopher even while mourning extinct animals, and Cole's Julius emerges from melancholy isolation as he watches starlings take off from trees in Central Park, locks eyes with a hawk who may be Pale Male, and traces the flights of geese, wrens, and rails.[31]

The Lost Zoo and *Open City* are, of course, artistic renderings of multi-species urban life, but they can help open our imaginations to possibilities for more-than-human kinship in the city. We also see such possibilities in community-engaged sciences, especially when scientists like Corina Newsome highlight the ways human movement, health, and justice are connected with the well-being of wildlife. Nineteenth-century park builders like those in New York thought that the advance of the city's grid meant that they would never again have the chance to set aside land for recreation and for urban animals. Over one hundred years later, however, communities are still claiming and transforming urban green spaces as part of their struggles for belonging and survival in broader webs of life.

Notes

Introduction

1. "A Dog's Guide to Central Park," Central Park Conservancy, accessed August 19, 2023, https://www.centralparknyc.org/activities/guides/dogs.
2. Sarah Nir, "How 2 Lives Collided in Central Park, Rattling the Nation," *New York Times*, June 14, 2020; Cooper, *Better Living Through Birding*, 243–44; Kimball, *Birders*.
3. Cooper, *Better Living Through Birding*, 239.
4. Nir, "How 2 Lives Collided"; Cooper, *Better Living Through Birding*, 239–49.
5. Cooper, *Better Living Through Birding*, 258–60.
6. Cooper, *Better Living Through Birding*, 245; see also 88 for description of tension between dog people and birders.
7. Watts, "Indigenous Place-Thought"; Belcourt, "Animal Bodies, Colonial Subjects"; Posthumus, "Lakota View," 278; Sakakibara, *Whale Snow*, 3–4, 12–18; Mavhunga, "Seeing the National Park."
8. Baker, *Lenapehoking*; Miller, *Before Central Park*, 47–48, 55–58, 90, 109–11; Burrows and Wallace, *Gotham*, 5–12, 37–40; Sanderson, *Mannahatta*, 106–34.
9. McNeur, *Taming Manhattan*, chapters 1, 5; Robichaud, *Animal City*, chapter 5; Tremante, "Livestock in Nineteenth-Century New York City," 5–7.
10. Robichaud, *Animal City*, 14.
11. McNeur, *Taming Manhattan*, chapter 2; Gandy, *Concrete and Clay*, 82.
12. Manevitz, "Rise and Fall of Seneca Village," 20, 214.
13. Foord, *Life and Public Services of Andrew Haswell Green*, 67; Rosenzweig and Blackmar, *Park and the People*, 272–73.
14. Olmsted and Kimball, *Forty Years of Landscape Architecture*, 100 (hereafter *FYLA*).
15. Board of Commissioners of the Central Park (hereafter BCCP), *Catalogue of the Plans for the Improvement of the Central Park, New York* (New York: C. W. Baker, 1858) (hereafter *CPICP*).

16. Hubbard and Brooks, "Animals and Urban Gentrification"; Checker, "Wiped Out by the Greenwave"; Curran and Hamilton, *Just Green Enough*, introduction; Palmer, "Colonization, Urbanization, and Animals"; Manevitz, "'Great Injustice.'"
17. Staeheli and Mitchell, *People's Property*, xxii; Blomley, "Enclosure, Common Right and the Property of the Poor."
18. Wolch, West, and Gaines, "Transspecies Urban Theory"; Wolch et al., "Constructing the Animal Worlds of Inner-City Los Angeles"; Kim, *Dangerous Crossings*, 3–23; Hobson, "Political Animals."
19. Barua, "Lively Commodities and Encounter Value"; Dempsey and Collard, "Capitalist Natures in Five Orientations." For discussions of migrants using urban green space to uphold or recreate rural outdoor traditions, see Fisher, *Urban Green*, 47, 99–100; Montrie, "'I Think Less of the Factory.'"
20. Collard, "Putting Animals Back Together"; Braverman, *Zooland*, 1–2, 6–7, 162–63; Wilson, "Mobile Bodies"; Collard, *Animal Traffic*, 4–7.
21. Steinberg, *Gotham Unbound*, especially 126–51.
22. Pasquier, "Interrupted Landscapes."
23. Eisenmann, "Frederick Law Olmsted."
24. Rosenzweig and Blackmar, *Park and the People*, 64–73; Taylor, "Central Park as a Model for Social Control"; Gandy, *Concrete and Clay*, chapter 2; Germic, *American Green*, chapter 1. See also Williams, *Country and the City*; Angelo, *How Green Became Good*.
25. Kim, *Dangerous Crossings*, 3–23; Boisseron, *Afro-Dog*, ix–xxi. See also Bennett, *Being Property Myself Once*; Jackson, "Animal."
26. For animal agency and sensation in history, see Brown, *City Is More than Human*, 12–13; Nance, *Historical Animal*, 3–6; Greene, *Horses at Work*, 7–8; Fudge, "Left-Handed Blow"; Gillespie and Collard, introduction to *Critical Animal Geographies*; Uddin, *Zoo Renewal*, 18–22; Mavhunga, *Mobile Workshop*, 89.
27. Mavhunga, "Seeing the National Park"; Lugones, "Toward a Decolonial Feminism"; Belcourt, "Animal Bodies, Colonial Subjects"; Posthumus, "Lakota View."
28. Alagona, *Accidental Ecosystem*, 38–39.
29. Zellmer and Goto, "Urban Wildlife Corridors"; Douglas et al., *Routledge Handbook of Urban Ecology*, 3–6; Blecha and Leitner, "Reimagining the Food System."

Part 1. Creating and Contesting the Animated Landscape

1. Board of Commissioners of the Central Park (hereafter BCCP), *Annual Report of the Board of Commissioners of Central Park* 12 (1869): 127–28 (hereafter *ARBCCP*).
2. Alexander Manevitz grapples with questions of memory and forgetting with reference to Seneca Village. "Rise and Fall of Seneca Village," chapter 5. Stories about the pre-park land emphasized memories of animals but seldom referenced the Black community there.

3. For discussions of valuation of animals, see, for example, Dempsey and Collard, "Capitalist Natures in Five Orientations"; Mighetto, *Wild Animals and American Environmental Ethics*, 17–19, 45–50.

4. "The Central Park—How It Looks Now," *New York Times*, March 5, 1856; McNeur, *Taming Manhattan*, chapter 2; Rosenzweig and Blackmar, *Park and the People*, 87–88. For further discussion of the park as built by and for elites, see Manevitz, "'Great Injustice,'" 1366.

5. For discussions of European models for the park, see Rosenzweig and Blackmar, *Park and the People*, 100, 107, 117–18, 216.

6. Schuyler, *Apostle of Taste*, 202–3.

7. Rosenzweig and Blackmar, *Park and the People*, 103–6.

8. *ARBCCP* 7 (1864): 35–36. For discussion of social control in the park, see Taylor, "Central Park as a Model for Social Control"; Germic, *American Green*, chapter 1. For universality of nature, see Angelo, *How Green Became Good*, 21.

9. Rosenwaike, *Population History of New York City*, 35, 36, 43.

10. Hodges, *New York City Cartmen*, 108, 158–61, 171.

11. Manevitz, "Rise and Fall of Seneca Village," 5; New York State Manuscript Census, 1855, ward 22, third election district. See also Viele, *Map of the Lands Included in the Central Park*.

12. Miller, *Before Central Park*, chapters 9 and 10, 444–47; Rosenzweig and Blackmar, *Park and the People*, 64–73; Manevitz, "Rise and Fall of Seneca Village," 6, 20, 55, 214; Copeland, Rothschild, and Wall, "Seneca Village Project"; Harris, *In the Shadow of Slavery*, 75, 119.

13. Miller, *Before Central Park*, chapters 14–16; McNeur, *Taming Manhattan*, 160–74, 187–88; Rosenzweig and Blackmar, *Park and the People*, 74–75.

14. Rosenwaike, *Population History*, 67, 78; Wang, *Surviving the City*, 11, 19.

15. Ziegelman, *97 Orchard*, 113–15; Davidson and Hatcher, *No More Separate Spheres*, 9–14; Peiss, *Cheap Amusements*, 3–9; Domosh, *Invented Cities*, chapter 2.

1. Reassembling a Rural City

1. I base these descriptions on BCCP, *First Annual Report on the Improvement of the Central Park* (New York: BCCP, 1857); "The Central Park," *Harper's Weekly*, November 28, 1857, 756–57; and H. C. Bunner, "Shantytown," *Scribner's Magazine*, October 1880. The Scribner's article allows for speculation about the landscape in which pre-park residents lived, though Bunner wrote it twenty-three years later. It is the most detailed and sympathetic firsthand account of a group of pastoralists similar to the pre-park residents.

2. Robichaud, *Animal City*, chapter 1.

3. McNeur, *Taming Manhattan*; Steinberg, *Down to Earth*, 157–72.

4. Rawson, *Eden on the Charles*, 29.
5. Hartog, "Pigs and Positivism."
6. McNeur, *Taming Manhattan*, chapters 3–4, especially 126–33.
7. Robichaud, *Animal City*, chapter 1.
8. Rosenwaike, *Population History of New York City*, 33–39.
9. Rosenzweig and Blackmar, *Park and the People*, 37–58.
10. Many of the so-called squatters actually owned their land; others rented theirs. See Bunner, "Shantytown"; Rosenzweig and Blackmar, *Park and the People*, 72–73. Some sources claim that a person with Indigenous and Black ancestry named Albro Lyons also resided in Seneca Village; see Cynthia Copeland, Nan Rothschild, and Diana Wall, "Seneca Village Project," accessed January 29, 2024, https://projects .mcah.columbia.edu/seneca_village/; however, Manevitz, "Rise and Fall of Seneca Village," 82–85, 214, indicates that the wealthy Lyons owned land and was active in social causes in Seneca Village but resided elsewhere.
11. US Census Office, "Census Schedules of New York State by Counties," Washington, DC, 1850, 1860, 1870; Bunner, "Shantytown."
12. Rosenzweig and Blackmar, *Park and the People*, 73; Bourke, "Agricultural Statistics of the 1841 Census of Ireland," 382, 386. Bellows et al. discuss urban livestock agriculture as a means of cultural survival for immigrants, even in host cultures that ban such practices in cities. Bellows et al., "Urban Livestock Agriculture," 8–9.
13. Several secondary sources discuss this practice. For example, see Radbill, "Role of Animals in Infant Feeding"; Naomi Baumslag, "Breastfeeding." Some cite Conrad Zweirlein, *The Goat as the Best and Most Agreeable Wet-Nurse*, a book published in German in 1816 for women unable or unwilling to breastfeed. Thanks to Molly Jones-Lewis for alerting me to this practice.
14. New York State Manuscript Census, 1855, ward 22, third election district.
15. Quoted in Rosenzweig and Blackmar, *Park and the People*, 63.
16. "Central Park: How It Looks Now," *New York Times*, March 5, 1856.
17. "The Central Park," *Harper's Weekly*, November 18, 1857, 756–57.
18. "A Cave Discovered in Central Park," *New York Times*, September 7, 1857; Manevitz, "Rise and Fall of Seneca Village," chapters 3-4, especially 167–69.
19. Rosenzweig and Blackmar, *Park and the People*, 100, 111, 342.
20. "Central Park: Exhibition of the Unsuccessful Plans for the Central Park," *New York Times*, May 13, 1858.
21. BCCP, *CPICP*, J. Lachaume, plan number 5, 13.
22. Stilgoe, "Town Common," 24; Gandy, *Concrete and Clay*, 94.
23. Stilgoe, "Town Common," 25.
24. Mazaraki, "Public Career of Andrew Haswell Green," 27; Foord, *Life and Public Services of Andrew Haswell Green*, 9, 20–21, 230–31.
25. *FYLA*, 86.

26. Frederick Law Olmsted to John Olmsted, July 1, 1846, in McLaughlin, *Papers of Frederick Law Olmsted*; Martin, *Genius of Place*, 46, 94; Olmsted, *Walks and Talks of an American Farmer*, 79, 88, 90, 99, 135–36, 224.

27. This sense of respite from change could be profoundly conservative, tending toward social control. For discussion of these tendencies in Olmsted's thought and Central Park's history, see Bender, *Toward an Urban Vision*, 163; Taylor, "Central Park as a Model," especially 426–30; Germic, *American Green*, chapter 1. See also Angelo, *How Green Became Good*, 39–53.

28. "A Cave Discovered in Central Park," *New York Times*, September 7, 1857.

29. Property owners on the borders of the area paid into a compensation fund for those who lost land. Those who used the land but did not own it could not seek compensation. Rosenzweig and Blackmar, *Park and the People*, chapter 3.

30. "New York City—Building Contrasts," *Frank Leslie's Illustrated Newspaper*, September 7, 1889.

31. Perris, *Maps of the City of New York*, accessed January 29, 2024, https://digitalcollections.nypl.org/items/510d47e0-bfd7-a3d9-e040-e00a18064a99, sheets 116–17.

32. Rosenzweig and Blackmar, *Park and the People*, 266–69.

33. *FYLA*, 33.

34. For discussion of goats on marginal land or arid, mountainous areas, and preference for sheep where environments are more favorable, see Zeuner, *History of Domesticated Animals*, 151–52. Zeuner also points to goats' better milk production, which helps explain their use for infant feeding. For goat behavior, see Miranda-de la Lama and Mattiello, "Importance of Social Behaviour."

35. *BCCP Minutes & Documents* (hereafter *BCCP M&D*), August 1858. Also cited in *FYLA*, 33.

36. Miranda-de la Lama and Mattiello, "Importance of Social Behavior."

37. For the commissioners' rulemaking power, see "An Act for the Regulation and Government of the Central Park in the City of New York," April 17, 1857, reprinted in *BCCP M&D for the Year Ending April 30, 1858*.

38. *ARBCCP* 1 (1857): 8. See also report by the chief engineer, document number 9, September 23, 1857, in *BCCP M&D*, two years ending April 30, 1859.

39. Wischermann, Steinbrecher, and Howell, *Animal History in the Modern City*, 2–9.

40. *BCCP M&D*, 1858–61, Report of the Architect-in-Chief, August 5, 1858; *ARBCCP* 4 (1860): 106.

41. BCCP, Scrapbook, 1858–70, Records of the Department of Parks, REC041, ACC 87-17, NYCMA.

42. Based on a survey of the *ARBCCP* and *ARBCDPP*.

43. *ARBCCP* 3 (1859): 18–19. Posters hung at park boundaries announced rules against gathering these resources. BCCP, Scrapbook, 1858–70, Records of the Department

of Parks, REC041, ACC 87-17, NYCMA. For mention of edible fruits planted in the park, see Demcker, *Central Park Plant List and Map Index of 1873*, for example, 12, 15, 17, 31, 35, 36, 40, 46.

44. Robichaud, *Animal City*, chapter 5.

45. Robert Dillon and August Belmont, "Objections of Two of the Commissioners to the Plan Adopted," *New York Times*, July 7, 1858.

46. Rosenzweig and Blackmar, *Park and the People*, 144–47. Rosenzweig and Blackmar interpreted Dillon and Belmont's protest against the combined paths not in terms of elitism but more as a push for more intensive use of the park space that served both practical and aesthetic goals and that ultimately fit with the overall purposes of the plan. While I agree that the separation also serves these ends, the elitist effect also seems clear.

47. BCCP, Scrapbook, 1858–70, ACC 87-17 NYCMA.

48. Greene, *Horses at Work*, chapters 2 and 5; Brown, *City Is More than Human*, 114–21; McShane and Tarr, *Horse in the City*, chapter 2. Thanks to Amy Smith Muise for the insight about horses becoming deaf.

49. Rybczynski, *Clearing in the Distance*, 175. Annual reports for the park also list laborers employed, but before 1867, cartmen were lumped with other semiskilled laborers.

50. Pooley-Ebert, "Species Agency."

51. "Municipal Oppression," *Colored American*, September 16, 1837.

52. Hodges, *New York City Cartmen*, 4–5, 103, 151–68; Brown, *City Is More than Human*, 114. Cartmen and horses formed close relationships marked by affection and even shared a common language of verbal and physical commands. However, horses might stop moving when they became fatigued. In this way, horses exercised a form of resistance, although the cartman possessed the power to physically injure a horse in response through whipping and other means.

53. *ARBCCP* 5 (1862): 67–72.

54. Haraway, *When Species Meet*, 46.

55. Black, *King of Fifth Avenue*, 8–17, 19–21, 30–33.

56. *BCCP M&D*, September 1, 1859. For discussion of Bois de Boulogne as a model, see Rosenzweig and Blackmar, *Park and the People*, 100, 109.

57. *Walks and Talks of an American Farmer* does not mention St. James Park but does discuss several rural farms and estates with their domestic animals, deer parks, and birds.

58. Benjamin West, *Milkmaids in St. James's Park, Westminster Abbey Beyond*, painting, 1801, Yale Center for British Art online, accessed January 28, 2024, https://collections.britishart.yale.edu/catalog/tms:67319.

59. *BCCP M&D*, 1858–61, document number 6, April 26, 1860.

60. For further discussion of enclosure, landscape, and cow commons, see Rawson, *Eden on the Charles*, 53–74.

61. *BCCP M&D*, 1861–63, February 6, 1862.

62. Rosenzweig and Blackmar, *Park and the People*, 252–53.

63. *BCCP M&D*, 1861–63, December 11, 1862. For Lawrence's donation of animal skins, see meeting minutes for November 13, 1862.

64. Moss, *Barbecue*, 76–78.

65. Board of Commissioners records do not indicate how many lambs they purchased each year, but expenditures lists include payments to Bryan Lawrence for animals in both 1862 and 1863. At J. C. Taylor's auction in 1862, lambs without pedigree but sired by "89" could go for as little as $14. That year, the commission report listed $123 in animal purchases, which could have purchased just seven lambs. The allocation for 1863 was only a few dollars more, but by that point, the lambs would be old enough to start breeding, thus increasing the flock. Prices increased rapidly in subsequent years; a report on a large auction in Dutchess County, New York, in late 1864, valued the youngest ewes, bred within the United States, at no less than $20 a head and on average in the $30 range. A prizewinning imported ram sold for $500. "Sale of Southdowns at Thornedale," *The Cultivator*, October 1, 1864, 305–6.

66. Walford-Lloyd, *Southdown Sheep*, 8–9.

67. Browne, *Trichologia Mammalium*, 150, 164–65.

68. Walford-Lloyd, *Southdown Sheep*, 9, 31.

69. Metcalfe, "American Livestock Improvers."

70. Stoykovich, "Culture of Improvement in the Early Republic"; Nash, "Breed Wealth."

71. Olmsted, *Walks and Talks of an American Farmer*, 136.

72. Solon Robinson, "The Best Sheep for the New York Market," *Prairie Farmer*, December 20, 1860, 387.

73. It is unclear which specific farmer Lawrence bought from this time or what was the price per animal, but there is a record of Lawrence buying from Thorne in 1864. See "Cattle Market," *Country Gentleman*, April 7, 1864, 229. For Belmont's detail-oriented approach to entertaining and dinner parties, see Black, *King of Fifth Avenue*, 72–74.

74. "Southdown Sheep," *New York Times*, September 5, 1862. For Jonas Webb's reputation as a Southdown breeder, see Walford-Lloyd, *Southdown Sheep*, 26.

75. "The Central Park," *New York Times*, July 25, 1863; see also Brenwall, *Central Park*, 110–11.

76. *ARBCCP* 8 (1965): 55.

77. Display ad, *New York Times*, December 24, 1864, 5.

78. See budget reports in *ARBCCP* (1866–69).

79. *ARBCCP 7* (1864): 37.

80. Cook, *Description of the New York Central Park*, 193–96. Meister (xiii–xviii) writes that Vaux and Olmsted closely advised Cook about his book's content.

81. "Central Park Dairy," *New York Times*, February 18, 1870.

82. Calvert Vaux, "The Central Park of New-York—Notes," *New York Times*, July 10, 1864.

83. *ARBCCP 9* (1866): 77.

84. *ARBCCP 9* (1866): 77; "Cattle at the Central Park," *Cultivator and Country Gentleman*, May 21, 1868, 274.

85. Steinitz and Wood, "World We Have Gained," 105–20.

86. Amendment to section 7 of Central Park ordinances, October 19, 1866, *BCCP M&D*, 1867–70.

87. Wang, *Mad Dogs and Other New Yorkers*, 19.

88. *ARBCCP 8* (1870): 47–48.

89. B. W. Kilburn, photographer, *Central Park, a Joy for Little Folks*, photograph, Central Park New York, 1895 (Littleton, NH: Photographed and published by B. W. Kilburn, 1895), accessed July 31, 2024, https://www.loc.gov/item/2017649059.

90. Rosenzweig and Blackmar, *Park and the People*, 263.

91. "Hilton as Landscape Architect," *New York Times*, March 6, 1872.

92. "The Dairy, Prospect Park, Brooklyn," *Hearth and Home*, July 22, 1871, 564.

93. Brenwall, *Central Park*, 110–11.

94. "Central Park: Plain Talk about the City's Great Pleasure-Ground," *New York Times*, November 25, 1872; *ARBDPP 1* (1870–71): 20. Amid its many offenses against the Greensward plan, the Tammany board also invested heavily in sheep, which seemed more in line with the architects' and other elites' hopes for animating the landscape. See *ARBDPP 1* (1870–71): 141–42, 399–400.

95. Forrester, *Little Peachblossom*. In using children's literature throughout this book, I draw upon Francesca Ammon's analysis of children's books as reflecting or attempting to shape attitudes toward landscape change. Ammon, *Bulldozer*, 221–50.

96. Forrester, *Little Peachblossom*, 208.

97. Forrester, *Little Peachblossom*, 33.

98. Meyer, *My Park Book*, 31–32.

99. C. W. Flanders, "Esther and the Miser," *Youth's Companion*, July 15, 1869, 42.

100. Bunner describes the area as between Sixty-Fifth and Eighty-Fifth Streets and Eighth Avenue and Central Park—but the latter two streets are the same. The remainder of his description seems to indicate that it is located east of the park, but the street location seems contradictory. Bunner, "Shantytown."

101. Bunner, "Shantytown," 855.

102. "Chinaman Anxious to Keep Ducks," *New York Tribune*, April 2, 1882, 2. For further discussion of racism against and segregation of early Chinese New Yorkers,

see Wang, *Surviving the City*; for racist stereotypes of food culture, see 1, 53; for discussion of tenements, see 67, 91. This example of Fain seeking approval for raising ducks and geese seems to exemplify Wang's emphasis on Chinese New Yorkers' agitation to protect their economic livelihoods. For further discussion of Asian Americans' influence on environment and landscapes amid racist portrayals of food culture and living arrangements, see Chiang, *Shaping the Shoreline*, 9, 25–26, 30–37, and chapter 2. See also Anderson, "Idea of Chinatown"; Anderson, "'Beast Within,'" 301–20.

103. "Southdown Bucks for Central Park," *Turf, Field, and Farm*, December 9, 1870.

104. Boyazoglu, Hatziminaoglou, and Morand-Fehr, "Role of the Goat in Society," paragraph 19. See also Gipson, "History of the US Goat Industry," 44; Stoykovich, "In the National Interest."

105. Brown and Johnson, *Twentieth Century Biographical Dictionary of Notable Americans*, 373–74; William Conklin, "Felidae in Captivity," *Archives of Comparative Medicine and Surgery* 1 (1880): 133.

106. Stoykovich, "Culture of Improvement," 36; Stoykovich, "In the National Interest," 8; Nash, "Breed Wealth," 850–51.

107. "Southdown Bucks for Central Park," 356. For transport times, see Rodrigue, *Geography of Transport Systems*, chapter 1.

108. American Southdown Breeders' Association, *American Southdown Record* 1 (1884): 64–65, 191.

109. "Twenty Fine Sheep," *New York Times*, July 31, 1885.

110. "Park Board Methods," *New York Times*, March 22, 1887.

111. "Park Board Privileges," *New York Times*, April 7, 1887.

112. Rosenzweig and Blackmar, *Park and the People*, 298–99, 309–10.

113. "Park Board Privileges," *New York Times*, April 7, 1887.

114. "Sale of Deer and Sheep," *New York Times*, June 27, 1896.

115. Connor, "Brief History of the Sheep Industry."

116. As late as 1894, Parks Department reports still referred to the Southdown flock as possessing "superior blood." By 1898, the zoological department was auctioning off Dorsets, including a prizewinning ram named Tranquility, who sold for twenty-six dollars. The 1898 annual report lists sale of fewer Southdowns than before and some Dorsets. *ARBDPP* (1898): 17.

117. "Building Contrasts," *Frank Leslie's Illustrated Newspaper*, September 7, 1889, 81–82.

118. "New-York's Tenement House Commission Is Doing Grand Work," *New York Tribune*, May 31, 1903.

119. Thanks to Steven Corey for pointing out the work of the Tenement Commission to me and for elucidating the continued presence of animal agriculture in Manhattan even after most outdoor farms were displaced. For further discussion of tenement-based livestock, see also Wang, *Mad Dogs*, 19; Ziegelman, *97 Orchard*, 113–17.

2. Free Animals in a Changing Landscape

1. "The Span-Worm or Measuring Worm," *Ohio Cultivator*, July 1, 1860, 202.

2. George Lawrence, "Catalogue of Birds Observed on New York, Long Island, Staten Island, and Adjacent Parts of New Jersey," *Annals of the Lyceum of Natural History of New York* 8 (1867): 287–88; "Our Feathered Friends," *New York Times*, November 22, 1868.

3. *ARBCCP* 7 (1864): 34.

4. *ARBCCP* 10 (1867): 45. For reference to the "German sparrow," see Central Park's animal inventory in *ARBCCP* 8 (1865): 40.

5. Lawrence, "Catalogue of Birds," 287.

6. For discussions of values relating to animals, see, for example, Mighetto, *Wild Animals*, chapter 1; Barua, "Lively Commodities and Encounter Value"; Dempsey and Collard, "Capitalist Natures in Five Orientations."

7. For tree and shrub species planted in the first several years of construction, see *ARBCCP* 7 (1864): 91–123. It is likely that some Manhattanites tried to keep guinea fowl, as agricultural and gentleman-farmer periodicals were starting to promote them. See, for example, "The Guinea Fowl," *Country Gentleman*, May 24, 1860, 333; "The Guinea Fowl," *Ohio Farmer*, May 3, 1856, 69.

8. *CPICP*, plan number 7, 23.

9. Greater London Council, *Alexander Pope's Villa*. See also Samuel Scott, "View of Alexander Pope's Villa, Twickenham" ca. 1759, Yale University Library, accessed March 20, 2023, https://collections.library.yale.edu/catalog/16721024.

10. George Kunhardt to R. M. Blatchford, May 9, 1860, in *ARBCCP* 4 (1860): 15–18. See also "Living and Breathing Icons: The Alster Swans," *Hamburg.com*, accessed August 11, 2023, https://www.hamburg.com/sights/maritime/13047284/alster-swans.

11. Worshipful Company of Vintners, "Swan Upping," n.d., accessed August 17, 2021, https://www.vintnershall.co.uk/swans. See also Gardner et al., *Swan Keeper's Handbook*, 1.

12. George Kunhardt to R. M. Blatchford, May 9, 1860, in *ARBCCP* 4 (1860): 15–18.

13. *ARBCCP* 4 (1960): 16.

14. *ARBCCP* 4 (1960): 15–18.

15. *ARBCCP* 7 (1864): 43.

16. Richards, *Guide to the Central Park*, 54–55.

17. Cook, *Description of the New York Central Park*, 60.

18. Cook, *Description of the New York Central Park*, 60–61.

19. Cook, *Description of the New York Central Park*, 106–7; Demcker, *Central Park Plant List and Map Index of 1873*; *ARBCCP* 7 (1864): 91–123.

20. For further firsthand description, see Cook, *Description of the New York Central Park*, 104–20.

21. *ARBCCP* 6 (1863): 43.

22. See, for example, *ARBCCP* 8 (1865): overleaf between 34 and 35.

23. Stoddard, *Domestic Waterfowl*, 62.

24. Stoddard, *Domestic Waterfowl*, 63. Two scientists who studied the flora and fauna of the large lake and the Harlem Meer in 1884 speculated that the "aquatic fowl" in the more southerly lake were controlling other aquatic species there. Gratacap and Woodward, *Freshwater Flora*, 5.

25. Richards, *Guide to the Central Park*, 55.

26. Several writers have pointed out growing popular desire for greater contact with nature among late-nineteenth- and early-twentieth-century city dwellers. See Mighetto, *Wild Animals*, chapter 1; Barrow, *Passion for Birds*, chapter 1.

27. Stoddard, *Domestic Waterfowl*, 61–62.

28. Entrant number 7 (anon.), *CPICP*, plan number 7, 23.

29. *Drawing of Swans Nests as Used upon the "Alster" in Hamburg*, Central Park Architectural Drawings, REC 041, ACC 1988-031, DPR-859 (microfilm), NYCMA.

30. *ARBCCP* 8 (1865): 53–54.

31. Goodman, "Animals in Gardens," 56–58.

32. Cook, *Description of the Central Park*, 144–47.

33. *BCCP M&D*, 1864–66, February 21, 1864; *ARBCCP* 9 (1866): 77. It is unclear whether Joshua Jones was related to the family that owned Jones Wood.

34. Gifford-Gonzalez and Hanotte, "Domesticating Animals in Africa," 16–17; Poole, "Bird Introductions," 155–65; Carney and Rosomoff, *In the Shadow of Slavery*, 157–60; Donkin, *Meleagrides*, 47–68, 79–87, 97–104; "The Guinea Fowl," *Country Gentleman*, May 24, 1860, 333; "The Guinea Fowl," *Ohio Farmer*, May 1856 3, 69; Tegetmeier and Weir, *Poultry Book*, 288–95. Guinea fowl deserve further research and discussion as important animals in the Atlantic world of empire, enslavement, and appropriation and in understanding distinct cosmologies, meanings, and uses of nature across societies.

35. Forrester, *Little Peachblossom*, 21; Cook, *Description of the New York Central Park*, 145–47; *Annual Report of the Director of the Central Park Menagerie* (hereafter *ARDCPM*) (1877): 7.

36. Numbers of peafowl and guinea fowl bred in the park were similar in 1877; see *ARDCPM* (1878): 5.

37. Although they were not kept in menagerie buildings, park administrators considered swans, peafowl, and guinea fowl part of the zoological collection. *ARBCCP* 10 (1867): 73–74; *ARBCCP* 12 (1869): 107–8.

38. Central Park Menagerie ledger, May 8, 1876, REC 041, ACC 1965-015: Department of Parks, Central Park Menagerie Records, 1876–1950, box 2, 3, NYCMA.

39. Minard, *All Things Harmless, Useful, and Ornamental*, 3–4; Ritvo, "Going Forth and Multiplying."

40. Ritvo, "Going Forth"; Dunlap, "Remaking the Land"; Crosby, *Ecological Imperialism*.

41. Barrow examines the fluidity of categories of amateur and professional ornithologists. Barrow argues that "ornithology provides a classic example of an inclusive scientific field"—meaning that amateurs and professionals frequently worked together, shared information, and sometimes as individuals moved between these categories. Barrow, *Passion for Birds*, 5.

42. Reynolds, *Genealogical and Family History*, 1296–1300; Nichols, "Review of the New York Markets," 70; "Society Proceedings," *New York Genealogical and Biographical Record* 38 (April 1907): 146.

43. Lawrence, "Catalogue of Birds," 287–88.

44. The commissioners cited London's Acclimatization Garden in their report on Olmsted's trip to European parks and zoos; see *ARBCCP* 6 (1863): 16.

45. *ARBCCP* 7 (1864): 34; *ARBCCP* 8 (1865): 37. Other sources state that the introductions in the park occurred in 1864, but this is the earliest reference and seems likely to be the most accurate. Also, a later speech by William Conklin, in 1877, indicated that the number of birds released was fifty, but the two board of commissioners reports cited here, which were prepared closer to the date, say seven pairs.

46. *ARBCCP* 8 (1865): 37.

47. Forrester, *Little Peachblossom*, 97; Cook, *Description of the New York Central Park*, 142.

48. "Our Feathered Friends," *New York Times*, November 22, 1868.

49. Lawrence, "Catalogue of Birds," quoted in *ARBCCP* 10 (1867): 46.

50. Lawrence, "Catalogue of Birds," quoted in *ARBCCP* 10 (1867): 46–47.

51. *ARBCCP* 12 (1869): 121.

52. Lawrence, "Catalogue of Birds," 287–88, 290; Elliot, "In Memoriam," 1–10; Foster, *Published Writings of George Newbold Lawrence*, vii–viii. In spite of his late career change, Lawrence was prominent in his generation of ornithologists, having studied birds in partnership with Spencer Baird, first curator of the Smithsonian Institution.

53. *ARBCCP* 7 (1864): 34; *ARBCCP* 10 (1867): 47.

54. See, for example, *ARBCCP* 7 (1864): 34; Lawrence, "Catalogue of Birds," quoted in *ARBCCP* 10 (1867): 47. See also Richards, *Guide to the Central Park*, 67.

55. Richards, *Guide to the Central Park*, 67.

56. "Our Feathered Friends," *New York Times*, November 22, 1868.

57. See, for example, Cronon, *Changes in the Land*, 53, 89–90. See also Smith, foreword to Walia, *Undoing Border Imperialism*. I am grateful to Yolanda Valencia for pointing out this connection between discourse about native birds and Indigenous people.

58. For example, see Catlin, *Illustrations of the Manner, Custom, and Conditions*, 6–8.

For a recent review of this trope and imagery that unsettles it, see Deloria, *Indians in Unexpected Places*, for example, 10, 50.

59. *ARBCCP* 10 (1867): 47.

60. *ARBCCP* 10 (1867): 45.

61. *ARBCCP* 9 (1866): 77; *ARBCCP* 12 (1869): 120. Later accounts reported on different donors and larger numbers of sparrows; see Conklin's 1877 speech to the American Acclimatization Society. I trust the earlier records more, as these occurred closer to the event.

62. *ARBCCP* 12 (1869): 120; Higgins, Peter, and Cowling, *Handbook of Australian, New Zealand & Antarctic Birds*, 7:1018–20.

63. American Acclimatization Society, "Charter, Articles of Association, and By-Laws," 1871.

64. Gentry, *House Sparrow at Home and Abroad*, 14.

65. Gibson and Lennon, "Historical Census Statistics on the Foreign-Born Population of the United States."

66. Barrow, *Passion for Birds*, 48–49.

67. Coates, "Eastenders Go West." See also Doughty, "English Sparrow"; Fugate and Miller, "Shakespeare's Starlings," 301–22.

68. I borrow the term *naturalist's gaze* from Cherry, *For the Birds*, 2. *ARBCCP* 12 (1869): 114; for the swan listing, see 109. It is possible that Gallatin actually wrote this section. For early pigeon donations, see *ARBCCP* 7 (1864): 57.

69. *ARBCCP* 7 (1864): 34.

70. *ARBCCP* 12 (1869): 114–24. It is possible that Gallatin actually wrote this section.

71. *ARBCCP* 12 (1869): 114–24. For birds elsewhere in New York, see Lawrence, "Catalogue of Birds."

72. Burrows and Wallace, *Gotham*, 5–12, 37–40; Baker, *Lenapehoking*; Sanderson, *Mannahatta*, 106–34.

73. Hall, "Central Park in the City of New York," 397–98. One mention of former Indigenous inhabitants in 1800s sources about the park came in *Little Peachblossom*, 22–26. The narrator, Uncle Nathan, calls the Indigenous Manhattanites a "low, sorry set" but does mention their agriculture and admits that the Dutch and the English mistreated them.

74. Benson, "Urbanization of the Eastern Gray Squirrel," 694.

75. *CPICP*, plan 1, 3. It is notable that this entrant assumed wild deer would be excluded from certain spaces, while deer were eventually placed in enclosures; see chapter 3.

76. Vague park records leave questions today about which animals were released and which were caged, especially before 1876, after which a massive logbook has survived, revealing each day's zoological events, bluntly noted in some scrolling hand—perhaps Conklin's or his wife Eliza O'Duffy's. NYCMA, accession number

1965-015, Department of Parks: Central Park Menagerie Records, 1876–1950, box 2, Central Park Menagerie ledger.

77. *ARDCPM* (1878): 10.

78. *ARBCCP* 12 (1869): 114, 123–24.

79. Conklin and Lawrence belonged to a generation of naturalists and scientists accustomed to shooting and skinning birds for collection, rather than viewing them live, and of course shooting was not permitted in Central Park. Affordable and user-friendly binoculars expanded access to bird-watching starting at the very end of the nineteenth century, continuing into the early twentieth century. See also Cook, *Description of the New York Central Park*, 82.

80. "The Migration of Birds," *Scribner's Monthly*, October 1881, 932–39.

81. *ARDCPM* (1877): 10.

82. "American Acclimatization Society," *New York Times*, November 15, 1877. The reporter covering this event likely confused some of the species names mentioned.

83. *ARDCPM* (1877): 10.

84. "American Acclimatization Society."

85. Anglophile animal enthusiasts erased the birds' more eastern origins with the name English pheasants. The Latin species name, *colchinis*, refers to a region in present-day Georgia. Oldys, *Pheasant Raising in the United States*, 11–13.

86. For a somewhat contemporary account of pheasant behavior and release in the United States, see Oldys, *Pheasant Raising*.

87. *ARDCPM* (1877): 10.

88. Goodman, "Animals in Gardens" (56–58), Barbara Simms, "Brown, Lancelot" (197–200), and David Cast, "Bridgeman, Charles" (191–92), in Shoemaker, *Chicago Botanic Garden Encyclopedia of Gardens*; Game Act 1831, UK National Archives, accessed January 29, 2024, https://www.legislation.gov.uk/ukpga/Will4/1-2/32 /contents.

89. *CPICP* (pseud. J. Lachaume), plan number 5; see also plan number 1, 3; plan number 3, 4; plan number 29, 71.

90. *ARBCCP* 6 (1863): 49.

91. *ARBCCP* 13 (1870): 98.

92. Ordinances of the Central Park, section 22, printed in "Public Notices," *New York Times*, June 3, 1870.

93. Gratacap and Woodward, *Freshwater Flora*, 10.

94. Gratacap and Woodward, *Freshwater Flora*, 7.

95. Gratacap and Woodward, *Freshwater Flora*, 6–9.

96. Robert Roosevelt, "Fish in the Park," *New York Times*, September 10, 1870. There were also periodic discussions of developing an aquarium in Central Park.

97. "American Acclimatization Society"; Tarleton Bean, "Fish Culture in New York," *Forest and Stream*, December 14, 1907, 941.

98. For examples of other fish exhibits drawing interest, see "Two Fish Exhibitions," *New York Tribune*, April 2, 1882.

99. At least one fly-fishing association held regular tournaments in the park in the nineteenth century. "Fly Fishers in Council," *New York Times*, January 9, 1887.

100. Gratacap and Woodward, *Freshwater Flora*, 5–9.

101. "Local Miscellany," *New York Times*, July 11, 1877; J.H.C., "Nuisance in Central Park," *New York Times*, June 9, 1878.

102. "Sunrise in Central Park," *New York Times*, June 28, 1891.

103. BCDPP, *Minutes and Documents* (hereafter *M&D*), July 19, 1876, 169.

104. Griffiths, "Feral Cats in the City"; Miltenberger, "Viewing the Anthrozoonotic City"; Grier, *Pets in America*, 60, 77–80; Wang, *Mad Dogs*, 11–49; Brown, *City Is More than Human*, 149–98.

105. "Bird Life in Central Park," *Forest and Stream*, June 14, 1883, 384.

106. *ARDCPM* (1877): 6.

107. *ARDCPM* (1875): 30–51.

108. *ARDCPM* (1877): 5.

109. Rome, "Nature Wars, Culture Wars," 434.

110. Lewis, *American Sportsman*, 91.

111. Lewis, himself a medical doctor based in Philadelphia, shared Olmsted's disdain for southern cultural ecologies; for example, he lambasted enslaved people for raiding partridge eggs to supplement meager diets, along with other hunting practices encouraged and forced by enslavers. Lewis, *American Sportsman*, xii, 90.

112. "Degenerate Nimrods," *New York Times*, October 27, 1867.

113. Richards, *Guide to the Central Park*, 67, 100; "Degenerate Nimrods."

114. *Oxford English Dictionary*, s.v. "Nimrod, (n.)" accessed March 2024, https://doi.org/10.1093/OED/2345435279.

115. For further discussion of Italian pothunters and criticism thereof, see Rome, "Nature Wars, Culture Wars"; Warren, *Hunter's Game*, 21–47. For a primary source from a slightly later time period with decidedly racist rhetoric, see also Hornaday, *Our Vanishing Wildlife*, 94–104.

116. Roosevelt, *Theodore Roosevelt's Diaries*. Roosevelt reported upsetting birds' nests with sticks at age eleven (7); at age twenty, he tallied sixty-eight birds (and dozens of other animals) in his yearly "bag count" (365).

117. Barrow, *Passion for Birds*, chapter 2.

118. Lawrence, "Catalogue of Birds," 280, 289, 293.

119. Price, *Flight Maps*, 30–36.

120. The *Times*, for example, continued to use the term *Nimrod* in a complimentary way when referring to the likes of, for example, Germany's Prince William, who killed thousands of large mammals and thousands more small mammals and birds over a lifetime of hunting. "An Imperial Nimrod," *New York Times*, May 13, 1878;

Anderson, "'Beast Within,'" 301–20; Wolch et al., "*Le Pratique Sauvage*," 72–90. Anderson shows that host cultures equate immigrants and others who transgress urban norms with animals. Wolch et al. discuss how host cultures cite violent animal-related practices to dehumanize immigrants and othered racial groups. They demonstrate that the classification of animal-related practices as violent relies upon the invisibility of violence against animals that is sanctioned by the host culture, for example slaughterhouses or laboratories, where brutality is considered only sacrifice.

121. Josephine Carter, "A Squirrel's Story," *The Independent*, May 1884, 22, 36.

122. Benson, "Urbanization of the Eastern Gray Squirrel," 705; "Three Boy Vandals Confess Their Raid," *New York Herald*, December 5, 1892. Many adult New Yorkers responded in media to boys tormenting squirrels; see, for example, two letters to the editor: Justitia (pseud.), "In Behalf of Squirrels," *New York Tribune*, August 21, 1898; AAC, "Cruelty in Central Park," *New York Times*, October 28, 1897.

123. "A Genial Day of Sunshine," *New York Tribune*, March 18, 1883; "The Balance of Animals," *New York Times*, March 23, 1883; "A Big Hunt in Central Park," *New York Tribune*, February 20, 1886. See also Benson, "Urbanization of the Eastern Gray Squirrel," 697. As we will see in chapters 3 and 5, killing was also a regular practice of managing captive animal collections. For discussions of killability and grievability, see Lopez and Gillespie, *Economies of Death*, chapter 1.

124. ARBCCP 7 (1864): 37; see also Gandy, *Concrete and Clay*, 91–94.

125. Cook, *Description of the New York Central Park*, 41.

126. Montrie, "'I Think Less of the Factory.'"

127. Taylor, "Central Park as a Model for Social Control," 427–28, 436, 441.

128. Bender notes Olmsted's particular concern for the future of women living in cities; Bender, *Toward an Urban Vision*, 170; however, Bender underemphasizes the role of xenophobia in attitudes toward parenting. Andrew Green, also, is noted for his emphasis on grand urban landscape projects while neglecting concerns such as social housing and labor. Mazaraki, "Public Career of Andrew Haswell Green," 14–15. For further discussions of gender dynamics and gendered expectations in urban life, see Domosh and Seager, *Putting Women in Place*, 7. See also Davidson and Hatcher, *No More Separate Spheres*. For discussion of emerging labor activism, see Marino, "A Woman Ahead of Her Time"; Brown, "Victims, B'hoys, Foreigners, Slave-Drivers, and Despots."

129. Cook, *Description of the New York Central Park*, 60–61. Both Harriet Ritvo and Katherine Grier have noted the nineteenth-century idea that birds could teach maternal values. See Grier, *Pets in America*, 164–65; Ritvo, *Noble Cows and Hybrid Zebras*, 32.

130. *ARBCCP* 10 (1867): 47–51; "Death of Joshua Fox," *Royal Cornwall Gazette*, April 6, 1877.

131. For discussion of popularization of bird love, see Barrow, *Passion for Birds*, especially 154–81.

132. N. B. Kinnear, "Dr. Frank Chapman," *Nature* 156, December 22, 1945, 741–42; Chapman, *Visitors' Guide to the Local Collection of Birds*; Barrow, *Passion for Birds*, 103–4.

133. Price, *Flight Maps*, 57–110.

134. Isabel Eaton, "For Teachers and Students: Bird-Studies for Children," *Bird-Lore* 1 (1899): 17.

135. "A Christmas Bird-Census," *Bird-Lore* 2 (1900): 192.

136. "The Christmas Bird Census," *Bird-Lore* 3 (1901): 30; "The Christmas Bird Census," *Bird-Lore* 4 (1902): 27–28.

137. "Bird Life in Central Park."

138. Olive Thorne Miller, "Spring Birds in the Park," *Christian Union*, May 7, 1892, 891.

139. Floyd Noble, "A February Walk in Central Park, New York," *Bird-Lore* 1, no. 2 (1899): 57–58.

140. Mary Allaire, "Some Boys in the Park," *The Outlook* June 1, 1895, 51.

141. Frank Chapman, "For Young Observers," *Bird-Lore* 1, no. 2 (1899): 55–56; E. M. Mead, "The Return of the Nuthatch," *Bird-Lore* 5, no. 1 (1903): 12–13; A. A. Crolius, "How the Central Park Chickadees Were Tamed," *Bird-Lore* 1, no. 6 (1899): 186.

142. "Bird Life in Central Park," *Forest and Stream*, June 14, 1883, 384.

143. Chapman, *Visitors' Guide to the Local Collection of Birds*, 56.

144. Miller, "Spring Birds in the Park."

145. Lawrence, "Catalogue of Birds," 290.

146. Barua, "Lively Commodities and Encounter Value."

147. Bunner, "Shantytown," 863–64.

148. Accession number 1965-015, RDP: Central Park Menagerie Records, 1876–1950, box 2, Central Park Menagerie ledger, March 1890, 100, NYCMA (hereafter zoo ledger); *ARDCPM* (1890): 7.

149. Fugate, "Shakespeare's Starlings."

150. Taylor, "Central Park as a Model for Social Control," 433–37.

151. Paine, "Dates of the Arrival of Migratory Birds," 109, 125.

152. "Urban Hunt Ends Well," *New York Times*, August 20, 1904.

3. Captive in the City

1. *ARBCCP* 6 (1862): 20.

2. *ARBCCP* 12 (1869): 31. The first bison donation was attributed to Charles Elleard or Ellard in 1864. This may have been a misspelling of the Allard family name; the Allards included Indigenous family members and raised buffalo. This animal disappeared from park records after 1866. See *ARBCCP* 8 (1865): 54; Schneider, "Decolonizing Conservation."

3. *ARBCCP* 12 (1869): 31.

4. Posthumus, "Lakota View."

5. By examining the multi-scalar connections of the Central Park Menagerie, I respond to cautions against "methodological cityism"—that is, a focus on only dynamics within the city as opposed to examining dynamics among cities and places ecologically connected with them through capitalist urbanization. Angelo and Wachsmuth, "Urbanizing Urban Political Ecology." I also follow the lead of environmental historians who trace commodities from "nature out there" into urban culture and economies, such as Cronon's *Nature's Metropolis* and Price's *Flight Maps*. This enlarged story field also builds upon the recent work of recent zoo studies scholars, such as Uddin's *Zoo Renewal* and Bender's *Animal Game*. Earlier research on zoos often emphasized their representational aspects, how animals symbolized the nature of nation or the exoticism and power of far-flung empires, *or* how zoo architecture changed over time to embrace more "naturalistic" displays. Uddin joins these threads, revealing that repeated rounds of "zoo renewals" in the twentieth century that sought to give urban zoo animals more space actually expressed white anxieties about crowded Black neighborhoods also being demolished by white authorities in the name of health and improved architecture. Bender traces what he calls "the animal game" from the capture of animals to their display throughout the twentieth century, including the labor of Indigenous hunters as well as zookeepers and their wives.

6. For discussion of European zoos, see Hoage and Deiss, *New Worlds, New Animals*, 33–72; Hanson, *Animal Attractions*, 2–3.

7. Kisling, "Development of American Zoological Parks," 114. The zoo historian Loisel terms this period the "classical" era of zoological gardens; for a review of Loisel's work, see Veltre, "Menageries, Metaphors, and Meanings," 20–21. Histories of zoos in the 1980s, 1990s, and early 2000s often focused on the scientific achievements and ways zoos "reflected" culture, but this chapter attempts to speak at least as much to questions of power relations among different humans and the way these became entangled with their relationships with animals. For example, the collection of essays on nineteenth-century zoo history in *New Worlds, New Animals*, exemplifies the field's former focus on "cultural reflection." See, for example, Veltre, "Menageries, Metaphors, and Meanings," 20, 28. Ritvo, "Order of Nature," discusses how the gardens in London represented "Britain's domination of the natural world," 47, 50. Hanson's *Animal Attractions*, Bender's *Animal Game*, and Uddin's *Zoo Renewal* address the material and symbolic aspects of zoos in more equal measure.

8. Downing, "New York Park," 162. For other discussions of zoos and national education, see Crang, "Nation, Region, and Homeland"; Stott, "Historical Origins of the Zoological Park." Stott recognizes the importance of zoos in the early

twentieth century for representing American identity, but he takes for granted that all zoo visitors would have equated nature and nation. He thus fails to acknowledge the power dynamic between elite zoo authorities and poor and often immigrant zoo visitors. Stott also argues that American zoological parks simply reflected growing environmental concerns but does not treat the parks as environments in themselves. See also Ritvo, "Order of Nature," 50.

9. Fleming and Halderman, *On Common Ground*, 5; Kisling, "Development of American Zoological Parks," 110.

10. Berger, *About Looking*, 7, 12–13, 21; Hancocks, *Different Nature*, xiv.

11. Hanson, *Animal Attractions*, 22, 53.

12. "Amusements," *New York Times*, March 10, 1860.

13. Betts, "P. T. Barnum," 353–68; Storey, "Spectacular Distractions," 107–23.

14. Schuyler, *Apostle of Taste*, 3–4, 189–90.

15. Several animal studies scholars have examined how relationships with animals have reiterated racial hierarchy. See, for example, Boisseron, *Afro-Dog*, xii–xxv; Jackson, "Animal," especially 672–74.

16. *American Anti-Slavery Society Annual Bulletin* 4 (1837): 109; Walker, *Afro-American in New York City*, 20; Freeman, *Free Negro in New York City*, 69–70.

17. *American Anti-Slavery Society Annual Bulletin* 4 (1837): 109; H. C. Wright, "Contemptible Meanness," *The Emancipator*, March 9, 1837, 179.

18. Wright, "Contemptible Meanness." There is much more to be said about viewing zoos and human-animal hierarchy through a Black studies lens; Uddin's *Zoo Renewal* is an important contributor to this dialogue, along with Boisseron, *Afro-Dog*; Jackson, "Animal"; Bennett, *Being Property Myself Once*, chapter 1.

19. Advertisements, *New York Times*, November 21, 1864, 7; McMillan, "Mammy–Memory," 29–46. McMillan notes that disability was also part of Heth's embodiment, and contemporary accounts compared her limbs and digits to animal body parts.

20. "Announcement for the Millions," *Scientific American* 7, August 23, 1862, 122.

21. The 1.25 million figure comes from 1864–65, immediately before a fire destroyed the American Museum. See "Destruction of Barnum's Museum by Fire," *New York Observer and Chronicle*, July 20, 1865, 230. This article expressed hopes that Barnum would rebuild, but just ten years earlier, religious and literary magazines responded to Barnum's autobiography by doubling down on their criticism. See "Barnum," *Eclectic Magazine of Foreign Literature*, March 1855, 410; Rev. T. M. Eddy, "Barnum," *Ladies' Repository*, March 1855, 170; WHH, "Barnum and Greeley's Autobiographies," *Christian Examiner and Religious Miscellany*, March 1855, 245. For additional discussion of elites' opinion of Barnum, see Rosenzweig and Blackmar, *Park and the People*, 343–44.

22. For discussion of these shifts, see Kasson, *Amusing the Million*, 36.

23. Hanson, *Animal Attractions*, 3–4; Kisling, "Development of American Zoological Parks," 115–16.

24. Olmsted and Kimball, *Forty Years of Landscape Architecture*, 85 (hereafter *FYLA*).

25. BCCP, *Catalogue of Plans for the Improvement of Central Park*, 1857 (hereafter *CPICP*). For examples of these descriptions, see plan 1, 3; plan 3, 4; plan 4, 7; plan 9, 27; plan 15, 7; plan 18, 5–6; plan 19, 11; plan 22, 13; plan 28, 13; plan 30, 28–29; and plan 31, 2.

26. Sykes et al., "Wild to Domestic and Back Again." For a roughly contemporary history of these parks, see Shirley, *Some Account of English Deer Parks*. Fisher, *Urban Green*, also discusses deer parks in Chicago as an expression of European elitism (13).

27. See, for example, *CPICP* plan 3, 4; plan 15, 7; plan 19, 11.

28. Plans that included these features anticipated later movements in zoo architecture. Karl Hagenbeck patented his "panorama" zoological garden design in 1896, well after entrants submitted designs for the Central Park competition—and after Olmsted and Vaux presented their alternative garden design. Reichenbach, "Tale of Two Zoos," 55–61. For spatial constraints on European zoos, see Hanson, *Animal Attractions*, 24.

29. *ARBCCP* 6 (1862): 22–23.

30. *Board of Commissioners of the Central Park Minutes & Documents* (hereafter *BCCP M&D*) 1858–61, minutes for May 26, June 19, November 17, and December 15, 1859, and February 6 and 13, 1860; see also document 4, December 31, 1859.

31. It is notable that in March 1860, shortly before the New York State Legislature chartered the society, Belmont actually rallied the commissioners to oppose the act, based on concerns that the society might destroy a portion of the landscape. It is interesting that Belmont led this charge because he was one of the minority of commissioners to vote for a different park plan less concerned with landscape design and because he recommended other changes to Olmsted and Vaux's Greensward plan. For discussion of the financial and landscape considerations of chartering a private entity to operate the zoo, see Mazaraki, "Public Career of Andrew Haswell Green," 112–14; *BCCP M&D*, 1858–61, minutes for March 21, 1860, 286.

32. New York State Laws of 1860, chapter 256, 25.

33. Rosenzweig and Blackmar, *Park and the People*, 340; Black, *King of Fifth Avenue*, 141.

34. For examples of Belmont's association with Barnum and performers, see Black, *King of Fifth Avenue*, 229, 290.

35. New York State Laws of 1860, chapter 256, 26, 28. Notably, just a few weeks before the passage of this bill, Belmont called for the commissioners to oppose it because it allowed the society to use sixty acres of the park. See *BCCP M&D*, 1858–61, March 21, 1860; *FYLA*, 84.

36. "American Zoological Society," *New York Observer and Chronicle*, May 17, 1860, 158.

37. "The Zoological Gardens in Central Park," *New York Herald*, May 28, 1860. See also Rosenzweig and Blackmar, *Park and the People*, 340–42.

38. "Zoological and Botanical Garden," *Scientific American*, February 18, 1860, 128.

39. *ARBCCP* 6 (1862): 22–23.

40. Rosenzweig and Blackmar, *Park and the People*, 340–42; Foord, *Life and Public Services of Andrew Haswell Green*, 20–21, 40, 63–64.

41. *ARBCCP* 12 (1869): 128.

42. *ARBCCP* 6 (1863): 23.

43. For further discussion of zoos, American national character, and early conservationism, see Stott, "Historical Origins of the Zoological Park," 54–58.

44. "Oldest Zookeeper Tells How He Started America's First Menagerie in Central Park," *New York Times*, March 10, 1912.

45. *ARBCCP* 6 (1863): 49. For the eagle donation, see *ARBCCP* 9 (1866): 77.

46. *ARBCCP* 6 (1863): 49.

47. *ARBCCP* 6 (1863): 22; *ARBCCP* 4 (1861): 74.

48. "The Central Park," *New York Times*, July 25, 1863

49. "The Central Park," *New York Times*, July 25, 1863.

50. "Amusements," *New York Times*, November 21, 1864.

51. *ARBCCP* 6 (1863): 15; Mazaraki, "Public Career of Andrew Haswell Green," 114.

52. *ARBCCP* 4 (1861): 74.

53. *ARBCCP* 4 (1861): 74.

54. *ARBCCP* 7 (1864): 56–57. As chapter 2 describes, park records prior to 1876 often omitted details about whether staff released animals into the park or confined them in cages.

55. Barrow, *Passion for Birds*, 9–17; Hanson, *Animal Attractions*, 48–52.

56. New York State Laws of 1864, chapter 319.

57. *FYLA*, 84.

58. Olmsted and Vaux, 1866, to president of the Board of Commissioners, in *ARBCCP* 10 (1867): 151.

59. Mazaraki, "Public Career of Andrew Haswell Green," 30; Foord, *Life and Public Services*, 58–59, 66, 216–18.

60. While Perris's map of 1857–62 stops to the south of Manhattan Square, other areas held by the city had pastoralist villages; H. C. Bunner's account indicates that a "shantytown" of primarily German and Irish folks persisted north of here well into the 1880s, with residents paying rent to landowners. Mazaraki, "Public Career of Andrew Haswell Green," 94, also asserts that Green had to evict "squatters." H. C. Bunner, "Shantytown," *Scribner's Magazine*, October 1880; McNeur, *Taming Manhattan*, 205–7.

61. *Annual Report of the Board of the Department of Public Parks* 1 (1870–71): 277 (hereafter *ARBDPP*).

62. Olmsted and Vaux, 1866, to president of the Board of Commissioners, in *ARBCCP* 10 (1867): 150.

63. *ARBCCP* 10 (1867): 40.

64. *ARBCCP* 9 (1866): 83–91.

65. Posthumus, "Lakota View"; Isenberg, *Destruction of the Bison*, 128–29; Smits, "Frontier Army," 318–19.

66. Quoted in Isenberg, *Destruction of the Bison*, 125.

67. Posthumus, "Lakota View," 280–81.

68. *ARBCCP* 6 (1862): 20.

69. Grier, *Pets in America*, chapter 3.

70. Isenberg, *Destruction of the Bison*, 130–32; Marsh, *Man and Nature*, 235–36.

71. *ARBCCP* 11 (1868): 91; *ARBCCP* 12 (1869): 31–33; *ARBDPP* 1 (1871): 134, 179. For discussion of the Union Pacific Railroad's role in the destruction of the bison, see Isenberg, *Destruction of the Bison*, 128, 131, 136.

72. *ARDCPM* (1875): 14, 16, 21, 53.

73. *ARBCCP* 10 (1867): 42.

74. *ARBCCP* 13 (1870): 30.

75. Parsons, *Memories of Samuel Parsons*, 68.

76. *ARBDPP* 1 (1871): 23.

77. *ARBDPP* 1 (1871): 277.

78. "The West Side," *New York Times*, February 4, 1872. For Green's endorsement of the museum, see, for example, Rosenzweig and Blackmar, *Park and the People*, 352.

79. *ARBCCP* 13 (1870): 87–99.

80. Rosenzweig and Blackmar, *Park and the People*, 344; *ARCDPP* 1 (1870–71): 21, 186–87, 310–11, 394–97.

81. *ARBDPP* 1 (1870–71): 171.

82. "Sunday at Central Park," *New York Times*, April 3, 1871.

83. Olmsted and Vaux to BCDPP, December 16, 1870, in *FYLA*, 505; see also *FYLA*, 88.

84. *FYLA*, 92.

85. *FYLA*, 499–517. Olmsted states in a later "catechism" on the zoo idea that an area farther north on the West Side would have been ideal (516).

86. Uddin, *Zoo Renewal*, 5–7; Hanson, *Animal Attractions*, 49; Kisling, "Development of American Zoological Parks," 116–17; Hancocks, *Different Nature*, xvii.

87. *ARDCPM* (1876): 3.

88. For numbers of animals "placed on exhibition," see tallies in *ARDCPM* and zoo ledgers. For more on the Reiche and the Ruhe families and circulation of zoo animals with circuses and vaudeville shows, see Hanson, *Animal Attractions*, 79, 83.

89. Grier, *Pets in America*, 104–5; Hanson, *Animal Attractions*, 54–59.

90. NYCMA-RDP, zoo ledger, 1876, 2–4. For a contemporary view of development in this part of New York, see Bromley & Company, *Atlas*, sheet 15. Olmsted recalled that many early donations were the pets of children who had died. *FYLA*, 512. I was unable to find an obituary for the O'Shea children in the *New York Tribune*.

91. NYCMA-RDP, zoo ledger, 1879, 147.

92. *ARDCPM* (1875): 40.

93. For turtles, see NYCMA-RDP, zoo ledger, 1876, 9, 11; for Grover Cleveland's raccoon, see NYCMA-RDP, zoo ledger, 1892, 227.

94. For further discussion of animal captivity, see Collard, "Putting Animals Back Together."

95. Souvenir alligators appeared in other zoos too; see Hanson, *Animal Attractions*, 49, 55.

96. *ARDCPM* (1875): 20.

97. *ARDCPM* (1876): 4; *ARDCPM* (1877): 5.

98. BCDPP, *M&D*, 1882–83, 55.

99. John Smith, "Central Park Animals as Their Keeper Knows Them," *Outing Magazine*, May 1903, 248.

100. NYCMA-RDP, zoo ledger, 1876, 4.

101. NYCMA-RDP, zoo ledger, 1892, 228.

102. Isenberg, *Destruction of the Bison*, 136.

103. Black Elk, *Black Elk Speaks*, see especially chapter 18.

104. NYCMA-RDP, zoo ledger, 1877, 44.

105. *ARDCPM* (1876): 25; NYCMA-RDP, zoo ledger, 1876, 5–6, 18; *ARDCPM* (1879): 20; *ARDCPM* (1888): 7, 17; *ARDCPM* (1890): 4, 20. There is some ambiguity about the date of the cow's purchase; at her death in 1890, the date is listed as November 1878, but the zoo ledger mentions the acquisition of a bison from New Jersey in early 1879, and the purchase is listed in the 1879 report as having occurred in January.

106. *ARDCPM* (1888): 9.

107. Parsons, *Memories of Samuel Parsons*, 67.

108. Uddin, *Zoo Renewal*, 5.

109. *FYLA*, 512.

110. Parsons, *Memories of Samuel Parsons*, 70. Parsons explained that the financial and physical accessibility of the menagerie to residents of the largely poor Lower East Side accounted for the demographics of menagerie attendance.

111. See photographic collections from 111 Mott Street, Museum of Chinese in America; Smith, "Central Park Animals."

112. Peiss, *Cheap Amusements*, introduction, 117.

113. For discussions of taste, class, and environmentalism, see, for example, Price, *Flight Maps*, chapter 2. See also Hanson, *Animal Attractions,* chapter 5, for discussions of tasteful zoo architecture.

114. For discussions of human dominance over animals, see Tuan, *Dominance and Affection*. Also, see two pieces in *New Worlds, New Animals*: Sally Kohlstedt's "Reflections on Zoo History" and Ritvo's "Order of Nature."

115. For more about Mike Crowley and the monkeys, see Fuller, *Mr. Crowley of Central Park*; Rosenzweig and Blackmar, *Park and the People*, 345–46.

116. Forester, *Little Peachblossom*, 131–39.

117. Frederick Law Olmsted and Calvert Vaux to the president of the Board of Commissioners, October 11, 1873, in *FYLA*, 506–7.

118. Demcker, *Central Park Plant List*; NYCMA-RDP, zoo ledger, November 13–19, 1876; "The Central Park Commission," *Turf, Field, and Farm*, December 1, 1876, 344.

119. Calvert Vaux, "A City Zoological Garden," *New York Times*, March 3, 1878.

120. Rosenzweig and Blackmar, *Park and the People*, 297; Salem H. Wales to Frederick Law Olmsted, November 1883, *Frederick Law Olmsted Papers*, General Correspondence Files, Library of Congress; BCDPP M&D, September 26, 1883, 295; "Zoology in the Central Park," *New York Times* November 24, 1883; "What to Do with the Central Park Menagerie," *New York Tribune*, October 12, 1883.

121. *FYLA*, 513; see also Rosenzweig and Blackmar, *Park and the People*, 347.

122. One of the People, "The Menagerie in the Park," *Christian Union*, April 24, 1890, 596.

123. BDPP M&D, February 11, 1891, 357.

124. Mazaraki, "Public Career of Andrew Haswell Green," 114.

125. Hanson, *Animal Attractions*, 28.

126. Hanson, *Animal Attractions*, 29–30.

127. Hanson, *Animal Attractions*, 28–30; Dehler, *Most Defiant Devil*, 8, 65–66, 96–98; Schneider, "Decolonizing Conservation," 810–11.

128. Parsons, *Memories of Samuel Parsons*, 70.

129. Quoted in Bridges, *Gathering of Animals*, 11.

130. Parsons, *Memories of Samuel Parsons*, 70.

131. "A Lively Buffalo Hunt," *New York Times*, June 29, 1899.

132. Orenstein, "Bronx Zoo," 190.

133. Schneider, "Decolonizing Conservation," 807.

134. Isenberg, *Destruction of the Bison*, 93–115.

135. *ARBDPP* 32 (1903): 24.

136. Hanson, *Animal Attractions*, 30–31.

137. Hancocks, *Different Nature*, chapter 7.

Part 2: Human and Animal Claims on a Plural Park

1. *Annual Report of the Department of Parks, Bureau of Manhattan* (1912): 7, 63–64 (hereafter *ARDPBM*).

2. *ARDPBM* (1927): 5, 14, 19–20, 32–33.

3. *ARDPBM* (1912): 7; *ARDPBM* (1927): 8–9, 36–42.
4. Lobo and Salvo, *Newest New Yorkers*, 9–10; America's Great Migrations Project, "New York Migration History, 1850–2018," University of Washington Civil Rights and Labor History Consortium, accessed August 30, 2023, https://depts .washington.edu/moving1/NewYork.shtml.
5. America's Great Migrations Project.
6. America's Great Migrations Project.
7. Steinberg, *Gotham Unbound*; see especially chapter 13.
8. *ARDPBM* (1927): 45–53.
9. Olmsted and Kimball, *Forty Years of Landscape Architecture*, volume 2, preface.
10. Gutman, "Race, Place, and Play"; Rogers, "Landscapes of Robert Moses."
11. Schwartz, *New York Approach*, xv–xxi.

4. Freedom, Joy, and Privilege in Multispecies Spaces

1. Anonymous, "YW to Take Up Horseback Riding," *New York Amsterdam News*, October 24, 1923.
2. Anonymous, "YWCA Notes," *New York Amsterdam News*, April 7, 1926.
3. Brownlow, "Archaeology of Fear and Environmental Change," 227–45; Finney, *Black Faces, White Spaces*, 53, 116–18; Glave, *Rooted in the Earth*, 59–60.
4. Weisenfeld, *African-American Women and Christian Activism*, 63–90; Hartman, *Wayward Lives, Beautiful Experiments*, 166–88.
5. For discussions of claims to citizenship through the supposed vulnerability of animals, see Uddin, "Canine Citizenship"; Kim, *Dangerous Crossings*, chapters 1 and 5.
6. Byrne and Wolch, "Nature, Race, and Parks."
7. *ARDPBM* (1927): 5, 14, 19–20, 32–33.
8. For discussion of the emergence of modern binoculars, see Barrow, *Passion for Birds*, 156–61.
9. Davis, *Dean of the Birdwatchers*, 22–23.
10. For further discussion of Griscom and his childhood, see Davis, *Dean of the Birdwatchers*, 3–7; for discussion of birding by sight, see 102–7.
11. Ludlow Griscom, "New York's Parks Are Bird Capitals in Maytime," *New York Times*, May 16, 1926.
12. Davis, *Dean of the Birdwatchers*, 8; Barrow, *Passion for Birds*, 178–79. The transition from gun to glass was an important one within ornithology that Griscom helped advance after initial advocacy by his colleague Frank Chapman. Shooting birds was, of course, prohibited in Central Park, so it appears that Griscom's unfriendly crowd was mocking him not for not using a gun but for something about his style of occupying public space.

13. Davis, *Dean of the Birdwatchers*, 18–24.
14. Davis, *Dean of the Birdwatchers*, 3–7.
15. Griscom, "New York's Parks."
16. Griscom, "New York's Parks."
17. For Griscom's praise of Crolius, see Griscom, *Birds of the New York City Region*, 45. For "bird-women" of Central Park, see, for example, "Spring Tours of Central Park Are Resumed by 'Bird Lady,'" *New York Times*, April 30, 1939. For Griscom's knowledge of the Ramble, see Griscom, "New York's Parks Are Bird Capitals in Maytime."
18. Staeheli and Mitchell, *People's Property*, xxii.
19. For discussion of Central Park's unhoused encampment, see Caro, *Power Broker*, 336; Roy Rosenzweig and Blackmar, *Park and the People*, 439–42.
20. Cook, *Description of the New York Central Park*, 112.
21. Chauncey, *Gay New York*, 146, 181–91.
22. Martin, *Genius of Place*, 153–54; "335 Seized as Annoyers," *New York Times*, October 7, 1929.
23. Chauncey, *Gay New York*, 182.
24. None of this is to say that people who slept, washed, defecated, or had sex in public spaces were somehow more "like animals" than other humans— an important caveat as we consider the ways white supremacist and heteronormative society has dehumanized Black and queer folks who are part of the focus of this chapter. While scholars of animal studies use the phrase *more-than-human* in part to call into question the boundaries between humans and our fellow creatures, Black, Indigenous, and queer scholars in animal studies have explored ways of human being in the world that dissolve hierarchies of race, sexuality, and species. Humans and other animals share the world as a habitat along with many bodily experiences through which we relate to environments and spaces. Jackson "Animal," 669–85; Bennett, *Being Property Myself Once*, 8, 32–35; Billy-Ray Belcourt, "Animal Bodies, Colonial Subjects," *Societies* 5 (2015): 1–11.
25. Chauncey, *Gay New York*, 98.
26. Chauncey, *Gay New York*, 5.
27. I am grateful to Craig Saper for talking with me about this distinction and to Bee Brown for explaining to me the culture of outdoor sex among queer youth. Thanks also to Mars Plater.
28. Chauncey, *Gay New York*, 172–73.
29. Chauncey, *Gay New York*, 173; Alexander and Strange, "Girl Problem."
30. "Thousands in Riot at Valentino Bier," *New York Times*, August 25, 1926; Anderson, *Twilight of the Idols*, 125–26.

31. Court of General Sessions of the County of New York, in the Matter of the People of the State of New York against Joseph A. Higgins, case number 166846, January 18, 1927.

32. "Actor Dies from Blows of Central Park Officer," *New York Amsterdam News*, September 1, 1926; "Postpone Sentence of Officer Who Killed DeForrest [*sic*]," *New York Amsterdam News*, January 26, 1927; "Roosevelt Frees Cop Who Slew Man," *New York Amsterdam News*, April 24, 1929.

33. I am grateful to Michelle Scott for discussing DeForest with me. See Scott, *T.O.B.A. Time*, 104.

34. Ireland, "Rendezvous in the Ramble"; see also Rosenzweig and Blackmar, *Park and the People*, 405, 479, 493.

35. Peet, *Trees and Shrubs of Central Park*, 187. See also Nicole Seymour on "gay pastoral" in *Strange Natures*, especially 105–46; Gandy, "Queer Ecologies."

36. For an example of media mocking the odd manner of bird-watchers, see Barrow, *Passion for Birds*, 163–64.

37. For discussions of deterioration of the park's landscape, see, for example, *ARBDPP* (1927): 5, 14, 19–20, 32–33.

38. For example, Chakenetsa Mavhunga writes of the ways British imperial agents in what they called Rhodesia reordered Indigenous Zimbabweans' relationships to land and animals through their cattle raising practices and programs for controlling wildlife that were both valued for nature preservation and also controlled as reservoirs of sleeping sickness. Mavhunga, *Mobile Workshop*.

39. Roger Pasquier, "Interrupted Landscapes: The Future of Bird Migration," *SiteLines* 13 (2017): 13–16; Winn *Red-Tails in Love*; Griscom, "New York's Parks."

40. Francis Gallatin to John Hylan, June 19, 1919, 2, Office of the Mayor of the City of New York (hereafter Mayor's Office) Correspondence Collection, box 132, folder 1427, Parks, Department of Manhattan, 1919, June–August, NYCMA.

41. Griscom, *Birds of the New York City Region*, 44.

42. Griscom, "New York's Parks."

43. Griscom, *Birds of the New York City Region*, 44.

44. Francis Gallatin to John Hylan, March 5, 1919, Mayor's Office Correspondence Collection, box 132, folder 1426, Parks, Department of Manhattan, January–May 1919, NYCMA.

45. Griscom, *Birds of the New York City Region*, 44.

46. *ARDPBM* (1912): 107.

47. Rosenzweig and Blackmar, *Park and the People*, 410–11.

48. Rosenzweig and Blackmar, *Park and the People*, 410–11.

49. *ARDPBM* (1927): 5–6.

50. For example, establishments such as "the Riding Club, which is one of the most

exclusive organizations of its kind" kept "the mounts of many of the matrons and young women, who can be seen hurrying thither and riding out quickly through the Plaza" and into an entrance across Fifth Avenue. WGR, "Spring in Central Park," *Town & Country*, April 11, 1903.

51.	Wilf P. Pond, "Turf, Field, and Ring," *The Spur*, November 15, 1929.

52.	Francis Gallatin to John Hylan, April 10, 1923, Mayor's Office Correspondence Collection, box 132, folder 1421, Parks, Department of Manhattan, 1923, NYCMA.

53.	*ARDPBM* (1927): 11.

54.	*ARDPBM* (1928): 36.

55.	*ARDPBM* (1927): 11; "Urge Resurfacing Park Bridle Path," *New York Times*, May 19, 1930.

56.	Unfortunately, equivalent statistics are not available to allow a true comparison of equestrian use of the park between any period after the first two decades of the park's existence to the 1930s.

57.	"Urge Resurfacing Park Bridle Path."

58.	"Requests $125,000 for Bridle Paths," *New York Times*, October 27, 1930.

59.	"Urge Resurfacing Park Bridle Path."

60.	For some examples of these complaints, see RDP, box 77, folder 71, NYCMA.

61.	"Park Equestrians Demand Reforms," *New York Times*, October 7, 1934; "Park Riders to Wait on Mayor in Costume," *New York Times*, January 3, 1936.

62.	"To 'Crash' Bridle Path," *New York Times*, January 5, 1936.

63.	"100 Park Hunters Ride to Hot Toddies," *New York Times*, April 20, 1936.

64.	Bernard Sandler to Allyn Jennings, May 6, 1939, REC 041 Department of Parks, box 77, folder 71, NYCMA.

65.	Robert Moses to Mayor Fiorello LaGuardia, May 27, 1939, REC 041, Department of Parks, box 77, folder 71, NYCMA.

66.	For letters, see REC 041 Department of Parks, box 77, folder 71, NYCMA.

67.	Socialite (pseud.) Sr., "Horseback Riding Replaces Skate and Bike as the Elite of Harlem's Haute Monde Go to Central Park," *New York Amsterdam News*, October 26, 1935.

68.	Geographer and food studies scholar Amie Breeze Harper has criticized similar positions by vegan and animal rights organizations that promote food products free from animal products without addressing unfree human labor practices of these "cruelty-free" companies, which disproportionately affect farm labors and factory workers of color. Harper, "Race as 'Feeble Matter.'" Claire Jean Kim similarly critiques political movements and academic disciplines that attack injustices from "separate bunkers," including especially animal advocates. Kim, *Dangerous Crossings*.

69.	Hartman, *Wayward Lives*, 108.

70.	McCammack, *Landscapes of Hope*, 3.

71.	Rosenzweig and Blackmar, *Park and the People*, 413–14.

72. Carby, "Policing the Black Woman's Body"; Hartman, *Wayward Lives*, 188.
73. Anonymous, "Traps for the Innocent," *New York Age*, October 17, 1925.
74. Weisenfeld, "Harlem YMCA and the Secular City."
75. Anonymous, "Health Education to Be Featured by 137th St. Y This Season," *New York Age*, March 20, 1926.
76. Anonymous, "Mrs. Emma Ransom Guest at the Emma Ransom YWCA Home Opening," *New York Age*, April 10, 1926.
77. "High Rents and Overcrowding Responsible for Many of the Ills Suffered by Harlemites," *New York Age*, August 11, 1923.
78. See five letters from Oscar Hauter to Allyn Jennings or Robert Moses, RDP, box 77, folder 71 (Bridle path, 1939), NYCMA.
79. "Y.W. to Take Up Horseback Riding."
80. "Frank Tucker's Riding Academy Does Big Business with Saddle Enthusiasts," *New York Amsterdam News*, October 26, 1935.
81. See Bennett, *Being Property Myself Once*, 1–17; Bénédicte Boisseron makes a similar argument about dogs in *Afro-Dog*.
82. Hotaling, *Great Black Jockeys*, introduction.
83. Rubenstein, *Harlem Riot of 1935*.
84. Socialite, "Horseback Riding Replaces Skate and Bike"; "For Riding Master," *New York Amsterdam News*, November 9, 1940.
85. Socialite, "Horseback Riding Replaces Skate and Bike."
86. Socialite, "Horseback Riding Replaces Skate and Bike."
87. For generalizations about horses in small operations and how they were trained, see, for example, Pooley-Ebert, "Species Agency"; McShane and Tarr, *Horse in the City*, 21–26, 40–54.
88. Socialite, "Horseback Riding Replaces Skate and Bike."
89. "Equestrians Not Wanted," *Pittsburgh Courier*, July 3, 1937; Lewis, *When Harlem Was in Vogue*, 130.
90. "Equestrians Not Wanted."
91. Bogle, *Heat Wave*, 201.
92. Wilson, *Bulldaggers, Pansies, and Chocolate Babies*, 59–60; see also mentions of Waters in Hartman, *Wayward Lives*, 337; Scott, *T.O.B.A. Time*, 104, 136.
93. "Protest against Ethel Waters Using Bridle Paths Flops," *Pittsburgh Courier*, June 19, 1937.
94. Johnson, *Lavender Scare*, 3.
95. Johnson, *Lavender Scare*, 3, 12, 55, 130–33.
96. REC 041, Department of Parks, box 503, folders 1 and 2, NYCMA; Rogers, *Saving Central Park*, 113, 142; personal communication with Sara Cedar Miller.
97. REC 041, Department of Parks, box 503, folders 1 and 2, NYCMA.
98. Cherry, *For the Birds*, chapter 7.

99. Personal communication with Robert DeCandido, August 2018; personal communication with Ohad Paris, April 2019.

100. Draft and final public statement, Robert Moses and Stuart Constable, "Statement re. Lasker Center for Times and Herald Tribune," August 25, 1955, Robert Moses Papers, box 100, folder 2, NYPL.

101. Memo, Constable to Moses, June 30, 1955, RDP, box 503, folder 1, NYCMA.

102. Sulzberger to Moses, July 11, 1955, RDP, box 503, folder 2, NYCMA; draft and final public statement, Moses and Constable, "Statement re. Lasker Center for Times and Herald Tribune." Notes on the draft statement make it clear that Moses and Constable were striving to show that both birds and the safety of birders were part of the reason to pursue the Lasker Center plans.

103. Cyrus Austin to Robert Moses, September 6, 1955, box 100, folder 2 Robert Moses Papers, NYPL.

104. Joseph Beller to Stuart Constable, October 2, 1955, REC 041, Department of Parks box 503, folder 3, NYCMA.

105. Seymour, *Strange Natures*, 2–5; Sandilands and Erickson, *Queer Ecologies*, 4–7.

106. Draft and final public statement, Moses and Constable, "Statement re. Lasker Center for Times and Herald Tribune."

107. Mundy to Moses, August 14, 1955, box 100, folder 2, Robert Moses Papers, NYPL; "Naturalists Win Battle of the Ramble," *New York Times*, December 1, 1955.

108. "Naturalists Win Battle of the Ramble."

109. Amelia Hull, "To Preserve the Ramble," *New York Times*, November 30, 1955.

110. Emanuel Perlmutter, "Night Made Safe in Central Park," *New York Times*, July 6, 1956.

111. Rosenzweig and Blackmar, *Park and the People*, 478–81. For crime as a threat to birders later in the twentieth century, see references to safety problems in Knowler, *Falconer of Central Park*, for example 27, 47.

112. Perlmutter, "Night Made Safe in Central Park."

113. Chauncey, *Gay New York*, epilogue.

114. Gandy, "Queer Ecologies."

115. Cooper, *Better Living Through Birding*, 5. Cooper also describes the gay cruising scene in the Ramble as "notorious" and not for him (81–82). Birder J. Drew Lanham also pointed out in 2013 that Black birders remained unusual in professional and leisure ornithology; he has faced suspicion while looking for birds and marginalization among birders because of his skin color. J. Drew Lanham, "9 Rules for the Black Birdwatcher," *Orion Magazine*, October 25, 2013.

116. Scholars in the fields of queer ecology argue that such ideas of what belongs in nature are also inseparable from the idea that heterosexual sex and binary gender are "natural." Many have shown that the pure category of "nature" obfuscates nonreproductive sex and denies strange mixtures of wild and humanized space.

Ecologists for decades observed same-sex couplings among charismatic megafauna but omitted them from their field notes; majestic wildlife have thrived in abandoned toxic waste sites; lesbians have led back-to-the-land movements; queer immigrants and butterfly watchers have formed alliances to protect a derelict urban cemetery where human couples, naturalists, and insects all find sanctuary. Krupar, *Hot Spotter's Report*, chapter 1; Seymour, *Strange Natures*, 35–40; Gandy, "Queer Ecologies"; Alaimo "Eluding Capture"; Bagemihl, *Biological Exuberance*, 122–67.

117. Bennett, *Being Property Myself Once*, 2; see also Jackson, "Animal."
118. The failure of white environmentalists to support Black access to natural resources is reminiscent of stories from Gary, Indiana; see Hurley, *Environmental Inequalities*, conclusion.

5. Modern Childhood and Modern Captivity

1. "New Zoo Opens," *New York Times*, December 3, 1934.
2. Mintz, *Huck's Raft*, especially chapters 10, 11, and 12. For the historical idea that "all children should have a childhood," see Lassonde, review of *Riding the Rails*, 156.
3. Mintz, *Huck's Raft*, 234.
4. For Moses, childhood, and play, see, for example, Gutman, "Race, Place, and Play."
5. "New Zoo Opens."
6. Correspondence file, 1935, REC 041, Department of Parks, box 34: Cheyne-Stout Case, folder 4, NYCMA.
7. Bender, *Animal Game*, chapter 4.
8. See Gillespie and Collard, *Critical Animal Geographies*, introduction; Uddin, *Zoo Renewal*, 13–22.
9. In tracing these parallels between zoos for animals and housing for human New Yorkers, I follow the lead of Uddin's *Zoo Renewal*; these parallels are both material and discursive. See particularly chapter 2 of *Zoo Renewal* on slum clearance.
10. See chapter 3.
11. Francis Gallatin to John Hylan, June 19, 1919, 3, Mayor's Office Correspondence Collection, Parks, Department of Manhattan, box 132, folder 1427, NYCMA.
12. "Cackling Geese Save Central Park Bison," *New York Times*, June 20, 1926.
13. *ARDPBM*, 1927, 5–6.
14. DeForest and Veiller, *Tenement House Problem*; see also Schwartz, *New York Approach*, 5–9.
15. Jackson, *Crabgrass Frontier*, 172–89. For parallels between suburbanization and zoo renewal, see Uddin, *Zoo Renewal*, 13, 71, 90, 172–79, though Uddin mostly references post–World War II suburbs.
16. See, for example, Rogers, "Landscapes of Robert Moses," 3.

17. Barua, "Lively Commodities and Encounter Value"; Uddin, *Zoo Renewal*, chapter 1; Bender, *Animal Game*, chapter 3.

18. Quoted in Hanson, *Animal Attractions*, 26.

19. "To Name Fatima's Baby," *New York Times*, March 9, 1896.

20. "Asks New Elephant and Hippo for Park," *New York Times*, February 8, 1923.

21. "Fox Chase Thrills Park's 'Huntsmen,'" *New York Times*, September 22, 1932. No one seemed to acknowledge the morbid side to this humor; fox hunters traditionally killed the fox.

22. Smith, "Central Park Animals," 42.

23. "Up to the Minute World Happenings," *New York Amsterdam News*, January 12, 1924.

24. Hinton and Cook, "Mass Criminalization of Black Americans."

25. Baldwin, *Go Tell It on the Mountain*, 195.

26. See, for example, "Negroes in Fantasia," *New York Amsterdam News*, October 22, 1930.

27. "Johnsons Return with Live Gorillas," *New York Times*, July 4, 1931; "Score Housing of Native Tribesmen," *New York Amsterdam News*, August 22, 1931. Many sources call both men Ugandans, but Imperato and Imperato distinguish Aussayne and Manuelli as being of different nationalities. Imperato and Imperato, *They Married Adventure*, 164.

28. Mitman, *Reel Nature*, 26–30; Imperato and Imperato, *They Married Adventure*, 164–65.

29. "Johnsons Return with Live Gorillas."

30. "Johnsons Return with Live Gorillas."

31. For Ota Benga at the Bronx Zoo, see Newkirk, *Spectacle*, 31–34; Dehler, *Most Defiant Devil*, 96–99. See also Enright, *Osa and Martin*, ix. Enright emphasizes the Johnsons' engagement with conservation and their openness to a diversity of people, omitting all reference to this incident, while Bender more closely compares the treatment of Aussayne and Manuelli to Ota Benga. Bender, *Animal Game*, chapter 6. Aussayne and Manuelli avoided Ota Benga's fate—he had planned to return to Congo after his release from the zoo, but his hopes were dashed when the Great War cut off ocean liner traffic. Stuck in the United States for what was then the foreseeable future, he committed suicide in 1916. Newkirk, *Spectacle*, 241–48.

32. Imperato and Imperato, *They Married Adventure*, xi, 164.

33. Johnson and Johnson, *Congorilla*, 1932.

34. "Two African Boys Find Harlem Odd," *New York Times*, July 6, 1931; "Harlem Sharpens Uganda Boys' Wits," *New York Times* July 20, 1931; "Score Housing of Native Tribesmen."

35. Maya Bengard, "Man in the Street Investigates," *New York Amsterdam News*, August 19, 1931.

36. Bender, *Animal Game*, 166–70.

37. "Big City Startles Two Africans," *New York Times*, July 5, 1931; "Curse of the Congo Claims Life of Dog," *New York Times*, January 26, 1934; "Deport Gorilla-Keepers after Near-Riot in Harlem," *Pittsburgh Courier*, October 8, 1931.

38. Johnson, *I Married Adventure*, 372. For more about gorillas and captivity, see Cincinnati, "Too Sullen for Survival."

39. See chapter 3.

40. Bender, *Animal Game*, 26.

41. Bender, *Animal Game*, 14.

42. Bender, *Animal Game*, chapters 3–4.

43. For zoo construction, see REC 041, Records of the Department of Parks, box 3, folder 34, NYCMA.

44. See Mintz, *Huck's Raft*, chapters 12, 13, and 14.

45. Chiles, "School Reform as Progressive Statecraft."

46. For an example of Depression-era concerns about children, see Murphy, "Children and the New Deal." See also Mintz, *Huck's Raft*, 234–36.

47. Murphy, "Children and the New Deal"; Caro, *Power Broker*, 234.

48. Jack Hansan, "The American Era of Child Labor," *Social Welfare History Project* (2011), https://socialwelfare.library.vcu.edu/programs/child-welfarechild-labor/child-labor; Lassonde, *Learning to Forget*, 192.

49. Mintz, *Huck's Raft*, chapter 12–13; Reiman, *New Deal and American Youth*, 99.

50. Gutman, "Race, Space, and Play"; Rogers, "Landscapes of Robert Moses."

51. Jackson, "Robert Moses and the Rise of New York," 67–71. As Rosenzweig and Blackmar describe, crime rates actually rose much later. Rosenzweig and Blackmar, *Park and the People*, 478–81.

52. Rogers "Landscapes of Robert Moses," 3.

53. For images of zoo cages, see Cheyne-Stout Scrap-Book, Wildlife Conservation Society Archives, Bronx Zoo.

54. Bender, *Animal Game*, 12, 23–26.

55. See chapter 4 of this book; Davis, *Dean of the Birdwatchers*, 3–7.

56. "Wallaby Mystery Has Zoo All Agog," *New York Times*, April 11, 1934.

57. College of New Jersey, "David Sarnoff Collection," accessed August 30, 2023, https://davidsarnoff.tcnj.edu/david-sarnoff/david-sarnoff-timeline.

58. "Wallaby Mystery."

59. "Sidelights of the Week," *New York Times*, August 2, 1936.

60. Hindle, foreword, vii.

61. Hindle, foreword, viii.

62. Collard, "Putting Animals Back Together"; Mavhunga, "Seeing the National Park"; Serrato, "Ecological Indigenous Foodways."

63. Bender, *Animal Game*, 64–65. For discussions of by-catch, see Mavhunga, *Mobile Workshop*, 190.

64. For examples of purchases from Ruhe, see, REC 041, Records of the Department of Parks, box 34: Cheyne-Stout Case, folder 4, NYCMA.

65. REC 041, Records of the Department of Parks, box 34: Cheyne-Stout Case, folder 8, NYCMA. For other instances of zoo director involvement in the animal trade, see Bender, *Animal Game*, chapter 7.

66. Bender, *Animal Game*, chapter 3; Hanson, *Animal Attractions*, 79–82.

67. Robert Moses to Dr. W. Reid Blair, April 5, 1935, REC 041, Records of the Department of Parks, box 34: Cheyne-Stout Case, folder 4, NYCMA.

68. Dr. W. Reid Blair to Robert Moses, April 8, 1935, REC 041, Records of the Department of Parks, box 34: Cheyne-Stout Case, folder 4 NYCMA.

69. James Sherry to Allyn Jennings, April 13, 1935, REC 041, Records of the Department of Parks, box 34: Cheyne-Stout Case, folder 4; A. L. Harris to Allyn Jennings, memo, box 34: Cheyne-Stout Case, folder 4, NYCMA.

70. Ronald Cheyne-Stout to Emil Schwartzhaupp, July 11, 1938, REC 041, Records of the Department of Parks, box 34: Cheyne-Stout Case, folder 4, New York City Municipal Archives.

71. Braverman, *Zooland*, chapter 6; Collard, *Animal Traffic*, 12.

72. Letters offering these animals and describing their situations are found in REC 041, Records of the Department of Parks, box 34: Cheyne-Stout Case, folder 4, NYCMA.

73. Hediger, *Wild Animals in Captivity*, 27.

74. REC 041, Records of the Department of Parks, box 34: Cheyne-Stout Case, folder 8, NYCMA.

75. "Zoo Honors Girl, 5, 6,000,000th Visitor," *New York Times*, April 20, 1936.

76. Dorothy Thompson, "People in the News," *Pall Mall Broadcast*, April 8, 1938, Robert Moses Papers, NYPL Special Collections, box 97, folder 10: Parks 1938.

77. "Things for Children to Do," *New York Times*, August 10, 1945.

78. "18 Animals at Zoo Have 'Baptism' Day," *New York Times*, June 4, 1938.

79. "Zoo Name Poll Closes," *New York Times*, August 28, 1935. Literary scholar Randy Malamud insists that in spite of popular opinion, children actually do not like zoos. Malamud, *Reading Zoos*, chapter 6.

80. "Zoo Chief Gets a Pet," *New York Times*, May 14, 1936.

81. "Frog Jumpers Here in a Dozen Hops," *New York Times*, May 13, 1935.

82. "Book Fair Stirred by Animal Stories," *New York Times*, November 14, 1937. Bender, in *Animal Game*, notes that story hours were common across New Deal–era zoos as keepers were encouraged to interact more with visitors (127).

83. Ronald Cheyne-Stout to Harry Sweeny, July 21, 1937, REC 041, Records of the Department of Parks, box 34: Cheyne-Stout Case, folder 4, NYCMA.

84. Flack, "'In Sight, Insane.'"

85. Henry Sweeny to Allyn Jennings, July 28, 1936, REC 041, Records of the Department of Parks, box 34: Cheyne-Stout Case, folder 7, NYCMA.

86. "Ousted Zoo Director Charges Unfairness," *New York Times*, April 5, 1939.

87. Harry Sweeny to W. R. C. Wood, November 10, 1936, REC 041, Records of the Department of Parks, box 34: Cheyne-Stout Case, folder 4, NYCMA.

88. REC 041, Records of the Department of Parks, box 34: Cheyne-Stout Case, folder 7, NYCMA.

89. REC 041, Records of the Department of Parks, box 34: folder 8, NYCMA.

90. "Zoo Head Ousted at Central Park," *New York Times*, April 4, 1939.

91. Hediger, *Wild Animals in Captivity*, 112–19.

92. REC 041, Records of the Department of Parks, box 34: Cheyne-Stout Case, folder 3, NYCMA.

93. Cheyne-Stout Scrapbook, Wildlife Conservation Society Archives, Bronx Zoo.

94. John Galm, memo to George Quigley, July 24, 1955 REC 041, Records of the Department of Parks, Zoo: Vital Statistics: Zoo Animals, 1929–80, accession number 91-14, box 503, folder 9, NYCMA

95. REC 041, Records of the Department of Parks, Zoo: Vital Statistics: Zoo Animals, 1929–80, accession number 91-14, box 503, folder 9, NYCMA.

96. For discussion of zoo babies in the spotlight, see Guro Flinterud, "Child Stars at the Zoo," in McDonald and Vandersommers, *Zoo Studies*, 191–210.

97. Theresa Robinson to Newbold Morris, December 9, 1961; Halle December to Parks Department, December 4, 1961, REC 041, Records of the Department of Parks, box 710, folder 5, NYCMA.

98. Hediger, *Wild Animals in Captivity*, 158–61.

99. Hediger, *Wild Animals in Captivity*, 37.

100. Hediger, *Wild Animals in Captivity*, 176. For further discussion of contemporary zoos and their use of animals, see Braverman, *Zooland*.

101. Salinger, *Catcher in the Rye*, 229–31.

102. Malamud, *Reading Zoos*, chapter 6.

103. Cat and Cullen, *Lost Zoo*, 12–15, 51–55. For further discussion of Cullen's affinity for animals, see Bennett, *Being Property Myself Once*, 6; Malamud, *Reading Zoos*, 318–23.

104. Bennett, *Being Property Myself Once*, 4.

105. These innocent though fallible animals missed their ride on Noah's Ark and were lost in the biblical flood, sent by God because of (some) humans' sins. Cat and Cullen, *Lost Zoo*, 19.

106. "Lehmans Give City Zoo for Children," *New York Times*, June 16, 1960.

107. Bender, *Animal Game*, 253–59, 270–71.

108. For discussion of the Lehman's intentions, particularly Edith Lehman's vision, in

creating the Children's Zoo, see REC 041, Records of the Department of Parks, box 709, folders 1–10, especially folder 9, NYCMA.

109. T. Boyle to A. Wirin, November 6, 1961, RDP, box 709, folder 1, NYCMA.

110. Hazen, *Visit to the Children's Zoo.*

111. See NYCMY-RDP zoo staff ledger, REC 041, RDP, Attendance Records of Employees, ACC 91-13, NYCMA; John C. Devlin, "Zoo for Children Is Opened in Park," *New York Times*, September 28, 1961. For further discussion of women zookeepers and children's zoos, see Bender, *Animal Game*, 256–71.

112. "History of Central Park Zoos," New York City Department of Parks and Recreation, accessed May 10, 2019, https://www.nycgovparks.org/about/history /zoos/central-park-zoo.

6. Animals Out and In

1. See chapter 1.

2. "What Might Be Done in Central Park," *New York Times*, June 13, 1909. See also "John D. Crimmins Dies of Pneumonia," *New York Times*, November 10, 1917.

3. John D. Crimmins, "Lenox Library in the Park," *New York Times*, June 1, 1912.

4. Caro, *Power Broker*, 335, 374.

5. Steven Corey (personal communication) has shown that livestock continued to flow through Manhattan slaughterhouses well into the twentieth century but remained mostly invisible to the general public.

6. "Central Park Sheep," *New York Tribune*, June 2, 1901.

7. See, for example, B. M. Kirschner, "Sheep Grazing in Central Park," *Popular Photography* 2 (February 1914): 198.

8. "John D. Crimmins Dies of Pneumonia," 13.

9. For discussion of the development of New York in the early twentieth century, see, for example, Schwartz, *New York Approach*, 9–14.

10. "New-York's Tenement House Commission Is Doing Grand Work," *New York Tribune*, May 31, 1903; Ziegelman, *97 Orchard*, 114–15.

11. *ARDPBM* (1912): 8, 45, 116, 348.

12. Bertram Reinitz, "A City Shepherd," *New York Times*, May 30, 1926.

13. "Central Park Is Pastoral," *New York Times*, October 16, 1927.

14. Reinitz, "City Shepherd."

15. "Park Lunches Poison Sheep," *New York Times*, June 4, 1921.

16. "Baa, Baa Park Sheep Lifted from the Fold," *New York Times*, October 19, 1928; "Sheep-Rustling in Central Park," *New York Times*, October 22, 1928.

17. Berger, *About Looking*, 7.

18. "Little Mary Gets Real Lamb at Zoo Auction," *New York Times*, June 16, 1927. Being won at auction ushered in major life changes for sheep, often leading to slaughter for ram lambs or use as a breeding dam for the ewes. The auction often separated ewes from their lambs, and the highest bidders introduced ewes to new rams for breeding. "Surplus" animals from the zoo were also auctioned the same day as the sheep. Some bidders purchased bison to start herds and later convert into steaks, others bought pigs for similar purposes. A few bidders took advantage of the auction, which was advertised with lists of animals a few days beforehand, to stock small local zoological collections with creatures from deer to coyotes. See also Gillespie and Collard, *Critical Animal Geographies*, introduction.

19. "Little Mary Gets Real Lamb at Zoo Auction."

20. "Insipid Sheep Top Zoo Auction," *New York Herald-Tribune*, June 14, 1928.

21. *ARDPBM* (1927): 19.

22. For records on manure contracts, see BDPP *M&D*, 1912, 192, 195. The reliance on outside manure indicates a reversal of former flows of fertilizer between city and suburbs; in the age of peak horsepower, cities' dense concentrations of horse manure were collected for export to suburban farms. See Steinberg, *Down to Earth*, 111–13.

23. ACM, "Spring in New York," *New York Herald-Tribune*, April 15, 1928; "Pastoral: Midtown," *New York Herald-Tribune*, May 7, 1928. See also ACM, "When Easter Comes," *New York Herald-Tribune*, March 31, 1929.

24. "Central Park's Sheep Join the Fold in Prospect Park," *New York Times*, March 18, 1934.

25. Caro, *Power Broker*, 399; Rosenzweig and Blackmar, *Park and the People*, 454–55.

26. Arnold Schleifer, Tavern on the Green menu, 1946, NYPL, Buttolph Collection of Menus, accessed July 24, 2019, http://exhibitions.nypl.org/treasures/items/show/145.

27. Brown, *City Is More than Human*, 200–201; Gillespie and Collard, *Critical Animal Geographies*, introduction.

28. "Central Park's Sheep Join the Fold in Prospect Park," *New York Times*, March 18, 1934.

29. Budget narrative, 1937, Robert Moses Papers, NYPL, Parks Department, box 97, folder 5.

30. For criticism and protests against the tavern, see Caro, *Power Broker*, 399, 614, 868; Rosenzweig and Blackmar, *Park and the People*, 454–55.

31. "Eclogue," *New York Times*, May 31, 1938.

32. Grizzly King, "The Top Rail," *Forest and Stream*, March 30, 1907, 501. From this time period, and given the publication, it is highly likely that this old-timer was white.

33. For discussions of fishing as environmental knowledge, see Bear and Eden, "Thinking like a Fish"; Giltner, "Slave Hunting and Fishing." For further

discussions of fishing among Chicagoans of multiple ethnicities, see Fisher, *Urban Green*, 99–100. For discussion of changing waterways in New York City, see Steinberg, *Gotham Unbound*.

34. "In Parks and Public Gardens," *American Gardening* June 11, 1904, 389; *ARBDPP* 1905, 31. Another sportsman suggested to an outdoor magazine that park engineers place salt in the park's waters to keep mosquitoes, pond scum, and other hazards in check. See Robert T. Morris, "The Central Park Lakes," *Forest and Stream*, June 25, 1904, 520.

35. See, for example, "Central Park Ordinances," *New York Times*, November 1, 1866.

36. See chapter 2.

37. See chapter 2.

38. Anglers' Club, *Anglers' Club Story*, 38–39.

39. Anglers' Club, *Anglers' Club Story*, 9–10; Fraser, "History of the Anglers' Club." Fraser's name is also spelled *Frazer* in some club literature.

40. Anglers' Club, *Anglers' Club Story*, 31, 35; see also *Anglers' Club Bulletin* for lists of new members, which include members' occupations.

41. See *Anglers' Club Bulletin* for examples of lobbying, especially spring 1922, April 1923, February 1935; see also Anglers' Club, *Anglers' Club Story*, 24.

42. Hurley, *Environmental Inequalities*, 93, 102.

43. For a meditation on why this abstracted competition came about, see "Switch-Reel" (pseud.), *Anglers' Club Bulletin*, February 1921, 1.

44. Fraser, "History of the Anglers' Club," 4.

45. Anglers' Club, *Anglers' Club Story*, 18. See also Fraser, "History of the Anglers' Club," 4.

46. Anglers' Club, *Anglers' Club Story*, 19.

47. *Forest and Stream*, June 1920; Anglers' Club, *Anglers' Club Story*, 24–27; "Boy Scouts," *New York Times*, November 2, 1924.

48. Anglers' Club, *Anglers' Club Story*, 30–31.

49. George Greenfield, "Boy of 13 Excels in Casting Tourney," *New York Times*, July 1, 1934; George Greenfield, "Rod and Gun," *New York Times*, July 8, 1934; "Throngs Here See Fly-Casting Meet," *New York Times*, June 16, 1935.

50. Meyer Berger, "About New York," *New York Times*, April 2, 1940; "One-Patrolmen Drive Traps 25 in Central Park," *New York Herald-Tribune*, May 24, 1938.

51. Sheu, *"Clean Water and Better Bass Fishing."* See also Giltner, "Slave Hunting and Fishing."

52. Hurston, *Mules and Men*, for example, 95. Historian Julian Rankin has highlighted the place of catfish in southern working-class cuisine and culture, particularly Black culture. Rankin, *Catfish Dream*, particularly 96–112. See also McCammack, who found multiple instances in which fishing was an important way for

Black Chicagoans to connect with nature, particularly during the Depression. McCammack, *Landscapes of Hope*, 29, 46, 85, 187–96.

53. Rankin, *Catfish Dream*, 89.

54. Catfish are reported as the most common fish in "Youth's Primal Urge to Catch Fish Brings Central Park's 'Open Season,'" *New York Times*, September 3, 1948.

55. See James F. Wilson for one interpretation of more adult stories of whites' curiosity about Harlem. Wilson, *Bulldaggers, Pansies, and Chocolate Babies*, 25.

56. "Central Park Fishing Season Ends as School Bell Rings," *New York Times*, September 16, 1928; "'Salmon' Season Closes in Central Park as Fishermen Are Called Back to School," *New York Times*, September 21, 1931; "Central Park Fish No Longer Sporting," *New York Times*, August 18, 1932.

57. For discussion of playgrounds, see Gagen, "Example to Us All." Thanks to Dena Aufseeser for suggesting this source to me.

58. Robert McCrean, "The Seagulls of Central Park," *New York Times*, January 23, 1925.

59. "Fence on Reservoir Due to Government," *New York Times*, March 16, 1926; "Park Reservoir Called a Menace," *New York Times*, March 20, 1926.

60. Rosenzweig and Blackmar, *Park and the People*, 439.

61. "10,000 Fish Motor to New Westchester Home," *New York Herald-Tribune*, March 16, 1930; "Seiners Second Central Park Foray Net Varied Catch of 2000 Fish," *New York Herald-Tribune*, February 26, 1930.

62. Draft public statement, n.d. (likely summer 1948), RDP, box 395, folder 13, NYCMA; "Youngsters Now Fishing Legally in Central Park," *New York Herald-Tribune*, September 5, 1948.

63. The first article describing allowed fishing in the park focused not on Harlem but on the Seventy-Second Street Lake and showed children who mostly appeared to be white; earlier articles about fishing in Harlem never included photos. "Youth's Primal Urge to Catch Fish Brings Central Park's 'Open Season,'" *New York Times*, September 3, 1948. See also draft public statement, n.d. (likely summer 1948), RDP, box 395, folder 13, NYCMA.

64. "New Supply of Fish in Central Park Lake Quickly Lures Small Boys with Bent Pins," *New York Times*, April 12, 1949; "Lake Is Restocked for Young Anglers," *New York Herald-Tribune*, April 12, 1949. One *Times* article said that Captain Cheyne-Stout would begin a fish breeding program in 1934, but I have found no further evidence of this. "Central Park to Have 3 Bird Sanctuaries; Fish for City Lakes Also to Be Hatched There," *New York Times*, July 19, 1934.

65. For Moses's bias against Harlem, see Caro, *Power Broker*, 510–12, 557–60, 779. For examples of questioning those slights, see, for example, Gutman, "Race, Space, and Play"; Jackson, "Robert Moses," 67–71.

66. For growth and shifts in pet culture around the turn of the twentieth century, see

Wang, *Mad Dogs*, 199; Grier, *Pets in America*, 76; Brown, *City Is More than Human*, 149–99; Pearson, *Dogopolis*, 31–46.

67. Pearson, in *Dogopolis*, explains that strays were becoming less acceptable to middle-class city dwellers at this time (13–17).

68. "The Dog Knew His Way," *New York Tribune*, February 7, 1902; "Fuss over Vanderbilt Dog," *New York Tribune*, March 11, 1902; "Ghost Dog in Park," *New York Tribune*, April 8, 1907. For further discussion of the idea that pampered pets could be a threat, see Pearson, *Dogopolis*, 41.

69. "Eagle-Hunting in Manhattan," *Youth's Companion*, April 24, 1913, 222.

70. For other discussions of regulations of urban dogs, see Wang, *Mad Dogs*, 193–226; Brown, *City Is More than Human*, 149–99; Grier, *Pets in America*, 74–76; Pearson, *Dogopolis*, 13–24, 58–64.

71. Wang, *Mad Dogs*, 231; Pearson, *Dogopolis*, 78–82. For an example of contemporary suspicion of the rabies vaccine for dogs, see William Bruette and Donald Stillman, "The Mad-Dog Hysteria," *Forest and Stream*, June 1927, 352.

72. Wang, *Mad Dogs*, 186–93.

73. Wang, *Mad Dogs*, 193–226; Pearson, *Dogopolis*, 78–82.

74. H. I. Brock, "The City's Dogs," *New York Times*, January 13, 1935. The article claimed that as wealthy households reduced their staff, many began to walk dogs themselves rather than leaving the job to their chauffeurs and maids. However, in the DPP files and newspapers, there were still several letters and public comments that mention maids and chauffeurs "airing" dogs.

75. Brock, "City's Dogs."

76. Bruette and Stillman, "Mad-Dog Hysteria." Wang points out that it could be hard to distinguish an actual rabies case and other kinds of nervous responses to a dog bite, including cases in which dog bite victims literally scared themselves to death. Wang, *Mad Dogs*, 4.

77. Kinney, *How to Raise a Dog*, 13–20.

78. Mrs. A. Cooper to Robert Moses, January 11, 1939, REC 041, Department of Parks Records, box 78: Borough of Manhattan, 1939, folder 11: Central Park Dogs, NYCMA. See this entire folder for additional examples of protests on all sides of dog walking debates.

79. John Heaslip Jr. to Mrs. A. Cooper, January 16, 1939, REC 041, Department of Parks Records, box 78: Borough of Manhattan, 1939, folder 11: Central Park Dogs, NYCMA.

80. Police Department memo from commanding officer of Twenty-Second Precinct to Joseph Bannon, copy filed in REC 041, Department of Parks Records, box 78: Borough of Manhattan, 1939, folder 11: Central Park Dogs, NYCMA.

81. Mrs. Gustave Wiegand to Robert Moses, May 17, 1939, REC 041, Department of Parks Records, box 78: Borough of Manhattan, 1939, folder 11: Central Park Dogs, NYCMA.

82. William Lathan to Mrs. Gustave Wiegand, May 20, 1939, REC 041, Department of Parks Records, box 78: Borough of Manhattan, 1939, folder 11: Central Park Dogs, NYCMA. For more on discussions of curb training in New York, see Pearson, *Dogopolis*, 173.

83. Dorothy Forbes to Robert Moses, May 5, 1939, REC 041 Department of Parks Records, box 78: Borough of Manhattan, 1939, folder 11: Central Park Dogs, NYCMA.

84. Mrs. A. Cooper to Robert Moses.

85. Kinney, *How to Raise a Dog*, chapter 14. For further discussion of discourse against dogs in cities, see Wang, *Mad Dogs*, 10–49, 193–226.

86. NYCMA-RDP, 1939, folder 11, NYCMA, contains such correspondence for just one year; the Parks Department records during Moses's administration has similar folders for most years. For an example of public comments, Herbert J. Wiener, "Dog Corrals Suggested," *New York Times*, July 16, 1949. Explanations for rejecting calls for fenced runs were often vague, and these rejections were particularly unusual given the other recreational pursuits for which Moses opened the park. This may have related to the Moses administration's concerns about cleanliness.

87. Meyer Berger, "About New York," *New York Times*, April 2, 1940. Dog walking violations came under section 20 of the sanitary code; failure to pick up dog feces violated section 227.

88. "Court Eases Mutt Fines," *New York Times*, November 18, 1939.

89. "Policeman Slapped; Woman Up in Court," *New York Times*, July 11, 1952.

90. "Would Muzzle Squirrels," *New York Times*, May 15, 1946; Brock, "City's Dogs."

91. "Kill of Stray Dogs to End Hydrophobia," *New York Times*, May 23, 1908.

92. Brown, *City Is More than Human*, 149–50.

93. Martha Kobbe, "Addressed to Dog Owners," *New York Times*, March 29, 1935.

94. Ernest L. Stebbins, Health Department press release, January 1, 1945, vi, REC 050 Health Department Records, Subgroup 3 (Ernest Stebbins administration), NYCMA; "Compulsory Vaccination of Dogs Will Go into Effect Here in Fall," *New York Times*, June 28, 1947.

95. "Rabies Test Ordered for Unleashed Dogs," *New York Times*, November 21, 1944.

96. Ernest L. Stebbins, Health Department press release, January 1, 1945, vi.

97. "All Dogs in City Face Vaccination," *New York Times*, December 11, 1946; "Dog Vaccinations Fought at Hearing," *New York Times*, January 28, 1947.

98. John Mahoncy, *Report of the Department of Health of the City of New York*, 1950, 108–9.

99. Hempel, *My Golden Age of Singing*, 301.

100. "Singer and Police in Row over Dog," *New York Times*, February 6, 1942; "Frieda Hempel's Wild Dog of Central Park," *New York Times*, December 3, 1942; "Mongrel That Kept 'Dates' with Frieda Hempel Dies," *New York Times*, May 22, 1952. What

finally led to Hempel seeking help was a fellow park goer who saw her rummaging in bushes and reported her to police, thinking that she might be planting a bomb.

101. Mrs. George Bethune Adams, "Mme. Hempel's Experience," *New York Times*, February 12, 1942. Pearson, in *Dogopolis*, discusses the idea that elite women were overly sentimental about their dogs (41); however, this is a distinct and important example of women humane activists bearing sympathy for stray dogs.

102. "Frieda Hempel's Wild Dog of Central Park."

103. Uddin, "Canine Citizenship"; Glave, *Rooted in the Earth*; and Finney, *Black Faces, White Spaces*, who have each written about how dogs have been used as agents by which whites controlled Blacks. See also Nast, "Pit Bulls, Slavery, and Whiteness."

104. Philip Dougherty, "Free Dog School Opens in Park," *New York Times*, August 23, 1966.

105. "Dog Lovers Here Waging the Battle of Cedar Hill," *New York Times*, September 15, 1968.

106. Homer Bigart, "Hoving Proposes Park Auto Curbs," *New York Times*, March 1, 1966.

107. David Avrick, "Dogs Must Run," *New York Times*, March 15, 1973.

108. Claire Berman, "New York: A City Going to the Dogs?" *New York Times*, September 27, 1970.

109. For one of many examples, see John Ewing Durand, "Dog Owner's Complaint," *New York Times*, February 3, 1968.

110. National Audubon Society Records, section B3, NYPL, Department and Divisional Files, box 576, file: New York City, Correspondence and Summary Report of Central Park Speak-Outs, January 27, 1979.

111. Savas, *Study of Central Park*, 243.

112. R. C. Jenkins to S. M. White, October 26, 1961, RDP, box 709, folder 3, NYCMA.

113. In Brooklyn, residents sued the Parks Department over Prospect Park's plans for a children's farm with livestock, considering it a waste of money. See clip file, NYPL, Audubon Society Papers, box B503, folder 9.

114. Lorrence Hargray, "Last Year's Fish-In," *New York Amsterdam News*, July 4, 1970; J. W. Durrah, "Park Lake Stocked," *New York Amsterdam News*, July 4, 1970; J. W. Durrah, "Youngsters Fishing Is Enjoyable," *New York Amsterdam News*, July 3, 1971.

115. John C. Devlin, "S.P.C.A. Takes Wild Dog Chase," *New York Times*, December 13, 1972.

116. Beck, *Ecology of Stray Dogs*.

117. Beck, "Public Health Implications of Urban Dogs"; Nast, "Pit Bulls, Slavery, and Whiteness."

118. Boisseron, *Afro-Dog*, chapter 2.

Conclusion

1. Ginger Otis, "Central Park Conservancy and Macaulay Honors College at CUNY Sponsor 'BioBlitz,'" *New York Daily News*, August 26, 2013.

2. For more on the idea that environmental agendas ask too much of cities, see Alagona, *Accidental Ecosystem*, 199–207; Angelo and Wachsmuth, "Why Does Everyone Think."

3. For discussion of an artistic take on the zoo's declining conditions in the 1970s and its visual parallels to urban renewal imagery, see Uddin, *Zoo Renewal*, 55–64.

4. Deirdre Carmody, "City Shows Its Design for Central Park Zoo," *New York Times*, April 6, 1982; Susan Heller Anderson, "At Last, a Joy for All Ages: The Central Park Zoo Is Back," *New York Times*, August 9, 1988.

5. Uddin, *Zoo Renewal*; Braverman, *Zooland*, chapter 6.

6. Francis X. Clines, "What's Three Letters and Zoologically Incorrect?" *New York Times*, February 4, 1993.

7. Joseph Lee, "Fortress Conservation Violently Displaces Indigenous People," *Grist*, June 15, 2022, accessed August 30, 2023, https://grist.org/article/fortress -conservation-violently-displaces-indigenous-people.

8. Douglas Martin, "Private Group Signs Central Park Deal to Be Its Manager," *New York Times*, February 12, 1998.

9. Savas, *Study of Central Park*, vii, 8, 21. For discussion of Central Park's separation from Harlem as an issue of environmental justice and exclusion from the environmental movement, see Vernice Miller-Travis, *Earth Day and Environmental Justice Teach Us That My Survival Is Inextricably Linked to Yours*, April 15, 2020, video, 33:00, Earth Month 2020 Conservation Café, Audubon Naturalist Society, https://conservationblog.anshome.org/blog/earth-day-and-environmental-justice -teach-us-that-my-survival-is-inextricably-tied-to-yours.

10. Byfield, *Savage Portrayals*; Rosenzweig and Blackmar, *Park and the People*, 520.

11. Daniele Selby, "New York City Unveils Gate of the Exonerated in Central Park Honoring Wrongly Convicted People," Innocence Project, December 19, 2022, https://innocenceproject.org/central-park-exonerated-five-gate-new-york-city.

12. Abby Ronner, "Giddy Out," *Village Voice*, April 20, 2016.

13. Gabrielle Birkner, "Claremont Riding Academy Closes Its Doors," *New York Sun*, April 30, 2007; Sam Roberts, "Paul Novograd, Who Owned Manhattan's Last Public Livery, Dies at 73," *New York Times*, March 27, 2017.

14. Katz, *Who Speaks for the Carriage Horses*.

15. Collard and Gillespie, *Critical Animal Geographies*, introduction; Haraway, *When Species Meet*, 16–19.

16. John Galm to R. C. Jenkins, September 6, 1961, RDP, Box 709, folder 7, NYCMA.

17. New York City Department of Health, "Animals Testing Positive for Rabies in New York City in 2010," map, accessed August 31, 2023, https://www.nyc.gov/site /doh/health/health-topics/rabies-stats.page.

18. Rachel Nuwer, "Illegal Traders Have Turned Baby Red-Eared Sliders into a Health and Environmental Threat," *Newsweek*, June 1, 2015, accessed August 30, 2023, https://www.newsweek.com/illegal-animal-traders-have-turned-baby-red-eared -sliders-health-and-337903. Claire Jean Kim has also examined imported turtles through the multiple optics of health, animal welfare, ecosystems, and cultural rights. See Kim, *Dangerous Crossings*, part 2. Thanks to Mariya Shcheglovitova for sharing this story with me.

19. Zellmer and Goto, "Urban Wildlife Corridors."

20. "A New Species in New York Was Croaking in Plain Sight," *New York Times*, March 13, 2012; Day, *Field Guide to the Natural World*.

21. Winn, *Red-Tails in Love*.

22. This does not mean that all conservationists and naturalists agree on how to manage spaces like Central Park. See, for example, the "mulberry wars" of the 1980s among birders, native flora advocates, and Olmstedian purists. Graff, *Central Park, Prospect Park*; Roger Starr, "The Mulberry Wars in the Park," *New York Times*, January 28, 1986; Albert F. Appleton, "What Misguided Overmanagement Did to Central Park's Ramble," *New York Times*, February 4, 1986.

23. Rosenberg, "Decline"; Cole et al., "Determining the Health Benefits of Green Space."

24. Staeheli, Mitchell, and Gibson, "Conflicting Rights."

25. Tenijah Hamilton and Corina Newsome, "The Zero Sum of It All," *Bring Birds Back*, podcast, season 4, episode 1, BirdNote, May 17, 2023, https://www.birdnote .org/podcasts/bring-birds-back/zero-sum-it-all-corina-newsome; Newsome, "Thing with Feathers."

26. *Open City*'s narrator, Julius, clearly loves Central Park, but Teju Cole has him observe that parks were "doted on, fussed over," while spaces such as the rivers surrounded Manhattan are "neglected." Perhaps this is a metaphor to correct the sole fixation on parks to solve social and environmental problems. Cole, *Open City*, 54.

27. Gould et al., "Seizing Opportunities to Diversify Conservation," accessed August 8, 2024, https://doi-org.proxy-bc.researchport.umd.edu/10.1111/con1.12431; Schneider, "Decolonizing Conservation"; "Intertribal Buffalo Council," accessed January 24, 2024, https://itbcbuffalonation.org.

28. Baker, *Lenapehoking*.

29. Schell et al., "Ecological and Evolutionary Consequences," 369; Andrea Thompson, "Black Birders Call Out Racism, Say Nature Should Be for Everyone," *Scientific American*, June 5, 2020, https://www.scientificamerican.com/article/black-birders -call-out-racism-say-nature-should-be-for-everyone; Cooper, *Better Living Through Birding*, 265, 269–76.

30. Carpenter, "Investigation of Urban Bat Ecology"; Schell et al., "Ecological and Evolutionary Consequences."

31. Cole, *Open City*, 4–5, 174, 185, 258–59.

Selected Bibliography

Archival Collections

New York City Municipal Archives (NYCMA)
    Office of the Mayor of the City of New York
    Records of the Department of Parks (RDP)
New-York Historical Society
    Annual Report of the Director of the Central Park Menagerie (*ARDCPM*)
New York Public Library
    National Audubon Society Records
    Robert Moses Papers

The following single and periodical reports are digitized and publicly available from the New York City Department of Parks and Recreation at https://www.nycgovparks. org/news/reports/archive. There is some discontinuity in this collection; reports missing from the online collection are at the New-York Historical Society or New York City Municipal Archives.
    Annual Report of the Board of Commissioners of Central Park (*ARBCCP*)
    Annual Report of the Board of the Department of Public Parks (*ARBDPP*)
    Annual Report of the Department of Parks, Borough of Manhattan (*ARDPBM*)
    Board of Commissioners of Central Park, Minutes and Documents (*BCCP M&D*)
    Board of Commissioners of the Department of Public Parks (*BCDPP M&D*)
    First Annual Report on the Improvement of Central Park

Published Sources

Acosta, Raúl, Joseph Adeniran Adedeji, Maan Barua, Matthew Gandy, L. Sasha Gora, and Kara Murphy Schlichting. "Thinking with Urban Natures." *Global Environment* 16, no. 2, September 25, 2023, 177–21.

Adams, Lowell, and Louise Dove. *Wildlife Reserves and Corridors in the Urban Environment: A Guide to Ecological Landscape Planning and Resource Conservation.* Columbia, MD: National Institute for Urban Wildlife, 1989.

Alagona, Peter. *Accidental Ecosystem.* Berkeley: University of California Press, 2023.

Alaimo, Stacy. "Eluding Capture." In *Queer Ecologies: Sex, Nature, Politics, Desire*, edited by Catriona Sandilands and Bruce Erickson, 51–70. Bloomington: Indiana University Press, 2010.

Alexander, Ruth, and Carolyn Strange. "The Girl Problem: Female Sexual Delinquency in New York, 1900–1930." *Labour* 39 (1997): 261–75.

America's Great Migrations Project. "New York Migration History, 1850–2018." University of Washington Civil Rights and Labor History Consortium. Accessed August 30, 2023. https://depts.washington.edu/moving1/NewYork.shtml.

Ammon, Francesca. *Bulldozer.* New Haven, CT: Yale University Press, 2016.

Anderson, Kay. "'The Beast Within': Race, Humanity, and Animality." *Environment and Planning D* 18 (2000): 301–20.

———. "The Idea of Chinatown." *Annals of the Association of American Geographers* 77 (1987): 580–98.

Anderson, Mark Lynn. *Twilight of the Idols: Hollywood and the Human Sciences in 1920s America.* Berkeley: University of California Press, 2011.

Angelo, Hillary. *How Green Became Good: Urbanized Nature and the Making of Cities and Citizens.* Chicago: University of Chicago Press, 2021.

Angelo, Hillary, and David Wachsmuth. "Urbanizing Urban Political Ecology: A Critique of Methodological Cityism." *International Journal of Urban and Regional Research* 39 (2015): 16–27.

———. "Why Does Everyone Think Cities Can Save the Planet?" *Urban Studies* 57 (2020): 2201–21.

Anglers' Club of New York. *The Anglers' Club Story.* New York: Anglers' Club, 1956.

Bagemihl, Bruce. *Biological Exuberance.* New York: St. Martin's, 1999.

Baker, Joe, curator. *Lenapehoking.* Exhibit. Brooklyn Public Library, 2022.

Baldwin, James. *Go Tell It on the Mountain.* New York: Random House, 1952.

Barrow, Mark. *A Passion for Birds: American Ornithology after Audubon.* Princeton: Princeton University Press, 1998.

Barua, Maan. "Lively Commodities and Encounter Value." *Environment and Planning D* 34 (2016): 725–44.

Baumslag, Naomi. "Breastfeeding: Cultural Practices and Variations." *Human Lactation* 2 (1986): 621–42.

Bear, Christopher, and Sally Eden. "Thinking Like a Fish? Engaging with Nonhuman Difference through Recreational Angling." *Environment and Planning D* 29 (2011): 336–52.

Beck, Alan. *The Ecology of Stray Dogs: A Study of Free-Ranging Urban Animals*. Baltimore: York Press, 1973.

———. "The Public Health Implications of Urban Dogs." *American Journal of Public Health* 65 (1975): 1315–18.

Belcourt, Billy-Ray. "Animal Bodies, Colonial Subjects: (Re)Locating Animality in Decolonial Thought." *Societies* 5 (2015): 1–11.

Bellows, A. C., V. Robinson, J. Guthrie, T. Meyer, N. Peric, and M. W. Hamm. "Urban Livestock Agriculture in the State of New Jersey, USA." *Urban Agriculture Magazine.* Special issue, Livestock in and around Cities. 1, no. 2 (2000): 8–9.

Bender, Daniel. *The Animal Game: Searching for Wildness at the American Zoo*. Cambridge: Harvard University Press, 2016.

Bender, Thomas. *Toward an Urban Vision: Ideas and Institutions in Nineteenth-Century America*. Lexington: University Press of Kentucky, 1975.

Bennett, Joshua. *Being Property Myself Once: Blackness and the End of Man*. Cambridge: Harvard University Press, 2020.

Benson, Etienne. "The Urbanization of the Eastern Gray Squirrel in the United States." *Journal of American History* 100 (2013): 691–710.

Berger, John. *About Looking*. New York: Pantheon, 1980.

Betts, John. "P. T. Barnum and the Popularization of Natural History." *Journal of the History of Ideas* 20 (1959): 353–68.

Beveridge, Charles E., and David Schuyler, eds. *Creating Central Park: 1857–1861*. In *The Papers of Frederick Law Olmsted*, edited by C. C. McLaughlin. Baltimore: Johns Hopkins University Press, 1983.

Black, David. *The King of Fifth Avenue: The Fortunes of August Belmont*. New York: Dial Press, 1981.

Black Elk. *Black Elk Speaks*. As told to John Neihardt. 1932. Reprint, Lincoln: University of Nebraska Press, 2014.

Blecha, Jennifer, and Helga Leitner. "Reimagining the Food System, the Economy, and Urban Life: New Urban Chicken-Keepers in US Cities." *Urban Geography* 35 (2014): 86–108.

Blomley, Nicholas. "Enclosure, Common Right and the Property of the Poor." *Social and Legal Studies* 17 (2008): 311–31.

Board of Commissioners of the Central Park. *Catalogue of the Plans for the Improvement of the Central Park, New York* (*CPICP*). New York: C. W. Baker, 1858.

Bogle, Donald. *Heat Wave: The Life and Career of Ethel Waters*. New York: HarperCollins, 2012.

Boisseron, Bénédicte. *Afro-Dog: Blackness and the Animal Question*. New York: Columbia University Press, 2018.

Bourke, P. M. Austin. "The Agricultural Statistics of the 1841 Census of Ireland." *Economic History Review* 18 (1965): 377–91.

Boyazoglu, J., I. Hatziminaoglou, and P. Morand-Fehr. "The Role of the Goat in Society: Past, Present and Perspectives for the Future." *Small Ruminant Research* 60 (2005): 13–23.

Boyd, Herb, ed. *The Harlem Reader*. New York: Three Rivers Press, 2003.

Braitman, Laurel. *Animal Madness: Inside Their Minds*. New York: Simon and Schuster, 2015.

Braverman, Irus. *Zooland: The Institution of Captivity*. Palo Alto: Stanford University Press, 2012.

Brenwall, Cynthia. *The Central Park: Original Designs for New York's Greatest Treasure*. New York: Abrams, 2019.

Bridges, W. *Gathering of Animals: An Unconventional History of the New York Zoological Society*. New York: Harper & Row, 1974.

Bromley, G. W. *Atlas of the Entire City of New York*. New York: Bromley and Robinson, 1879.

Brown, Frederick L. *The City Is More than Human: An Animal History of Seattle*. Seattle: University of Washington Press, 2016.

Brown, John Howard, and Rossiter Johnson. *The Twentieth Century Biographical Dictionary of Notable Americans*. Boston: Biographical Society, 1904.

Brown, Joshua. "Victims, B'hoys, Foreigners, Slave-Drivers, and Despots: Picturing Work, Workers, and Activism in 19th-Century New York." In *City of Workers, City of Struggle: How Labor Movements Changed New York*, edited by Joshua Freeman, 64–77. New York: Columbia University Press, 2019.

Browne, Peter. *Trichologia Mammalium; Or, A Treatise on the Organization, Properties, and Uses of Hair and Wool*. Philadelphia: J. H. Jones, 1853.

Brownlow, Alec. "An Archaeology of Fear and Environmental Change in Philadelphia." *Geoforum* 37 (2006): 227–45.

Bunner, H. C. "Shantytown." *Scribner's Magazine*, October 1880.

Bureau of Manhattan, Department of Parks. *Annual Report of the Department of Parks, Bureau of Manhattan*, 1912.

Burrows, Edwin, and Mike Wallace. *Gotham: A History of New York City to 1898*. New York: Oxford University Press, 1999.

Byfield, Natalie. *Savage Portrayals: Race, Media, and the Central Park Jogger Story*. Philadelphia: Temple University Press, 2014.

Byrne, Jason, and Jennifer Wolch. "Nature, Race, and Parks: Past Research and Future Directions for Geographic Research." *Progress in Human Geography* 33 (2009): 743–65.

Carby, Hazel. "Policing the Black Woman's Body in an Urban Context." *Critical Inquiry* 18 (1992): 738–55.

Carney, Judith, and Richard Nicholas Rosomoff. *In the Shadow of Slavery: Africa's Botanical Legacy in the Atlantic World*. Berkeley: University of California Press, 2009.

Caro, Robert A. *The Power Broker: Robert Moses and the Fall of New York*. New York: Random House, 1974.

Carpenter, Ela Sita. "An Investigation of Urban Bat Ecology in Baltimore, MD." PhD diss., University of Missouri, 2019.

Cat, Christopher, and Countee Cullen. *Lost Zoo*. Englewood Cliffs, NJ: Silver Burdett Press, 1940.

Catlin, George. *Illustrations of the Manner, Custom, and Conditions of the North American Indians*. London: Henry Bohn, 1845.

Chauncey, George. *Gay New York: Gender, Urban Culture, and the Making of the Gay Male World, 1890–1940*. New York: HarperCollins, 1994.

Checker, Melissa. "Wiped Out by the Greenwave: Environmental Gentrification and the Paradoxical Politics of Urban Sustainability." *City & Society* 23 (2007): 210–29.

Cherry, Elizabeth. *For the Birds: Protecting Wildlife through the Naturalist Gaze*. New Brunswick: Rutgers University Press, 2019.

Chiang, Connie. *Shaping the Shoreline: Fisheries and Tourism on the Monterey Coast*. Seattle: University of Washington Press, 2008.

Chiles, Robert. "School Reform as Progressive Statecraft: Education Policy in New York under Governor Alfred E. Smith, 1919–1928." *Journal of the Gilded Age and Progressive Era* 15 (2016): 379–98.

Cincinnati, Noah. "Too Sullen for Survival." In *The Historical Animal*, edited by Susan Nance, 166–83. Syracuse: Syracuse University Press, 2015.

Cleaveland, Henry. "The Central Park." *Appleton's Journal of Popular Literature, Science, and Art* 3, no. 64 (June 18, 1870): 691–92.

Coates, Peter. "Eastenders Go West: English Sparrows, Immigrants, and the Nature of Fear." *Journal of American Studies* 39 (2005): 431–62.

Cole, Helen V. S., Margarita Triguero-Mas, James J. T. Connolly, and Isabelle Anguelovski. "Determining the Health Benefits of Green Space: Does Gentrification Matter?" *Health and Place* 57 (2019): 1–11.

Cole, Teju. *Open City*. New York: Random House, 2012.

Collard, Rosemary-Claire. *Animal Traffic: Lively Capital in the Global Exotic Pet Trade*. Durham, NC: Duke University Press, 2020.

———. "Putting Animals Back Together, Taking Commodities Apart." *Annals of the American Association of Geographers* 104 (2014): 151–65.

Connor, L. G. "A Brief History of the Sheep Industry in the United States." *Agricultural History Society Papers* 1 (1921): 89–197.

Cook, Clarence, with introduction by Maureen Meister. *A Description of the New York Central Park*. 1869. Reprint, New York: NYU Press, 2017.

Cooper, Christian. *Better Living through Birding*. New York: Random House, 2023.

Copeland, Cynthia, Nan Rothschild, and Diana Wall. "Seneca Village Project." Media

Center for Art History, Columbia University. Accessed August 30, 2023. https://projects.mcah.columbia.edu/seneca_village.

Corey, Steven. "King Garbage: A History of Solid Waste Management in New York City, 1881–1970." PhD diss., New York University, 1994.

Crang, Mike. "Nation, Region, and Homeland: History and Tradition in Dalarna, Sweden." *Ecumene* 6 (1999): 447–70.

Cronon, William. *Changes in the Land*. New York: Hill and Wang 1983.

———. *Nature's Metropolis: Chicago and the Great West*. New York: Norton, 1991.

———. "The Trouble with Wilderness." In *Uncommon Ground: Rethinking the Human Place in Nature*, edited by William Cronon, 69–90. New York: Norton, 1995.

Crosby, Alfred. *Ecological Imperialism: The Biological Expansion of Europe, 900–1900*. 2nd ed. Cambridge: Cambridge University Press, 2004.

Curran, Winifred, and Trina Hamilton. *Just Green Enough: Urban Development and Environmental Gentrification*. New York: Routledge, 2017.

Davidson, Cathy, and Jessamyn Hatcher, eds. *No More Separate Spheres! A Next Wave American Studies Reader*. Durham, NC: Duke University Press, 2002.

Davis, William E., Jr. *Dean of the Birdwatchers: A Biography of Ludlow Griscom*. Washington, DC: Smithsonian Institution Press, 1994.

Day, Leslie. *Field Guide to the Natural World of New York City*. Baltimore: Johns Hopkins University Press, 2007.

Deforest, Robert, and Lawrence Veiller. *The Tenement House Problem*. New York: Macmillan, 1903.

Dehler, Gregory. *The Most Defiant Devil*. Charlottesville: University of Virginia Press, 2013.

Deloria, Philip J. *Indians in Unexpected Places*. Lawrence: University Press of Kansas, 2004.

Demcker, Robert. *Central Park Plant List and Map Index of 1873*. New York: Frederick Law Olmsted Association and the Central Park Community Fund, 1979.

Dempsey, Jessica, and Rosemary-Claire Collard. "Capitalist Natures in Five Orientations." *Capitalism Nature Socialism* 28 (2016): 78–97.

Domosh, Mona. *Invented Cities: The Creation of Landscape in Nineteenth-Century New York & Boston*. New Haven, CT: Yale University Press, 1996.

Domosh, Mona, and Joni Seager. *Putting Women in Place: Feminist Geographers Make Sense of the World*. New York: Guilford, 2001.

Donkin, Robert. *Meleagrides: An Historical and Ethnogeographical Study of the Guinea Fowl*. London: Ethnographica, 1991.

Doughty, Robin. *The English Sparrow in the American Landscape: A Paradox in Nineteenth Century Wildlife Conservation*. Oxford: School of Geography, University of Oxford, 1978.

Douglas, Ian, David Goode, Mike Houck, and Rusong Wang, eds. *The Routledge of Urban Ecology*. 2nd ed. New York: Routledge, 2010.

Downing, Andrew Jackson. "The New York Park." Reprinted in Board of Commissioners of the Central Park. *The First Annual Report on the Improvement of the Central Park*. New York: C. W. Baker, 1858.

Dunlap, Thomas. "Remaking the Land: The Acclimatization Movement and Anglo Ideas of Nature." *Journal of World History* 8 (1997): 303–19.

Eisenmann, Theodore. "Frederick Law Olmsted, Green Infrastructure, and the Evolving City." *Journal of Planning History* 12 (2013): 287–311.

Elder, Glen, Jennifer Wolch, and Jody Emel. "*Le Pratique Sauvage*: Race, Place, and the Human-Animal Divide." In *Animal Geographies: Place, Politics, and Identity at the Nature-Culture Borderlands*, edited by Jennifer Wolch and Jody Emel, 72–90. New York: Verso, 1998.

Elliot, D. G. "In Memoriam: George Newbold Lawrence." *The Auk* 8 (January 1896): 1–10.

Enright, Kelly. *Osa and Martin: For the Love of Adventure*. Guilford, CT: Lyons Press, 2011.

Finney, Carolyn. *Black Faces, White Spaces: Reimagining the Relationship of African Americans to the Great Outdoors*. Chapel Hill: University of North Carolina Press, 2014.

Fisher, Colin. *Urban Green: Nature, Recreation, and the Working Class in Industrial Chicago*. Chapel Hill: University of North Carolina Press, 2015.

Flack, Andy. "'In Sight, Insane': Animal Agency, Captivity and the Frozen Wilderness in the Late-Twentieth Century." *Environment and History* 22 (2016): 629–52.

Fleming, Ronald, and Lauri Halderman, eds. *On Common Ground*. Cambridge, MA: Townscape Institute, 1982.

Foord, John. *The Life and Public Services of Andrew Haswell Green*. New York: Doubleday, 1913.

Forrester, Francis [Daniel Wise]. *Little Peachblossom; or, Rambles in Central Park*. New York: Nelson and Phillips, 1873.

Foster, Lyman Spalding, ed. *The Published Writings of George Newbold Lawrence, 1844–1891*. Washington, DC: Government Printing Office, 1892.

Fraser, Perry. "History of the Anglers' Club of New York." *Anglers' Club Bulletin* (January 1926): 1.

Freeman, Rhoda. *The Free Negro in Negro in New York City in the Era before the Civil War*. New York: Garland, 1994.

Fudge, Erica. "A Left-Handed Blow: Writing the History of Animals." In *Representing Animals*, edited by Nigel Rothfels, 3–18. Bloomington: Indiana University Press, 2002.

Fugate, Lauren, and John MacNeill Miller. "Shakespeare's Starlings." *Environmental Humanities* 13 (2021): 301–22.

Fuller, H. S. *Mr. Crowley of Central Park*. New York: H. F. Clinton, 1888.

Gagen, Elizabeth. "An Example to Us All: Child Development and Identity Construction in Early 20th-Century Playgrounds." *Environment and Planning A* 32 (2000): 599–616.

Gandy, Matthew. *Concrete and Clay: Reworking Nature in New York City*. Cambridge, MA: MIT Press, 2002.

———. *Natura Urbana: Ecological Constellations in Urban Space*. Cambridge, MA: MIT Press, 2022.

———. "Queer Ecologies." *Society and Space* 30 (2012): 727–47.

Gardner, Geoffrey R., Fanchon F. Funk, Sheila A. Bolin, Rebecca Webb Wilson, and Shirley A. Bolin, eds. *Swan Keeper's Handbook: A Guide to the Care of Captive Swans*. Malabar, FL: Krieger Publishing, 2003.

Gentry, Thomas. *The House Sparrow at Home and Abroad*. Philadelphia: Claxton, 1878.

Germic, Stephen. *American Green: Class, Crisis, and the Deployment of Nature in Central Park, Yosemite, and Yellowstone*. Lanham, MD: Lexington Books, 2001.

Gibson, Campbell, and Emily Lennon. "Historical Census Statistics on the Foreign-Born Population of the United States: 1850–1990." US Census Bureau Working Paper POP-WP029, 1999.

Gifford-Gonzalez, Diane, and Olivier Hanotte. "Domesticating Animals in Africa: Implications of Genetic and Archaeological Findings." *Journal of World Prehistory* 24 (2011): 1–23.

Gillespie, Kathryn, and Rosemary-Claire Collard, eds. *Critical Animal Geographies: Politics, Intersection, and Hierarchies in a Multi-Species World*. London: Routledge, 2015.

Giltner, Scott. "Slave Hunting and Fishing in the Antebellum South." In *To Love the Wind and the Rain: African-Americans and Environmental History*, edited by Dianne Glave and Mark Stoll, 21–36. Pittsburgh: University of Pittsburgh Press, 2005.

Gipson, Terry. "History of the US Goat Industry." *Professional Agricultural Workers' Journal* 6 (2019): 41–49.

Glave, Dianne. *Rooted in the Earth: Reclaiming the African American Environmental Heritage*. Chicago: Chicago Review Press, 2010.

Glave, Dianne, and Mark Stoll. *To Love the Wind and the Rain*. Pittsburgh: University of Pittsburgh Press, 2006.

Gould, Rachelle, Indira Phukan, Mary Mendoza, Nicole Ardoin, and Bindu Panikkar. "Seizing Opportunities to Diversify Conservation." *Conservation Letters* 11 (2018). https://doi.org/10.1111/conl.12431.

Graff, M. M. *Central Park, Prospect Park: A New Perspective*. New York: Greensward Foundation, 1985.

Gratacap, L. P., and A. Woodward. *The Freshwater Flora and Fauna of Central Park*. New York: MacGowan and Slipper, 1884.

Greater London Council. *Alexander Pope's Villa*. London: Greater London Council, 1980.

Greene, Ann Norton. *Horses at Work*. Cambridge: Harvard University Press, 2008.

Grier, Katherine. *Pets in America: A History*. Chapel Hill: University of North Carolina Press, 2010.

Griffiths, Huw, and Ingrid Poulter. "Feral Cats in the City." In *Animal Spaces, Beastly Places: New Geographies of Human-Animal Relations*, edited by Chris Philo and Chris Wilbert, 56–70. London: Routledge, 2000.

Griscom, Ludlow. *Birds of the New York City Region*. New York: American Museum of Natural History, 1923.

Guild, W. H., and F. B. Perkins. *The Central Park*. New York: Carleton, 1864.

Gutman, Marta. "Race, Place, and Play: Robert Moses and the WPA Swimming Pools in New York City." *Journal of the Society of Architectural Historians* 67 (2008): 532–61.

Hall, Edward Hagaman. "Central Park in the City of New York." *American Scenic and Historic Preservation Society Annual Report* 16 (1911): 379–490.

Hancocks, David. *A Different Nature*. Berkeley: University of California Press, 2001.

Hanson, Elizabeth. *Animal Attractions*. Princeton: Princeton University Press, 2004.

Haraway, Donna. *When Species Meet*. Minneapolis: University of Minnesota Press, 2007.

Harper, Amie Breeze. "Race as 'Feeble Matter' in Veganism." *Journal of Critical Animal Studies* 8 (2010): 5–27.

Harris, Leslie M. *In the Shadow of Slavery: African-Americans in New York City, 1626–1863*. Chicago: University of Chicago Press, 2003.

Hartman, Saidiya. *Wayward Lives, Beautiful Experiments*. New York: Norton, 2019.

Hartog, Hendrik. "Pigs and Positivism." *Wisconsin Law Review* (July–August 1985): 899–935.

Hazen, Barbara Shook. *A Visit to the Children's Zoo*. New York: Golden, 1963.

Hediger, Heini. *Wild Animals in Captivity*. Translated by G. Sircom. New York: Dover Publications, 1964.

Hempel, Frieda. *My Golden Age of Singing*. Portland, OR: Amadeus Press, 1998.

Higgins, P. J., J. M. Peter, and S. J. Cowling, eds. *Handbook of Australian, New Zealand & Antarctic Birds*. Vol. 7. Melbourne, Victoria: Oxford University Press, 2006.

Hindle, Edward. Foreword to *Wild Animals in Captivity*, by Heini Hediger. Translated by G. Sircom. New York: Dover Publications, 1964.

Hinton, Elizabeth, and DeAnza Cook. "The Mass Criminalization of Black Americans: A Historical Overview." *Annual Review of Criminology* 4, no. 1 (2021): 261–86.

Hoage, R. J., and William A. Deiss, eds. *New Worlds, New Animals: From Menagerie to Zoological Park in the Nineteenth Century*. Baltimore: Johns Hopkins University Press, 1996.

Hobson, Kersty. "Political Animals? On Animals as Subjects in an Enlarged Political Geography." *Political Geography* 26 (2007): 250–67.

Hodges, Graham. *New York City Cartmen, 1667–1850*. New York: NYU Press, 2012.

Hornaday, William. *Our Vanishing Wildlife*. New York: Scribner's, 1913.

Hotaling, Edward. *The Great Black Jockeys: The Lives and Times of the Men Who Dominated America's First National Sport*. Rocklin, CA: Prima, 1999.

Hubbard, Phil, and Andrew Brooks. "Animals and Urban Gentrification: Displacement and Injustice in the Trans-Species City." *Progress in Human Geography* 45 (2021): 1490–1511.

Hurley, Andrew. *Environmental Inequalities*. Chapel Hill: University of North Carolina Press, 1995.

Hurston, Zora Neale. *Mules and Men*. 1935. Reprint, New York: Harper & Row, 1990.

Imperato, Pascal, and Eleanor Imperato. *They Married Adventure*. New Brunswick, NJ: Rutgers University Press, 1999.

Ireland, Doug. "Rendezvous in the Ramble." *New York Magazine*, July 24, 1978. https://nymag.com/news/features/47179.

Isenberg, Andrew. *The Destruction of the Bison: An Environmental History, 1750–1920*. New York: Cambridge University Press, 2000.

Jackson, Kenneth T. *Crabgrass Frontier*. New York: Oxford University Press, 1985.

———. "Robert Moses and the Rise of New York: The Power Broker in Perspective." In *Robert Moses and the Modern City: The Transformation of New York*, edited by Hilary Ballon and Kenneth T. Jackson, 67–71. New York: Norton, 2007.

Jackson, Zakiyyah. "Animal: New Directions in the Theorization of Race and Posthumanism." *Feminist Studies* 39 (2013): 669–85.

Jacoby, Karl. *Crimes against Nature: Squatters, Poachers, Thieves, and the Hidden History of American Conservation*. Berkeley: University of California Press, 2014.

Johnson, David. *The Lavender Scare*. Chicago: University of Chicago Press, 2006.

Johnson, Martin, and Osa Johnson. *Congorilla*. Canute, KS: Safari Museum, 1932.

Johnson, Osa. *I Married Adventure: The Lives and Adventures of Martin and Osa Johnson*. 1940. Reprint, New York: Morrow, 1989.

Kasson, John. *Amusing the Million: Coney Island at the Turn of the Century*. New York: Hill and Wang, 1978.

Kastner, Joseph. *A World of Watchers*. New York: Knopf, 1986.

Katz, Jonathan. *Who Speaks for the Carriage Horses: The Future of Animals in Our World*. New York: Roadswell, 2015.

Kim, Claire Jean. *Dangerous Crossings: Race, Species, and Nature in a Multicultural Age*. Cambridge: Cambridge University Press, 2015.

Kimball, Jeffrey, dir. *Birders: The Central Park Effect*. Chicago: Music Box Films, 2012.

Kinkead, Eugene. *Central Park, 1857–1995: The Birth, Decline, and Renewal of a National Treasure*. New York: Norton, 1990.

Kinney, James R. *How to Raise a Dog: In the City, in the Suburbs*. New York: Simon and Schuster, 1938.

Kisling, Vernon, Jr. "Origin and Development of American Zoological Parks." In *New Worlds, New Animals: From Menagerie to Zoological Park in the Nineteenth Century*, edited by R. J. Hoage and W. A. Deiss, 109–25. Baltimore: Johns Hopkins University Press, 1996.

Knowler, Donald. *The Falconer of Central Park*. New York: Karz-Cohl, 1984.

Kohlstedt, Sally Gregory. "Reflections on Zoo History." In *New Worlds, New Animals: From Menagerie to Zoological Park in the Nineteenth Century*, edited by R. J. Hoage and W. A. Deiss, 3–7. Baltimore: Johns Hopkins University Press, 1996.

Korda, Michael. *Horse People: Scenes from Riding Life*. New York: HarperCollins, 2003.

Krupar, Shiloh. *Hot-Spotters Report: Military Fables of Toxic Waste*. Minneapolis: University of Minnesota Press, 2013.

Lanham, J. Drew. "9 Rules for the Black Birdwatcher." *Orion Magazine*, October 25, 2013.

Lassonde, Stephen. *Learning to Forget: Schooling and Family Life in New Haven's Working Class, 1870–1940*. New Haven, CT: Yale University Press, 2005.

———. Review of *Riding the Rails: Teenagers on the Move during the Great Depression*, by Errol Lincoln Uys. *Histoire Sociale / Social History* 37, no. 73 (2004): 153–56.

Lawrence, George. "Catalogue of Birds Observed on New York, Long Island, Staten Island, and Adjacent Parts of New Jersey." *Annals of the Lyceum of Natural History of New York* 8 (1867): 279–300.

Lewis, David Levering. *When Harlem Was in Vogue*. New York: Penguin, 1997.

Lewis, Elisha. *The American Sportsman*. 3rd ed. Philadelphia: Lippincott, 1857.

Lobo, Arun, and Joseph Salvo. *The Newest New Yorkers*. New York: Department of City Planning, 2013.

Lopez, Patricia, and Kathryn Gillespie. *Economies of Death: Economic Logics of Killable Life and Grievable Death*. London: Routledge, 2015.

Lugones, Maria. "Toward a Decolonial Feminism." *Hypatia* (2010): 742–59.

Malamud, Randy. *Reading Zoos: Representations of Animals and Captivity*. New York: NYU Press, 1998.

Manevitz, Alexander. "'A Great Injustice': Urban Capitalism and the Limits of Freedom in Nineteenth-Century New York City." *Journal of Urban History* 48 (2021): 1365–82.

———. "The Rise and Fall of Seneca Village." PhD diss., New York University, 2016.

Marino, Kelly. "A Woman Ahead of Her Time: Augusta Lewis Troup and Local Women's Activism in New York City and New Haven, Connecticut." *Society of Historians of the Gilded Age and Progressive Era* blog. Accessed May 25, 2024, https://www.shgape.org/a-woman-ahead-of-her-time-augusta-lewis-troup.

Marsh, George Perkins. *Man and Nature*. New York: Scribner's, 1864.

Martin, Justin. *Genius of Place: The Life of Frederick Law Olmsted*. Boston: Da Capo, 2011.

Mavhunga, Chakenetsa. *The Mobile Workshop: The Tsetse Fly and African Knowledge Production*. Cambridge, MA: MIT Press, 2018.

———. "Seeing the National Park from Outside It." *Rachel Carson Center Perspectives* 1 (2014): 53–60.

———. *Transient Workspaces: Technologies of Everyday Innovation in Zimbabwe.* Cambridge, MA: MIT Press, 2014.

Mazaraki, George. "The Public Career of Andrew Haswell Green." PhD diss., New York University, 1966.

McCammack, Brian. *Landscapes of Hope: Nature and the Great Migration in Chicago.* Cambridge: Harvard University Press, 2018.

McDonald, Tracy, and Daniel Vandersommers, eds. *Zoo Studies: A New Humanities.* Montreal: McGill-Queens University Press, 2019.

McLaughlin, C. C., ed. *The Papers of Frederick Law Olmsted.* Baltimore: Johns Hopkins University Press, 1983.

McMillan, Uri. "Mammy-Memory: Staging Joice Heth, or the Curious Phenomenon of the 'Ancient Negress.'" *Women & Performance: A Journal of Feminist Theory* 22 (2012): 29–46.

McNeur, Catherine. *Taming Manhattan: Environmental Battles in the Antebellum City.* Cambridge: Harvard University Press, 2014.

McShane, Clay, and Joel Tarr. *The Horse in the City: Living Machines in the Nineteenth Century.* Baltimore: Johns Hopkins University Press, 2007.

Metcalfe, Robyn. "American Livestock Improvers and Urban Markets in the Nineteenth Century." *Journal of the Historical Society* 7 (2007): 475–92.

Meyer, Annie Nathan. *My Park Book.* New York: Edwin W. Dayton, 1898.

Mighetto, Lisa. *Wild Animals and American Environmental Ethics.* Tucson: University of Arizona Press, 1991.

Miller, L. *Lewis Miller's "Guide to Central Park."* 1864. Reprint, Dearborn, MI: Henry Ford Museum, 1977.

Miller, Sara Cedar. *Before Central Park.* New York: Columbia University Press, 2022.

Miltenberger, Scott. "Viewing the Anthrozoonotic City." In *The Historical Animal*, edited by Susan Nance, 261–71. Syracuse: Syracuse University Press.

Minard, Pete. *All Things Harmless, Useful, and Ornamental: Environmental Transformation through Species Acclimatization, from Colonial Australia to the World.* Chapel Hill: University of North Carolina Press, 2019.

Mintz, Steven. *Huck's Raft: A History of American Childhood.* Cambridge: Harvard University Press, 2006.

Miranda-de la Lama, G. C., and S. Mattiello. "The Importance of Social Behaviour for Goat Welfare in Livestock Farming." *Small Ruminant Research* 90 (2010): 1–10.

Mitman, Gregg. *Reel Nature: America's Romance with Wildlife on Film.* Seattle: University of Washington Press, 1999.

Montrie, Chad. "'I Think Less of the Factory Than of My Native Dell.'" *Environmental History* 9 (2004): 275–95.

Moss, Robert. *Barbecue: The History of an American Institution.* Tuscaloosa: University of Alabama Press, 2020.

Muñoz, José Esteban. "Theorizing Queer Inhumanisms." *GLQ* 21 (2015): 2–3.

Murphy, J. Prentice. "Children and the New Deal." *Annals of the American Academy of Political and Social Science* 176 (1934): 121–30.

Nance, Susan, ed. *The Historical Animal.* Syracuse: Syracuse University Press, 2015.

Nash, Catherine. "Breed Wealth: Origins, Encounter Value and the International Love of a Breed." *Transactions of the Institute of British Geographers* 45 (2020): 849–61.

Nast, Heidi J. "Pit Bulls, Slavery, and Whiteness in the Mid- to Late-Nineteenth-Century US." In *Critical Animal Geographies: Politics, Intersection, and Hierarchies in a Multi-Species World,* edited by Kathryn Gillespie and Rosemary-Claire Collard, 127–45. London: Routledge, 2015.

Naughton-Treves, Lisa. "Wild Animals in the Garden: Conserving Wildlife in Amazonian Agroecosystems." *Annals of the Association of American Geographers* 92 (2002): 488–506.

Neumann, Roderick. *Imposing Wilderness.* Berkeley: University of California Press, 2002.

Newkirk, Pamela. *Spectacle: The Astonishing Life of Ota Benga.* New York: HarperCollins, 2015.

Newsome, Corina. "The Thing with Feathers." In *Rooted and Rising: Voices of Courage in a Time of Climate Crisis,* edited by Leah Schade and Margaret Bullitt-Jonas, 69–74. Lanham, MD: Rowman & Littlefield, 2019.

Nichols, F. B. "Review of the New York Markets." *American Druggists' Circular and Chemical Gazette,* March 1, 1860.

Oldys, Henry. *Pheasant Raising in the United States.* Washington, DC: US Government Printing Office, 1910.

Olmsted, Frederick Law, Jr., and Theodora Kimball, eds. *Forty Years of Landscape Architecture: Central Park.* 1928. Reprint, Cambridge, MA: MIT Press, 1973.

Olmsted, Frederick Law, Sr. *Description of the Plan for the Improvement of the Central Park, New York.* New York: Aldine Press, 1858.

———. *Walks and Talks of an American Farmer in England.* 1851. Reprint, Ann Arbor: University of Michigan Press, 1967.

Orenstein, Alison F. "Bronx Zoo / Wildlife Conservation Park." In *Encyclopedia of the World's Zoos,* edited by Catharine Bell, 190–95. Chicago: Fitzroy Dearborn, 2001.

Paine, A. G., Jr. "Dates of the Arrival of Migratory Birds in the Spring of 1886." *Ornithologist and Oologist* 11 (1887): 109, 125.

Palmer, Clare. "Colonization, Urbanization, and Animals." *Philosophy and Geography* 6 (2003): 47–58.

Parsons, Mabel, ed. *Memories of Samuel Parsons.* New York: Putnam, 1926.

Pasquier, Roger. "Interrupted Landscapes: The Future of Bird Migration." *Sitelines: A Journal of Place* 13 (2017): 13–16.

Pearson, Chris. *Dogopolis: How Dogs and Humans Made New York, London, and Paris.* Chicago: University of Chicago Press, 2021.

Peet, Louis. *Trees and Shrubs of Central Park.* New York: Manhattan Press, 1903.

Peiss, Kathy. *Cheap Amusements: Working Women and Leisure in Turn-of-the-Century New York.* Philadelphia: Temple University Press, 1986.

Perris, William. *Maps of the City of New York.* 3rd ed. New York Public Library Digital Collections. Accessed January 29, 2024. https://digitalcollections.nypl.org/items/510d47e0-bfd7-a3d9-e040-e00a18064a99.

Philo, Chris, and Chris Wilbert, eds. *Animal Spaces, Beastly Places: New Geographies of Human-Animal Relations.* London: Routledge, 2000.

Poole, Kristopher. "Bird Introductions." *Extinctions and Invasions: A Social History of British Fauna* (2010): 155–65.

Pooley-Ebert, Andria. "Species Agency." In *The Historical Animal*, edited by Susan Nance, 148–65. Syracuse: Syracuse University Press, 2015.

Posthumus, David. "A Lakota View of Pté Oyáte (Buffalo Nation)." In *Bison and People on the North American Great Plains*, edited by G. Cunfer and B. Waiser, 278–310. College Station: Texas A&M University Press, 2016.

Prest, John. *The Garden of Eden: The Botanic Garden and the Re-Creation of Paradise.* New Haven, CT: Yale University Press, 1981.

Price, Jennifer. *Flight Maps: Adventures with Nature in Modern America.* New York: Basic Books, 1999.

Radbill, Samuel X. "The Role of Animals in Infant Feeding." In *American Folk Medicine: A Symposium*, edited by Wayland D. Hand, 21–30. UCLA Conference on American Folk Medicine, 1973. Berkeley: University of California Press, 1976.

Rankin, Julian. *Catfish Dream: Ed Scott's Fight for His Family Farm and Racial Justice in the Mississippi Delta.* Athens: University of Georgia Press, 2018.

Rawson, Michael. *Eden on the Charles: The Making of Boston.* Cambridge: Harvard University Press, 2010.

Reed, Hope Henry, and Sophia Duckworth. *Central Park: A History and a Guide.* New York: Clarkson and Potter, 1967.

Reichenbach, Herman. "A Tale of Two Zoos." In *New Worlds, New Animals: From Menagerie to Zoological Park in the Nineteenth Century*, edited by R. J. Hoage and W. A. Deiss 51–62. Baltimore: Johns Hopkins University Press, 1996.

Reiman, Richard. *The New Deal and American Youth: Ideas and Ideals in the Depression Decade.* Athens: University of Georgia Press, 1992.

Reynolds, Cuyler. *Genealogical and Family History of Southern New York and the Hudson River Valley.* New York: Lewis, 1914.

Richards, T. A. *Guide to the Central Park.* New York: J. Miller, 1866.

Riker, James. *Harlem: Its Origins and Early Annals.* New York: New Harlem, 1904.

Ritvo, Harriet. "Going Forth and Multiplying: Animal Acclimatization and Invasion." *Environmental History* 17 (2012): 404–14.

———. *Noble Cows and Hybrid Zebras: Essays on Animals and History*. Charlottesville: University of Virginia Press, 2010.

———. "The Order of Nature." In *New Worlds, New Animals: From Menagerie to Zoological Park in the Nineteenth Century*, edited by edited by R. J. Hoage and W. A. Deiss, 43–50. Baltimore: Johns Hopkins University Press, 1996.

Robichaud, Andrew. *Animal City: The Domestication of America*. Cambridge: Harvard University Press, 2020.

Rodrigue, Jean-Paul. *The Geography of Transport Systems*. 5th ed. New York: Routledge, 2020.

Rogers, Elizabeth Barlow. "The Landscapes of Robert Moses." *Sitelines: A Journal of Place* 3 (2007): 3–12.

———. *Saving Central Park: A History and a Memoir*. New York: Knopf, 2018.

Rome, Adam. "Nature Wars, Culture Wars: Immigration and Environmental Reform in the Progressive Era." *Environmental History* 13 (2008): 432–53.

Roosevelt, Theodore. *Theodore Roosevelt's Diaries of Boyhood and Youth*. New York: Charles Scribner's Sons, 1931.

Rosenberg, Charles. *The Cholera Years: The United States in 1832, 1849, and 1866*. Chicago: University of Chicago Press, 1987.

Rosenberg, Kenneth. "Decline of the North American Avifauna." *Science* 366 (September 2019): 120–24.

Rosenwaike, Ira. *Population History of New York City*. Syracuse: Syracuse University Press, 1972.

Rosenzweig, Roy, and Elizabeth Blackmar. *The Park and the People: A History of Central Park*. Ithaca: Cornell University Press, 1992.

Rubenstein, Richard, ed. *The Harlem Riot of 1935*. New York: Arno Press, 1969.

Rutherford, Stephanie. *Villain, Vermin, Icon, Kin: Wolves and the Making of Canada*. Montreal: McGill-Queens University Press, 2022.

Rybczynski, Witold. *A Clearing in the Distance: Frederick Law Olmsted and America in the Nineteenth Century*. New York: Scribner, 1999.

Sakakibara, Chie. *Whale Snow: Iñupiat, Climate Change, and Multispecies Resilience in Arctic Alaska*. Tucson: University of Arizona Press, 2020.

Salinger, J. D. *The Catcher in the Rye*. New York: Little, Brown, 1951.

Sanderson, Eric W. *Mannahatta: A Natural History of New York City*. New York: Abrams, 2009.

Sandilands, Catriona, and Bruce Erickson, eds. *Queer Ecologies: Sex, Nature, Politics, Desire*. Bloomington: Indiana University Press, 2010.

Savas, Emanuel. *A Study of Central Park*. New York: Columbia University Center for Government Studies, 1976.

Saxton, Baker, and Company. *A Guide to the Central Park with a Map of the Proposed Improvements*. New York: C. M. Saxton, Baker and Company, 1859.

Schell, Christopher J., Karen Dyson, Tracy L. Fuentes, Simone des Roches, Nyeema C. Harris, Danica Sterud Miller, Cleo A. Woelfle-Erskine, and Max R. Lambert. "The Ecological and Evolutionary Consequences of Systemic Racism in Urban Environments." *Science* 369, no. 651018, September 18, 2020, DOI: 10.1126/science .aay4497.

Schlichting, Kara. *New York Recentered: Building the Metropolis from the Shore*. Chicago: University of Chicago Press, 2019.

Schneider, Lindsey. "Decolonizing Conservation? Indigenous Resurgence and Buffalo Restoration in the American West." *Environment and Planning E: Nature and Space* 6 (2023): 801–21.

Schuyler, David. *Apostle of Taste: Andrew Jackson Downing, 1815–1852*. Baltimore: Johns Hopkins University Press, 1996.

Schwartz, Joel. *The New York Approach: Robert Moses, Urban Liberals, and Redevelopment of the Inner City*. Columbus: Ohio State University Press, 1993.

Scott, Michelle. *T.O.B.A. Time: Black Vaudeville and the Theatre Owners' Booking Association in Jazz-Age America*. Urbana: University of Illinois Press, 2023.

Serrato, Claudia. "Ecological Indigenous Foodways and the Healing of All Our Relations." *Journal of Critical Animal Studies* 8 (2010): 52–60.

Seymour, Nicole. *Strange Natures: Futurity, Empathy, and the Queer Ecological Imagination*. Urbana: University of Illinois Press, 2013.

Sheu, Sherri. *"Clean Water and Better Bass Fishing": Bass Angling and Bass Culture, 1968–1980*. Report to the Graduate Faculty at University of Texas at Austin, 2013.

Shirley, Evelyn Philip. *Some Account of English Deer Parks with Notes of the Management of Deer*. London: John Murray, 1867.

Shoemaker, Candice, ed. *Chicago Botanic Garden Encyclopedia of Gardens*. Chicago: Fitzroy Dearborn, 2001.

Sinclair, James. *Sheep: Domestic Breeds and Their Treatment*. London: Vinton & Company, 1896.

Smith, Andrea. Foreword to *Undoing Border Imperialism*, by Harsha Walia. Chico, CA: AK Press, 2013.

Smits, David D. "The Frontier Army and the Destruction of the Buffalo: 1865–1883." *Western Historical Quarterly* 25 (1994): 318–19.

Spirn, Anne W. "Constructing Nature: The Legacy of Frederick Law Olmsted." In *Uncommon Ground: Rethinking the Human Place in Nature*, edited by William Cronon, 91–113. New York: Norton, 1996.

———. *The Granite Garden: Urban Nature and Human Design*. New York: Basic Books, 1984.

Spooner, Walter W., ed. *Historic Families of America*. New York: Historic Families Publishing Association, 1907.

Staeheli, Lynn, and Don Mitchell. *The People's Property? Power, Politics, and the Public.* London: Routledge, 2008.

Staeheli, Lynn, Don Mitchell, and Kristina Gibson. "Conflicting Rights to the City in New York's Community Gardens." *GeoJournal* 58 (2002): 197–205.

Stefanics, Barbara. "Clarence Cook's Role as Art Critic." PhD diss., University of Maryland, 1997.

Steinberg, Ted. *Down to Earth: Nature's Role in American History.* New York: Oxford University Press, 2000.

———. *Gotham Unbound: The Ecological History of Greater New York.* New York: Simon and Schuster, 2014.

Stewart, Ian. "Central Park, 1851–1871: Urbanization and Environmental Planning in New York City." PhD diss., Cornell University, 1973.

Steinitz, M., and J. S. Wood. "A World We Have Gained: House, Common, and Village in New England." *Journal of Historical Geography* 18, no. 1 (1992): 105–20.

Stilgoe, John. "Town Common and Village Green in New England: 1620 to 1981." In *On Common Ground*, edited by Ronald Fleming and Lauri Halderman, 7–36. Cambridge, MA: Townscape Institute, 1982.

Stoddard, H. H. *Domestic Waterfowl: Ducks, Geese and Swans. How to Rear and Manage Them.* Hartford, CT: Stoddard, 1885.

Storey, Mark. "Spectacular Distractions: P. T. Barnum and American Modernism." *Modernism/modernity* 21, no. 1 (January 2014): 107–23. https://doi.org/10.1353/mod.2014.0027.

Stott, R. Jeffrey. "The Origins of the Zoological Park in American Thought." *Environmental Review* 5 (1981): 52–65.

Stoykovich, Eric. "The Culture of Improvement in the Early Republic: Domestic Livestock, Animal Breeding, and Philadelphia's Urban Gentlemen, 1820–1860." *Pennsylvania Magazine of History and Biography* 134 (2010): 31–58.

———. "In the National Interest: Improving Domestic Animals and the Making of the United States, 1815–1870." PhD diss., University of Virginia, 2009.

Sturgeon, Noel. "Penguin Family Values." In *Queer Ecologies: Sex, Nature, Politics, Desire*, edited by Catriona Mortimer-Sandilands and Bruce Erikson, 102–33. Bloomington: Indiana University Press.

Swyngedouw, Erik, and Maria Kaika. "The Environment of the City . . . or the Urbanization of Nature." In *A Companion to the City*, edited by Gary Bridge and Sophie Watson, 567–80. Malden, MA: Blackwell, 2000.

Sykes, Naomi, et al. "Wild to Domestic and Back Again: The Dynamics of Fallow Deer Management in Medieval England." *Science & Technology of Archaeological Research* 2 (2016): 113–26.

Taylor, Dorceta. "Central Park as a Model for Social Control: Urban Parks, Social Class and Leisure Behavior in Nineteenth-Century America." *Journal of Leisure*

Research 31 (1999): 420–77. http://www.rochester.edu/in_visible_culture/Issue_6/issue6title.html.

———. *Zoo Renewal: White Flight and the Animal Ghetto*. Minneapolis: University of Minnesota Press, 2015.

Urbanik, Julie. *Placing Animals: An Introduction to the Geography of Human-Animal Relations*. Lanham, MD: Rowman and Littlefield, 2012.

US Census Office. "Agricultural Schedules of New York State by Counties." Washington, DC, 1850.

———. "Agricultural Schedules of New York State by Counties." Washington, DC, 1860.

———. "Agricultural Schedules of New York State by Counties." Washington, DC, 1870.

Veltre, Thomas. "Menageries, Metaphors, and Meanings." In *New Worlds, New Animals: From Menagerie to Zoological Park in the Nineteenth Century*, edited by R. J. Hoage and W. A. Deiss, 19–31. Baltimore: Johns Hopkins University Press, 1996.

Viele, Egbert. *Map of the Lands Included in the Central Park, from a Topographical Survey, June 17th, 1856; Plan for the Improvement of the Central Park, Adopted by the Commissioners, June 3rd, 1856*. New York: Mayer and Company, 1856.

Walford-Lloyd, E., ed. *The Southdown Sheep*. Chichester, UK: Southdown Sheep Society, 1922.

Walker, George. *The Afro-American in New York City, 1827–1860*. New York: Garland, 1993.

Wall, Diana diZerega, Nan Rothschild, and Cynthia Copeland. "Seneca Village and Little Africa: Two African-American Communities in New York City." *Historical Archaeology* 42 (2008): 97–107.

Wang, Jess. *Mad Dogs and Other New Yorkers*. Baltimore: Johns Hopkins University Press, 2019.

Wang, Xinyang. *Surviving the City: The Chinese Immigrant Experience in New York City, 1890–1970*. Lanham, MD: Rowman and Littlefield, 2001.

Warren, Louis. *The Hunter's Game: Poachers and Conservationists in Twentieth-Century America*. New Haven, CT: Yale University Press, 1997.

Watts, Vanessa. "Indigenous Place-Thought & Agency amongst Humans and Non-Humans (First Woman and Sky Woman Go on a European World Tour!)." *Decolonization: Indigeneity, Education & Society* 2 (2013): 20–34.

Weisenfeld, Judith. *African-American Women and Christian Activism: New York's Black YWCA, 1905–1945*. Cambridge: Harvard University Press, 1997.

———. "The Harlem YMCA and the Secular City, 1904–1945." *Journal of Women's History* 6 (1994): 62–78.

Williams, Raymond. *The Country and the City*. New York: Oxford University Press, 1973.

Wilson, James. F. *Bulldaggers, Pansies, and Chocolate Babies: Performance, Race, and Sexuality in the Harlem Renaissance*. Ann Arbor: University of Michigan Press, 2010.

Wilson, Robert. "Mobile Bodies: Animal Migration in North American History." *Geoforum* 65 (2015): 465–72.

Wing, Joseph. *Sheep Farming in America*. Chicago: Sanders, 1905.

Winn, Marie. *Red-Tails in Love: A Wildlife Drama in Central Park*. New York: Pantheon, 1998.

Wischermann, Clemens, Aline Steinbrecher, and Philip Howell, eds. *Animal History in the Modern City: Exploring Liminality*. London: Bloomsbury, 2019.

Wolch, Jennifer. "Zoopolis." *Capitalism Nature Socialism* 7 (1996): 21–47.

Wolch, Jennifer, Alec Brownlow, and Unna Lassiter. "Constructing the Animal Worlds of Inner-City Los Angeles." In *Animal Spaces, Beastly Places: New Geographies of Human-Animal Relations*, edited by Chris Philo and Chris Wilbert, 73–98. London: Routledge, 2000.

Wolch, Jennifer, and Jody Emel, eds. *Animal Geographies: Place, Politics, and Identity at the Nature-Culture Borderlands*. New York: Verso, 1998.

Wolch, Jennifer, Kathleen West, and Thomas E. Gaines. "Transspecies Urban Theory." *Environment and Planning D: Society and Space* 13 (1995): 735–60.

Worshipful Company of Vintners. "Swan Upping." Accessed August 17, 2021. https://www.vintnershall.co.uk/swans.

Wright, Mabel Osgood. *Citizen Bird: Scenes from Bird Life*. New York: Macmillan, 1897.

Zellmer, Amanda J., and Barbara S. Goto. "Urban Wildlife Corridors: Building Bridges for Wildlife and People." *Frontiers in Sustainable Cities* 14 (October 2022). https://doi.org/10.3389/frsc.2022.954089.

Zeuner, Frederick. *A History of Domesticated Animals*. London: Hutchinson, 1963.

Ziegelman, Jane. *97 Orchard: An Edible History of Five Immigrant Families in One New York Tenement*. New York: HarperCollins, 2010.

Index

Page numbers in *italics* refer to illustrations

Abney Park Cemetery, 195–96
acclimatization movement, 80, 83, 85–86, 92, 95
Adams, Helen Balfour, 259
aesthetic, 11, 24, 41, 142, 169; African, 78; Asian, 78; European, 78; pastoral, 42, 47–48, 52, 62–63, 66, 68–69, 72, 266; picturesque, 14, 35, 42, 74, 102, 169, 195
agency, 13
Akeley, Carl, 205
Allaire, Mary, 105
alligators, 137, *139*, 218
Alster Lake, Hamburg, 72–73
American Acclimatization Society, 85, 95
American Botanical and Zoological Society, 119
American Museum of Natural History, 103, 205
American Sportsman, The (Lewis), 98
Andrews, W. Earle, 199
anglers, 245–48
Anti-Slavery Society, 115–16
Arsenal, *55*, 122–23, 125–26, 131, *134*, 201
Asian Americans, 62
ASPCA (American Society for the Prevention of Cruelty to Animals), 100, 137, 254, 258, 267
Astor, John Jacob, IV, 150
Audubon Society, 103, 106, 161
Augusta, Bessie, 185, 197
Aussayne (Ugandan man), 204–6
austerity, 178–80

Baldwin, James, 204
Barnum, P. T., 64, 115–16, 119, 128, 132–33, 135, 138
Barrett Park Zoo, 208
Barrow, Mark, 99
bear, grizzly, 129–30
Beck, Alan, 267
Belmont, August: finances, 45, 50, 68; horses, 41, 44; sheep, 48; zoo plans, 118, 119–20, 270
Bender, Daniel, 207
Benga, Ota, 146, 205
Bennett, Joshua, 196, 231
Benson, Etienne, 90, 100
Bergh, Henry, 100–101, 137, 278
Berkeley, William, 244
Berman, Claire, 262
BioBlitz, 269–70, 276, 279
birders, 158, 161–64, *165*, 171, 180, 189–91, 276–77
Birders: The Central Park Effect (J. Kimball), 1
Bird-Lore, 104–5
birds, *87*; houses, *84*, *107*; meaning of, 101–6, 108–10; migration of, 82, 170, 189–90; protection of, 97–99, 136–37, 218, 276; sanctuaries for, 192, *194*; shelter seeking, 8, 170–71, 197
bison, xi–xii, 131, 147–48, *149*, 150; and Indigenous people, 111–12, 128–30, 140, 278
blackbird, English, 85
Black ecology, 196
Black Elk (Lakota leader), 140
Blackford, Eugene, 137
Blackmar, Elizabeth, 11, 144

Black New Yorkers, 25–26, 32, 146

Blair, W. Reid, 216

Board of Commissioners, 22, 34, 37, 45; agricultural animals, 48, 56, 65, 67; bird introductions, 78, 81, 86; menagerie and zoo plans, 119–22, 126, *127*, 128, 130–31, 133, 141, 144–45; Sweeny board, 56–57, 131, 133

Bogle, Donald, 186

Bois de Boulogne, 45–46

Boisseron, Bénédicte, 13

Boone and Crockett Club, 146

Bridgeman, Charles, 93

bridle path, 68; construction, 6, 41–44; maintenance, 154, 174–75, 177–78, 182, 185; use and exclusivity of, 24, 158, 159–60, 164, 174, 180, 183–84

Bronx Zoo, 146–48, 202–3, 205, 207, 211, 216, 270

Brown, Capability, 93

Brown, Fred, 258

Brownie (dog), 259–60, 267

Buck, Frank, 223

Buenroste, Vincent, 240–41

buffalo. *See* bison

Bunner, H. C., 60, 107

Burritt, Elihu, 102

cages, 121–22

Calvé, Emma, 253

capitalism, 9, 101–2

captivity, 139–40, 141–42, 143–47

Carter, Josephine, 100–101

cartmen, 25, 43

Catcher in the Rye, The (Salinger), 228–29

Catlin, George, 83

cats, 97

Cave, Edward, 245

Cedar Hill, 261–62

Central Park Board. *See* Board of Commissioners

Central Park Conservancy, 15, 16, 269, 272

Central Park Zoo, 16, 157, 201–6, 250, 271

Chapman, Frank, 103, 104–6, 109

Chauncey, George, 165, 167

Cherry, Elizabeth, 189

Cheyne-Stout, Ronald, 213–14, 215, 216–18, 219, 221–24, *222*, 225, 232–33

chickadees, 105, 111

childhood, 26, 200–201, 205, 209–10, 212–14, 228–29, 231–33

children, *194*, *251*; education of, 58, 104–5, 229, 239; and recreation, 154, 156, 173, 206–11, 219, 221–24, 237–38, *249*, 250; safety of, 233, 262; and spaces, 188–89; and zoos, xii, 229, 232–33

Children's District, 56–57, 266

Children's Zoo, 232–33, 263, 266, 275

chimpanzee, 144

Chinese immigrants, 26, 141, 155

Christmas Bird Census, 104, 276

Christopher (cat), 229, 231, 279–80

Ciccia, Louis, 260–61

citizenship, 259–60

Cleveland, Grover, 137

Cogswell, Cynthia, 219

Cole, Teju, 279–80

colonialism, 4–5, 22, 80, 83, 109, 112, 128, 140, 148, 150

Colonial Park, 179–80

commons, 30–31, 47

Congorilla (Johnson and Johnson), 205, 207–8

Conklin, William, 14, 94–96; birds, 78, 80–82, 85, 88, 89, 92–93, 97, 108; hunting, 100–101; menagerie, 22, 90–91, 132, 135–38, 140, 141; sheep, 63–66, 67–68

conservation, 101–7, 129, 146, 150–51, 228, 244, 271–72, 277

Conservatory Lake, 247

Cook, Clarence, 52, 58, 74–75, 78, 81, 101–2, 109, 165

Cooper, A. (1930s dog owner), 256–57

Cooper, Amy (2020 dog owner), 3

Cooper, Christian, 1, 3, 196, 278

Cooper-Davis, Lizzy, 233

Cotton Club, Harlem, 186–87

COVID-19, 1

cows, 5–6, 46–47, 52, 54, *55*, 57–58, 241

Crimmins, John, 65–66, 234–35, 237–39, 250, 252, 270

Crolius, Anne, 105, 109, 164

cruising, 195–96

Cullen, Countee, 229, 231, 279–80

culture of collecting, 82, 99–100, 124–25, 162

Curley (lion), 223–24

Curtis, Gertrude, 182–83

Custer, George Armstrong, xi–xii, 130

dairy, 5–6, 31, 47, 52

Dancer, Maurice, 185

Davis, Epiphany, 25

Davis, Gordon, 233, 271–72

Davis, William, 162

Deas, Barbara, 184

DeBlasio, Bill, 274

December, Halle, 227–28

decolonial scholarship, 14

deer, 122, *123*, 137

DeForest, Clinton, 168–69, 182

Depression. *See* Great Depression

Dillon, Robert, 41, 44

Dismond, Binga, 184

displacement, 7–8, 17, 23, 30, 235, 252, 271. *See also* pastoralism: displacement

dogs, 1, 3, 41, 97–98, 237–42, *255*, *265*, 275; and rabies, 253–63

Dom Pedro (sheep), 64–65

Downing, Andrew Jackson, 24, 37, 52, 114, 127

Dresden Zoo, 217

ducks, 89, *194*

Durant, Thomas C., 129–30

Durfee, Elias Hicks, 129–30

Dutch West India Company, 4–5

eagles, 99, 121–22, 124, 137, *138*, 149

Early Risers Club, 177–78

Eaton, Isabel, 104

Ellman, John, 49, 64

Embury, Aymar, II, 200

empire, 11, 22, 79–80, 85, 113–14, 129, 150–51

encounter value, xi, 22, 30, 45, 68, 74, 111, 114, 214

Enright, John, 246

enslavement, 13, 79, 115–16, 183

environmentalism, 158

erosion, 160–61, 169, 170–73

European values, 23, 34, 114, 119, 169; birds and, 72–74, 79, 93, 100, 108–9

exploitation of animals, 13

Fairmount Park, 134

Falstaff (hippo), 225

Fane, Yein, 62, 69

Fatima (hippo), 203

Federation of Black Cowboys, 274

Fifth Avenue, 39

fish, xi, 71, 94–96, 109, 137, *249*, 250, 252–53

Flaco (owl), ix–x, xiii

Flanders, C. W., 60

fly casting, 96, 245–48

Forbes, Dorothy, 256–57, 261

Forrester, Francis. *See* Wise, Daniel

Fox, Joshua, 102

foxes, 90, 139, 203

Fraser, Perry, 245

Fry, Gladys, 164

Gallatin, Albert, 63, 111–12, 128

Gallatin, Francis, 170, 172, 174, 202–3

Gandy, Matthew, 11, 195–96

Geddes, George, 36, 50, 66

geese, 29, 30, 60, *61*, 62, 68–69

gender, 26

General Scott (ox), 48

gentrification, 11, 17, 272–73

Gentry, Thomas, 85

Germic, Stephen, 11

Glenarm (horse), 182

goats, xi, 38–39, 54–55, 56, *57*, 60, *61*

Google, 269

Go Tell It on the Mountain (Baldwin), 204

Gratacap, Louis Pope, 96

Great Depression, 157, 173, 175, 242, 247, 254, 262; and children, 199–200, 209

Great Migration, 154–55, 180, 181, 248

Green, Andrew Haswell, 14, 22; agricultural animals, 52, 54, 68; conservation, 111–13, 125, 126, 129, 148, 150, 270–71; early life, 35–36; science, 48, 66; zoology, 120, 131–32, 142, 146, 151

Greensward plan, 6–7, 41

Grier, Katherine, 97, 129

Griscom, Ludlow, 161–63, 168, 170–72, 188, 211

guinea fowl, 78–79, *79*, 108, 136

Gunther (dog), 237, 240

Gustin, Samuel, 34–35

habitat loss, 11–12, 114, 149, 156, 170–72, 189–90, 270

Hall, Minna, 103

Hanson, Elizabeth, 135

Harlem, 79, 145; equestrians, xii, 159–60, 179–80, 181–86; fishing, 248, 252, 266–67; immigrants, 5, 155; neglect, 90, 180, 197, 272–73; recreation, 204–5; resistance, 206

Harlem Meer, 94, 96, 181, 246–47, 250, 252, 266, 273

Harlem Renaissance, 204, 279

Hartman, Saidiya, 180, 181

Hattie (elephant), 203

Hauter, Oscar, 182, 274

hawks, 89, 91, 123, 130, 277, 280

health. *See* public health

Hearst, William Randolph, 222

Heckscher Playground, 257

Hediger, Heini, 218, 227–28

Hemenway, Harriet, 103

Hemings, James, 79

Hempel, Frieda, 259–60

Herrick, Walter, 154, 177

Herrmann, Moses, 245–46

heterosexuality, 165

Heth, Joice, 116

Higgins, Joseph, 168–69

Hindle, Edward, 214–15, 218, 228

hippos, 203, 225–27, *226*, 228

Hoey, Thomas, 237–42, *239*

hogs, 5, 31. *See also* pigs

Holmes, Philip, 121, 147

homosexuality, 158, 161, 164–65, 167–70, 187–88, 191–93, 195–96

Hoover Dam, 209

Hornaday, William Temple, 146, 148, 150, 203, 205, 278

horses: Black women, xii, 3, 159–60, 180–87; bridle paths, 174–75, *176*, 177–80, *179*, 197; carriages, *20–21*, 34, 41, 43–44, 59, 274; elites, 24, 41–42, 158, 173, 274; working, xi, 34, 43–44, *44*, 237

Horticulturalist, The (Downing), 24, 37

Hoving, Thomas, 260–63

How to Raise a Dog (Kinney), 256

hunting, 98–99

Hurston, Zora Neale, 248

Hylan, John, 174, 250

immigrants, 24–25, 60, 62, 86, 99, 108, 141–42, 144, 155

Irish immigrants, 25–26, 32, 33, 43, 62, 65

Isenberg, Andrew, 129

Italian Americans, 142, 146, 155, 248, 252

Jackie Robinson Park, 179–80

Jacque (dog), 253

Johnson, Martin, 204–6, 215–16

Johnson, Osa, 204–6, 215–16

Jones, Joshua, 78, 85

Joseph, Elias, 217

Kasin, Louis, 216

Kimball, Jeffrey, 1

Kimball, Theodora, 156

Kim, Claire Jean, 13

Kinney, James, 256–57

Kinsey, Alfred C., 188

Kobbe, Martha, 258

Kunhardt, George, 73

labor, xi, 42–44

LaBranche, George, 246

Lachaume, J., 35, 48, 94

LaGuardia, Fiorello, 199

Lake (Central Park), 74–76, 78–79, 94, 96, 98

Lakota people, 129, 140

Lasker, Loula, 189

Lasker Recreation Center, 189–93, *190*, 197

Lavender Scare, 187–88, 195

Lawrence, Bryan, 48–51

Lawrence, George, 70, 81–82, 83, 86, 88–89, 106, 121, 162, 171

Lehman, Edith, 232

Lehman, Herbert, 232

Lenapehoking, 4–5, 22, 90

Lenape people, 4–5, 9

Lenox Library, 234–35

Lepow, Benjamin, 223–24

Lepow, Raymond, 223–24

Lewis, Elisha J., 98

Linnaean Society of New York, 103, 161, 170, 191, 193

lions, *143*, 223–24

Little Peachblossom; or, Rambles in Central Park (Forrester [Wise]), 58–59, 79, 81, 144

Lorenz, Konrad, 227

Lost Zoo, The (Cullen), 229, *230*, 231, 279–80

Lyceum of Natural History, 103

Malamud, Randy, 229

Manevitz, Alexander, 33

Manhattan Square, *2*, 125–26, *127*, 133

Manuelli (Kenyan man), 204–6

Marsh, George Perkins, 129

masculinity, 104

Mattachine Society, 195

Mbuti people, 205–6

McCammack, Brian, 180

McCray, Antron, 273

McDonald, Edwin, 241

McNeur, Catherine, x, 30

media, 204

Meili, Trisha, 273

menagerie, *124*, *132*; cages, 97; construction, 131–32; donations, 136–39; and empire, 111–13, 139–40, 144, 150–51; funding, 67, 134–35, 145–47, 201–6; recreation, 63, 149

Metropolitan Riding Club, 174

Meyer, Annie Nathan, 59, 62

miasma theory of disease, 96

Mike Crowley (chimpanzee), 144

Miller, Olive Thorne (Harriet Mann Miller), 104–6, 278

Milton, John, 52

Mitchell, Don, 8

mobility, 4, 9–10, 44, 170–71

Mohawk people, 155

Moon, Henry Lee, 206

Moore, Victor, 257

Moses, Robert: birders and, 191–93; childhood and, 207, 209, 219, 225, 231; dogs and, 256–57; equestrians and, 177–78, 182; exclusionary policies, 15, 157, 188, 195, 252; sheep and, 241–42; and zoo, 199–200, 208, 210–11, 213–14, 216, 222–24

mosquito, 244

motherhood, 225–27

Mould, Jacob Wrey, 58

Nash, Catherine, 49–50

Native American trope, disappearing, 85, 109

New Deal, 199–200, 201, 207–10, 231

Newsome, Corina, 277, 280

New York Zoological Institute, 115, 142–44

New York Zoological Society (1860s, defunct), 122

New York Zoological Society (new), 201, 207, 270–71

Noble, Floyd, 105

North Meadow, 133, 145

O'Brien, John, 242

Olmsted, Frederick Law, 11, 14, 66; cows, 45–50, 54, 56, 58; early life, 36–37; encounter value, 22, 74, 77, 97, 101–2, 144–45; Greensward Plan, x, 6–7, 41–42; pastoralism, 38–39, 67, 109; zoo plans of, 112, 117–18, 120, 125–26, 133, 141–42, 270

Olmsted, Frederick Law, Jr., 156

Open City (Cole), 279–80

O'Shea, Arthur, 136
O'Shea, Mary, 136
owls, 88

Pale Male (hawk), 277, 280
Parsons, Samuel, 141
pastoralism, 8, 243; displacement, 14, *40*, 56; persistence, 54, *61*, 107, 126, 130; traditional, 22, 26, 30, 33, 37–38, 39. *See* aesthetic, pastoral
peafowl, 78–79, 121
Peet, Louis, 169
Peiss, Kathy, 142
Perry, Matthew, 119
pheasants, 65, 93
Philadelphia Zoological Society, 134–35
pigeon: fancy, x, 86; passenger, 89, 99, 125
pigs, 29, 33. *See also* hogs
Pilat, Ignaz, 121
place making, 3–4
Plains peoples, 112, 128–29, 150
Poey, Gonzalo, 246
police, 100–101, 163–64, 193, 195, 237, 261–62
Pope, Alexander, 72
Price, Jenny, 99–100
Proskauer, Joseph, 178
Prospect Park, 58, 208, 218, 231–42
public health, 279; dogs, 254–58, 259, 262; livestock, 5–6, 28, 29–30, 31, 55; sanitation, 62; waterways, 244, 275

queer communities, 158, 161, 164–65, 167–70, 187–88, 191–93, 195–96
queer ecology, xii, 196

rabies, 254–56, 258
raccoons, 139, 275
racial geography, 262, 267
Ramble, 1, 3, 74–75, 77, 91, 102, *166*, 167; birders, 105–6, 109, 158, 160–64; Lasker Center controversy, 187–93
rats, x, 244, 259
real estate, 31, 38, 155, 270
recreation, 8, 173, 210

red-eared slider, 275–76
Red Scare, 187–88
Regent Park Zoo, 214
rehabilitation, 156–57, 273
Reiche brothers, 135, 140
reservoir, 27, 94–96, 234, 244, 247, 250, 252, 256
restoration, 154
Richards, T. Addison, 83, 99
Richardson, Kevin, 273
Robichaud, Andrew, 31
Robinson, Joyce, 184
Robinson, Theresa, 226–28
Rogers, Elizabeth Barlow, 272
Rome, Adam, 98
Roosevelt, Franklin, 168
Roosevelt, Robert B., 95
Roosevelt, Theodore, 99, 104, 137, 146
Rose (hippo), 225
Rose II (hippo), 225–27
Rosenzweig, Roy, 11, 144
Ruhe, Louis, 135, 216, 219
Rushing Nola (horse), 184

Salaam, Yusef, 273
Salinger, J. D., 228–29
Sandler, Bernard, 177
San Juan Hill, 25, 142
Sargent, Henry Winthrop, 78
Sarnoff, David, 212
Sarnoff, Tommy, 211–14
Sarreals, Escobeda, 182–83
Savas Report (Columbia University), 272–73
scarcity, 158, 178–80
Schaefer Brewing Company, 266
Schieffelin, Eugene, 80–82, 85, 92–93, 106, 108
Schneider, Lindsey, 148
Schwartz, Joel, 157
Schwartzhaupt, Emil, 217, 219
science, 80, 82, 114, 201, 227–28, 277
scientific farming, 36, 45, 48–50
sea lions, 219
seals, *220*
segregation, 16, 202

Seneca Village, 6, 8, 25–26, 32, 37–38
Seventh Cavalry, 111–12, 128, 129–30, 140
Sexual Behavior in the Human Male (Kinsey), 188
sexual violence, 160
sex work, 167
sheep: decline, 234–36, 237–43, 266, 274; Dorsets, 68, 238, *239*; elitism, 35–37, 45–46; nostalgia, 59, 67–69; Southdown, xi, 49–52, *53*, 63, 64–66
Sheepfold, 58, 235, 238–39, *239*, 242
Sheep Meadow, xiii, 54, 207, 236
Silver Queen (horse), 184
Skelton, Kathleen, 193
slavery, 13, 79, 115–16, 183
Smith, Al, 199–200, 209, 211, 222
Smith, John, 141–42
Smithsonian Zoo, 224
Snoopy (horse), 184
Southwick, E. B., 244
spanworm, 70–71, 85, 90
sparrow, 106; house, 81, 82, 83, 85–86, 88, 91–93, 108–9
squirrels, *92*, 100, 110, 257, 276
Staeheli, Lynn, 8
starlings, 92, 108–10, 280
Steinberg, Ted, 30
St. James's Park, 46–47
Stoykovich, Eric, 49
Straus, Nathan, Jr., 175, 177
Sultan (horse), 182
Sulzberger, Iphigene Ochs, 188–89, 191
Sutherland, John, 85, 93
swans, 72–80, *75, 76*, 97–98, 102
Sweeny, Harry, 223
Sweeny, Peter, 131–33

Tammany Hall, 56–57, 63, 131
tastemaking, 41
Tavern on the Green, xiii, 242
Taylor, Dorceta, 11, 102
Taylor, J. C., 51
Tenement Commission, 69
tenements, 62, 69, 114

Thompson, Dorothy, 219
Thorne, Samuel, 50
Tilden, Samuel, 94
Treadwell, Charles, 25
Tucker, Frank, 183–84, 196
turtles, 123, 137, 218, 275–76
Tweed, William, 56–57, 133, 146

Uddin, Lisa, 134, 260
union, labor, 102
urban greening, 16–17
urbanization, 11

Valentino, Rudolph, 168
Van Amburgh, Isaac, 115, 122, 128
Van Rensselaer, Thomas, 116, 142, 144
Vaux, Calvert, 11, 14; cows, 45–48, 52, 56, 58; encounter value, 22, 54–55, 74, 77, 97, 101–2, 144–45; Greensward Plan, x, 6–7, 41–42; pastoralism, 37, 67; zoo plans, 112, 117–18, 120, 125–26, 133, 270–71
Viele, Egbert, 34, 41
Visit to the Children's Zoo, A, 233
von Uexküll, Jakob, 227

wallaby, 212–13, *213*
Walsingham, Baron, 64–65
Walton, Izaak, 245
warblers, 88
Waters, Ethel, 3, 186–87, 197
Watson, Elkanah, 35
Webb, Jonas, 51
Weisenfeld, Judith, 181
West, Benjamin, 46
West Drive, 237
White, G. Granville, 121, 124
white supremacy, 183, 262
Wild Animals in Captivity (Hediger), 227–28
Wildlife Conservation Society (WCS), 16, 271–72
Williams, Andrew, 25
Wilson, James F., 187
Wise, Daniel, 58–59, 79, 81, 144

Wise, Korey, 273

women, 142; Black, xii, 160, 181–87; wealthy, 103; working class, 102

Wood, Fernando, 38

Woodward, Anthony, 96

Works Progress Administration (WPA), 199, 208

Worshipful Company of Dyers, 73–74

Worshipful Company of Vintners, 73–74

Wright, H. C., 116

YWCA (Young Women's Christian Association), 159, 181–82, 185

zoos, 113–18, 120–21, 151, 271; Central Park Zoo, 16, 157, 201–6, 250, 271

Weyerhaeuser Environmental Books

Animating Central Park: A Multispecies History, by Dawn Day Biehler

Cleaning Up the Bomb Factory: Grassroots Activism and Nuclear Waste in the Midwest, by Casey A. Huegel

Capturing Glaciers: A History of Repeat Photography and Global Warming, by Dani Inkpen

The Toxic Ship: The Voyage of the Khian Sea *and the Global Waste Trade*, by Simone M. Müller

People of the Ecotone: Environment and Indigenous Power at the Center of Early America, by Robert Michael Morrissey

Charged: A History of Batteries and Lessons for a Clean Energy Future, by James Morton Turner

Wetlands in a Dry Land: More-Than-Human Histories of Australia's Murray-Darling Basin, by Emily O'Gorman

Seeds of Control: Japan's Empire of Forestry in Colonial Korea, by David Fedman

Fir and Empire: The Transformation of Forests in Early Modern China, by Ian M. Miller

Communist Pigs: An Animal History of East Germany's Rise and Fall, by Thomas Fleischman

Footprints of War: Militarized Landscapes in Vietnam, by David Biggs

Cultivating Nature: The Conservation of a Valencian Working Landscape, by Sarah R. Hamilton

Bringing Whales Ashore: Oceans and the Environment of Early Modern Japan, by Jakobina K. Arch

The Organic Profit: Rodale and the Making of Marketplace Environmentalism, by Andrew N. Case

Seismic City: An Environmental History of San Francisco's 1906 Earthquake, by Joanna L. Dyl

Smell Detectives: An Olfactory History of Nineteenth-Century Urban America, by Melanie A. Kiechle

Defending Giants: The Redwood Wars and the Transformation of American Environmental Politics, by Darren Frederick Speece

The City Is More Than Human: An Animal History of Seattle, by Frederick L. Brown

Wilderburbs: Communities on Nature's Edge, by Lincoln Bramwell

How to Read the American West: A Field Guide, by William Wyckoff

Behind the Curve: Science and the Politics of Global Warming, by Joshua P. Howe

Whales and Nations: Environmental Diplomacy on the High Seas, by Kurkpatrick Dorsey

Loving Nature, Fearing the State: Environmentalism and Antigovernment Politics before Reagan, by Brian Allen Drake

Pests in the City: Flies, Bedbugs, Cockroaches, and Rats, by Dawn Day Biehler

Tangled Roots: The Appalachian Trail and American Environmental Politics, by Sarah Mittlefehldt

Vacationland: Tourism and Environment in the Colorado High Country, by William Philpott

Car Country: An Environmental History, by Christopher W. Wells

Nature Next Door: Cities and Trees in the American Northeast, by Ellen Stroud

Pumpkin: The Curious History of an American Icon, by Cindy Ott

The Promise of Wilderness: American Environmental Politics since 1964, by James Morton Turner

The Republic of Nature: An Environmental History of the United States, by Mark Fiege

A Storied Wilderness: Rewilding the Apostle Islands, by James W. Feldman

Iceland Imagined: Nature, Culture, and Storytelling in the North Atlantic, by Karen Oslund

Quagmire: Nation-Building and Nature in the Mekong Delta, by David Biggs

Seeking Refuge: Birds and Landscapes of the Pacific Flyway, by Robert M. Wilson

Toxic Archipelago: A History of Industrial Disease in Japan, by Brett L. Walker

Dreaming of Sheep in Navajo Country, by Marsha L. Weisiger

Shaping the Shoreline: Fisheries and Tourism on the Monterey Coast, by Connie Y. Chiang

The Fishermen's Frontier: People and Salmon in Southeast Alaska, by David F. Arnold

Making Mountains: New York City and the Catskills, by David Stradling

Plowed Under: Agriculture and Environment in the Palouse, by Andrew P. Duffin

The Country in the City: The Greening of the San Francisco Bay Area, by Richard A. Walker

Native Seattle: Histories from the Crossing-Over Place, by Coll Thrush

Drawing Lines in the Forest: Creating Wilderness Areas in the Pacific Northwest, by Kevin R. Marsh

Public Power, Private Dams: The Hells Canyon High Dam Controversy, by Karl Boyd Brooks

Windshield Wilderness: Cars, Roads, and Nature in Washington's National Parks, by David Louter

On the Road Again: Montana's Changing Landscape, by William Wyckoff

Wilderness Forever: Howard Zahniser and the Path to the Wilderness Act, by Mark Harvey

The Lost Wolves of Japan, by Brett L. Walker

Landscapes of Conflict: The Oregon Story, 1940–2000, by William G. Robbins

Faith in Nature: Environmentalism as Religious Quest, by Thomas R. Dunlap

The Nature of Gold: An Environmental History of the Klondike Gold Rush, by Kathryn Morse

Where Land and Water Meet: A Western Landscape Transformed, by Nancy Langston

The Rhine: An Eco-Biography, 1815–2000, by Mark Cioc

Driven Wild: How the Fight against Automobiles Launched the Modern Wilderness Movement, by Paul S. Sutter

George Perkins Marsh: Prophet of Conservation, by David Lowenthal

Making Salmon: An Environmental History of the Northwest Fisheries Crisis, by Joseph E. Taylor III

Irrigated Eden: The Making of an Agricultural Landscape in the American West, by Mark Fiege

The Dawn of Conservation Diplomacy: U.S.-Canadian Wildlife Protection Treaties in the Progressive Era, by Kurkpatrick Dorsey

Landscapes of Promise: The Oregon Story, 1800–1940, by William G. Robbins

Forest Dreams, Forest Nightmares: The Paradox of Old Growth in the Inland West, by Nancy Langston

The Natural History of Puget Sound Country, by Arthur R. Kruckeberg

Weyerhaeuser Environmental Classics

Debating Malthus: A Documentary Reader on Population, Resources, and the Environment, edited by Robert J. Mayhew

Environmental Justice in Postwar America: A Documentary Reader, edited by Christopher W. Wells

Making Climate Change History: Documents from Global Warming's Past, edited by Joshua P. Howe

Nuclear Reactions: Documenting American Encounters with Nuclear Energy, edited by James W. Feldman

The Wilderness Writings of Howard Zahniser, edited by Mark Harvey

The Environmental Moment: 1968–1972, edited by David Stradling

Reel Nature: America's Romance with Wildlife on Film, by Gregg Mitman

DDT, Silent Spring, and the Rise of Environmentalism, edited by Thomas R. Dunlap

Conservation in the Progressive Era: Classic Texts, edited by David Stradling

Man and Nature: Or, Physical Geography as Modified by Human Action, by George Perkins Marsh

A Symbol of Wilderness: Echo Park and the American Conservation Movement, by Mark W. T. Harvey

Tutira: The Story of a New Zealand Sheep Station, by Herbert Guthrie-Smith

Mountain Gloom and Mountain Glory: The Development of the Aesthetics of the Infinite, by Marjorie Hope Nicolson

The Great Columbia Plain: A Historical Geography, 1805–1910, by Donald W. Meinig

Cycle of Fire

Fire: A Brief History, second edition, by Stephen J. Pyne

The Ice: A Journey to Antarctica, by Stephen J. Pyne

Burning Bush: A Fire History of Australia, by Stephen J. Pyne

Fire in America: A Cultural History of Wildland and Rural Fire, by Stephen J. Pyne

Vestal Fire: An Environmental History, Told through Fire, of Europe and Europe's Encounter with the World, by Stephen J. Pyne

World Fire: The Culture of Fire on Earth, by Stephen J. Pyne

Also available:

Awful Splendour: A Fire History of Canada, by Stephen J. Pyne